Foster Family Care

Theory and Practice

Judith A. Martin

University of Wisconsin–Green Bay

Allyn and Bacon

Boston • *London* • *Toronto* • *Sydney* • *Tokyo* • *Singapore*

Senior Editor: *Judy Fifer*
Editor in Chief, Social Sciences: *Karen Hanson*
Editorial Assistant: *Julianna Cancio*
Marketing Manager: *Jackie Aaron*
Editorial-Production Administrator: *Annette Joseph*
Editorial-Production Service: *Holly Crawford*
Composition Buyer: *Linda Cox*
Electronic Composition: *Peggy Cabot, Cabot Computer Services*
Manufacturing Buyer: *Julie McNeill*
Cover Designer: *Jenny Hart*

Library of Congress Cataloging-in-Publication Data

Martin, Judith A.
    Foster family care : theory and practice / Judith A. Martin
        p. cm.
    Includes bibliographical references and index.
    ISBN 0-205-30491-5
    1. Foster home care—United States. I. Title.
HV881 .M245 2000
362.73'3'0973—dc21
                                                      99-056023
                                                        CIP

Printed in the United States of America

10 9 8 7 6 5 4 3 2 1   05 04 03 02 01 00

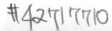

Contents

Foreword

During the last 150 years, foster family care has been a topic of importance and an issue of concern to the public, the media, the courts, legislators, religious organizations, public and private social service agencies, researchers, and many, many children and families. Interest would rise and wane from time to time; the focus of attention shifted often; public policy lurched from fad to fad and crisis to crisis; adults frequently made decisions and policies based on adult, economic, or other interests, rather than the best interests of children; and ideas were sometimes recycled decades after they were introduced and fell from favor.

Indeed, many ideas and initiatives dating back to the 1850s have a familiar ring, and some remain firmly in place today. Charles Loring Brace (1826–1890), for example, may have trampled parents' and children's rights and promoted child involuntary servitude, or he may have been an early prophet of permanency planning. Charles Birtwell (1860–1932) recognized the dangers of institutionalization for most children and advocated elements of what much later came to be called family preservation. The First White House Conference on the Care of Dependent Children (1909) recommended family-based care over institutional care for dependent children and urged an early version of "reasonable efforts" to keep children with their biological families insofar as possible. Courts became more and more involved in the lives of dependent children when, in just eighteen short years (1899–1917), forty-five states enacted juvenile court statutes. The Social Security Act (1935) and its subsequent amendments created massive public child and family support and child welfare systems.

Since the mid–twentieth century, a small but influential series of research studies on foster care, child abuse and neglect, and adoption heightened public awareness of the plight and needs of children at risk in our society. Part of the public response was the passage of several major pieces of legislation between 1974 and 1997. Each was more reactive to the pressures of the time than proactive, but each had a powerful effect on foster care. Notable among these were the Child Abuse Prevention and Treatment Act (1974), the Indian Child Welfare Act (1978), the Adoption Assistance and Child Welfare Act (1980), the Child Abuse Prevention and Family Services Act (1988), and the Adoption and Safe Families Act (1997).

During the last century and a half, many child welfare controversies have been generated. Each had an impact on foster care. Among these, states' rights, parents' rights, and children's rights continue to arouse passion. Transracial placements and adoptions, termination of parental rights, child custody and child support, and the emergence and acceptance of gay and lesbian foster parents continue to attract public attention. Foster family care has been buffeted about by shifts in public opinion and public policy as family preservation, permanency planning, reasonable efforts, and child safety took turns at center stage. The proper balance between family privacy and state intervention in the family to protect children has continued to trouble families, the public, legislators, and the courts.

Foster family care is closely tied to other child welfare services. Yet, as one of the oldest and largest areas of child welfare practice, foster family care has its own history, issues, legislative mandates, practice standards, and practice methods. Dr. Martin has captured the essence of foster care by integrating these threads into a meticulously documented, research-based and practice-oriented volume. As we enter the twenty-first century, more than half a million children are living in foster family homes. Many of these children have serious, multiple problems. The challenge of meeting their needs will require all the knowledge and skills professionals can muster, along with the support and resources of the public at large. Fortunately, a great deal is known about how to provide effective foster family services. What has been most lacking has been the public will to provide the resources for best practice. Public support for victims in this society is fickle, and most of the children in need of foster care qualify as victims of one or another personal or social tragedy beyond their control.

Despite the challenges (or perhaps because of them), foster care is an essential, constructive, and rewarding service for foster families and agency personnel. This volume is a good place to start for families and workers alike as they seek to understand what contemporary foster family care is, how it has been shaped, and how it might be improved.

Edward W. Sites, Ph.D.
University of Pittsburgh

Preface

In the early 1980s, I had the wonderful opportunity to work with Dr. Alfred Kadushin on the fourth edition of his text, *Child Welfare Services*. Part of my responsibility involved updating the chapter in that text on foster family care. Because this work is encyclopedic in its focus, I read widely in the field of foster care practice and research. As I read and thought about this material, I came to believe that foster family care is not so much a service in disarray as a field of practice in need of articulation. I came to see that the core of foster family care lies in the concept of "family" and that foster parents were often "doing" what we were not yet writing—or were only writing in fragmentary ways. This book reflects an attempt to present this field of service from a more comprehensive and wholistic perspective. I hope it proves helpful to child welfare practitioners and to the families they serve.

In writing the text, I owe a debt of gratitude to those whose perspectives profoundly affected my own and whose writing challenged my thinking on this subject. I want to thank in particular Alfred Kadushin, Anthony Maluccio, Edith Fein, Vera Fahlberg, and Paul Steinhauer. To my mentors, my colleagues, and my best critics—Edward W. Sites and Sandra Wexler—there is no way to adequately express my appreciation. I especially want to thank Judy Fifer of Allyn and Bacon for her patience, her endurance, and her support in seeing this book to publication. Many people did the tough work of helping me find and catalog the resources that were so essential to this effort and to prepare the manuscript for publication. I want to acknowledge with gratitude the help provided by Tina Naylor-Riston, Eleanor Barry, Alice Shapiro, Mary Ann Robbins, Valerie Flickinger, Mary Cardamone, and Terry Stoops. Thanks are also due to the reviewers of the proposal: George W. Caulton, Western New England College; John M. Herrick, Michigan State University; and Lois Pierce, University of Missouri–St. Louis.

This book is dedicated to the foster care workers who, on a daily basis, make this service "work" for families. It is dedicated to the birth families and their children who need foster family services and to the foster parents whose love and support are essential to successful foster care. It is dedicated to the members of my extended family who have had their own need of foster family services—and who have both benefited and suffered in the process. I thank Nancy, Keyavonne, Jayron, and Nadine for teaching me a great deal about what "really goes on."

Finally, I want to express my gratitude to the members of my family for putting up with my preoccupations and responsibilities in getting this task accomplished—my thanks to Ian and Gaven and Jean with love.

                                                                    J. M.

1

The Nature of Foster Family Care

When we pulled up, on March 16, 1967, I stood for a spell, stretching from the long drive down, looking around, wondering which house it was on the block, as the social worker gathered what few things I had from the car. I asked myself what the foster parents would be like and if they would want me. The social worker then took my hand and said, "This is a nice family. You should do well here!"

—Jones, 1990, p. 12

This chapter presents an orientation to foster family care as a service for vulnerable children and families. Foster family care as a child welfare service is defined, and its goals and service philosophy are outlined. The various service settings and contexts within which foster family care is provided are also described.

What Is Foster Family Care?

The term *foster care* has been applied to a range of substitute care alternatives—boarding homes, adoptive homes, and group or residential facilities. To distinguish our use of the term to refer to substitute care services provided only in a family setting, we refer in this text to *foster family care*.

Foster family care involves supplementing the care provided by the child's own family with that made available in the home of another family, so that two sets of parents share responsibility for basic parenting functions—nurturing, protection, socialization, and guidance. When a child welfare agency is responsible for placing a child in foster family care, this move is necessitated by the parents' inability to provide the child with minimally adequate social, emotional, or physical care. If left in the home, the child would suffer from serious abuse or neglect or would be in immediate danger of doing so (Besharov, 1986; Wald, Carlsmith, & Leiderman, 1988; Plumer, 1992; Child Welfare League of America, 1995). The Child Welfare League of America (CWLA) defined the value of this service in the following way:

> When children and parents must be separated because of the tragedy of physical abuse, sexual abuse, neglect, maltreatment, or special circumstances, family foster care provides a planned, goal-directed service in which the care of children and youths takes place in the home of an agency-approved family. The value of family foster care is that it can respond to the unique, individual needs of infants, children, youths, and their families through the strength of family living, and through family and community supports. (1991, p. 51)

Goals and Philosophy of Foster Family Care in Child Welfare

The primary goal of foster family care is to provide short-term care in circumstances in which parents are unable to provide minimally adequate care for their children. Foster carers offer protection and nurturance to children in a family setting and contribute to the long-term developmental needs of children while facilitating family reunification or other permanent outcomes. Meeting these developmental needs also requires that decisions be made with regard to permanency in a timely fashion.

The Bill of Rights of Foster Children (1973) outlines the responsibilities of foster care toward the children receiving services:

Every foster child has the inherent right:

Article of the first: to be cherished by a family of his own, either his family helped by readily available services and supports to reassume his care, or an adoption family, or by plan a continuing foster family.

Article of the second: to be nurtured by foster parents who have been selected to meet his individual needs and who are provided services and supports, including specialized education, so that they can grow in their ability to enable the child to reach his potential.

Article of the third: to receive sensitive, continuing help in understanding and accepting the reasons for his own family's inability to take care of him, and in developing confidence in his own self-worth.

Article of the fourth: to receive continuing loving care and respect as a unique human being . . . a child growing in trust in himself and others.

Article of the fifth: to grow up in freedom and dignity in a neighborhood of people who accept him with understanding, respect, and friendship.

Article of the sixth: to receive help in overcoming deprivation or whatever distortion in his emotional, physical, intellectual, social, and spiritual growth may have resulted from his early experiences.

Article of the seventh: to receive education, training, and career guidance to prepare himself for a useful and satisfying life.

Article of the eighth: to receive preparation for citizenship and parenthood through interaction with foster parents and other adults who are consistent role models.

Article of the ninth: to be represented by an attorney-at-law in administrative or judicial proceedings with access to fair hearings and court review of decisions, so that his best interests are safeguarded.

Article of the tenth: to receive a high quality of child welfare services, including involvement of the natural parents and his own involvement in major decisions that affect his life. (Carrieri, 1991, pp. v–vi)

Embedded in these goals are the following principles of foster care practice:

1. Children are to be placed in foster family care only when there is clear-cut evidence that their parents are unable to care for them adequately in their own homes.
2. Children are to be placed only when it is clear that other options, short of placement, are not effective in keeping children safe from further harm and in helping parents change harmful practices.
3. Adequate placement services are built on the notion of family-centered practice.
4. Adequate placement services support the developmental needs of the growing child.
5. Adequate placement services are structured so that they move the child and parents toward some permanent decision with regard to the child's future.
6. Adequate placement services are adapted to meet the needs of families coming from varied racial, cultural, and socioeconomic groups.
7. Adequate placement services must be developed for three different clients of foster family care: the children in care, their parents, and the foster families with whom these children live.

We will consider each of these principles in order to describe effective practice in foster family care.

The Need for Services

Parenting Insufficiencies

Public child welfare services are designed to help families in which children have been mistreated by parents or other adult caretakers. Most of the "parenting figures" with whom this agency works are the child's biological mothers or fathers, stepparents, parents' partners who live in the home but who are not married to the parents, and grandparents, aunts or uncles, or other adult relatives. Mistreatment involves one or more of the following types of behavior: physical abuse of children, child neglect, child sexual abuse, and emotional mistreatment (Meriwether, 1988; Besharov, 1990; Howing & Wodarski, 1992; Tower, 1996).

Parents who physically injure their children and who intend to hurt their children are considered physically abusive. Frequently, this type of maltreatment occurs while the parents are using some type of physical discipline. Most physically abused children are not severely hurt, but the parent's choice of disciplinary techniques (use of a switch or extension cord; chasing the child through the house and throwing objects at him or her) has the potential for inflicting greater harm. Physical abuse is found in approximately one in four families served by public child welfare. Children of all ages are mistreated in this way, and mothers and fathers are equally likely to inflict this type of harm (Pecora, Whittaker, & Maluccio, 1992, p. 103).

Child sexual abuse occurs when parents engage in sexual activities with their sons or daughters. While these activities may be appropriate with consenting adult partners, children are considered incapable of giving informed, noncoerced consent to participation. Parents who fondle their children's breasts or sexual organs, who engage in sexual intercourse with them, or who insist that their children be subjects for pornography are included in this group. These families comprise approximately 15 percent of child welfare cases. Most of the parents who sexually abuse their children are fathers or other male caretakers; most of the children who are sexually abused are female.

In contrast to the two previous categories, in which parents actively engage in behavior considered abusive, child neglect involves parents' failure to act in circumstances in which a child's needs and welfare demand action. Parents who do not routinely provide their children with sufficient food, a safe and protective place to stay, proper clothing, or needed medical care may be considered neglectful. Child neglect is found in more than half of the cases dealt with by public child welfare agencies. While the children may be of any age or gender, most of the parents considered neglectful are mothers. Most of these families live in dire poverty as well.

Emotional or psychological maltreatment of children involves the failure of parents to provide their children with a loving and nurturing home environment. Instead, a child may be constantly criticized, isolated from peers and other family members, and made the object of constant rejecting and denigrating comments. These cases comprise less than 10 percent of all child welfare families.

Options Short of Placement Are Not Effective

Within the child welfare system, foster family care is recognized as one of a group of services that are necessary for carrying out the mandate to protect children (Pecora, Whittaker, & Maluccio, 1992; Usher, Gibbs, & Wildfire, 1995). The continuum of care described in Figure 1.1 reflects the need to provide services that are least intrusive into family life but meet the needs of the child. Because the child remains at home while the family receives help, family preservation services are considered least disruptive of family life. The family gets help either by going to a social service agency or by having agency staff come into the home. When such assistance offers insufficient protection for children, placement in foster family care is considered.

For children whose problems are too severe to allow them to benefit from such care, a more therapeutic placement is sought. This may be offered in a therapeutic foster home, a group home, a mental hospital, or a residential treatment facility. These children may return to their family's home or to foster placement after completing their treatment. For those families whose children cannot be returned, placement in a new permanent home, through adoption or the transfer of legal guardianship, is the primary service need. Adoption reflects a legal recognition that the child's new caretakers are his or her legal parents in every sense of the term, and all rights of the child's birth parents are terminated. Guardianship involves the transfer of custodial rights to the caretaker, but the child's parents still retain some rights.

When the child welfare agency finds that some type of maltreatment is occurring in a family, every effort is made to have the child remain at home and to have the family stay together while receiving services. Using substitute care involves, for the child, a major upheaval in his or her life circumstances. The child experiences not only total separation from the family but also adjustment to a new set of caretakers, a change of location, a change of school, and a change of peer and sibling groups. Because of this, every "reasonable" effort has to be made to keep the home intact for the child and to keep the child in the home before making a removal decision (Williams, 1972; Bryce & Lloyd, 1981; Hardin, 1983; Ratterman, 1987; CWLA, 1995). Seaberg (1986) suggested that a reasonable effort includes "evidence of sustained activity with and in behalf of the parents to engage and maintain them in relevant services" (p. 474). "Sustained" activity requires that the child welfare worker persevere in offering services, even in the face of overt rejection by the parents, for up to one year and that the worker follow up with the family to determine whether services have been made available

Family Services: Children Stay Home	Family Services: Children Out of Home	New Homes for Children

Examples:
   Home-Based Programs
   Family Preservation Services
   Family Support Centers
	Examples:
	   Foster Family Care
	   Family Reunification Services
	   Residential Treatment Services
		Examples:
		   Adoption
		   Guardianship
		   Informal Adoption

FIGURE 1.1 *Child Welfare Continuum of Services*

and have been used by the parents. "Relevant" services are those that directly address the parental and child issues that made the child vulnerable to maltreatment; these services must also be readily accessible to the families needing them.

Despite these efforts, no home-based program would claim to be able to adequately assist all maltreating families (Bath & Haapala, 1993). A residual group of children will need placement, even if the best and most adequate community-based services are available. Because of its ability to sustain a child in an atmosphere most like that of an ordinary family, foster family care is the preferred choice for children who cannot remain with their own mothers and fathers.

The Provision of Services

Family-Centered Practice

The need to understand children in the context of their family life has been clearly articulated by John Bowlby (1969, 1973, 1988). In his view, effective intervention with the child requires that the type and quality of the child's interpersonal relationships with caretakers, particularly the mother, be assessed. Using the term *attachment*, which describes "an enduring affectional tie or bond, specific in its focus" (Lamb, Thompson, Gardner, & Charnov, 1985, p. 16), Bowlby argued that the child needed a predictable, nurturant, sustained relationship with a particular parent in order for optimal development to occur (*secure* attachment). Children can face problems when the relationship with their parents is not predictable and nurturant (*insecure* attachment) or when the loving relationship with a parent has to be interrupted. Loss or insufficiency in a parental relationship can have consequences for the child's sense of self-esteem (positive feelings about the worth of one's existence), for maintenance of a coherent sense of identity (an integrated and meaningful set of ideas about one's characteristics and beliefs), for the ability to build other supportive attachments (Aldgate, Maluccio, & Reeves, 1989; Siu & Hogan, 1989; Bretherton & Waters, 1985; Bretherton, 1990; Cicchetti, Cummings, Greenberg, & Marvin, 1990; Palmer, 1990; Steinhauer, 1991; Downes, 1993), and for the development of other behavioral problems (Greenspan & Greenspan, 1985; Belsky & Nezworski, 1988, p. ii).

Attachment theory highlights the centrality of the birth family in child welfare services, even in instances where the child and family cannot live together (CWLA, 1990). Foster family care is usually considered a short-term resource for the child while his or her family struggles to remedy the problems that led to removal and placement (Tolfree, 1995). By continuing efforts to reunite the birth family, foster family care becomes a "service to families" rather than a "substitute for families" (Fein & Maluccio, 1992; see also Fisher, Marsh, & Phillips, 1986; Packman, 1986).

An important aspect of foster family care is the maintenance of ties between the child and family while the child is in care. To sustain secure attachments and to strengthen attachments that are in jeopardy, the child welfare agency encourages and supports visitation between the child and family.

Attachment theory also recognizes the child's need to be part of a family, even in circumstances in which parental insufficiencies necessitate the move into a new home. In the past, it was considered preferable to institutionalize children when their parents objected to the use of foster care or when they were part of a sibling group and a single home could not be found for them. These criteria are not considered acceptable reasons for refusing a child a foster family experience today. The present feeling is that all children requiring care should be considered for foster family care, since it is the "least restrictive" substitute care environment. The need for continuous, close parenting dictates this. Even in instances in which children have serious reservations about entering foster care because they feel divided loyalty to parent figures, it is considered more appropriate to place the children in a foster family setting and provide services to help them, the birth family, and the foster parents make a mutually satisfactory adjustment.

While some teenagers, struggling to develop independence from adult caretakers, may find the more impersonal atmosphere of a group setting more congenial (Janchill, 1983), most of these youngsters continue to value and need the support and guidance provided by parenting figures. Therefore, a foster family setting is preferable for the majority of adolescents needing placement.

Attachment theory also provides a rationale for preferring kinship care over placement in the home of strangers. Particularly in instances in which the child already has a strong and supportive relationship with a grandmother or other relative, a move to that home comprises a recognition of secure attachments rather than a threat to them.

Meeting Other Developmental Needs

Effective foster family care services go beyond the placement of a child in a foster home to examination of the quality of life the child has experienced, both before going into care and afterward. Called "enhancing developmental value" (Berrick, Needell, Barth, and Johnson-Reid, 1998, p. 141), the ultimate objective is that of "providing alternative living arrangements for the child that offer a sufficient commitment of financial, social, and interpersonal resources to help the child achieve and sustain self-sufficiency as an adult" (Barth, 1995, p. 8).

Members of the foster family are expected to welcome the child into the family and to develop close relationships with that child. In addition, the child's need to grow and develop cognitively, affectively, socially, and physically is recognized (Berrick, Needell, Barth, & Johnson-Reid, 1998). The family's role in helping the child to do well academically, to develop and enjoy new friendships, and to find exciting challenges in play and work is also important. For those children whose relationships with their own family have not included such experiences, foster care services work to improve parenting so that the child can develop in healthier ways once he or she returns home.

Finding a Permanent Home

Foster family care is used when there is some possibility that the child's family can, with sufficient assistance, eventually be reunited (Maluccio & Fein, 1983; Plumer, 1992). When reunification is not possible, the search for a permanent family for the child is conducted by the adoption worker. Reunification decisions are to be made within a relatively brief period, since indefinite stays in foster family care, especially when accompanied by limited outreach to birth families, can seriously jeopardize the child's ability to build and maintain permanent attachments (Wiltse, 1985; Jones, 1990; Solnit, Nordhaus, & Lord, 1992; Berrick, Needell, Barth, & Johnson-Reid, 1998). Carrying out the monitoring and planning work that will insure that the child has a permanent family within a reasonable period of time is called *permanency planning* (Maluccio, Fein, & Olmstead, 1986; Pecora, Whittaker, & Maluccio, 1992).

Reunification with the child's family and adoption are considered the most "permanent" outcomes of foster family care. "Long-stay" or "permanent" foster family homes have also been used by child welfare agencies, primarily for children whose parents are unable to maintain them in their birth home but who, for one reason or another, are not in a position to be adopted. As a child remains in foster care for longer and longer periods of time, contact with the birth family typically diminishes, and the foster parents are increasingly perceived as primary caretakers (Rowe, 1980). We will examine the impact of long-term foster family care at a later point in the text.

Racially and Culturally Relevant Practice

Commitment to an ecological framework requires an understanding of and respect for the child's cultural and racial heritage and an analysis of steps to be taken in order to provide effective services within the context of that heritage (Cohen, 1992; Everett, Chipungu, & Leashore, 1991; McPhatter, 1997). Effective practice requires:

> a knowledge base in a client's history, culture, traditions, customs, value orientations, and spiritual orientations. Child welfare workers must be knowledgeable about the dynamics of oppression and how social problems affect different client groups. They must understand and be open to the diversity of family structure and the functionality of diverse family forms and childrearing practices. (Folaron & Wagner, 1998, pp. 115–116)

Culturally relevant foster care practice is integrated into all aspects of the service delivery system, from daily activities to long-term planning. It involves all practice participants: children and their families, the professionals providing services, administrators, and planners.

Meeting the Needs of Three Client Groups

In this text, we present the view that three distinct groups must receive service whenever children enter foster family care: the children themselves, the children's birth families, and the foster families in which the children are placed. Foster care workers have the complex responsibility to support and guide the children in care; assist the birth families to develop skills that will allow for the children's return home; and support, counsel, and collaborate with the foster parents in their role as caretakers for their foster children. In order to do this, workers develop partnerships with both the birth and foster parents to help both the children and their families resolve the issues that led to placement and to develop meaningful permanency plans:

> The goal is to create a continuing cooperative network around the child, a network in which agency personnel and the members of both families remain in contact to share information, handle problems together, and create a kind of extended kinship system that will last through, and perhaps beyond, the period of placement. (Minuchin, 1992, p. 2)

This professional orientation has widespread support—from the Child Welfare League of America, the National Commission on Family Foster Care, and the National Foster Parent Association, among others (Maluccio, 1985; CWLA, 1991). However, there is considerable variation in the extent to which the children's parents and the foster families are actually treated as service recipients while the children are in care. Actual practice may reflect the assumption that the needs of children require most attention (Kufeldt, Armstrong, & Dorosh, 1989; Schatz & Bane, 1991). The children's parents may be seen as the responsibility of a different service delivery system—home-based care, for example; some parents, especially fathers, are simply ignored (Kahkonen, 1997). Foster families may be defined as useful "resources" for the children while their own needs for services go largely unrecognized.

In its *Out-of-Home Care: Agenda for the Nineties* (1990), the Child Welfare League of America argued for "recognition of the out-of-home provider as a support service for families, not as a substitute for families" (p. 15). "The goal now is not to eliminate families of children in care, but to recognize them; it is not to exclude them, but to involve them; it is not to do something to them, but to do something with them" (Plumer, 1992, p. 192; see also Fisher, Marsh, & Phillips, 1986). In order to implement this, the League recommended that treatment plans be modified "from a child-only orientation to a child-centered and family-focused orientation" (p. 15). This should encompass "comprehensive services to the child's biological family, especially the parents," according to Maluccio and Fein (1985b, p. 128).

Failure to consider the birth family as a primary service recipient often reflects the belief that the parents are incapable of developing even minimal ability to care for the child. From this perspective, the primary purpose of foster family care is "to identify 'not good enough' parents and to transfer the child's care and parental rights to 'good enough' substitutes" (Packman, 1986, p. 6; see also Kates, Johnson, Rader, & Strieder, 1991). As an alternative, some foster care workers consider the child their only client, thereby "focus[ing] on the young person in care, with the family reappearing, as it were, when care was ending" (Fisher, Marsh, & Phillips, 1986, p. 114). However, without careful service coordination and ongoing parental support provided by the foster care agency, these practices can too easily result in "losing the parents, in abandoning them, in provoking or encouraging them to abandon or neglect their children" (Maluccio, 1991, p. 23; see also Weiner & Weiner, 1990). Research suggests that the ability to keep children from reentering the foster care system, once they have been returned home, is dependent on the quality of the work that was done with parents before the child was returned (Lindsey, 1982; Block & Libowitz, 1983; Turner, 1984; Aldgate, Maluccio, & Reeves, 1989; Bullock, Little, & Millham, 1993).

Since foster care services were first developed in the United States, foster families have been seen as "resources" for children, but their own needs as service recipients have been deemphasized. However, the changing nature of the population of children coming into care makes this approach far less tenable than it once was:

> Most children needing foster care today require foster parents who have—or can develop—the skills to parent youngsters who have been sexually abused, have drug-related or school problems and who will need help moving into independent living. Work in these areas cannot wait for a weekly meeting with a therapist, or a quarterly or even monthly meeting with a caseworker. This work must occur every day in the daily life of the child or youth. (Pasztor, Shannon, & Buck, 1989, p. II-4)

This responsibility can make enormous demands on the foster parents and stress the entire foster family (Humphrey & Humphrey, 1988). Expectations that the foster parents work with the child's birth family only exacerbate the need for ongoing support from and collaboration with the foster care worker.

The reality for children is that the move to foster care challenges them to live with two families; foster care services must embrace this reality by incorporating both families as key service participants throughout the process (Minuchin, 1992).

Community Contexts and Agency Auspices

A wholistic or "ecological" assessment of the needs of children and their families requires that their circumstances be understood within the context of the family network, neighborhood, community, and broader society within which they live (Pecora, Whittaker, & Maluccio, 1992). For families needing child welfare services, this frequently means that the supportiveness of schools, health services, employment opportunities, and welfare services *(formal systems)* as well as clergy, neighborhood groups, and kin *(informal systems)* must be evaluated. The complex nature of these relationships is reflected in Figure 1.2.

Foster family care is sometimes offered by social service agencies, who take on the responsibility for recruiting foster families, evaluating them, placing children in their homes, and supporting and monitoring the families throughout the placement. This is considered *formal* foster care.

In many communities and cultures, there are also strong patterns of using *informal* foster family care, a circumstance in which the child's family works out an arrangement for placement with relatives, neighbors, or friends, but no agency officially sanctions the placement (Hegar, 1999). Informal kinship placements have a long history in the African American, Native American, and Hispanic communities. Informal care has been used, in part, because these children have been excluded from or underserved by formally funded substitute care programs

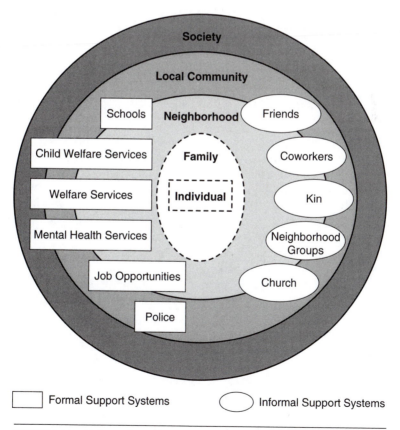

FIGURE 1.2 *Informal and Formal Systems of Support for Families in Child Welfare*

(Hauswald, 1987; Vidal, 1998; Berrick, Barth, & Needell, 1994). Informal kinship placements are common practice in many other countries throughout the world as well (Kilbride & Kilbride, 1994; Hegar & Scannapieco, 1995). Today, informal and formal placement systems may exist side by side in the same community.

Formal foster care services in child welfare may be linked to two other major service delivery systems: the mental health system and the juvenile justice system. Mental health services are offered to children and families in an effort to address psychiatric problems and severe emotional difficulties. The juvenile justice system addresses the needs of children and adolescents who have broken the law. The nature of services made available by each of the three systems is largely a political matter, one heavily influenced by federal and state funding resources. Because many vulnerable families have multiple problems, they may receive services in two or three of these systems simultaneously. Children may be in a foster family home funded by the child welfare system and simultaneously receive mental health services. A mother might be receiving inpatient services from a local mental health agency while her older son is incarcerated in a juvenile institution and her younger daughter is placed in a foster family home by the child welfare agency. Relationships among these systems are complicated, and concerns about service coordination and access to services are widespread (CWLA, 1990; Halpern, 1990; Fanshel, 1992; Farley, 1993; Johnson, Day, & Cahn, 1993; Ratterman, 1993; Glisson & Hemmelgarn, 1998). Some of these difficulties will be discussed later in this text.

Families may be provided formal child welfare services by the public agency or by private agencies in the community. The public child welfare agency can be found in every state. Mandated by the Social Security Act, its public charge is threefold: to investigate and substantiate allegations of mistreatment made against a child's parents or other individuals with caretaking responsibility *(investigative function),* to make decisions on behalf of children to insure their safety from further maltreatment *(protective function),* and to provide services to the child's caretakers to help remedy the parenting problems that created such vulnerability for the child *(treatment function).* Some of the children in care and some foster parents may also need treatment resources.

Treatment services may be provided by the agency itself, or the public agency may pay private agencies in the community to serve the children and their families. Some private service providers have a religious affiliation (Jewish Family Services and Catholic Charities are examples of these); others are nonprofit agencies without religious affiliation (examples include Child Guidance Clinics and Parents Anonymous programs). For-profit private providers are not common in child welfare today.

In recent years, public agencies have made increased use of private agency services. Some public child welfare agencies no longer carry out any treatment functions themselves; instead they rely exclusively on private providers to offer this support. In this situation, the public agency pays the private agency to give needed assistance to a family. However, the public child welfare agency still retains ultimate responsibility for that child and family. The public agency becomes a manager of services, coordinating services for the family that may be offered by several different agencies and providing oversight to insure that children continue to be protected and needed treatment work is being done.

Types of Foster Family Homes

When selecting a foster family home for children, child welfare agencies may use one of the following options:

1. Receiving or shelter homes

In this type of placement, foster families agree to care for children on short notice for limited periods of time. In the past, this service was offered primarily to babies and younger children, for whom an institutional arrangement was felt to be undesirable, even for a short period of time, and in situations requiring emergency removal of a child from a home (Rowe, 1980). It is now routinely used for older children and teenagers as well (Fullbright, 1988). At times when foster family homes are in short supply, children may remain in shelter homes for lengthy periods, waiting for placement with regular foster families or in adoptive homes (Sellick, 1992).

2. Kinship foster homes

Kinship care involves the placement of foster children in the homes of relatives.

Kinship care may be defined as the full-time nurturing and protection of children who must be separated from their parents by relatives, members of their tribes or clans, godparents, stepparents, or other adults who have a kinship bond with the child. (CWLA, 1994, p. 2)

In contrast to shelter placements, the length of time a child remains in kinship care is dependent upon the ability of the child's mother and father to strengthen their parenting capabilities and to change practices that are detrimental or harmful to their children. While some children may remain with kin for only a few months, others may stay for years or even into adulthood.

The use of kinship care has increased substantially in recent years, and this type of care is now preferred over placement of the child in the home of strangers. It is believed that the child benefits from strong family connections and supports that are not initially available in non-kin homes. Scannapieco and Jackson (1996) described it as a "resilient, natural system of child rearing," part of the African American community's effort to protect and preserve the family (p. 194).

3. Non-kin foster homes

Children are placed in the homes of nonrelatives when their parents cannot care for them and placement with relatives is not a viable option. Relatives may not be available in the community, they may be unwilling or unable to assume this responsibility, or they may, themselves, struggle with problems that would jeopardize the children's welfare. For many years, non-kin care was considered the preferred option for children, in part because it was assumed that vulnerable parents usually came from dysfunctional family systems. Now it is recognized that the capacity of kin to care for a child may be strong, even though the child's parents have many problems. Whether the child should be placed with kin needs to be assessed on a case-by-case basis.

In much of the literature on foster care, it is difficult to determine whether the term *foster family care* refers only to non-kin care or to both kin and non-kin homes. In this text, we will use the term in a comprehensive sense to refer to both types of placements with families.

4. Specialized or treatment foster homes

These placements are designed for children who have severe emotional, developmental, or behavioral problems. Foster parents in these families are specially trained to work with the children, and much of the parenting work they do is considered therapeutic (Testa & Rolock, 1999).

Rather than examining foster parenting using a "therapeutic" approach, this book explores the ways "regular" parents nurture and support children whose families cannot care for them adequately. Detailed discussion of the unique needs, issues, and challenges of severely emotionally disturbed foster children is beyond the scope of this text. However, because so many children in regular foster care do have some type of problem—behavioral, educational, or medical—the ways in which "regular" foster parents deal with these issues will be explored.

Voluntary and Involuntary Placements

Children may be placed in care with the voluntary consent of their parents or involuntarily, without their agreement. Voluntary placements may be sought by parents for children whom they perceive as "out of control." The child welfare agency may also solicit a voluntary placement in instances in which there is strong concern for the welfare and safety of the child but insufficient proof of maltreatment to seek involuntary placement through the courts. At times, youths can choose to place themselves in care. In Boston, for example, "teen mothers without homes tend to come to DSS for voluntary foster care arrangements, some quite brief" (Kamerman & Kahn, 1990, p. 75). Involuntary placements are more likely to be sought when risk to the child of remaining in the home is perceived as high and the parents are uncooperative in planning with the agency to address maltreatment issues.

Placements without parental consent are the more common type of arrangement. Evidence from one state (Hubbell, 1981) indicated that only 8.5 percent of all placements were voluntary (p. 62). However, there is considerable variation in this practice from community to community (National Black Child Development Institute, 1989; Carrieri, 1992).

Questions for Discussion and Debate

1. What difference does it make in the field of foster family care that these services for children are publicly mandated?
2. What impact has the shift from non-kin to kinship foster homes had on the provision of public child welfare services?
3. What is the effect on services of having "parental insufficiency" as a basis for decisions to remove children from their parents' homes?
4. What alternative service philosophies might there be for foster family care other than "family-centered practice"?

2

Foster Family Care Policies and Programs

This chapter describes the historical and contemporary context for the development of foster family care services in the United States. A review of past practice prefaces a description of the size of today's foster care population. Current political, professional, and legislative concerns in the field are then reviewed.

The Early History

Foster family care "is a time-honoured practice, going back at least to the rescue of Moses from the bulrushes" (Humphrey & Humphrey, 1988, p. 16). "Under ancient Jewish laws and customs, children lacking parental care became members of the household of other relatives, if such there were, who reared them for adult life" (Slingerland, 1919, p. 27). The early Christian church boarded destitute children with "worthy widows."

Indenture was another widely used form of early foster family care. The Elizabethan Poor Laws provided for the apprenticing of dependent children until their twenty-first year. The master accepted the dependent child into his home, provided him or her with food, clothing, and the necessities of life, and accepted the responsibility for teaching the child a craft or trade. In addition, provision was usually made for some extra payment in the form of clothes and/or money at the termination of the indenture. In return, the child worked for the master around the house and in the craft or trade as an "employee." Indenture was recognized as a "business deal from which the person accepting a poor child on indenture was expected to receive from the child, a full equivalent in work for the expenses of his support, care and teaching" (Thurston, 1930, p. 10).

"It is morally certain that the experiences of indentured children varied all the way from that of being virtual slaves to that of being real foster sons or daughters" (Thurston, 1930, p. 17); there was little guarantee of protection for the child other than public indignation or the foster parents' desire to keep the good opinion of their neighbors. Despite the fact that indenture permitted all sorts of abuses and exploitation, it persisted in the United States until the first decade of the twentieth century. For many children, it did provide placement with a family and at least minimal care.

Indenture eventually declined in popularity, in part because it grew less profitable for the foster family. With growing industrialization and the movement of crafts and trades out of the home, the value of bringing laborers into the home diminished. But perhaps of greater importance was the impact of the abolition of slavery, after which it was hard to justify an indenture that required the apprehension and return to the master of a runaway apprentice and that had some of the characteristics of bondage arrangements. Folks (1902) noted, "It has been seriously suggested that, with the adoption of the Constitutional Amendment in 1865, forbidding 'involuntary servitude,' the indenture system became unconstitutional" (p. 42).

The origin of modern foster family care lies with Charles Loring Brace and the Placing Out System of the New York Children's Aid Society. In the middle of the nineteenth century, New York City faced a problem in dealing with the large numbers of vagrant children. In the mid-1800s, some 10,000 of these children lived on the city's streets and in its institutions. In 1849, the New York City chief of police called attention to the fact that:

> there was a constantly increasing number of vagrant, idle, and vicious children of both sexes who infest our public thoroughfares, hotels, docks, etc., children who are growing up in ignorance and profligacy, only destined to a life of misery, shame, and crime and ultimately to a felon's doom. (quoted in Langsam, 1964, pp. 1–2)

Brace, a young minister who became the first secretary of the New York Children's Aid Society upon its organization in 1853, decided the society would "drain the city of these children by communicating with farmers, manufacturers, or families in the country who may have need of such for employment." The appeal was to Christian charity and to the need for labor on the farms, relocating children from the pernicious influences of urban areas, where there was little for them to do, to rural areas, where there was much for them to do and where the environment was regarded as morally healthier. There evolved a particular program of group emigration and placement that resulted in finding free foster family homes for as many as 150,000 children between 1854 and 1929 (Jackson, 1986).

The procedure was first to collect a group of children in New York City. Some of the children were known to be orphans; others had been abandoned; still others were half-orphans or children with both parents living. In the latter cases, an attempt was made to obtain parental consent to the child's relocation. "Mr. S. a widower, worked as a hostler at a New Jersey hotel where he earned ten dollars a month. On such wages he could not afford to supply both his aged parents and his three children, and consequently he relinquished the youngsters to the Home

Missionary Society" (Clement, 1979, p. 413). The largest numbers of children were provided by institutions in the city, but the Society's agents also had responsibility for locating vagrant children living on the streets.

After making some effort to eliminate the physically ill, the mentally handicapped, and the incorrigible, the organizers sent the children out West or to the South in the company of one of the Society's workers. The community to which the children were to be sent was encouraged by the Society to set up a committee of prominent citizens who had the responsibility to publicize the coming of the children, to encourage families to take them in, and to evaluate the suitability of those families who indicated interest. A report by the pioneer child welfare worker, Dr. Hastings Hart, to the National Conference of Charities and Corrections in 1884 described the "placement" procedure:

> I was a witness of the distribution of forty children in . . . County, Minnesota. . . . The children arrived at about half-past three p.m. and were taken directly from the train to the Court House, where a large crowd was gathered. Mr. Matthews set the children, one by one, before the company, and in his stentorian voice gave a brief account of each. Applicants for children were then admitted in order behind the railing and rapidly made their selections. Then, if the child gave assent, the bargain was soon concluded on the spot. It was a pathetic sight, not soon to be forgotten, to see those children, tired young people, weary, travel-stained, confused by the excitement and the unwonted surroundings, peering into those strange faces, and trying to choose wisely for themselves. And it was surprising how many happy selections were made under such circumstances. In a little more than three hours nearly all those forty children were disposed of. Some who had not previously applied selected children. (Hart, 1884)

The Society rated the Placing Out System a success. "A 1910 survey concluded that 87 percent of the children sent to country homes had 'done well,' while eight percent had returned to New York and the other five percent had either died, disappeared or soiled the record by getting arrested" (Jackson, 1986, p. 98).

However, the distances over which the Society operated and the limited number of workers employed created difficulties for the system because they prevented careful selection and supervision of homes:

> There was little time for consultation, and refusal would be embarrassing, and I know that the Committee consented to some assignments against their better judgment. . . . The evil is proved by the fact that, while the younger children are taken from motives of benevolence and are uniformly well treated, the older ones are, in the majority of cases, taken from motives of profit, and are expected to earn their way from the start. (Hart, 1884)

Opposition of Western states to the "extraditing" and "dumping" of dependent children in their area, opposition of the Catholic Church to what was regarded as an attempt by a Protestant organization to wean children from their Catholic heritage through placement in non-Catholic homes, and criticism by a growing number of child welfare professionals contributed to declining use of these placement procedures. "It is the wolf of the old indenture philosophy of child labor in the sheepskin disguise of a so-called good or Christian home" (Thurston, 1930, p. 136).

Brace's program stimulated the development of similar services elsewhere. The State Children's Home Societies originated in 1883 in Indiana and Illinois with the work of Martin Van Buren Van Arsdale, who, like Brace, was a minister. By 1923, there were Societies in thirty-four states. The activities of these agencies were supplemented by sectarian agencies in larger cities, such as the Jewish Child Care Association in New York City, and nonsectarian agencies, such as the Boston Children's Aid Society.

At the same time, public agencies were pioneering other alternatives. The Michigan State Public School (in reality, an orphanage) opened in 1874; it was created as a temporary home for all destitute children who had become public charges until the children could be placed in foster family homes. Nineteen other states soon adopted similar plans. In the late 1860s, Massachusetts pioneered in paying board money to foster families for the maintenance of children who might otherwise have been placed in institutions and who were too young to be profitably indentured. This state also pioneered in more careful supervision of those children who had been indentured by the state.

The Boston Children's Aid Society, under the leadership of Charles Birtwell in the late 1800s, carried foster family care a step further. For each child, Birtwell asked, "What does the child really need?" rather than "Where shall we put the child?" He developed a systematic plan for studying foster home applicant families and a systematic plan of supervision once the child was placed. An effort was made to keep detailed records and to develop principles of action. His approach required individual study of the child and a variety of different kinds of substitute care—an individualization of need and diversification of services. Birtwell was, in effect, attempting to build a science of foster family care and to professionalize practice.

Birtwell also showed an appreciation for the potentialities of the preventive placement aspects of supportive and supplementary services. For Brace, long-term placement suggested that the foster parent was, in fact, replacing the birth parent in a pseudo-adoptive situation. Given Birtwell's approach, the foster parent–foster child relationship became something distinctively different—a means through which the child could be ultimately restored to the family.

The closing of mixed almshouses at the end of the nineteenth century gave further impetus to the use of foster family care (Folks, 1902). Orphanages also used foster family services as a supplementary resource. For infants, before the advent of pasteurized milk and formula feeding, the institution had to provide nursing care, often in a foster family home. When the child reached early adolescence, institutions had to "dismiss their wards and the usual method when that age arrives is to obtain a place for a child in a private home as an accepted inmate or paid worker before withdrawing institutional care and support" (Slingerland, 1919, p. 39).

Throughout the nineteenth century and the early part of the twentieth century, controversy raged between the advocates of institutional care and the supporters of foster family care over which was the more desirable method. Foster family care was given official sanction in 1899 by the National Conference of Correction and Charities. The First White House Conference on the Care of Dependent Children in 1909 stated that "the carefully selected foster home is, for the normal child, the best substitute for the natural home." The child welfare field had come to adopt the perspective that it is only when the child cannot function in this type of environment that residential care is to be contemplated. Pelton (1989) argued that, if impact is measured by results, "the shift in foster care patterns from institutions to foster homes has been the only true major reform that has occurred in child welfare practice in modern times" (p. xi).

The twentieth century saw a gradual expansion of the impact of public agencies and governmental policies on the delivery of foster family services. "Public child welfare was to develop largely as a system of foster homes and institutions" (Kamerman & Kahn, 1990, p. 24). As foster family care changed from a system of free wage homes to one in which foster families were paid for opening their homes to children, funding, particularly public funding, became of increasing concern to service providers. Since the 1930s, changes in the size and nature of the foster care population have been tied to expansion or contraction of public services for poor families. At some points, provision of readily available public assistance monies, like AFDC, contributed to decreases in foster care populations. On the other hand, increases in funding for public child welfare programming and for staff were associated with increases in the size of that population (Pelton, 1989).

Patterns of use of foster family care were not the same for African American, Native American, and Hispanic children as they were for Caucasian children. Until the 1950s, African American, Native American, and Hispanic children were largely excluded from services, especially those delivered by private social service programs (Stehno, 1988; Pelton, 1989).

> ADC opened the way for states' Mothers' Pensions to be given to African-American families, and by midcentury, children of color began to appear in the group of dependent children cared for publicly. Because of the linkage of Aid to Families with Dependent Children (AFDC) funds to foster care placements, African-American, Hispanic, and Native American children soon began to appear in ever-increasing numbers in publicly financed foster care. (Davidson, 1994, p. 79)

Exclusionary practices made the development of alternative, more informal means of care an imperative in many African American communities, and these resources are still used today. Native American children have a long history of removal and placement in boarding schools, obstensibly for educational purposes (Matheson, 1996). Such placements, in effect, cut children's ties to their families and communities while at the same time denying them the right to any other normative family experiences.

The Size of Today's Foster Care Population

While effective policy development and program planning necessitates an accurate count of the number and types of children for whom foster family services are used, no such figures are, as yet, available for the country as a whole. While the federal government recognizes the need for such statistics, implementation of nationwide mandatory data collection is just beginning to come to fruition. Regulations for a 1986 amendment to Title IV-E of the Social Security Act were finally published in 1993, requiring all states to participate in the Adoption and Foster Care Analysis and Reporting System (AFCARS). Data for 1995 and 1996 are now available from this source. However, serious problems with production and promulgation of the data remain (Barth, Courtney, Berrick, & Albert, 1994). An October 9, 1998 U.S. Children's Bureau web page noted,

> Although a total of 38 States submitted foster care data for the period, data from up to 22 States were excluded from each table because of data quality issues and/or specific requests by some States not to have their data included. The data are estimated to represent 55 percent of the total number of children served by State child welfare foster care systems in FY 1996.

Michigan, Pennsylvania, Indiana, Minnesota, Wisconsin, Texas, and Virginia were among the states excluded from the 1996 figures. The Children's Bureau described 382,017 children in care as of September 30, 1997 (web page, March 12, 1999).

Estimates of the size of the foster care population for the earlier years of the 1990s were generated by the Voluntary Cooperative Information System (VCIS), which operated under the auspices of the American Public Welfare Association and began publishing data voluntarily provided by the states in 1982. Unfortunately, states decided individually whether or not to contribute data for each report.

Of even greater consequence for examination of foster family statistics, VCIS had only aggregate data from each state to work with. These data reflected the total number of children

> in substitute care under the management and responsibility of the State child welfare agency, including: foster family care (relative and nonrelative), group homes, child care facilities, emergency shelter care, supervised independent living, nonfinalized adoptive placements, and any other arrangement considered 24-hour substitute care by the State agency. (U.S. House of Representatives Committee on Ways and Means, 1992, p. 904)

The data were not disaggregated for the various types of substitute care options. Therefore, when we describe characteristics of children in care using these data, the reader is cautioned that the extent to which this material reflects use of foster family services is unknown. Recent VCIS data are described in Table 2.1.

TABLE 2.1   *Trends in the Use of Substitute Care Services, 1982–1994*

Year	Total Number of Children Served	Number in Care, End of Year	Placement Rate (per 1000)	Percent in Family Care[*]
1982	434,000	262,000	2.5	72.0%
1984	456,000	276,000	2.4	67.7
1986	456,000	280,000	2.4	71.3
1988	511,000	340,000	2.7	73.7
1989	565,000	383,000	2.9	76.1
1990		407,000		71.4
1991	636,000	414,000		
1992		427,000		
1993	657,000	445,000		
1994	698,000	468,000		
1995		494,000 (estimated)		

Sources: Tatara, 1993, pp. 33, 98; U.S. House of Representatives Committee on Ways & Means, 1992, p. 903; Tatara, 1994, 1995, 1996.

[*]Includes foster homes and nonfinalized adoptive placements.

Beginning in 1987, an ambitious attempt to address these data problems was begun by investigators representing a five-state consortium: Illinois, New York, California, Michigan, and Texas. This Multi-State Foster Care Data Archive incorporates material on children in "foster family homes, group homes, and congregate care facilities" (Wulczyn, Goerge, & Harden, 1993). However, the nature of data collection will eventually allow for disaggregation of the data based on type of care. The archive published its first report in 1993. Plans include expansion of the survey to include information from ten states within the next few years.

Summarizing available data on use of substitute care services over the years, Pelton (1989) concluded, "The foster care population increased from 1910 until 1933, declined until sometime before 1961, increased until its high point during 1975–77, and declined until 1982" (p. 8). Since that time the figures have been rising (Table 2.1), and, in the case of some states, increasing in dramatic fashion. The number of children in substitute homes in California rose 143 percent between 1983 and 1992; Illinois's population rose 135 percent, New York's 125 percent, Texas's 124 percent (Wulczyn, Goerge, & Harden, 1993); and between 1985 and 1995, Washington's 70 percent (English & Clark, 1996). The national placement rate increased 60.7 percent between 1986 and 1992 (Tatara, 1994). The period of greatest growth occurred between 1987 and 1989 (Wulczyn, 1994; Courtney, 1994). Estimates are that by the turn of the century, more than half a million children will be in substitute care (Lindsey, 1992).

These figures are, in some ways, deceptive since they denote the number of children living in care on a given day. This does not give consideration to the turnover factor—the flow of children in and out of care. For example, VCIS data suggest that while 429,000 children were in care at the end of 1991, 636,000 children were actually in care at some point during that year (Tatara, 1994). Since the mid-1980s, more children have entered care than have left care, reversing a trend toward greater discharge rates found in the early 1980s. The 1996 AFCARS data indicated that 62,816 children came into care between April and September of that year, but only 43,585 children left care (U.S. DHHS Children's Bureau web page, October 9, 1998). The substitute care figures also fail to indicate children placed in homes privately or informally by families. In any one year, then, the number of children served by the foster family care system is likely to be much higher than the official figures—how much higher, nobody really knows.

The federal government annually tracks the number of children in substitute care for whom it makes maintenance payments under the Title IV-E AFDC Foster Care Program (U.S. House of Representatives Committee on Ways and Means, 1993). These are children who would have been eligible for AFDC if they had been able to remain in their own parents' homes. They may be placed in foster family care with kin or non-kin, in private child care agencies, or in public institutions housing fewer than twenty-six children. Because this database reflects information from all fifty states, it can be used to evaluate changes in the need for substitute services in recent years. The average estimated number of such children doubled between 1982 and 1991, from 93,000 to 203,000; the Committee on Ways and Means of the U.S. House of Representatives estimated that by 1998 the number would double again, rising to 304,000. Federal expenditures for AFDC-eligible children are estimated to have increased 1300 percent between 1981 and 1999 (Courtney, 1995).

In the 1970s and early 1980s, the average age of children in substitute care settings was increasing, and adolescents comprised the fastest growing group of children in care (Kadushin & Martin, 1988). This picture now appears to be changing. Wulczyn, Goerge, and Harden (1993) remarked, "When the five state data are pooled together, the most striking feature of the age distribution is the overwhelming number of infants admitted to foster care. For the entire period (1983–1992), one out of every five first admissions was a child who had yet to experience his or her first birthday" (p. 17). Between 1982 and 1989, the proportion of infants in care rose 139 percent, and those between the ages of one and five rose 133 percent.

> A study conducted by the U.S. General Accounting Office (GAO) revealed that in New York City, Los Angeles County, and Philadelphia County, the total population in out-of-home care increased by 66 percent between 1986 and 1991, while the number of children under three years of age in care in these cities increased by 110 percent. (Gleeson, 1999, p. 42)

(See also English & Clark, 1996.) Berrick, Needell, Barth, and Johnson-Reid (1998) estimated "nearly 3 percent of all young children will experience such grave threats to their well-being that they will be placed in foster care at some point before age six" (p. 4). A 1986 study of African American children in care in five cities

throughout the United States also found that infants were entering care in dispro-
portionate numbers (National Black Child Development Institute, 1989).

The proportion of children who are in care during their middle school years
has remained relatively stable. Teens comprised 30.6 percent of all children in
care at the end of 1989, a decrease from 45.3 percent in 1982 (Tatara, 1993, p. 88).
The 1997 AFCARS data described 40 percent of the children as teens (age eleven
or older), 33 percent as babies and preschoolers, and the remainder (28 percent) as
elementary school age (U.S. DHHS Children's Bureau web page, March 12, 1999.
See also Wulczyn, 1994; Albert, 1994; Barth, Courtney, Berrick, & Albert, 1994;
Schwartz, Ortega, Guo, & Fishman, 1994).

In 1988, the average age of children in all types of substitute care was nine
and a half years. The median age of children in foster family homes is, however,
younger than that of children in other forms of substitute care, such as group
homes and institutions. California data (Barth, Courtney, Berrick, & Albert, 1994)
describe their average age as between seven and eight (p. 244).

Data collected over the past several years indicate that boys and girls are
equally likely to be referred for foster family care services (Fitzharris, 1985;
Lindsey, 1992; U.S. DHHS Children's Bureau AFCARS data, web page, March 12,
1999). Because racial and gender-based differences might emerge in comparisons
among various types of substitute care settings, it is unfortunate that such statistics are unavailable.

African American, Native American, and Hispanic children continue to be
greatly overrepresented in substitute care (Cox & Cox, 1984; Barth, Courtney,
Berrick, & Albert, 1994; English & Clark, 1996). About one-third of all children in
care at the end of 1989 were African American and 10 percent were Hispanic
(Tatara, 1993). The 1997 AFCARS data described 32 percent of the children in care
as white, 47 percent as Black, 14 percent as Hispanic, and 1 percent as Asian/
Pacific Islanders (U.S. DHHS Children's Bureau web page, March 12, 1999). "In
1990, African American children in Texas were 3 times as likely as European
American children to be in foster care, and over 10 times as likely in New York"
(Courtney, 1995, p. 30). One study estimated that Native American children are
placed at a rate 3.6 times that of other children in care (Wares, Dobrec, Rosenthal,
& Wedel, 1992). The number of minority children is particularly high among sub-
stitute care populations from large cities (Jenkins & Diamond, 1985).

Substitute care services are not evenly distributed throughout the country.
The considerable variation existing from state to state suggests differing political
and professional milieus, varying economic and social climates, as well as historical differences in the use of services (Humphrey & Humphrey, 1988; Goerge,
Wulczyn, & Harden, 1996). Two-thirds of all children in substitute care live in ten
states, primarily in the Northeast and Southeast: California, Florida, Georgia, Illinois, Massachusetts, Michigan, New Jersey, New York, Ohio, and Pennsylvania
(Besharov, 1990). New York and California are responsible for almost half of the
children in care and for half of the federal funds expended for substitute services.
However, federal expenditures for IV-E eligible children have been increasing
most dramatically in the Southeast. Urban caseloads in some states are increasing

at a far greater rate than those of suburban or rural areas (Goerge, Wulczyn, & Harden, 1996).

Courtney (1995) estimated that federal expenditures for twelve months for support payments to a foster family and administrative costs for a child's care were $10,945 in 1993 (p. 28). Once again, there is considerable variation in this figure from state to state. In 1992, payments to Alaskan foster parents for a 16-year-old averaged $621 and to Alabaman parents averaged $234; the national average was $385 (U.S. House of Representatives Committee on Ways & Means, 1993, p. 895).

Current Policy and Practice Concerns

The more recent history of foster family care reflects widespread concern about the effectiveness of this service for children and families as well as a deepening conviction that this option for children is too easily accessed when other, more useful services remain underutilized. Today, as in Brace's time, foster family care is challenged for its inability to provide some critically important aspects of family life, including a sense of predictability and continuity. Concern with the rights of children has made us sensitive to the entitlement of such children to some regularization of their status (Freud, Goldstein, & Solnit, 1973). Since the 1970s, national evaluations by various child advocacy groups have indicted the system for its failure in meeting children's need for permanence (Children's Defense Fund, 1978, 1992; National Commission for Children in Need of Parents, 1979; National Commission on Children, 1991). Studies conducted over the last forty years have repeatedly shown that the longer a child has been in placement, the greater the likelihood that he or she will continue in placement (Maas & Engler, 1959; Shapiro, 1972; Fanshel & Shinn, 1978; Goerge, 1990).

At the same time, children in care for long periods are more likely to lose contact with their birth families than are those who stay only short periods. Without sufficient agency support, parents' motivation to see their children can diminish. Many families gradually reorient their lives to the reality that they are no longer actually caring for their children; having reorganized their lives in this way, they may find it increasingly difficult to welcome the idea of the child's return (Musewicz, 1981). All of these factors threaten the foster child's right to family permanency.

The decreasing number of white, nonhandicapped infants available for adoption also prompted reexamination of the status of all children in substitute care in an effort to determine if some of those children could be made available for adoption. Increasing public resentment in the 1970s against being taxed to support social programs added concern about program costs and impelled efforts to free more children for adoption and to more rapidly reunify others with their families.

Criticism has been extensive and often harsh, particularly over the last thirty years, as the foster care population has grown rapidly. The sense of frustration is evident in the argument of some critics that perhaps the system should be disbanded and replaced by old-style "orphanages" (Aldgate, 1987; American Humane Association, 1994; Smith, 1995). The system's limitations are emphasized and claims about the harm done to children have been exaggerated (Wald, Carlsmith, & Leiderman, 1988; Steinhauer, 1991).

Initiatives Designed to Reduce the Use of Foster Care

A variety of initiatives—programmatic, judicial, legislative, and administrative—have attempted to deal with the burgeoning scope of the foster care system. These include:

Development of programs designed to prevent the placement of children in foster family care

Increased use of kinship caretakers, who are seen as both foster parents and family-based caretakers

Development of reunification services designed to move children out of care and into permanent homes more quickly

Efforts to reduce payments for foster family care, especially for kinship care

Changes in judicial procedures to make children more readily available for adoption

Development of better tracking and monitoring procedures for children in care

Efforts to reduce the size of foster family care through use of managed care principles

Explicit changes in federal legislation designed to force states to implement procedures that minimize foster care placements, move children out of care more quickly, and move them on to permanent homes

Preventing Placement

Local, state, and federal initiatives have focused on efforts to prevent children from entering foster family care, primarily through the use of *family preservation* services. Sometimes providing services to families in their homes (*home-based* programs) and sometimes bringing families together at some convenient neighborhood location (*family support centers*), these programs share a common philosophy of practice:

1. Services should be *family centered* rather than child centered, that is, services should be directed at enhancing family functioning as a whole so that the child can remain in the famiy.

2. Services should be *home based,* that is, insofar as possible they should be delivered in the home, not in an agency office.
3. Services should be *crisis oriented,* taking advantage of the dynamics of crisis to bring about change. . . .
4. Services should *empower* families, which we take to mean developing in families the ability to solve their own problems. . . .
5. Services should be *community oriented.* (Schuerman, Rzepnicki, & Littell, 1994, p. 19. Italics in original.)

(See also Wells & Biegel, 1990; Kinney, Haapala, & Booth, 1991; Allen, Brown, & Finlay, 1992; Morton & Grigsby, 1993; Melina, 1997.)

Family preservation is seen as the "front line" service of public child welfare. For all families (except those whose parenting practices place children in severe jeopardy), agencies create service plans that attempt to correct insufficiencies and prevent further mistreatment while keeping the family together. Foster family care is only to be used in instances where family preservation services fail—in situations where parents continue to mistreat their children, even though they have been provided with appropriate supports and interventions in their own homes.

Using Kinship Care

While the number of children in care is rising, the number of foster homes licensed to care for these children has been on the decline. "In some areas, the shortage of foster homes is so severe that children are sleeping overnight in the child welfare office because no homes are available" (McFadden, 1990, p. 2). The licensed capacity of these homes has also been decreasing. A survey of more than 1,900 foster families conducted by James Bell Associates (1993) found the average capacity of homes licensed before 1980 was 3.0 children; between 1980 and 1985 the capacity diminished to 2.9; after 1985, homes could take even fewer children, 2.6 on the average. The study estimated that 65,000 additional families would be needed just to retain the spaces provided by existing foster homes (p. iv). In California, the lack of sufficient foster family homes has resulted in increased use of group care, especially for young children. "The percentage of children under the age of five in group home care more than doubled over the five years between 1985 and 1990. During the same period the percentage of group home children who were infants (under one year old) grew by more than 50%" (Courtney, 1994, p. 187).

Kinship placements began to be seen as more viable resources at a time when the need for foster family homes had grown desperate and new funding opportunities for kinship care became available (Danzy & Jackson, 1997). In a 1979 U.S. Supreme Court ruling (*Youakim* v. *Miller*), relatives were granted the opportunity to receive the same foster family payment rates as nonrelatives. Prior to the ruling, relatives might be told they could only receive support through AFDC, where payments are considerably lower than foster care board rates (CWLA, 1991a; Johnson, 1994).

Kinship foster care now represents more than half of all placements in several states, including California, Illinois, Florida, and New York (Gebel, 1996). In California, two-thirds of the increase in foster care use between 1984 and 1992 involved kin placements (Berrick, Barth, & Needell, 1994). AFCAR statistics from 1997 (U.S. DHHS Children's Bureau, web page, March 12, 1999) indicated that kin placements made up 32 percent of foster family care. (See also Hegar & Scannapieco, 1999.) Interestingly, data from the AARP's Grandparent Information Center suggests kinship care may be part of a general trend for grandparents to take on more responsibility for raising their grandchildren (Woodworth, 1996).

The steepest rise in use of such care occurred since 1986 (Testa, 1992; Gleeson, 1996; Testa, Shook, Cohen, & Woods, 1996). In New York City, for example, 151 kin homes were used in 1985; by 1991, 23,591 were in use (Scannapieco & Jackson, 1996). In California, the foster care population as a whole grew 2.5 times larger between 1984 and 1994; however, the kinship care population grew 6.6 times (Barth, Courtney, Needell, & Johnson-Reid, 1994, p. 3). Private foster care providers have also documented a major increase in use of such care (Massinga & Perry, 1994).

There has been strong support for the notion that kinship care is more than a foster care service; it also must be seen as a means of keeping families together:

> For the African American community, the terms *family preservation* and *kinship care* are interchangeable. Both are ways of sustaining and maintaining the family system. (Danzy & Jackson, 1997, p. 36. Italics in original.)

Kinship services are seen as such a vital resource for children who must be placed away from their families that most child welfare agencies now routinely explore whether kin can take a child needing care before turning to non-kin resources.

Enhancing Family Reunification and Permanency

Some programmatic efforts enhanced permanency and continuity for children by developing a cadre of social workers committed to permanency objectives and skilled in implementing them. The most notable examples were the Alameda Project in California (Stein, 1976; Stein, Gambrill, & Wiltse, 1978) and the Oregon Project (Emlen et al., 1977; Pike et al., 1977). The Alameda Project used three specially assigned workers with a limited caseload (twenty cases "defined as families") who "offered intensive service to the natural parents using behavioral methods of treatment while county child welfare workers provided their usual services to the child in the foster home" (Stein, 1976, p. 39). At the end of two years, a significantly greater percentage of the experimental group children had been returned home or had achieved or were headed for adoption than was true for the control group children. The researchers attributed experimental group success to early systematic planning by the demonstration workers, facilitating early decision making on the part of the parents. Contracts provided the specific framework and content for worker-client interaction. They also provided the evidence needed for active steps taken to terminate parental rights in planning for adoption.

The Oregon Project employed a somewhat different set of procedures in dealing with problems of the foster care system. The project emphasized intensive, systematic casework in achieving permanent planning for children and active, aggressive pursuit of the termination of parental rights. The project design also involved limited caseloads (twenty-five children per worker as opposed to the usual caseload of fifty to sixty children in Oregon) and full-time legal assistance to free children for adoption. The 509 children selected for the project had been in care one year or more; were twelve years of age or younger; were not likely, in the worker's judgment, to return home; and were considered adoptable. At the end of the three-year period, an impressive 79 percent of the children were out of foster family care; 27 percent had been returned home, and an additional 52 percent either were in adoptive homes or their adoption was being actively planned (Emlen et al., 1977, p. 5). Procedures that were effective in the Alameda and Oregon Projects have been subsequently employed in other established programs with the help of federal funding.

Statistics from states that developed well-organized programs whose explicit objective is permanence showed a drop in total foster care caseloads following initiation of such efforts—in South Carolina, from 4,000 to 3,500 and in Virginia, from 11,876 to 10,369 over a two-year period; in Oregon, from 4,400 in 1972 to 3,600 in 1976; and in New York from 44,000 in 1979 to 25,000 in 1984. These efforts also resulted in substantial reductions in the cost of services to children (State of California, 1981, p. 21).

Reducing Payments and Services for Foster Family Care

Efforts to reduce the cost of foster family care by making reductions in supports to or funding for foster families have targeted kinship foster homes. Under the assumption that kinship care is actually a form of family preservation, several state and county child welfare agencies have explored one or more of the following options (Gleeson & Craig, 1994; Gleeson, 1995, 1999; Hornby, Zeller, & Karraker, 1996).

1. Some agencies have reduced the extent to which kinship care placements are monitored. Arguing that such monitoring is unnecessary and represents unwanted intrusion into family life, these programs have chosen to reduce administrative costs by reducing oversight services in these cases.
2. "Some states are considering a two-tiered system for reimbursing kinship caregivers, with the full foster care payment for kinship homes meeting approved standards and a reduced rate for those not yet approved" (Gleeson, 1995, p. 189).

3. Some agencies do not offer kinship caretakers any financial support unless the caretaker explicitly requests it.
4. Some agencies will place children with kin who, because of their own backgrounds or living circumstances, do not meet the criteria for foster care licensure. These kin are denied foster care payments because they do not meet foster care standards; however, the children remain in their homes (Gleeson, 1999).

Kin who are not offered or who do not receive foster care payments may be encouraged to apply for welfare funding instead (Scannapieco, 1999). However, support from this source continues to be substantially less than that provided by foster care board rates (Gleeson, 1995). Welfare reform has also made continuation of these payments uncertain.

Expanding Opportunities for Adoption

One set of initiatives relates to changes in the laws regarding the termination of parental rights so that foster children who are unlikely to return home can be freed for adoption. The termination of parental rights is more readily available now for the child who is "permanently neglected," whose parents fail, despite the diligent efforts of the agency, to maintain any kind of meaningful contact with the child. However, organizational barriers in both the child welfare agency and the court system can impede or prevent termination efforts (Cahn & Johnson, 1993). Lack of knowledge of the whereabouts of the parents, active or anticipated opposition by the parents to termination, or the continuing interest of the parents in the child, however vague or intermittent, can make freeing the child for adoption more difficult (Meyer, 1985).

Enhanced Tracking and Monitoring Efforts

To obtain greater control over the entry and exit of children from the foster care system, child welfare agencies have made explicit plans to monitor permanency efforts internally; child welfare agencies have also collaborated in extra-agency monitoring activities carried out by citizen review boards. Courts, particularly juvenile courts, have also played oversight, evaluative, and advocacy roles designed to insure timely permanency planning for children.

Child welfare agencies now pay more attention to documentation of essential information about children in care. All case files should include an explication of current plans for the child and family, documentation of the child's placement history, and other essential medical and personal data (National Black Child Development Institute, 1991). Agencies have made increased use of computers to assist in this work (Fanshel & Finch, 1985).

Because permanency decisions are complex, forms and computers cannot, by themselves, be relied on to monitor a child's progress toward permanency. Instead, professional judgments must be made with regard to relevance and timeliness. To provide oversight of permanency planning processes and outcomes, one approach has been to utilize volunteers who form a citizen review board. Board members are responsible for evaluating permanency plans in individual cases (Dodson, 1983; Wiltse, 1985; Lindsey & Wodarski, 1986; Jordan & Franklin, 1994). The Children in Placement Project (CIP), sponsored by the National Council of Juvenile and Family Court Judges, is a program of this type.

Another approach relies on both outside and internal participants to do this work. Maryland has used a system of this type (Kamerman & Kahn, 1990), as has Children's Services of San Mateo County, California. Children's Services established a Placement Review Board comprised of three members, at least one of whom came from outside the agency (Ten Broeck & Barth, 1986). The committee carried out a "regular review of children in placement, screening of all children referred for group or institutional placement, and children placed in shelter care more than 30 days" (p. 284).

The role of juvenile court judges is highlighted by the Michigan Agency Attorney Project (Herring, 1993). In this program, private attorneys were hired to represent the Department of Social Services (DSS) and to advocate for the caseworker's plan for each family in juvenile court. Juvenile court judges were also required by law to pay close attention to permanency plans and timely decision making during court hearings. Project efforts resulted in substantially earlier permanency decisions on behalf of children (p. 34). (See also Festinger 1975, 1976; Wert, Fein, & Haller, 1986.)

The CASA (Court Appointed Special Advocates) model uses specially trained volunteers to serve as advocates for children in juvenile court proceedings. This is a popular approach; in 1992 there were more than 450 CASA programs in 47 states (National Court Appointed Special Advocates Association mimeo, 1992). A study of its impact in one community "indicated that, overall, CASA volunteers performed at least as well as specialized attorneys in representing children in juvenile court" (Poertner & Press, 1990, p. 547; see also Jordan, 1989; White, 1994; Leung, 1996).

Another approach used to advocate for more effective decision making has been to sue public child welfare agencies who are not carrying out required permanency planning mandates. "As of mid-1992, cases have been settled or decided in Massachusetts, Maryland, Connecticut, the District of Columbia, Kansas City, New Mexico, Alabama, Louisiana, Los Angeles, Illinois, Cincinnati, and Arkansas" (Hansen, 1994, p. 226. See also Mushlin, Levitt, & Anderson, 1986; Stein, 1991; Kopels & Rycraft, 1993). Cases were pending in six other communities or states. Hansen (1994) suggested that this litigation has at least enhanced the service delivery process in foster care; whether children and families have benefited is more difficult to determine.

Taken together, all of these efforts are seen as having had a positive impact on the delivery of child welfare services to children and their families:

The review of cases, the representation of clients and the lawsuits brought against agencies for violating their statutory obligations all have resulted in more systemic change in children's services than almost any other aspect of permanency planning reform (Elizabeth Cole cited in *NASW News,* July, 1993, p. 9).

Using Managed Care

In a recent survey of child welfare agency administrators, the Child Welfare League of America found 41 out of 49 states were considering "applying or planning to apply managed care principles to the financing and delivery of child welfare services" (*NASW News,* June, 1996, p. 3; see also Mordock, 1996). Although states and communities differ in their definition of the term *managed care,* most would include *privatization* (using the private instead of the public sector to provide or manage services) and *oversight* (use of a particular agency or service to set standards for and limits on service delivery). In 1997, Kansas "became the first state in the country to privatize its child-welfare system" (Tyson, 1997, p. 1). In this state, private agencies are paid a one-time "capitated" rate of about $13,000 per client. Limiting payments in this way is designed to motivate agencies to move clients toward permanency in as timely a fashion as possible.

Concerns about the potential impact of managed care on child welfare are manifold (Petr & Johnson, 1999). There are worries that this type of system will undermine efforts to keep children safe, will prematurely terminate parental rights, and will force families and children into accepting short-term services when longer-term care is actually needed. It is not clear how children will be treated if their funding limit has been reached but they are not in (or have reentered care from) a permanent placement. Serious questions about monitoring the quality of services have also been raised, as have concerns about diversion of funds from needed services into oversight and management activities. Concerns about adequacy of service delivery under managed care in the health and mental health service sectors also create unease about its impact on the child welfare field. Gleeson (1999) noted that, under managed care,

> Any efforts to reduce caseloads and costs are likely to be evaluated with measures of case status. However, lower caseloads, shorter length of service, and higher discharge rates are not necessarily measures of success, unless the only goal is to reduce costs. Success should not be equated with merely providing less service, to fewer recipients, for lower costs. Costs of services are interpretable only in relationship to the safety, permanence, and well-being experienced by children and families affected by cost reduction policies. (p. 46)

(See also *NASW News,* February, 1999, p. 5.) Whether children can be well served and remain safe is yet to be seen.

Legislative Underpinnings

The many concerns about adequacy of services and the size of the foster care system fueled important federal legislation which created standards for child welfare services that emphasized the importance of permanency, created guidelines for better management and oversight of services, emphasized the significance of timely decision making, and validated the importance of kinship care for children. These principles are embodied in PL 96-272, the *Adoption Assistance and Child Welfare Act of 1980;* PL 100-485, the *Family Preservation and Support Provisions,* adopted in 1988; and PL 105-89, the *Adoption and Safe Families Act of 1997.*

Legislators sought a major revision in foster care standards and practice with passage of PL 96-272. This law codified service delivery provisions designed to enhance permanence. Each child must have an individualized case plan that includes

> (1) a description of the placement setting, (2) an explanation of the appropriateness of the placement, (3) a description and explanation of the appropriateness of the services aimed at achieving permanence to be provided the child, the parents, and the foster parents, and (4) an explanation of the appropriateness of such services with respect to the child's needs while in foster care. (Musewicz, 1981, p. 728)

Public Law 96-272 also described requirements for intensive efforts to assist parents in remediating problems that led to removal of their children from their home. These requirements have as their objective prevention of inappropriate use of substitute care and, in cases in which it is required, use of care for as short a period of time as possible.

This legislation outlined procedures for assessing an individual child's progress through the system. After the child has been in care for six months, his or her situation was to be reviewed, using either court or administrative procedures. Within eighteen months after placement, a dispositional hearing was to be held in order to evaluate the agency's achievement of permanency-planning objectives and to clarify the child's future. The child's record also had to contain basic medical and educational information (U.S. House of Representatives Committee on Ways & Means, 1992, p. 881).

Under the law, states were encouraged and, in some instances, mandated to carry out a series of monitoring procedures in order to receive AFDC-FC and Title IV-B funding. States are now responsible for developing inventories of children who have been in substitute care for more than six months, for disseminating information about basic characteristics of these children, and for monitoring and evaluating utilization of federal funds to maintain them in settings other than their birth family or an adoptive home. States are, furthermore, responsible for developing a tracking system, so that information is readily available about all children in care. This provision is aimed at preventing children from becoming "lost in the system."

Concerns that federal funding has been more readily available for foster family care than for home-based services led to passage of the Family Preservation and Support Services Provisions of the Social Security Act in 1993. This legislation targeted funds for states to develop intensive preplacement services programs to prevent placement; respite care for children whose parents have no other option; and services to teach parents to develop confidence in their own strengths, recognize where they need to improve, and learn skills in child development, financial management, coping with stress, and health and nutrition. (Early & Hawkins, 1994, p. 311)

Funds are to be used by states to evaluate and overhaul their system of services for families, focusing their greatest effort on areas of greatest need, and encouraging "cross-cutting community-based strategies" (Early & Hawkins, 1994, p. 311). This legislation has resulted in

a growing number of effective partnerships involving family preservation and family support services, as well as a lot of valuable prevention projects and support programs—all attributable to the FPSSP. (Mannes, 1998, p. 2)

Federal attention to adoption as a second approach to ensuring permanency for children is reflected in the Adoption and Safe Families Act (ASFA) of 1997 (PL 105-89). Zlotnik (1998) summarized the purpose of this legislation:

The new law, effective since November 1997, reinforces the need for permanency planning efforts to begin as soon as the child enters foster care. The emphasis on permanency includes:
- expedited termination of parental rights
- promotion of concurrent planning
- emphasis on placement with kin, legal guardians, or adoptive families
- identification of situations in which "reasonable efforts" may be waived (1998, p. 17)

This legislation emphasized child safety as a criterion for decision making in child welfare. Agencies may not be required to make or extend reasonable efforts toward family preservation or reunification if a judge has determined that the child's safety is jeopardized because the parent has "subjected the child to aggravated circumstances," such as "abandonment, torture, chronic abuse, and sexual abuse," the parent has committed murder or voluntary manslaughter, or the parent has "committed a felony assault that results in serious bodily harm to the child or another child of the parent" (111 Stat. 2116), or the parent has had parental rights to a sibling involuntarily terminated. Permanency hearings for such children must occur within thirty days after such a judicial determination.

This legislation also shortened the time period in which options short of termination of parental rights may be explored for all children in care. While PL 96-272 gave agencies eighteen months to create a permanency plan, PL 105-89 requires they be developed within twelve months. Alternative permanent placements must be sought for children who have been in care for fifteen of the last twenty-two months. The legislation adds explicit financial incentives for states to pursue adoption for children in such circumstances.

Reducing the Use of Foster Family Care: A Final Comment

Terpstra and McFadden (1993) outlined the major reasons for the substantial rise in the use of substitute care services over the past five years. They noted that economic factors (the recessions of the 1980s and 1990s, with the concomitant increase in both poverty and homelessness among families with children), political factors (declining commitment to helping those in need through governmental programs), professional factors (such as deinstitutionalization), and social factors (increased drug use, for example) have played major roles (pp. 3–4). (See also National Black Child Development Institute, 1989; Testa, 1992; Wulczyn 1994; Tatara, 1994.)

In its *Blueprint for Fostering Infants, Children, and Youths in the 1990s* (1991a), the Child Welfare League of America argued for the need for a more realistic view of the social conditions that underlie expansion of the foster family care population:

> The problems that family foster care is struggling to handle are the logical result of two decades of national neglect in providing funding and services for children, youths, and their families. Numerous national studies report that the quality of life for children and their families has deteriorated over the past 20 years, particularly during the last decade. (CWLA, 1991a, p. 3)

There is a growing realization that efforts to address the endemic problems of foster care require that we also address the myriad problems of families served by the child welfare system (Meyer, 1985; Tatara, 1994) as well as making a commitment to providing needed services to all vulnerable families so that they can more easily avoid becoming clients of this system (Werner, 1994).

Given the clear association between economic and social stresses on the one hand and use of substitute care services on the other, it is difficult to hazard a prediction about future trends in the use of foster family care. Mounting concerns about the costs of such services, coupled with growing evidence that funds to pay for such services are not limitless, suggest that efforts to curb the use of these programs will continue. Such efforts may well result in renewed attempts to prevent placement of children and to remove as many children from care as possible, resulting in lower overall placement rates. On the other hand, continuation of the severe economic difficulties and lack of opportunity that have plagued this nation over the last decade may well result in expanded demand for services, particularly if alternative programs, such as welfare, home-based care, drug treatment, or outpatient mental health services, do not receive additional funding (National Black Child Development Institute, 1989; Courtney, 1995). The fact that most of these alternative programs are either overutilized, with long waiting lists, or are actually facing budget cuts does not suggest that families will be readily diverted away from the substitute care system.

Questions for Discussion and Debate

1. What are the links between early views of "best practice" in foster family care and views in vogue today?
2. What are the societal implications of the enormous and expanding size of our foster care population?
3. Despite its huge size, we still have very limited information about children and families needing foster family services. What are the consequences of this situation?
4. There is a tension between those who advocate for reunification approaches and those who press for other permanency options, such as adoption. What are the consequences of stressing (and financing) one or the other of these approaches?
5. What factors have contributed to the loss of non-kin foster care resources for children?
6. What are the pros and cons of using outside resources—such as citizen review boards or CASA programs—to help move children toward permanency more rapidly?

3

Overview of Practice in Foster Family Care

This chapter provides a broad view of service goals and objectives and describes the stages of the service delivery process for children and their families. These goals and stages will be examined in greater detail in the chapters that follow. Because an adequate understanding of practice requires information about the professionals responsible for engaging in that practice, the chapter also gives a snapshot of the foster family worker.

Service Goals and Objectives

The principles of practice described in Chapter 1 serve as guides during all phases of foster care practice and suggest specific objectives to be accomplished with each of the primary groups of foster family service recipients (Table 3.1). These objectives are complex and multifaceted, and they require coordinated efforts by the child's birth parents, foster parents, and service providers if they are to be accomplished.

Stages in the Service Delivery Process

Although the goals of insuring children's safety, working toward permanency, maintaining family attachments, and remediating family problems guide practice in all phases of foster family work, different phases of service delivery require that somewhat different tasks be accomplished. The stages of this process—intake, intervention, and leave-taking—are summarized next.

Intake. Intake with children and their families comprises two main functions. Workers perform a screening task to determine that foster family care is only used

TABLE 3.1 *Foster Family Service Objectives*

Client	Service Needs	Child Welfare Service
Children	Adapt to foster care Build more effective ties to birth family Maintain sense of personal, racial, and cultural identity Participate in permanency planning Work on personal problems resulting from maltreatment Work on developmental tasks	Worker provides some direct services and coordinates services delivered by foster parents or other providers; family-oriented services; more specialized services tend to be provided by outside agencies.
Birth Parents	Adapt to child's move to foster care Work on parenting issues that led to placement Work on personal problems that resulted in child maltreatment Make critical decisions about permanency for the child Work on own developmental tasks Manage relationship with foster parent and agency	Worker provides direct services through building partnerships with family members; foster parents work directly with birth parents; some services provided by other agencies.
Foster Parents	Adapt to child's move into foster home Help child with personal and interpersonal issues and concerns Work directly with birth parents and facilitate visiting Maintain own family and help own children grow and develop Work on own developmental tasks and concerns Manage relationship with foster agency	Worker provides direct services by developing intervention team with foster parents as key members; foster parents may also be recruited and supervised by other agencies.

by clients for whom other home-based service options are clearly inappropriate and dangerous for the child. Workers also carry out a variety of orientation activities, to help both the children and their parents understand the nature of foster family care and begin to adjust to changes in the children's living situation. Planning for the child's future originates in activities begun with both the child and family at intake.

The goal of intake with foster parents, in contrast, is to "screen in" potential applicants. Efforts are made to recruit interested applicants, acquaint them with the foster care and child welfare systems, assess, and train them. Intake eventuates in placement of the child in the foster family home.

Intervention.   Interventions with both the child and parents are primarily concerned with developing and carrying out permanency planning goals, remediating problems and issues that developed prior to placement and that precipitated it, and promoting healthy development during the placement period (CWLA, 1991a). For the children, establishing relationships with foster parents is a major challenge. For the children's parents, managing relationships with the foster family agency and participating effectively in plans for the children's future become additional tasks of importance.

Interventions with the foster family serve a two-fold function—(1) helping the foster parents become and remain effective supports and intervention aides for the children and birth families, and (2) helping the foster families maintain their own growth and health. Like birth parents, foster parents must learn to effectively manage their relationships with the foster care agency in order to carry out their role.

Leave-Taking.   This stage is not so much an "ending" as a "moving on" to a new set of life tasks for participants in these services. For children, their families, and the foster families, leave-taking involves making the decision to move on to the next stage of permanency planning. The children may be returned to birth family homes, placed for adoption, emancipated from care, or stabilized in planned long-term foster family settings. Leave-taking can also occur for unforeseen and unwelcome reasons, when the children or foster parents ask that the children be removed, for example.

The Foster Care Worker

We have no count of the number of foster family workers employed by public and private child welfare agencies; however, they number in the thousands. While some more general research has been done on child welfare agency staff, studies have not examined the qualifications or other characteristics of those specifically providing substitute care services in these agencies. Information about their backgrounds is, for all intents and purposes, nonexistent.

The many responsibilities of foster care workers are outlined by Hubbell (1981):

> Being a foster care caseworker demands intelligence, fairness, good judgment, empathy, and determination. The job entails being responsible for the safety of foster children, being the target of angry or bewildered biological parents, consoling confused or anxious children, and handling the demands and irritations of foster parents. Among the multitude of duties are removing a child from his family; securing a foster home; developing plans for a child and his family; working with the biological parents for the return of a child; arranging visits, treatment, and medical care; providing transportation; preparing for and attending judicial proceedings; terminating parents' rights; and arranging for adoption. Endless reams of paperwork accompany all of these tasks. (p. 110)

Workers are also required to make appropriate referrals to other agencies for services and to monitor clients' progress as they receive these services. The effective foster care worker must have extensive knowledge about the functioning of individuals, families, and agencies and skills in direct intervention, case management, and advocacy.

Child welfare workers describe this work as "'exciting,' 'challenging,' and 'rewarding'" (Gold, 1998, p. 705) because it provides them with the opportunity to work with people and see lives change for the better. A survey of social worker graduates who received National Child Welfare Training Center traineeships (Vinokur-Kaplan, 1991) found them generally satisfied with their work, particularly their efforts with clients and "feelings of accomplishment" (p. 86).

Workers' many complex responsibilities can also make this work exhausting, frustrating, and, at times, upsetting. In this child-welfare arena, as in others, workers complain about the amount of time they have to spend fulfilling obligations other than direct client service work. Hubbell (1981) asked fourteen workers to keep a daily log of their activities. She found that, during an eight-hour day, caseworkers spent almost two hours doing paperwork and more than an hour traveling to and from client interviews (pp. 116–117). Similar figures were cited in a more recent study conducted by Stein, Callaghan, McGee, and Douglas (1990).

The need for intensive family contact, particularly with families who can potentially move toward reunification with their children, and the need to respond to frequent crises suggest that the ideal caseload size for the foster care worker should be very small. The Child Welfare League of American (1995) recommended that foster care workers have twelve to fifteen children as clients (p. 113). Others have advocated for use of a caseload weighting approach, whereby the amount of direct intervention work, administrative effort, and travel time are taken into account in determining a realistic caseload size (Stein, Callaghan, McGee, & Douglas, 1990; Mills & Ivery, 1991).

Although there is general agreement that small caseloads are necessary, this is clearly "the ideal" and not reality in many agencies. Caseloads of as many as eighty clients are not uncommon (CWLA, 1991a); in some agencies, caseloads have been so unmanageable that judges have ordered that they be reduced (Mushlin, Levitt, & Anderson, 1986). Gold (1998) found workload concerns a frequently cited problem for many child welfare workers in her sample. Problems with caseload size are seriously exacerbated when workers leave their jobs, since, in many agencies, prolonged periods of time may elapse before positions are refilled. The children formerly served by these workers either are unserved or are added temporarily to the already heavy loads of the workers who remain (Cox & Cox, 1984).

Proper preparation for this job requires a strong academic background reinforced by periodic on-the-job training. In its *Standards of Excellence for Family Foster Care Services* (1995), the Child Welfare League of America recommended that workers have a bachelor's degree in social work or a related discipline and, for more advanced work, a master's degree in social work (pp. 109–110). However, many foster care workers function without this type of preparation. According to one study, "the number of child welfare staff with undergraduate or graduate degrees in social work has declined in the last 10 years to less than 28 percent" (Pecora, Whittaker, & Maluccio, 1992, p. 437). The problem is even more pronounced in rural areas.

The CWLA (1991a) argued that all child welfare practice needs to be seen as a professional specialty and recommended that only certified social workers be used for this work. The Texas Department of Human Services has developed certification procedures for child protective services staff.

> The department expects that certification will strengthen staff credibility in the agency, the courts, and the community by ensuring that each certified staff member has demonstrated a basic mastery of the specialized knowledge and skills necessary to adequately carry out the tasks in child protective services. (Birmingham, Berry, & Bussey, 1996, pp. 730–731)

Public law in Pennsylvania requires that all child welfare workers, supervisors, and administrators be certified, and their training must be updated annually.

Availability of on-the-job training varies widely from agency to agency and from state to state. A national study (Vinokur-Kaplan, 1987) revealed that 14 percent of workers had no opportunity for inservice training in their agencies; another 30 percent had not received training within the last year. Only 4 percent of workers had had specific training in foster care. However, 70 percent cited the need for training in "decision making in child placement and family reunification" (p. 301). The Child Welfare League of America (1995) noted that workers need initial (preservice) training to prepare them for their jobs and continuing (inservice) training to expand their basic knowledge and skills, to prepare them for more advanced work, and to apprise them of new developments in the field. (See Breitenstein, 1998, for a description of one state's efforts in this regard.)

Salaries for child welfare workers tend to be lower than those of workers in similar positions in other types of agencies. The Child Welfare League of America (1991a) recommended that guidelines for beginning salaries developed by the National Association of Social Workers be followed—which, in 1990, were $20,000 for those with a bachelor's degree and $25,000 for those with advanced degrees.

The many stresses and limited rewards of this job contribute to the very high turnover rate and widespread burnout. One recent estimate (CWLA, 1991a) is that one in three child welfare workers leaves the job every year. A study of African American children in care in five cities (National Black Child Development Institute, 1989) reviewed outcomes for children who had been in care between twelve and forty months. The children had an average of 2.5 caseworkers during that time (p. 85). Recent efforts to license social workers have made this situation worse, according to Pecora, Whittaker, and Maluccio (1992):

> Licensing programs in many states have contributed to a situation where child welfare agencies become a training ground that enables new graduates to accrue

the necessary clinical hours, but not stay with the agency beyond the point of clinical licensing. (p. 441)

Under these working conditions, the individual child welfare worker, no matter how committed, cannot successfully handle job demands unless he or she receives effective supervision and has available the support of colleagues and the agency.

> Supervision and consultation are specific sources of support that should be available on a regular basis. Supervision can be defined as a process in which two people participate in a joint effort to establish and maintain or elevate a level of performance. The supervisor uses empathy and his or her knowledge of theory and practice to assist the worker in dealing with the intricacies of a difficult case. (Solnit, Nordhaus, & Lord, 1992, p. 23)

Supervisors cannot create a positive work environment without the support of agency management, whom they represent. Administrators of foster care programs who recognize the peculiar demands of this type of work can help create a manageable and supportive environment in which workers—and clients—can thrive.

Questions for Discussion and Debate

1. What are the reasons behind practices that hire workers with minimal qualifications, pay them poorly, and watch them quickly leave their child welfare agencies?
2. How do workers manage their jobs when their caseloads are too large?
3. Given the challenges and difficulties of being a foster care worker, what do you think attracts people to—and keeps them in—these jobs?

4

Recruitment and Assessment of Foster Family Homes

In order to successfully recruit appropriate foster families, the foster care worker must have a clear understanding of the types of families that will be most successful in this role. Thus, this chapter begins with a discussion of "ideal" foster parents. Strategies for seeking out such parents and encouraging them to request to become foster parents (recruitment strategies) and approaches to evaluating foster care applicants (assessment strategies) are also discussed. The chapter ends with an explanation of the work to be done with families considered inappropriate for providing foster care services to children.

Seeking Foster Parents: The Ideal

Foster parent selection is determined, in part, by the worker's and agency's vision of a "good" foster parent. The traditional conception suggests that foster parents perform their most valuable service by offering a child a "normal" home environment. "The family is God's Reformatory; and every child of bad habits who can secure a place in a Christian home is in the best possible place for his improvement" (Charles Loring Brace, cited in Jackson, 1986, p. 96). It was assumed that "good" foster parents would do an adequate job at this and that they needed little or no assistance from the worker in managing the child or in carrying out their duties. Historically, Pasztor, Shannon, and Buck (1989) argued, such expectations worked well for most children.

> Foster parents were recruited as volunteers to serve young, dependent children.... In fact, early foster care—from its inception in the 1860s through the 1930s—looked much like adoption with considerable congruency among children's needs, foster parents' abilities and foster parents' responsibilities. (p. II-4)

Under this traditional system, parents were recruited who saw parenting as a primary source of psychic satisfaction and who were, therefore, willing to carry out caretaking responsibilities, even when they are accompanied by inadequate pay (CWLA, 1991a; Plumer, 1992). Descriptions of "ideal" foster parents evoked general images of "good" parents: child-centered, flexible and developmentally appropriate in their childrearing, relatively independent and self-sufficient, evincing considerable stability personally and interpersonally within the family, and good providers. Foster parents were expected to develop attachments to the foster child much as they would to their own birth children.

This traditional depiction of the foster parent role also encouraged the foster care worker to rely on broadly supported social views regarding preferred parenting styles in recruiting and selecting foster mothers and fathers (Shaw, 1989). A study of 542 foster care applicants who contacted the Henepen County Community Services Department between 1979 and 1981 found that workers were more likely to license individuals living in suburban rather than urban settings, those who were married rather than single, those living in homes they owned rather than rented, and those who were more educated (Moore, Grandpre, & Scoll, 1988).

An alternative to the traditional approach suggests that foster parenthood is a job title and that the foster parent is an employee of the agency (Harling, 1981; Testa & Rolock, 1999). These foster parents, when adequately trained and provided sufficient input in decision making about the child, become "professionals" or "paraprofessionals" who work alongside the foster care worker as part of the team that intervenes directly with the child to alter problematic behavior and with the birth family to develop more functional childrearing skills (Schachter, 1989; Walsh & Walsh, 1990; CWLA, 1991a; Lowe, 1991; Pecora, Whittaker, & Maluccio, 1992).

The image of the "ideal" foster parent evoked by this conceptualization generates a somewhat different list of critical qualities. Greater stress is placed on tolerance for children and birth families whose upbringing, interpersonal styles, and values may be at odds with those of the foster family. Foster parents are expected not only to engage in "normal" parenting but also to help deeply distressed and emotionally injured children once again attain some sense of normalcy in their lives. Greater emphasis is placed on interest in becoming part of an intervention team and being open to input from professionals and from the birth parents; less emphasis is placed on independence. While stability remains important, it must be balanced with the capacity to tolerate crises, to live with the unexpected, and to take pride in learning about and growing with the foster child (Cautley & Aldridge, 1975; Rowe, 1976; Cohen & Westhues, 1990; Stahl, 1990; Walsh & Walsh, 1990; CWLA, 1995). Expectations concerning attachment are also at variance with those embodied in the traditional framework. Professional foster parents are expected to care for children who may reject attachment overtures and whose notions of intimacy and loving may be at odds with those of the foster family. They must allow for the possibility that the foster child may never develop feelings of closeness (Fahlberg, 1991).

While the perspective that foster parents should function as professionals is now widely supported (CWLA, 1990; Costin, Bell, & Downs, 1991; Minuchin, 1992), current foster care practice actually reflects a sometimes confusing mix of more traditional and more contemporary beliefs (Gil, 1984; Meyer, 1985; Armstrong, 1989; Pelton, 1989; Fein, Maluccio, & Kluger, 1990; Kates, Johnson, Rader, & Strieder, 1991; James Bell Associates, 1993). The foster parent is expected to be a willing member of a treatment team but to function fairly independently with minimal training. The foster parent is expected to develop warm, loving feelings for the foster child but to be able to let go of the child at a moment's notice from the agency. Blurring of the boundaries between foster care and adoption serves to exacerbate these contradictions. Although foster families are expected to care for children only on a short-term basis, they may find the children remaining in their homes for several years. In addition, their relationship to the children in their care can, at some point, shift dramatically, since, if these children become available for adoption, foster parents are usually considered primary applicants (Mica & Vosler, 1990). These conflicting expectations are responsible for much of the tension in the foster family care system today (Berridge & Cleaver, 1987).

It is interesting to note that neither traditional nor professional ideals clarify expectations concerning kin foster placements. In fact, there has been considerable ambivalence in child welfare practice about using kinship placements, primarily because of the assumption that troubled parents must, themselves, have come from troubled kinship systems. The last decade has seen a transformation in this regard. Today, kinship placements are the preferred option for children who cannot live with their birth parents, and child welfare workers are routinely expected to explore these placement possibilities before putting the child in the home of nonrelatives (CWLA, 1991a; Plumer, 1992). It is now assumed that kin homes offer a sense of connection and continuity that may be more valuable for the child than middle-class childrearing norms or professional care. Consideration of kin placements as a first option has been interpreted as a requirement under PL 96-272, the *Indian Child Welfare Act* (PL 95-608), and some state regulations (Carrieri, 1992; Gleeson & Craig, 1994; Gleeson, 1995). The Child Welfare League of America (1994) cited a 1992 GAO study indicating a written preference for such care in 29 states (p. 27).

Foster Care Applicants: The Reality

While choice of foster parents is guided by expectations concerning the type of role they are to play, choice is also influenced by the numbers and types of individuals available to become foster carers. In their survey of several public child welfare programs throughout the country, Kamerman and Kahn (1990) found foster parents in Baltimore "very difficult to recruit and retain" (p. 71), a "severe shelter and foster home shortage" (p. 72) in Boston, and, in Los Angeles, "a need for trained, professional foster parents" (p. 80). "Today, the number of at-home mothers is dwindling, houses and families are smaller, and the time and income needed to care for additional children are not so available" (Phelps, 1989, p. 7). As a consequence, selection of foster parents is undertaken by the worker who has limited options but a severe need.

> One can hardly begin to study a couple in depth if the child has to be placed as a matter of urgency and there is no well-tried foster home available. Child care was ever a crisis service, with decisions having to be made at a speed that would be unthinkable for adoption workers. (Humphrey & Humphrey, 1988, pp. 19–20)

There is a continued appeal of fostering among working-class and lower-middle-class families (James Bell Associates, 1993). Studying 386 families who were caring for children in the New York City area, Fanshel (1982) found that 44 percent of the foster mothers and 46 percent of the fathers had not completed high school. Almost half of the fathers worked as laborers, service workers, or operatives, and only one in four functioned in a white-collar or professional role. Most of these families lived in "modest material circumstances" (p. 227). Data from a Virginia survey (Hampson & Tavormina, 1980), constituting 90 percent of the active foster parents in a particular region, also point to their limited educational attainment. The average income of the 34 participating families was $794 a month (p. 109). Researching long-term foster parents providing homes for difficult youngsters in Montana, Walsh and Walsh (1990) described the average mother and father as lacking a high school education (p. 50). Recent research comparing characteristics of more than 1,900 foster parents (James Bell Associates, 1993) pointed out that "childless, higher income, better educated families are less likely to remain as foster parents" (p. 79).

This study also found that contemporary foster mothers are more likely to be employed, on either a full- or part-time basis. The number of mothers working prior to 1989 was 42 percent; this figure rose to 60 percent for those fostering since 1985 (p. v). Using Holland's Vocational Preference Inventory, Wiehe (1983) contrasted the personality characteristics of younger foster mothers with those of mothers over forty. Older respondents were "more dependent, less assertive, and adventurous." They were also more traditional than mothers from a control group of nonfoster parents. Wiehe recommended that recruitment efforts be cognizant of the changing attitudes and values of younger parents.

Data from several communities across the country provide a picture of the "typical" kinship placement (Table 4.1). Most often, the child is placed with a maternal grandmother or aunt. These women are usually poorer, older, and less well educated than other foster mothers. Many are single parents, and some struggle with personal health problem while raising children with medical, emotional, and behavioral problems of their own (Dubowitz, Feigelman, & Zuravin, 1993; LeProhn, 1994; Scannapieco & Hegar, 1994; Gebel, 1996; Link, 1996; McLean & Thomas, 1996; Gleeson, O'Donnell, & Bonecutter, 1997; Pecora, LeProhn, & Nasuti, 1999; Scannapieco, 1999).

Contemporary data that can be used to compare the role perceptions and parenting approaches of actual foster parents with those considered "ideal" are in

TABLE 4.1 *Kinship Care Studies: General Characteristics*

Source	Characteristics of Sample	Study Goals
Lewis & Fraser (1987)	137 "specific" and 335 regular foster homes	Compare general characteristics of & services provided to the homes
National Black Child Development Institute (1989); Walker, Zangrillo, & Smith (1994)	401 Black children from 5 major cities	Describe children placed with or discharged to kin; compare results for different cities
Testa (1992)	Illinois data collected between 1986–1990	Explore whether kin care reflects children previously in informal care or families newly vulnerable
Wulczyn & Goerge (1992)	Illinois and New York data, 1983–1989	Examine reasons for growth in use of foster care
Dubowitz, Feigelman, & Zuravin (1993); Dubowitz et al. (1994); Sawyer & Dubowitz (1994)	524 Baltimore children with relatives at end of April, 1989; comprehensive assessment of 407 children	Describe family characteristics & services provided; assess health, mental health, & educational status of children
Barth, Courtney, Berrick, & Alpert (1994)	8,748 children who entered care over 3-year period, kin & non-kin care, California	Examine reunification from kinship care
Berrick, Barth, & Needell (1994)	600 kin & non-kin homes, children in care from 1988–present	Compare family characteristics & services provided
Goerge, Wulczyn, & Hardin (1994)	Data from 5 states over 5–10 year period	Explore duration of placement in kin homes
Inglehart (1994)	352 adolescents in kin homes; 638 adolescents in non-kin homes	Compare placement history, adjustment, & agency monitoring
LeProhn (1994); LeProhn & Pecora (1994)	129 kin & 175 non-kin homes used by Casey Family Program, January, 1992	Compare role conceptions of kin & non-kin foster parents
Scannapieco & Hegar (1994)	Children in kin homes in City & Baltimore County	Compare two different management models for kinship care
Wulczyn (1994)	Infant placements in New York City, 1984–1989	Kin placement as one factor describing infants in care
Berrick & Lawrence-Karshi (1995)	Survey of 1,096 child welfare administrators	Survey attitudes about kin placements as one of a number of emerging issues
Ritter (1995)	447 cases from agency in Florida; open & closed cases	Examine changes in placement for children & caretakers
Gebel (1996)	140 kin homes & 140 non-kin homes, Florida	Compare attitudes toward child care, children in care, and agency services
James Bell Associates (1993)	National sample of 203 current & 333 former foster parents	Examine licensure & other characteristics of kin homes
Pecora, LeProhn, & Nasuti (1999)	506 foster parents from Casey Programs and Louisiana	Compare role perceptions of kin and non-kin foster parents
Starr, Dubowitz, Harrington, & Feigelman (1999)	66 adolescents in kinship care homes in Baltimore	Study emotional and behavioral problems of teens

very short supply. Walsh and Walsh (1990) described foster parents for 51 children placed through the Casey Family Program in Montana. While there was evidence of marital stability, strong "executive capacity," and high stress tolerance, there were also indications of a "modest degree of ease and comfort in their several roles" (p. 50), limited use of physical affection in the family, and only average ability to share feelings. "There was a moderate tendency for the foster home to be child-centered and for a smothering, overnurturing climate to exist in it. . . . The foster parents' overall attitude toward the child was accepting and positive, but not parental" (p. 51). A study of 506 kin and non-kin foster families (Pecora, LeProhn, & Nasuti, 1999) found:

> the majority of foster parents in this study stated that their role was "the same as parents." Few foster parents, either relative or nonrelative, described their role as that of a "professional therapeutic caregiver," although many identified with tasks that may require specialized expertise, such as "helping foster child with emotional problems," "selecting the child's counselor or therapist," and "helping the child with issues related to being separated from his/her birth parents." (pp. 172–173)

These data indicate some disparity between the qualities the child welfare agency would prefer to find and those that actually characterize foster caregivers. However, study of this question has been so minimal that it is impossible to determine the extent to which these results apply to foster families in general. Describing "average" foster parents is of only limited utility, since this provides no clear picture of the range of different types of fostering capabilities that might exist. Because there has not been an in-depth examination of the connection between "ideal" fostering and success in fostering, we are hard-pressed to determine whether these various characteristics of foster families make any discernible difference to the children who need care. Would more "ideal" parents treat children in ways that seem unfamiliar, even alien to the children? Would more "ideal" parents handle the children more effectively or be able to commit to them more deeply? At this point, we do not know.

Motives for taking on the foster parent role are both altruistic and personal (Plumer, 1992). Foster parents are most likely to point to "love of children, desire to help someone else, and interest in children's well-being" (Hampson & Tavormina, 1980, pp. 109–110). In a 1987 study of 10 San Francisco area counties, Anderson (cited in Pasztor & Wynne, 1995) asked foster parents to describe the most rewarding aspects of their experience. "Success in improving a child's life" was listed by 39 percent, "giving or receiving love" by one-quarter, and "altruism/selfless concern for others" by one in five (p. 14). Successful foster parents in the Casey Family Program were motivated by "liking children and/or a feeling of closeness to young people" and "social commitment, as to a better world or to do something useful" (Walsh & Walsh, 1990, p. 70; see also James Bell Associates, 1993).

Other, more personal forces also propel individuals to assume this responsibility (Cautley, 1980). This in no way implies a derogation of foster parents' readiness to accept a child or the capacity to do a good job. Even a desire to find a "replacement" or a companion for one's own child does not necessarily imply failure. If the parents' needs are complementary to those of the child, the child can be provided the best kind of foster family experience. Individuals who consider personal motives their primary or exclusive reasons for taking this step may, however, find themselves in more difficulty than those who combine personal needs with more altruistic, child-oriented objectives (Hampson & Tavormina, 1980).

Examination of motives for fostering suggests that most foster parents do not arrive at the agency seeking to be professionals or team members (Tinney, 1985; Pecora, LeProhn, & Nasuti, 1999). Their wishes are to help children, to serve society, and to meet some personal needs of their own. It is the task of the assessment process to help them understand how their parenting role will be different with foster children than with their own birth children and to learn to use agency services to enhance their caretaking role.

The J Case

Rod Tedesco is a junior high school teacher who heard about the growing need for foster parents from a colleague who has been a foster mother for several years. Because she knew of Rod's enjoyment of children and his ability to teach children who are atypical, she strongly encouraged him to apply. Rod is both excited and frightened about this idea. Having lived alone, he wonders if he can share his home with a child, commit his time and energy to childrearing. Having taught children who have not been well cared for by their parents, he worries about whether he could see them return to their homes, whether he can really recognize their need to love their mothers and fathers. He has heard that the agency can take the child away at any time and wonders if he can develop a trusting relationship with a foster care worker.

Rod comes from a large family. While he was growing up, his cousins and friends sometimes stayed at his home for extensive periods of time. Rod feels this gives him some sense of what foster family care is like. He has for many years spent time with children, as a Boy Scout leader, a summer camp coordinator, and a Big Brother. He is eager to learn more about the agency's expectations and requirements.

Recruitment

Recruitment of non-kin foster parents involves a program of interpretation to the public of the need for foster homes for children and the satisfactions to be derived from fostering a child. All mass communication media have been used by agencies in recruitment efforts: newspaper ads, radio, television, billboards, and placards in buses and subway trains. Evidence suggests that the mass media, particularly television, may be far more effective than printed material in reaching the widest possible audience (Moore, Grandpre, & Scoll, 1988). On occasion, advertisements have been supplemented by presentations before church groups, PTA groups, women's clubs, and so on. Such activity is reinforced by the visible enhancement of the symbol of the foster parent. In some areas, the mayor proclaims "Foster Parent Week," and an award is given to a couple selected as the "Foster Parents of the Year." All of this activity develops a "climate of awareness" of the need for foster parents in the community.

Studies of the outcome of foster care recruitment show a high attrition rate among the families that express initial interest. Usually, less than 10 percent of the original group are licensed and very rarely more than 20 percent. An extensive effort begun in the Washington, D.C. area in 1987 resulted in "less than 5% of those who inquired" actually becoming foster parents (Pasztor & Wynne, 1995, p. 11).

Given the shrinking pool of potential foster care applicants and the large number who express some interest but who fail to complete the application process, agencies find that more intensive recruitment efforts are required. Using sophisticated marketing strategies and multidimensional outreach efforts, agencies have successfully found new homes for waiting children. For greater effectiveness, multiagency and multistate recruitment efforts have also been organized (Radinsky et al., 1963; Pasztor, 1985). Keeping track of the impact of various recruitment approaches can help an agency discover those that are most useful in recruiting and retaining families (Moore, Grandpre, & Scoll, 1988; Phelps, 1989).

Of special benefit are efforts to develop more rapid agency responses to inquiries and to maintain continual recruitment campaigns. Delayed agency responses severely frustrate potential applicants, and intermittent or one-shot recruitment efforts tend to overtax the agency and substantially increase response delays (Pasztor & Wynne, 1995). Concentrating on more timely responses to requests for information about foster care in Prince George's County, Maryland, meant

> the usual time between initial phone call and licensing for families who followed through quickly was reduced to about three and one-half months, and the percentage of families who continued from initial inquiry to placement of children doubled. (Phelps, 1989, p. 8)

Eight years of recruitment experience led Pasztor (1985) to comment:

> Recruitment themes usually reflected an "open your home and your heart" message, implying that love is all it takes to be a foster parent. Recruitment posters tended to picture a young female waif with blonde hair and sad eyes. The underlying message was that this obviously uncared for child needed someone to replace her uncaring parents and that the children needing homes were primarily very young, white, and female. (p. 195)

More useful, she argued, are strategies that focus on the foster cargiver, not the child, depicting the role that foster parents play, the impact they have, and the rewards of the job.

People who have "been there" have a special capability as recruiters because they have greater credibility for the applicant. Current foster parents can participate in and help develop advertising campaigns and other recruitment initiatives (CWLA, 1991a; James Bell Associates, 1993). Current foster parents are also important "informal" recruiters. Through their social contacts, they raise the consciousness of others about foster care and offer support to those willing to explore the possibility of becoming foster parents. A study of more than 1,900 foster parents (James Bell Associates, 1993) found that 37 percent had learned of the need for foster care from other foster families (p. 46); those who had opportunities to share information with other foster parents were also less likely to quit caring for children than those who were more isolated from their fostering colleagues. Assessing the process whereby 106 foster families from England and Wales eventually had children placed in their homes, Palmer (1981) discovered that 33 percent had close friends or relatives who were foster parents, and 37 percent had close associates who were adopters. One in three foster families had also known substitute parents while they were growing up (p. 42). The state of Maryland has paid a finders fee of $50 to foster parents who recruit new families for children (Phelps, 1989).

There is increased need for agencies to develop homes for specific types of foster children—teenagers, those with developmental or physical handicaps, medically fragile children and those who are HIV+, children with severe emotional and behavior problems, groups of siblings who need to be in care together, and children of specific cultural or racial backgrounds (Goldstein, Gabay, & Switzer, 1981; Knitzer & Olson, 1982; Engel, 1983; Hazel, Schmedes, & Korshin, 1983; Davis et al., 1984; Humphrey & Humphrey, 1988; CWLA, 1992a; Pasztor & Wynne, 1995). Many foster parents are not willing to care for such children. In the survey conducted by James Bell Associates (1993), one in four of parents said they would not care for a child who was emotionally disturbed, seriously ill, or handicapped; one-third were unwilling to care for a drug-exposed infant; almost half would not parent teenagers; and three out of four would not accept children who had AIDS (p. v; see also Downs, 1990, p. 25).

"Targeted recruitment strategies" involve the search for parents most likely to be interested in children with special characteristics. One such approach is to seek out parents who are already involved with such children. The foster parent survey (James Bell Associates, 1993) found that 26 percent of the foster mothers had worked with retarded, handicapped, or emotionally impaired children before deciding to take on the foster parent role; 15 percent had family members with such problems (p. 49). For developmentally disabled children who do not need nursing care, Coyne (1986) recommended seeking

> people in their 30s or 40s who live in small cities, who finished 11th or 12th grade, are of lower middle-class status, have strong church connections, have children still at home but no preschoolers, and have added to their family by ways other than birth. (p. 31)

To find homes for medically fragile children, she recommended people in their late 20s or 30s who live in urban areas, have some college and/or nursing training, are middle or upper middle class, are childless or have only one or two school-age children, and intent to be foster parents for only a short time (two to three years). (p. 31)

When culturally similar homes are not available for Indochinese refugee unaccompanied minors, Porte and Torney-Purta (1987) suggested recruiting families with cross-cultural experience, such as former Peace Corps volunteers.

Because it is preferable that minority group children be placed in homes that are ethnically and racially similar to that of their own families, many agencies are concerned about the need to increase recruitment of African American, Hispanic, and Native American foster parents. Because minority group children are overrepresented in care, the need for such homes is especially acute. Once minority foster homes are licensed, they are more likely to be used and more likely to be filled to capacity than are white homes (James Bell Associates, 1993). Efforts to enlist the assistance of the African American, Hispanic, and Native American communities and to rely on existing foster parents in recruiting new foster families for these children are particularly important. Agency adaptations, including hiring of bilingual staff and staff identified with the community are often necessary steps in enhancing recruitment possibilities. Moore, Grandpre, and Scoll (1988) reported that in Henepen County, "A black licensing social worker was hired to work exclusively with black foster families and the preliminary results have been overwhelmingly positive" (p. 159).

Recruiting foster homes from among the child's kin follows a different process than that used for non-kin. Instead of focusing on the larger community, the worker looks within the family for placement resources. Research on child welfare practice in California (Berrick, Needell, & Barth, 1999) revealed:

> that the majority of staff first asked the birth parent with whom he or she wanted the child placed. This began the selection process and was considered the best means of locating viable kin. If the relative made the allegation against the parent, the relative making the claim was first reviewed as a potential caregiver. Many workers also indicated that they asked the child where she wanted to live. (p. 186)

When the worker encountered strong opposition from the parent or child to placement with these relatives, the search for an appropriate kin placement expanded to other, more distant relatives.

Assessment and Training Approaches

The agency has the grave responsibility of finding the best possible substitute home for the child needing care. A detailed study of all applicants is necessary, not only because the agency has an ethical and professional responsibility to children and their birth parents but also because it has a legal responsibility to the community. Foster homes are licensed by the state, and the agency must certify that the home meets licensing requirements.

The assessment process typically involves the applicant's participation in both group meetings and in individual agency-based and home-based interviews with the worker. Group meetings have grown in popularity as an assessment/training device (Pasztor, 1985). Cohen and Westhues (1990) noted the importance of the potential foster father's participation in these meetings and recommended separate interviews with children already living in the foster home as well. Research examining foster care outcomes for especially demanding children (Walsh & Walsh, 1990) noted,

> Whether the foster father was emotionally involved with the child appeared to be an important determiner of placement success, including also how strong a masculine role model the foster father provided, whether it was he who had initiated taking on a foster child, and whether he was in the process of mid-life reassessment. (p. 31)

In addition to participating in interviews and home visits, applicants are required to provide references who can comment on their character and parenting abilities. Routine checks are conducted to determine that these individuals have no history of child mistreatment. Applicants are also required to complete a medical examination to establish that they are physically capable of caring for a child and have no infectious diseases. The state may require that applicants have income sufficient to meet their own needs. The state also stipulates that the home provide adequate space for a child, that it meet adequate sanitary and safety standards, and that it be located in a community that offers access to necessary academic, health, religious, and recreational resources (James Bell Associates, 1993).

Requirements with regard to income, housing, and community resources for kinship placements are not always as stringent as those in force for non-kin homes. A California survey of child welfare workers (Berrick, Needell, & Barth, 1999) found that "about 29 percent of kinship homes fell below the standards they regularly witnessed in average foster family homes" (p. 185). This is not surprising, in light of the evidence that kin foster parents have far less income than non-kin parents do. Workers sometimes struggle with the decision whether to place a child with a loving grandparent who lives in substandard housing in a dangerous neighborhood or to place the child with strangers living in neighborhoods where housing and safety are more adequate.

The assessment process involves mutual exploration on the part of the foster care worker and the foster parent applicant. While the worker evaluates family motives and capabilities, he or she also helps the family evaluate its own needs and desires. Areas of evaluation include current and historical background of the applicants, their children, and their family; personal and family-related reasons for bringing a new child into the home; childrearing attitudes and practices; reactions to children coming from abusive or neglectful backgrounds; willingness to work with and handle visits by birth parents who may have maltreated their children; and potential reaction to the child's eventual departure. The applicants' willingness to work cooperatively with the agency is another critical part of assessment (Walsh & Walsh, 1990; Touliatos & Lindhome, 1992; CWLA, 1995; Berrick, Needell, & Barth, 1999).

Assessment of parental and family dynamics for kinship placements differs somewhat from that for non-kin homes. The worker makes a "triad assessment" (Jackson, 1999) of the applicant's current and past relationships with the child and birth parents in order to determine whether the placement will be appropriate. The foster care worker is concerned about "kin who have an agenda to obtain custody of a child, who have a personal vendetta, or who don't get along with parents" (Berrick, Needell, & Barth, 1999, p. 185). They also worry about kin who cannot be sufficiently protective of the child, who "are too soft with parents and allow unlimited access to the child" (p. 185).

In gathering this information, much more emphasis is placed on the applicant's evaluation of whether his or her own needs and goals can be met through a fostering experience; less emphasis is placed on the worker's judgment that the applicant is "good enough" to be approved. Except in unusual cases, the worker does not decide for the applicant that she or he is able to carry out this role.

> Foster parent applicants come to the agency, in the main, as mature and competent people offering their skills in partnership with the agency—there should be nothing in the agency's response at any stage which might de-skill or induce unhealthy dependence in the foster parents. (Shaw, 1989, p. 145)

During assessment, the worker tries to give sufficient information about fostering and foster children so that the family can make a more fully informed choice about becoming involved. This typically includes an overview of the child welfare agency and its foster care policies, material on the causes and consequences of child maltreatment, common adjustment reactions of foster families when foster children move into the home, and some material on preferred childrearing approaches. This aspect of assessment is usually termed *preservice orientation* or *training* (CWLA, 1995; Triseliotis, Sellick, & Short, 1995).

Various training curricula are available to help structure the information-giving and decision-making aspects of foster parent assessment. The earliest of the nationally distributed programs was "Parenting Plus," developed by the Child Welfare League of America. The Model Approach to Partnership in Parenting (MAPP) curricula (Pasztor, Shannon, & Buck, 1989), distributed by the Child Welfare Institute, has been used in several states and adapted for use internationally (van Pagee, van Miltenburg, & Pasztor, 1991). Also widely used is the "Eastern Michigan Foster Parent Curriculum" disseminated through the National Foster Care Resource Center in Ypsilanti. Patricia Minuchin (1990) developed training materials based on "An Ecological Perspective on Foster Care." Jackson

(1999) described a curriculum specifically developed for kin foster caregivers. Special curricula are available on fostering adolescents (Pine & Jacobs, 1989) and other types of special needs children. Recently, there has been greater recognition that material on cultural competence is an essential part of these training programs (CWLA, 1990; Triseliotis, Sellick, & Short, 1995).

Preservice training is most typically offered in a group context, although it has also been used in individual sessions with applicants. Titterington (1990) found training more effective when it was combined with efforts to build ongoing support networks for applicants.

There is only limited evidence as to the impact of training curricula on recruitment and retention of potential foster parents (Hampson, 1985).

> Few studies have compared the effectiveness of various approaches to foster-parent training. In fact, one of the common features for many of these foster-parent training programs is the lack of an evaluative element. Without evaluation, it is unclear which treatments are more effective and with which populations. (Berry, 1988, p. 314)

It is highly likely that training will be found to be only one essential component of effective assessment, imbedded in and affected by the overall programming of the agency and the ongoing relationship between workers and applicants (James Bell Associates, 1993; Pasztor & Wynne, 1995).

Assessment Outcome

Assessment standards need to be flexibly applied and adapted so that they fit the circumstances of applicants. Applicants may need the active help of the agency in meeting minimum standards, even to the point of agency support in improving their homes so that more and safer space is available. Agencies still prefer what is considered a "traditional" family—a nuclear, heterosexual couple living in fairly comfortable economic circumstances and espousing middle-class values. The greater the extent to which families deviate from this model, the more anxious agencies are about selecting them as homes for children. Recently revised CWLA foster care standards (1995) state, "The family foster care agency should not reject foster parent applicants solely due to their age, income, marital status, race, religious preference, sexual orientation, physical or disabling condition, or location of the foster home" (p. 97). There is currently a greater willingness to place foster children in one-parent and low-income homes. In 1984, two children placed with a gay couple after careful agency screening were removed when a story about the placement appeared in the *Boston Globe*. The National Association of Social Workers Massachusetts Chapter joined a class-action suit against the governor for subsequently ordering the State Department of Social Services to refuse foster care applications from gays and lesbians, however well qualified (*N.A.S.W. News*,

May, 1985). Massachusetts subsequently revised these regulations (Ricketts, 1991).

Applicants who are uninterested in foster care or who fail to meet requirements may either withdraw themselves at some point during the application process or may be formally rejected by the worker. Applicant withdrawal accounts for by far the largest proportion of attrition cases (Soothill & Derbyshire, 1981). A small percentage is rejected, often for very clear and unambiguous reasons, such as overage, poor health, or an abusive background. Soothill and Derbyshire (1981) found that rejection situations tended to fall into two categories—those who appeared to meet agency standards but who, upon closer assessment really did not; and those who were poor candidates from the beginning but who insisted that they complete the application process.

Formal rejection situations require that the worker produce a written document stating her reasons for refusing the family a license.

> In helping couples and families withdraw their request to an agency, it is important that the withdrawal request be part of the ongoing process and work with the family, the couple, and the social worker. If the withdrawal can be done in this context, it can be constructive and will provide the family with an opportunity to save face. (Cohen & Westhues, 1990, p. 69)

Once these procedures and requirements have been completed, the family is issued a license that certifies their home is authorized to accept children for foster care. In many states, the license indicates the number of children that the home may accept at any one time. Generally, no more than four older children are allowed, with not more than two under the age of two. A license is usually issued for a one-year period. At the end of that time, the agency must review the situation and relicense the home.

An agreement usually must be signed with the agency as part of the licensing procedure. A study (Festinger, 1974) of such agreements used by state departments of social services throughout the United States noted some uniformities. Agreements generally include a statement of the foster parents' responsibilities for caring for the foster child, helping with the agency's plan for the child, and keeping the agency informed of accidents, illness, or changes in the child's location, such as vacations. It restricts the rights of the foster parents to accept other children or to take action for the adoption of the foster child without agency permission. Procedures regarding the birth parents' visits are spelled out. A key aspect of the agreement, appearing in almost all contracts, is the requirement that foster parents acquiesce in the removal of a child and relinquishment of contact with the child at the request of the agency.

Kinship foster homes may be licensed or unlicensed, and most public foster care programs have both types of homes (James Bell Associates, 1993; Gleeson, 1996). National data (Tatara, 1993) indicate that some 18 percent of children in care in 1989 were living in unlicensed kin homes. Licensed homes must achieve the same standards of care required of non-kin homes; unlicensed homes may be unable to meet these standards, sometimes because the foster home lacks sufficient space or the foster parent has insufficient resources to relocate to a better home. At times, the worker is reluctant to license the home because the child's grandmother or aunt has had personal problems in the past. For example, a grandmother may have struggled with her own addictions and had trouble caring for her own children as a younger woman. Because these difficulties would not lead to licensure of a nonrelative home, the agency may refuse to license the kinship placement. At times, agency policies discourage licensure of kinship care because this would result in a substantial increase in costs for the agency. Agencies may, for example, require the family to ask to be licensed and paid rather than routinely offering this option to them (Gleeson & Craig, 1994; Gleeson, 1995).

A primary benefit for kin of having a licensed home is that they qualify for reimbursement at regular foster care rates; kin in unlicensed homes must attempt to qualify for other types of welfare support (Berrick, Barth, & Needell, 1994; Scannapieco & Hegar, 1994; Hegar & Scannapieco, 1999). In 1991, some 10 percent of AFDC recipients were the child's kin (McLean & Thomas, 1996). Because of their responsibility to monitor licensed placements, agencies also tend to be more intrusive with these families. Kin may see this in a positive light because they can rely on the foster care worker's guidance and because they may receive additional resources or services for the child (McLean & Thomas, 1996). At other times, kin consider such oversight to be unwanted interference.

The J Case

The foster family recruitment worker does a careful assessment of Rod Tedesco's background, references, and work performance. There is universal agreement among his colleagues, friends, and associates that he is an excellent teacher, a fine person, and a good candidate for foster parenthood. The worker hesitates because it is somewhat unusual for men to consider this role; a single man's motives are questioned much more closely than those of a single woman. The worker finally decides to license his home but to recommend that an older child be placed there. If problems should develop, an older child would be in a better position to speak up and to seek help.

Rod finds it difficult to have his motives so closely scrutinized. He realizes he can do little to instill confidence in his fostering ability until a child is in placement in his home. He agrees to the placement of an older child, since he has worked with older children so extensively. However, he would welcome a younger child as well and hopes the agency will eventually consider this for him.

The worker notes that Rod continues to feel ambivalent about the birth family and that he will need to have assistance from the foster care worker in learning to work effectively with the child's mother and father.

Questions for Discussion and Debate

1. How do your expectations concerning "best" parenting practices compare with those cited in the foster care literature as "ideal"?
2. What kinds of difficulties would you expect foster parents to encounter when they approach their tasks as "just parents" but must deal with a child welfare agency that has different expectations?
3. What are the ramifications of having somewhat different housing and income requirements of kin and non-kin foster homes?
4. How can the foster worker manage the tension between his or her desire to respect the foster applicant as a mature and informed individual, on the one hand, and the need to evaluate and make decisions about the applicant on the other hand?

5

Moving a Child into Foster Family Care

This chapter describes the process of placing a child into a foster family home. In order to understand the experiences families have with this type of care, we first examine the kinds of problems families have at the time of placement. The child welfare worker's initial responsibilities toward the family are then explored. These include making the decision that foster family care is the most appropriate resource for the family at this time, obtaining court sanction for the placement decision, selecting the most appropriate foster family home for the child, and helping the children and their parents make the actual move into care. Early placement concerns to be addressed after this move is effectuated are described in Chapter 6.

Family Circumstances and the Need for Foster Family Care

While governmental regulations and professional philosophies defining the role of foster family care services suggest that parent-related deficiencies and needs should determine when these services are to be used, child-related issues and environmental circumstances are factors of additional importance in placement decisions (Sauber & Jenkins, 1966; Shyne, 1969; Vasaly, 1978; Shyne & Schroeder, 1978; Hubbell, 1981; Gershenson, 1982; Becker & Austin, 1983; Packman, 1986; Seaberg, 1988; Lindsey, 1992). To obtain a clear picture of the types of families using foster care services, it is, therefore, important to explore parenting problems, characteristics of the children, and the social and economic circumstances in which these families find themselves. The role of agency policies and other factors affecting access to services are also important considerations in understanding the paths to placement.

Parent Characteristics and Entry into Care

Problematic parenting is evident in the majority of instances in which foster family care is used (Cautley, 1980; Fitzharris, 1985; Costin, Bell, & Downs, 1991; U.S. House of Representatives Committee on Ways & Means, 1992). Kamerman and Kahn (1990) estimated that "about 90 to 95 percent of the children now going into foster care are placed away from home because of some form of alleged child abuse or severe neglect" (p. 8). Using 1977 data on 9,507 children from the National Social Services for Children and Family sample, Seaberg (1988) provided evidence that

> only the most extreme cases seem to be placed in foster care—extreme in the sense that the child is abandoned or neglected or the parent is unavailable or incapable of caring for the child because of the parent's own problem. (p. 7)

Using newer national data, Tatara (1994) noted that "families from which children were removed in recent years are more severely 'damaged' and have more complex multiple problems than families in past years" (p. 141). A study of child welfare cases in Queensland, Australia (Dalgleish & Drew, 1989) found "aspects of parenting, aspects of the marital relationship, and family's lack of cooperation" most strongly contributing to the placement decision (p. 495). "Severity of abuse" was also a strong placement predictor. (See also Fanshel, 1982; Wald, Carlsmith, & Leiderman, 1988; Benedict & White, 1991; Jones, 1993; Weisz, 1994.)

Findings on the pervasive importance of parent-related factors are not consistent across all studies, however. Examining 59 families experiencing first-time placements in foster care, Kliman, Schaeffer, and Friedman (1982) found 25 percent were without a "history of mental illness, alcohol or drug abuse, or abuse and/or neglect of own children" (p. 48). Other researchers (Packman, 1986; Lindsey, 1992) found children's problems to be as significant or even more significant contributors to placement than parenting difficulties in some instances.

Jenkins and Norman (1975) distinguished between more "socially acceptable" reasons for placement, such as the parent's physical or mental illness, and "socially unacceptable reasons," which include neglect, parental incarceration, "unwillingness, or inability to continue care, abandonment, or family dysfunction" (pp. 14–15). Marital discord, spousal violence, and substance abuse are not uncommon challenges faced by the latter type of families.

Placement is more often used for families in which parents have engaged in "socially unacceptable" behavior (National Black Child Development Institute, 1989, p. 36). Drug-related problems are now widespread among families using foster care services, especially those with infants being placed (Besharov, 1990; Weiner & Weiner, 1990; Staff & Fein, 1991; Davis, English, & Landsverk, 1995). These are families in which parental addiction contributes to severe child neglect, abuse, or abandonment. Addicted parents may be unable to gain access to overburdened drug treatment programs or may be insufficiently motivated to participate in them. Lack of education and economic opportunities, coupled with the "intense pleasurability of cocaine," can make some addicts "exceedingly difficult to reach" (Besharov, 1990, p. 22).

A CWLA survey of member agencies "indicated severe strains in the family foster care system resulting from the impact of AOD" (Curtis & McCullough, 1993, p. 538). (AOD stands for alcohol and other drugs.) The National Black Child Development Institute (1989) found this a contributing factor in placement of more than one-third of the Seattle and Detroit families and half of the families living in Miami and New York. The Child Welfare League of America (1990) estimated that "as many as 75% of the families of the children placed in out-of-home care are chemically dependent" (p. 4). In California, the number of affected families rose from 55 percent in 1985 to 88 percent in 1989 (Courtney, 1994, p. 186). For every 1,000 drug-related arrests in that state, it is estimated that 665 children will enter the foster care system (Albert, 1994, p. 235).

When children are placed for "socially unacceptable" reasons, parents tend to feel angrier with and less supported by the child welfare agency. When they appear to the worker to be uncooperative, unconcerned about the child, or unmotivated to change, this, in turn, provides greater impetus to place the child (Packman, 1986; Dalgleish & Drew, 1989).

The J Case

The Jelico family is a blended family. Mr. J has three children by a previous marriage; Marsha aged nine, Joey aged eleven, and Janet, who is fourteen. Mrs. J also has children—Timothy aged ten and Monica, who is twelve. The Js have been married for three years and have a sixth child, Frank, who is now two years old.

The neighbors have repeatedly called the police and the child welfare agency about this family. There is extensive conflict among the older children and between the parents. Mr. J has been physically abusive of Mrs. J, particularly when he has been drinking. He has a history of using severe physical discipline with his own children and with Timothy. The teachers have seen bruises on these children on several occasions.

The family has been asked to participate in home-based programs over the last year. These have had limited impact, in part because Mr. J refuses to participate. He was also belligerent toward and verbally abusive with the home-based worker. As a rather passive person, Mrs. J has little authority in the home.

Last week, neighbors again called the agency because of fighting in the home. Mr. J had beaten Mrs. J so that she needed hospitalization. In an effort to protect his mother, Timothy had tried to intercede and had been repeatedly hit in the face by his father. Mr. J refused to talk with the child welfare worker. He refused to leave the home and repeatedly threatened the worker and Timothy. Mrs. J was too frightened to consider forcing her husband to leave the home.

Timothy is in the hospital emergency room, getting stitches for a cut on his face after being hit by Mr. J. The child welfare worker must make a decision as to whether he should be discharged to his home or taken into care.

Child Characteristics and Entry into Care

Recent evidence suggests that the level of disability faced by children entering the foster care system is now more severe than in the past, in part because home-based services have allowed some more functional children to be maintained in their own homes. Deinstitutionalization of the mentally ill and decriminalization of status offenders have placed added burdens on families trying to cope with these children and have, in some instances, resulted in foster family placement. (The range and severity of children's problems will be considered in greater detail in Chapter 8.)

Child-related problems can contribute to the placement process in two ways. In some instances, the emotional and behavioral difficulties of children can tax family resources beyond their limits. When informal and formal supports are insufficient to help parents care adequately for these children, foster family care might be considered as an option. These are children whose needs might burden any family; for parents with many vulnerabilities or limitations, the challenge can be overwhelming (Kamerman & Kahn, 1990, pp. 12–13). Fanshel (1982) noted that "even where children required placement away from their homes because of adjustment difficulties, the inability of the parents to be effective in their efforts to impose discipline was usually an important causal factor in the situation which made placement necessary" (p. 8). Sometimes parents actively seek placement in a desperate attempt to obtain treatment for the child and respite for the family.

Child-related problems can also contribute to placement when parenting insufficiencies have resulted in emotional or behavioral problems in their children. Experiences with "physical abuse, sexual abuse, neglect, maltreatment, and/or exposure to alcohol and other drugs and HIV infection" (CWLA, 1991a, p. 36) will lead some children to rely on rigid defensive and protective measures when approached by intimates, even in situations where they need not do so; some of these children will themselves become hostile and abusive (Stahl, 1990; Fanshel, Finch, & Grundy, 1990). Berrick, Needell, Barth, and Johnson-Reid (1998) described the impact of neglect on children found in one study:

> it was the neglected children who had the severest and widest variety of problems at the time of kindergarten. Their ratings on cognitive assessments were lower than those of the control group, the group with psychologically unavailable mothers, and the sexually abused group. They were anxious and inattentive, lacked initiative, and had trouble understanding their work. Socially, they were both aggressive and withdrawn. They were uncooperative, insensitive, and rarely had a sense of humor. (p. 19)

(See also Russell, 1986; Crittenden, 1988, 1993; Salter, 1988; Asen, George, Piper, & Stevens, 1989; Bolton, Morris, & MacEachron, 1989; Gomes-Schwartz, Horowitz, & Cardarelli, 1990; Vissing, Straus, Gelles, & Harrop, 1991; Ney, Fungt, & Wickett, 1994.) For some children, it is the "chronic discord and disharmony" in the birth family home (Steinhauer, 1991, p. 15), often accompanied by drug or alcohol abuse and marital violence, that produce disturbed behavior (Kliman, Schaeffer, & Friedman, 1982; Hulsey & White, 1989; CWLA, 1992a). Personal vulnerability of the child may also play a part, leading one child from a maltreating family to develop many problems while that child's sibling remains in far better mental health. (See also Weisz, 1994.) Parents in these types of families are less likely to consider placement of their children a useful resource for resolving family strain.

Using data collected for the national Social Services for Children and Family sample, Lindsey (1992) described an association between the reasons why placement requests were initiated and the ultimate placement decision. Both child-related and parent-related reasons contributed to the outcome, but child dependency (children whose parents cannot care for them or with no one to care for them), child problems (behavioral, physical, or mental health difficulties), and neglect were more likely to result in placement than parental drug or alcohol abuse, mental or physical problems of the parent, or abuse (p. 31). Examining placement decisions reached in two administrative districts in southern England, Packman (1986) found child characteristics (delinquency, truancy, sexual problems, self-injury) more likely to be associated with placement but parenting problems (including abuse and neglect) more often associated with maintenance of the child in the home (pp. 51–52). The author noted the "child's own behavior" was considered an important precipitant of placement in 35 percent of the placements (p. 46). In its study of African American children in foster family care in five major cities in 1986, the National Black Child Development Institute (1989) found the child's emotional problems to be far more pervasive contributors to placement than health or mental health difficulties.

Whatever the origins of the child's difficulties, parental feelings of frustration and defeat are common at the time of placement. In an examination of 350 children who were older than seven and came into care in three social service divisions in Sheffield, England, Fisher, Marsh, & Phillips (1986) found:

> A sense of bitterness and frustration characterized these mothers' accounts of trying to convince others that they needed help. Underlying this was a sense of never having anything good back from their children. . . . There was an overwhelming feeling from these parents of distance between themselves and their children . . . and constant reference was made to lack of 'respect' and of 'manners.' As the need for discipline increased, parents became less sure how to exercise it effectively. (pp. 34, 36)

Fisher and his colleagues found these mothers fatalistic about their capacity to manage successfully, convinced that any new effort on their part would probably fail.

Children's physical and medical problems may also be important concerns at the time of placement. Some children come to placement after being injured by their parents. For others, the child's physical limitations and needs have overtaxed parents. Practitioners and policy makers describe a need for expanded foster family services for physically or developmentally delayed children and for those with "serious, chronic illnesses" who have been "spending many months—in some cases, their entire lives—in acute care hospitals because alternative home care is unavailable" (Yost, Hochstadt, & Charles, 1988, p. 22; Webb, 1988; Luginbill & Spiegler, 1989; Myers, 1989). A 1990 Child Welfare League of America survey of its member agencies estimated 5,791 of these children had been served within the past twelve months (CWLA, 1992b). Research conducted jointly by the CWLA and the National Association of Public Hospitals in 1992 called these infants the "youngest of the homeless." Lack of sufficient foster family resources prevented half of the 607 "boarder babies" in the survey from being discharged from the hospital in a timely fashion. Concern about children experiencing these problems led to passage of the Abandoned Infants Assistance Act (PL 100-505 [S.945]) in 1988. The act describes as its major purpose the development of demonstration projects:

> to assist abandoned infants and young children, particularly those with acquired immune deficiency syndrome, to reside with their natural families or in foster care, as appropriate;

> to recruit, train, and retain foster families for abandoned infants and young children, particularly those with acquired immune deficiency syndrome; . . .

> to carry out programs of respite care for families and foster families of infants and young children with acquired immune deficiency syndrome; and

> to recruit and train health and social services personnel to work with families, foster care families, and residential care programs for abandoned infants and young children, particularly those with acquired immune deficiency syndrome. (Sec. 101)

The need to develop resources for children who are drug-exposed and for children with HIV or AIDS is also acute (Merkel-Holguin, 1996). AIDS has had differential impact on minority children and families. A 1989 report described 60 percent of all childhood AIDS cases as African American and 22 percent as Hispanic (Taylor-Brown, 1991, p. 197). As with drugs, there are wide variations from state to state and community to community in the significance of the impact of AIDS on the child welfare population. New York City, which has the most widespread problem, has taken the most direct steps to develop child welfare policies to address it (Tourse & Gundersen, 1988).

In the past, child welfare workers considered the child's age to be an important consideration in the placement decision, believing that younger children had a greater need for placement in a family rather than an institutional setting. Today, however, children of all ages are seen as in need of a substitute family's nurturance and support. Children who are very young are moving into care in record numbers, and they are far more likely to be moved to the homes of kin than are older children needing care (Inglehart, 1994; Gleeson 1996). Two-thirds of the children in kin homes in Baltimore were placed because of parental neglect (Dubowitz, Feigelman, & Zuravin, 1993); data from Los Angeles reveals similar trends (Inglehart, 1994). Abuse of substances, particularly crack/cocaine, is especially likely to result in such placement (Walker, Zangrillo, & Smith, 1994; Benedict, Zuravin, & Stallings, 1996; Gleeson, 1996; McLean & Thomas, 1996; Woodworth, 1996).

Using assessments of caseworkers and foster parents, in-depth interviews with adolescents, and independent case reviews, Hornby and Collins (1981) found that, compared to their younger counterparts, teenagers were more likely to be in care because of their own personal difficulties—behavior problems, delinquency, emotional illness, or substance abuse. Whereas 29 percent of the younger children were considered difficult to place, 49 percent of the adolescent group was perceived this way (pp. 12–14). (See also Fitzharris, 1985.) A study of 46 children aged seven to sixteen in care in Southern Ontario (Palmer, 1990) concluded that "difficulty in managing older children is becoming a significant reason for foster care" (p. 233). Once in care, the older children were more likely to experience multiple moves, to be placed in foster care before or after being in residential treatment, and to remain in any one foster family home for short periods of time.

In view of these data, it is not surprising that social workers describe availability of suitable foster families as one of the most significant factors influencing placement decisions for children in this older age group (Melotte, 1979, p. 56). Nevertheless, evidence suggests that, under appropriate circumstances, foster parents can be highly effective with even the most difficult adolescents. Following the progress of some two hundred teenagers placed by the Kent Project in foster family settings in Great Britain, Hazel, Schmedes, and Korshin (1983) found almost three-quarters were functioning very well or in a generally positive fashion and only 15 percent were considered to be worse or in "disastrous condition" at the end of the demonstration period. (See also Rosenblum, 1977; Hazel, 1981.) The large number of older children in care suggests the need for further development of family resources that can meet the special needs of this client group (James Bell Associates, 1993).

The J Case

Timothy Jelico is a ten-year-old boy being considered for placement in foster family care. He is belligerent with adults and peers, particularly with men. He has had considerable trouble at school in the last year, getting into several fights with his classmates and being verbally aggressive with some of his teachers. Although he was an A student in his early school years, his grades have dropped substantially, and he is now failing in three classes. He has also been suspended from school for fighting.

Timothy had difficulty talking to the clinician to whom he was referred by the home-based service worker six months ago. He expressed considerable rage toward his stepfather, and it is clear that he would like to see Mr. J leave the home. However, he was reticent to talk about any other family members, particularly his mother. He seemed to the clinician to be excessively protective of her. When asked about his difficulties at school, Timothy said he hated school and didn't want to go.

continued

> Timothy is insistent that he needs to return home and that he can take care of himself there. When asked how he will do that, he shrugs. He tells the worker he will run away from any foster home in which he is placed.

Family Circumstances and the Need for Care

The third set of factors associated with use of foster family care, those associated with environmental stress and deprivation, are primary precipitating factors in a very limited number of cases (3 to 5 percent of the cases). However, when combined with parental and/or child factors, these problems are endemic among the families whose children are in care (Jenkins & Diamond, 1985; Packman, 1986; Humphrey & Humphrey, 1988; Hessle, 1989; Pelton, 1989; Barth, Courtney, Berrick, & Albert, 1994; Davis, English, & Lansverk, 1995; National Black Child Development Institute, 1995). African American children are particularly likely to face placement because of environmental factors (Olsen, 1982; Becker & Austin, 1983; Lindsey, 1992). Serious financial need, inadequate housing, chronic unemployment, and lack of sufficient social supports may prevent a parent from appropriately caring for a child or from having access to critical community resources and services. The National Black Child Development Institute (1989) found that poverty contributed to foster placements among 25 percent of the families studied. His analysis of a large sample of 1977 child welfare cases led Lindsey (1992) to conclude that "an unstable income source is the best predictor of removal of a child and placement in foster care" (p. 34). Examining placement data from New York, Wulczyn (1994) reported a strong association between poverty and the likelihood of infant placements. In some of the city's lowest income neighborhoods, more than one in ten infants were in care in 1988 (p. 157). Davis and Ellis-MacLeod (1994) added the following:

> At present, over 40% of all children in foster care come from the very poorest socioeconomic households, from families that qualify for federal subsidies. Once in foster care, research has shown that the families of placed children are less likely to receive supportive or remedial services. . . . Therefore, for many parents living in poverty, any economic and social hardships that may have contributed to the removal of their children are not improved by the placement of their children in substitute care. (p. 132)

Homelessness, a growing problem for parents using child welfare services, is clearly tied to increased use of foster family care, according to Homes for the Homeless, a New York–based service agency. Its survey of 400 such parents found 20 percent had children in substitute care. A study by the National Alliance to End Homelessness (Roman & Wolfe, 1997) found a relationship between the homeless parents' own foster care history and the use of this care for their children:

> Of the homeless individuals for whom data were obtained, 36.2 percent had a foster care history. Of the parents with a foster care history, 77 percent had at least

one child who had been or currently was in foster care; in comparison, 27 percent of the parents without a foster care history had at least one child who had been or currently was in foster care. (p. 7)

One program for the homeless described a typical client as "a twenty-nine year old woman" with "4 children, 3 of whom are currently in foster care" (Institute for Children and Poverty, 1993).

In most cases, it is actually a combination of circumstances—involving adult caretakers struggling with personal disabilities, who have extremely limited financial, personal, and social resources, who find themselves unable to care for children whose needs sometimes make them especially demanding and difficult to deal with—that precipitates the need for placement. A long history of such stress is not uncommon.

> Although it is usually a specific crisis that brings children into social agency foster care, during the year prior to placement these families by and large were functioning marginally and had experienced difficulties so severe that it might have been anticipated that further stress could not be tolerated. (Sauber & Jenkins, 1966, p. 111)

In their research on children eight years old or older who were placed in foster care in Sheffield, Fisher, Marsh, and Phillips (1986) came to similar conclusions:

> The difficulties over the care of their children which brought families into contact with social services were extremely long-standing. Almost without fail, parents would describe their current difficulties as having started many years ago when the child was much younger. (p. 33)

Whereas workers tend to emphasize the role played by parental disability, the parents themselves stress the importance of the child's behavior or situational stressors (Phillips et al., 1971; Jones, Neuman, & Shyne, 1976; Three Feathers Associates, 1989).

The J Case

Mr. and Mrs. Jelico are raising their six children in a small three-bedroom house. Three girls sleep in one room and two boys and the baby in another, leaving the older children little chance for privacy or opportunity to study. Despite its dilapidated condition, the Jelicos have attempted to purchase this home, since that would reflect some residential and occupational stability for the family. However, Mr. J's uncertain employment has precluded this. Mr. J is an unskilled laborer; his sometimes uncontrolled temper has resulted in his being fired from several jobs. Mrs. J has not worked in recent years, due to medical problems and intermittent depression. Mr. J prefers that his wife stay at home with the children and has, during her periods of employment, exerted considerable pressure on her to quit. The Js have had to rely on public assistance and food stamps to feed the family over the past several months. The landlord is now trying to evict the family for nonpayment of rent.

Service Availability

The movement of children into substitute care has sometimes been perceived as a political act "to rescue poor children from their parents as opposed to providing money and social services to children in their own homes" (Mandell, 1973, p. 36; Meyer, 1985; Pelton, 1989). In some instances, foster family care has been utilized because the community has not made services or specialized programming available to families who could not afford to pay for them; the parents, having no other available options, felt they must relinquish their children to obtain help.

Evaluating the hypothesis that availability of alternative services influences placement decisions of child welfare workers, Rapp (1992) used case simulations in a study involving 538 workers. Some were randomly provided with a list of preventive services they were to assume would be available to the families, while others were not given this information. Rapp noted that "virtually no association was found between the decision to place and the experimental condition of optimal availability of services" (p. 23).

Runyan and his colleagues (1981) found that highly potent correlates of removal included the type of referral resource and the community in which the abuse occurred. When the courts or police initiated the placement request, the child was far more likely to be removed than when the referral came from other sources. This relationship held, even when controlling for seriousness of the abuse. Some communities were far more likely to utilize placement services than others, although racial and economic factors did not explain these differences. In England, Packman (1986) also found "enormous variability in rates of children in care (and in the use of voluntary and compulsory powers) between one local authority and another" (p. 5).

The reasons for the differential placement rates across communities remain unclear. We can speculate that political attitudes affect a particular community's decision about the extent to which foster family care resources will be available for its vulnerable children. However, this question clearly requires further study.

Initiating the Placement Process

Exploration of the need for foster family care is most often initiated by the child's family, by the child welfare agency, or by the police or the courts. Birth parents and close relatives most often make this request when the parents' physical or mental illness or severe social stress prevent them from adequately caring for their children. Parents sometimes request placement when their children's behavior or emotional difficulties severely strain their caretaking capacities.

Relatives, the police, the courts, schools, and social service agencies already involved with the family more frequently initiate placement in cases of neglect and abuse. Where the behavior of parents poses a clear threat to the life or health of the child, or in situations where extensive use of home-based services has failed to help the family address critical problems, the child welfare agency explores the need for foster care services.

In making placement decision for maltreating families, the child welfare worker makes an assessment of (1) the danger to the child's biological, social, and emotional development of the current living situation, (2) the competence of the child's birth parents and their motivation and capacity to make necessary changes, (3) the formal and informal support system that might be mobilized to help in maintaining the child in the home without damage, and (4) the strengths and the vulnerability of the child that determine the level of stress with which he or she can cope without adverse effects (Steinhauer, 1991; Plumer, 1992). The worker's task here is to seek placement for children whose family circumstances are such that they cannot be protected from further abuse or neglect; however, the worker must also insure that children who can receive help while remaining in their own homes are not placed in care.

Whether to provide a child with foster family care is one of the most complex and difficult decisions a child welfare worker can participate in, particularly when there is insufficient or incomplete information about important aspects of family life. Agency standards and governmental regulations are often too vague to provide helpful decision-making guidelines (Melotte, 1979; Hubbell, 1981). The weightiness of the consequences of this decision exacerbates its difficulty for the worker. "Willingness to gamble upon the parent's restraint can lead to grim tragedy if the judgment is wrong. On the other hand, placing the child in foster care when the home is essentially safe is a costly solution for society and may not really serve the child's welfare" (Fanshel, 1981, p. 685). Faced with this dilemma, workers may choose to be cautious and recommend placement of the child, preferring the risk of discontinuity in parent-child relations. However, with increased emphasis on the use of home-based services, there is greater pressure on workers to avoid placement unless it is deemed absolutely necessary.

Public Law 96-272 requires that "reasonable efforts" to maintain a child in his or her own home must be proven ineffective (or shown to be dangerous for the child) before the decision can be made to place the child in care (Ratterman, 1987; U.S. House of Representatives Committee on Ways and Means, 1993; Portwood & Reppucci, 1994). There is some indication that families experiencing placement were offered in-home services prior to this decision (Smollar, no date; Bullock, Little, & Millham, 1993), although the range of services actually provided them may have been quite limited. In a study of 104 children coming into care for the first time in Westchester County, New York, Kliman, Schaeffer, and Friedman (1982) found that only 59 percent of the parents had been previously known to the social service delivery system. However, more recent research (Davis, English, & Landsverk, 1995) describes "an overwhelming majority (74.8%)" of their families who had prior referrals, with an overall mean of 2.8 prior contacts (p. 45). Studying the experiences of African American children in care in five cities, the National Black Child Development Institute (1989) found six in ten had received casework services and one in four had participated in crisis counseling, but fewer than one in six had received financial help, drug counseling, or other services.

Houston, the city with the most complete records, had offered preplacement services to 72 percent of the families of children in care (p. 42). A study of children coming into care in England (Packman, 1986) described almost all of the families as previously known to the agency or actively receiving services at the time of placement (p. 43). In addition, "children who had already been in care were more likely to be admitted again. . . . It is as if resistance to admission diminishes once a child or members of his family have already crossed the threshold" (Packman, 1986, p. 52).

Regardless of the factors creating the need for placement, evidence suggests that many parents and children believe that placement was the right choice for the family. Jenkins and Norman (1975) posed the following question to 125 mothers of children in foster family care: "Looking back at everything that has happened would you say that placement of your child was absolutely necessary, very necessary, somewhat necessary, or not necessary at all?" Forty-seven percent considered the placement to be "absolutely necessary," 17 percent said it was "very necessary," 13 percent "somewhat necessary," and 23 percent said placement was "not necessary at all" (p. 111). The negative responses were primarily contributed by those mothers for whom the placement was involuntary (p. 52). A more recent study using a smaller sample (Colton, 1988) reported similar results for birth mothers but a great deal of indifference among birth fathers (p. 147). When interviewed regarding their perception of the experience, foster children themselves thought the placement was a desirable alternative to their own home situations (Jacobsen & Cockerum, 1976). A study of 101 children placed in Ontario, Canada (Kufeldt, Armstrong, & Dorosch, 1989) found, "Respondents overwhelmingly agreed with the agencies' decisions to remove the children. 89% of the social workers, 85% of the children, and a surprising 72% of the biological parents believed that care was the best solution at that time" (p. 357). (See also Yoshikami, 1984; Johnson, Yoken, & Voss, 1995.)

The experience of coming into care varies, depending upon the amount of time the family and worker have had to assess the situation prior to placement and the degree to which parents themselves accept the need for placement. (See Figure 5.1.) In some situations, the worker has sufficient time to prepare the family, and the parents voluntarily agree to put the child in foster care. This occurs, for example, when a pregnant adolescent realizes she will not be able to provide appropriate care for her newborn infant. At other times, parents realize they do not have the resources to provide adequate care for their children and voluntarily seek placement, but placement must be done during a family crisis. A parent may suddenly be hospitalized or suspected of a crime and incarcerated. One study of older children in care in Southern Ontario (Palmer, 1990) found 58 percent of the parents had requested the placement; another 20 percent were said to be accepting.

Involuntary placements may also be made after extensive planning or precipitously, in response to a family crisis. Perhaps the most widely publicized involuntary placement circumstances are those surrounding the removal of children from their home after the worker discovers they have been severely mal-

		Timing	
		Noncrisis Situation	*Crisis Situation*
Parental Initiative	*Voluntary*	Example: Adolescent unwilling to care for newborn	Example: Parental need for hospitalization for illness
	Involuntary	Example: Gradual deterioration in alcoholic parents	Example: Child hospitalized because of severe neglect

FIGURE 5.1 *Intake Circumstances*

treated. Drug or alcohol abuse issues may further complicate these situations. "In all but a few cases, the parents will express a desire to retain custody of the child, and the decision will have to be made on the basis of the child's safety and well-being" (CWLA, 1992a, p. 58).

While it is preferable that placement involve sufficient time to carefully assess family needs and prepare the child, the birth parents, and the foster family, many moves take place under conditions where this may not be possible. Palmer's (1990) study found only 16 percent of the children had a preplacement visit prior to their move into care. One study found that "non-urgent requests for consideration of possible placement were frequently ignored until resubmitted on an emergency basis some weeks later" (Steinhauer, 1991, p. 134).

Voluntary placements are preferable, since they maximize the family's involvement in the placement process (Packman, 1986; Schachter, 1989). Paying attention to this participatory role of parents is termed a *liaison casework strategy* (Hubbell, 1981). The agency indicates the critical role parents continue to play in their child's life and strives to work collaboratively with them (Blumenthal & Weinberg, 1984). When parents are not considered full partners in planning, they tend to view placement goals as impositions that are irrelevant to their circumstances and insensitive to their needs.

Placement of a child in care must be sanctioned by the juvenile court. Changing the child's temporary caretakers involves a change in legal custody of the child. Legal custody is concerned with the rights and duties of the person having custody to provide for the child's daily needs—to feed and clothe the child, provide shelter, put the child to bed, send him or her to school, and to see that the child's face is washed and teeth are brushed. Legal custody permits the agency having custody to determine where and with whom the child shall live and when the child will receive routine medical care and mental health services. But the child still legally "belongs" to the parent, and the parent retains guardianship. This means that, in some crucial areas of the child's life, the agency cannot act without parent authorization. Only the parent can consent to surgery for the child, consent to the child's marriage, permit the child's enlistment in the armed forces, or represent the child at law. Only with a change of guardianship are the birth parents' legal ties to their child completely severed.

Considering Potential Foster Homes

The placement of a child involves the selection of a potential home for a particular child and participation of the foster parents in this placement decision. Possible kinship placements are now explored as a first priority in this process. Ideally, selection of kin and non-kin homes is on the basis of complementarity of needs. This is not entirely a new idea. In 1867 the Massachusetts Board of State Charities recommended "that a child of passionate temper should not be placed in a family where the master or mistress is of a similar disposition. When such instances do occur there is apt to be trouble pretty soon."

Placement options are affected by a decision to place siblings together in the same home. "Siblings are placed together in anywhere from 25% to 77% of cases, depending on how shared placements are defined" (Davis & Ellis-MacLeod, 1994, p. 144; see also Festinger, 1994). After reviewing the meager research literature on sibling placements, Hegar (1988) concluded that placing related children together should be undertaken whenever possible because "brothers and sisters usually have meaning for each other that unrelated children lack" and because "loss of a sibling is a traumatic experience, while presence of a brother or sister may ease adjustment to other stresses or losses" (p. 460). Fahlberg (1991) noted that joint placement can facilitate healthy identity formation while separation of siblings accentuates "the impression that family relationships are not really important" (p. 274). Research by Staff and Fein (1991) suggests that fostering brothers and sisters in the same home may also reduce the likelihood of replacements for the children.

The Child Welfare League of America has recently taken a much stronger stand with regard to this issue, stating that "the destruction of sibling relationships resulting from separation is too harmful to tolerate except in the most unique circumstances" (1991a, p. 39). The League noted that sibling groups are now more likely to come into care as a result of placements linked to parental drug abuse.

However, when sibling relationships will "prevent the development of healthier attachments" (Fahlberg, 1991, p. 274) or in cases where the needs of all siblings cannot be met in one placement setting, separate homes may become necessary. The attitudes of foster parents concerning the difficulties involved in parenting sibling groups may also play a role in placement decisions (Smith, 1996).

Unfortunately, it is often the practical difficulty of finding a home that can accommodate the sibling group that prevents brothers and sisters from being placed with one another (Kufeldt, Armstrong & Dorosch, 1989; Weiner & Weiner, 1990). James Bell Associates's (1993) extensive survey found that, among children who had most recently come to their foster homes, 25 percent had been placed with siblings but 42 percent had siblings living in another foster home (p. 68). Research conducted by Testa and Rolock (1999) found that one in four children in sibling groups of three who were in regular foster care were placed with siblings; kinship placements maintain sibling groups more effectively, keeping 56 percent of these children together (p. 117).

The age, sex, and developmental stage of the foster parents' own children may be significant if they are the same as that of the foster child, since this might create undesirable competition (Berridge & Cleaver, 1987; Humphrey & Humphrey, 1988; Steinhauer, 1991; CWLA, 1995). Cautley (1980) reported that "position of the foster child as the youngest in the family group" was associated with success of the placement (p. 252).

Choice of a foster home involves not only assessment of congruence between needs of the child and the foster family, but also evaluation of the degree to which needs of the birth and foster families mesh. Birth families have a right to insist that a substitute home maintain their racial, cultural, and religious heritage (Hubbell, 1981; Blumenthal, 1983), and many would prefer such placements (Barn, 1993). Children should be "placed in homes where they will find compatibility with their family life styles and affiliations" (Meyer, 1985, p. 256). Typically this involves choosing a foster family whose racial composition and economic circumstances are as similar as possible to those of the birth family. The value of kinship placements in this regard is evident.

Pragmatically, foster homes must also be located at some navigable distance from the birth home if parents are to have any reasonable opportunity to meet regularly with their children (Cox & Cox, 1984; Lewis & Fraser, 1987; Barn, 1993; CWLA, 1995). When children are placed in homes some distance from their birth family home or in inaccessible locations, birth parents, who tend to be very poor, are forced to decrease the frequency of visitation unless they are provided with funds or transportation by the agency. In his research on foster care children in New York City, Fanshel (1982) found that only one in five parents had been given this type of assistance (p. 73). In his five-state survey, Yoshikami (1984) discovered obstacles to visiting (distance, high transportation costs, and so on) in 70 percent of child welfare agency records. (See also Jenkins & Norman, 1975; Thoburn, 1980.) However, data collected by Testa and Rolock (1999) indicate that kinship placements offer the greatest opportunity for parents to remain in close proximity to their children. When children are placed in their home community, Meyer (1985) argued, the families receive better support and are more likely to be challenged to improve their situation. (See also Children's Defense Fund, 1992.)

The selection of a home is not always a conscious, deliberate process. It is often a "search, seek, find" operation, one of expediency rather than an exercise of professional judgment (Fahlberg, 1991). Workers may be faced with providing the child with "the best plan possible rather than the best possible plan." Inappropriate placements are often the result of the lack of availability of appropriate homes rather than a consequence of a worker's faulty decision making.

The child's family usually does not play an active role in choosing the child's new home. In Fisher, Marsh, and Phillips's (1986) English study, "placement selection was seen primarily as a professional/administrative decision about the disposition of agency resources, involving consultation with colleagues rather than clients" (p. 65). Interviewing twelve birth families, Hubbell (1981) discovered

> ten said they had no involvement in a placement decision. "I asked them to please keep them (her two children) together, but they didn't," said Mrs. Sonners. "I never had any say. I didn't know who it was they were living with," commented Mrs. Carey. (p. 82)

In Plumer's (1992) research on child placement, parents were asked "whether or not they were given a realistic picture of foster care by the social worker prior to placement"; results indicated that "42.5% of the parents reported that it was not talked about at all" (p. 86). Children have even less knowledge about the selection process or influence on its outcome than their parents do.

Preparing for Placement

Once a potential home for the child is chosen, the worker presents information about the child and the birth family and the need for placement to the foster parents. Providing the foster parents with accurate and detailed data allows them to think realistically about their potential for living comfortably with the child and interacting effectively with the child's birth family. This material allows them to anticipate the types of stresses placement might engender and consider the type of skills they might need to respond adequately.

Kin being considered for placement may or may not already know some or all of this information, so the extent of their current knowledge about the child's circumstances needs to be assessed. Sharing information about the birth parents with kin can raise dilemmas about confidentiality, as the worker struggles to balance the right of kin to have access to crucial information with the responsibility to protect the birth parents from unnecessary invasion of their privacy.

Unfortunately, in many instances, both kin and non-kin foster parents may be offered insufficient background material on the child's family. Frequently, they are given insufficient time to explore with the worker the meaning of placement for their families. In a detailed examination of the placement experiences of 145 new foster parents, Cautley (1980) discovered that "two-thirds of all the families had no more than a total of one or two contacts (joint or individual) with the worker in preparation, and less than a total of three hours was devoted to these" (p. 55). Eight percent of the families had no preparation whatsoever, "other than a brief telephone call on the same day." (See also Rowe, Cain, Hundleby, & Keane, 1984.) A study of thirty-six foster care workers in Ontario (Palmer, 1995) found that "to avoid discussing the reason for admission with children and foster carers is the usual approach" (p. 139). When foster mothers and fathers are not allowed an opportunity to evaluate and discuss their reactions to this material, breakdown of the foster placement is more likely (Berridge & Cleaver, 1987; Steinhauer, 1991).

In preparation for placement and in helping the family with the critical adjustment to the child's entrance into the family, the foster care worker's meetings with both foster father and foster mother are more likely to contribute to the success of the placement than contact with the mother only. Although foster fathers may be seen as "passive partners" by many child welfare workers, they are "quite strong and firm in the areas they perceive to be within their proper area of functioning" (Fanshel, 1966, p. 151; see also Davids, 1968).

Because children benefit from concrete evidence of their parents' recognition of the need for placement, packing belongings with the child, including favorite toys, and providing photos of the family are some of the means whereby this can be communicated (Jones & Biesecker, 1980; Fahlberg, 1991; CWLA, 1995). In a study of older children in care (Kufeldt, Armstrong, & Dorosch, 1989), 95 percent of the children considered bringing favorite possessions an important transitional task; 86 percent thought family pictures were also important. Unfortunately, fewer than half of these children had had an opportunity to bring such possessions, and fewer than two-thirds brought family photos with them to placement (p. 358).

When parents accompany the child on preplacement visits to the foster home, all family members benefit (Triseliotis, Sellick, & Short, 1995). For parents, there is evidence that they have a voice in what happens to their children, while for children, there is evidence of parental acceptance of the move (Plumer, 1992; Palmer, 1995). Younger children are especially in need of direct contact between the two families; gradual movement between the two homes, involving several visits of increased duration, is also particularly beneficial for them. Only three percent of the children in Palmer's (1990) study were accompanied by their parents when they moved into care.

The J Case

After talking repeatedly with Mr. and Mrs. Jelico and with Timothy, the child welfare worker discusses the family situation with his supervisor and decides to recommend that Timothy be placed in foster family care. After reviewing the limited number of homes available for placement of a teenager, the foster care worker recommends that Timothy be placed with Rod Tedesco. Although the worker realizes that Rod is an inexperienced foster parent and Timothy a challenging child, she also feels that Rod will have the time and energy to devote to this lonely and frightened adolescent. The worker also hopes that placement with a male will help Timothy, since he will not be asked to replace his mother with another female caretaker. Although Timothy will be several miles from home and have to attend a new school, the worker believes this will make it less tempting for him to run away from the foster home.

The worker warns Rod that Timothy harbors considerable anger toward his father and may treat Rod poorly as a result. She also reminds him that she will be asking

continued

him to relate to Timothy's parents, who have not been adequate caretakers for him. Rod reluctantly says he will do his best with the J family. He thinks it will be very difficult for him to be pleasant toward Timothy's father.

In the hospital emergency room, Timothy is very reluctant to go anywhere but back home. The worker patiently explains that concerns about his safety will not allow for this at the present time. The worker tries to make the need for placement clear to him, explaining that neither his mother nor his father are in a position to protect him adequately right now. Very reluctantly, after a great deal of protest, Timothy accompanies the worker to the Tedesco foster home. The foster care worker realizes he will need to spend considerable time with Timothy immediately after placement in an effort to help him accept the situation and make the best of it.

Timothy arrives at the foster home with nothing but the clothes he is wearing, which are torn and bloody. His father has refused to let the foster care worker take any of Timothy's belongings from the J home. The worker will need to provide emergency funds so Rod can buy Timothy clothes and school supplies.

Timothy is surly and silent when he first arrives at Rod's home. He refuses food, refuses to shop for clothes, and asks to call his mother. He then goes to his room and stays there for several hours. Rod realizes that this is not at all the way he expected a child coming into his home to behave. He wonders how he will get Timothy to think about going to a new school in a few days.

Questions for Discussion and Debate

1. What are the practice and policy implications of the fact that so many families using foster care resources are desperately poor?
2. How would you go about finding out why foster family services are widely available in some communities but in very short supply in others?
3. What is the impact on birth parents of having custody of their children placed with the child welfare agency?
4. How would you go about deciding what might be the best type of foster family home for Timothy, the child in our case example?
5. What is the experience like for children when they have to be removed from home during a crisis and placed with a family they do not know?
6. If you were a prospective foster parent and were called about a child whom you had to decide whether to take immediately, what would you do? Why?

6

Intervention with Birth Parents and Their Children

Early Placement Issues

Separation of a child from his or her family is often thought of as an individual issue for that child and, sometimes, for that child's parents. However, removal of a child produces a major family crisis, one that creates problems that must be addressed by all its members (parents, siblings, grandparents, other relatives, and even close friends). All family members must grieve for the losses that separation engenders, and each must struggle to give meaning to the separation experience. All family members must cope with the altered family circumstances in which they subsequently find themselves. Finally, the family must respond to the fact of child welfare agency involvement. The task of the foster care worker is to assist parents, foster children, and other family members in addressing these concerns and to provide support as members help one another move toward a positive resolution of the situation that resulted in placement.

Losses

While not all separation experiences imply challenges to major life attachments, a move into substitute care is experienced as loss by many children and parents. This is especially true for children placed with non-kin or with kin whom they do not know well. Siu and Hogan (1989) described this as a crisis of "dismemberment—losing a member of the family, either temporarily or permanently" (p. 343). At the time of placement, family members begin to deal with feelings precipitated by distance from loved ones, with substantial changes in core roles as "someone's mother" or "someone's child," and with loss of familiar routines and predictable environments.

The move away from family represents traumatic loss for many children. As Glatz (1998) pointed out, "most children deeply resent being taken away from home. More to the point, they are furious, horribly homesick, and terrified" (p. 37). Losses for the child are of many types—encompassing removal from a familiar community, loss of friends and familiar routines, and changes in school and child care locales. A study of foster care in five metropolitan communities (National Black Child Development Institute, 1989) found 81 percent of the children were placed in a new school situation (p. 22). In an Ontario study of 101 children between the ages of nine and sixteen (Kufeldt, Armstrong, & Dorosch, 1989), two-thirds went to new schools. A Chicago study (Johnson, Yoken, & Voss, 1995) found 95 percent of the children had been moved to new neighborhoods (p. 966). (See also Berrick, Barth, & Needell, 1994.)

Individuals undergoing loss experiences typically pass through a series of stages of mourning. Children share with grieving adults the need to deny initially the reality of their loss, the task of eventually facing it, and, ultimately, the need to move beyond it and reintegrate their lives (Norton, 1981; Jewett, 1982; Bayless, 1990; Stahl, 1990; Fahlberg, 1991; Steinhauer, 1991; Wolfelt, 1991):

> *Stage 1: Shock and Denial.* During this stage, the individual is overwhelmed by the loss. Adaptive strategies involve attempts to ward off or minimize recognition of the loss and powerful feelings of anger, fear, and despair that accompany its recognition.
>
> *Stage 2: Protest.* During this "bargaining" stage, individuals attempt to manage the loss by undoing it. The loss is now recognized, but the person continues to feel overwhelmed and unable to cope with the fact of its irreversibility.
>
> *Stage 3: Despair.* During this stage, the individual fully confronts the loss and its meaning. Grief, rage, and hopelessness are fully experienced.
>
> *Stage 4: Detachment.* This is a stage of readjustment. Affectively, there is a sense of mastery—"I've arrived; I've made it." There is a deep sense of pride present as the hope in the future replaces the hopelessness and despair that have been part of the past.

Steinhauer is doubtful whether a child younger than six months old "will experience the full force of the acute distress precipitated by disruption of an existing selective attachment" (p. 18). He believes that reactions will be most intense when the child is between the ages of six months and four years. Fahlberg (1991) found clear evidence of grief reactions among children older than four-and-a-half.

In this chapter, we will deal primarily with the first stage of grieving, since it reflects children's (and parents') typical reactions in the early part of placement. In subsequent chapters, later stages of grieving will be addressed.

Denial involves a refusal to recognize or admit the loss and the sad, angry, and frightened feelings that accompany it (Terr, 1990; Steinhauer, 1991). In an effort to manage difficult feelings, children discount them. During this stage, some children present the superficial picture of adaptation to the placement with a notable absence of any kind of behavior—physical or verbal—that might indicate discomfort. For other children, excessive activity or emotions serve to divert them from thoughts of loss and grief (Norton, 1981; Jewett, 1982). Wakefulness, sleep walking, nightmares, night terrors, teeth grinding, and upper respiratory infections are common. "The shock and denial stages will be most prominent when the separation has been abrupt" (Fahlberg, 1991, p. 164).

Denial is a normal and adaptive response during the early stages of loss. However, if relied upon for too long, children cannot resolve grief issues and move on with their lives (Folaron, 1993).

Parents may withdraw, appear numb and unresponsive, or deny the importance of the placement for the family. "Their feelings may be expressed inappropriately, leading us to think that they are uncaring. Parents may resort to drinking or drug use to dull their senses and decrease pain. During the stages of shock and denial, forgetfulness is common" (Fahlberg, 1991, p. 192). Unresolved feelings about their own past placements may surface at this time.

Only minimal attention has been paid to children's attempts to cope with separation from siblings, extended family members, teachers, friends, and other individuals of significance in their lives (Hegar, 1988). In their study of children in placement in Israel, Weiner and Weiner (1990) described sibling support as a "potentially important resource that was insufficiently used for the children's benefit" (p. 123). Kahan (1979) described the outcome for one sibling group who had been inseparable as young children:

> Both children had been through experiences of loss and disappointment in the foster home and their own relationship suffered. "In the end we were apart. We are very apart now, my brother and me. There is, a sort of, I don't know, a very wide gap between us. . . . It sounds an awful thing to say but I've given him up as a brother. As an acquaintance, well, we keep in touch; as a brother I don't think he'll ever be a brother to me." (pp. 26–27)

Both parents and children require help to acknowledge their losses, and this help must be given by adults whom they find trustworthy and supportive (Wolfelt, 1991). The foster care worker can be one such resource, helping family members by validating individual feelings, by recognizing their impact on behavior, and by teaching family members to anticipate and understand their reactions (Maluccio, Fein, & Olmstead, 1986; Stahl, 1990). The worker also encourages and facilitates early contacts between parents and children. Parental visitation at this stage provides an opportunity for family members to support one another in their grief and to realize that separation need not mean abandonment. Agency support of visitation also provides an acknowledgment of the importance of ongoing attachments among family members (Hardin, 1983). Evidence suggests that this early encouragement is instrumental in maintenance of parent-child ties throughout the placement (Fanshel, 1982; Festinger, 1983; Rowe et al., 1984; Weiner & Weiner, 1990).

Making Sense of the Move

Both the children and their families face a task of assigning meaning to the need for the child's placement. Family members can attempt to understand this need in a variety of ways:

1. *Personal failure* ("I am so incapable as a parent that they took away my child." "I was a bad boy, so my parents got rid of me.")
2. *Inability to live up to others' expectations* ("I've let my family down." "Everybody says I'm not good enough to keep my child." "Why can't my parents be like other parents and take care of me?")
3. *Attribution of responsibility to others* ("My child just doesn't want to listen, so I had to send her away." "My mom runs around and drinks all the time, so they took me away." "That agency just snatches children for no good reason.")

Guilt, shame, and rage are among the powerful emotions associated with the struggle to understand "Why did this happen to me?" (Tunnard, 1989).

Children may feel ambivalent about their birth families: On the one hand they desperately miss them and want to be with them, and on the other they may be ashamed of their parents' inadequacies and angry about their parents' failure to provide them with a safe home. One former foster child commented, "I've got very divided loyalties about my mother. . . . When she says something about 'Oh, it's hard for you on your own with two children,' I'll turn round and say 'Yes, well you got rid of me and there was only me' and I say it even now. I feel very bitter about it still" (Kahan, 1979, p. 30). Yet, this young woman "could not bear other people to criticize her mother and as an adult had a continuing sense of responsibility for her." Children are also ambivalent in that they appreciate some aspects of care (better material circumstances, greater freedom, decreased family stress) while missing their home and wanting to return there (Fisher, Marsh, & Phillips, 1986).

Conflicted feelings are equally common for parents, who may feel saddened and worried about their children's removal but relieved about not having to care for them on a daily basis. "Parents often described with some pleasure the first few days, or sometimes weeks, after a child's departure into care. Instead of a constant stream of minor crises, a relative peace descended and some parents relaxed in this relative calm" (Fisher, Marsh, & Phillips, 1986, p. 68). Parents typically feel responsible for the move but angry with the worker for making the removal happen.

Analyzing the reactions parents had at the time of placement, Jenkins and Norman (1975) described three general types. Although expressing sadness, nervousness, and worry, Group A, the largest group, was distinguished by feelings of anger and bitterness. This anger may be directed toward the agency, toward the child who seems uncooperative and untrustworthy, and toward the self. This group tended to include parents whose children were placed involuntarily for less socially acceptable reasons (such as abuse or neglect). Angry parents were more likely to come from the most deprived economic circumstances, to be African American or Puerto Rican, and to already feel alienated for other reasons.

Group B was, in many ways, the antithesis of Group A. These mothers primarily felt relieved and thankful and had children who were placed for more "socially acceptable" reasons, such as uncontrollable behavior of the child or physical illness of the mother. Members of this group tended to have higher incomes, to be white, and to feel less alienated. Group C, a relatively small group, included mothers who were distinguished for their feelings of guilt. Included here were a substantial number who were unable to care for their children due to mental illness. These mothers tended to live in economic circumstances midway between those of Groups A and B, and their beliefs about the need for placement were more midrange as well (pp. 52–53).

Many children feel confused about the reasons for their placement (Rice & McFadden, 1988). A study of 59 young adolescents in Cook County, Illinois (Johnson, Yoken, & Voss, 1995) found 40 percent either did not know or were unclear about what had precipitated their move into care. Stahl (1990) explained why confusion is widespread:

> Part of the reason for this is that she is often given conflicting messages, since biological parents, social workers, and foster parents may tell her different things about why she is in care. At the same time, even if the child is told the "truth" about her placement, her ability to understand and deal with its ramifications may be somewhat limited. (p. 40)

It is not uncommon for children, especially young children, to feel fully responsible for the placement.

> Preadolescent children think what is, ought to be. They are not capable of distancing from events or of understanding the many possible explanations for things that happen to them. When they consider the reasons for placement, they rarely understand that their parents could have handled things differently. Moreover, these children are acutely aware of their own limitations and failings. This means that when they cast about for answers to the questions posed by placement, they usually find the answers within: Placement is a punishment for real or fancied misdeeds. (Levine, 1988, p. 302)

(See also Rosenberg, 1991.) Adolescents may also blame themselves, particularly when their own misbehavior has played some role in the conflicts precipitating placement.

A special challenge for parents and the worker during the intake process is to help the child sort out the reasons for having to leave the birth family. It is preferable that the parents take primary responsibility for providing explanations and that the worker serve as an assistant to them. What parents tell (and fail to tell) children about this is of central importance, but how they act toward the child also has substantial impact. Do their actions convey that placement is "a blessing? Is it a curse? Or, is it so noncommittal that the implication is that the child was unimportant to the caretaker?" (Fahlberg, 1991, p. 153). The child welfare literature gives minimal guidance as to ways the worker can be of help to parents in this effort. Perhaps this explains why, in Plumer's (1992) study, "60% of the parents stated that they felt as if they were excluded from participating in the process with their children when it came to dealing with their reactions" (p. 87).

Kinship caretakers face their own responsibilities in coming to terms with the purpose of placement and communicating with the children about this issue. The process of understanding the reasons for placement is affected by their own attitudes toward the birth parents. If kin caretakers are angry or frustrated with birth parents, children may come to believe it is wrong to love their parents or to miss them. When kin caretakers blame the agency for the move and insist the parents had no responsibility for it, children may feel uncertain about the meaning of their mistreatment.

The child welfare worker repeatedly communicates to parents, foster parents, and children that understanding why the move occurred is an important and discussable issue (National Commission on Children, 1991). The worker offers ongoing assistance as the family struggles to develop a realistic understanding of the need for foster care—one that does not generate debilitating levels of guilt or an insufficient level of parental responsibility for change. Ideally, as a result of this process, children will begin to develop a clearer and more realistic understanding of the need for placement, will realize that their parents can and do still care for them, and will come to believe that all the adults responsible for their welfare will be working together to create a stable, permanent future for them.

The J Case

Both Mr. and Mrs. Jelico had a very difficult time during intake, both with the worker and with Timothy. Mr. J was very angry and repeatedly blamed Timothy for his placement. He could not tell Timothy that he supported this move, and he handled his fears and frustrations by refusing to talk to his stepson. He said he would let his wife "take care of this" but hovered nearby and became enraged with her if she said anything that appeared supportive of Timothy. Increasingly, Mrs. J had trouble saying much of anything to the worker, except that she missed Timothy a great deal and "didn't know what to do about it all." She grew increasingly hopeless and frightened. Although Mrs. J "sneaked" phone calls to Timothy when her husband wasn't home, neither parent could provide much support for Timothy at this time.

The worker was concerned about ways to help this family and keep Mrs. J safe. She considered talking to Mrs. J when Mr. J was not at home, but his vigilance made this difficult and potentially dangerous for Mrs. J. She finally decided to deal more directly with Mr. J, telling him that he was a very important parent whose input was needed but making it clear that his aggressiveness continued to raise problems for himself and for Timothy. She talked about the fact that most parents feel guilty, worried, and angry when their children go into care. Mr. J began to gradually calm down and to participate directly in the interviews. After a month, Mr. J agreed that both he and his wife should sign a "Thinking of You" card for Timothy.

Family Readjustment

Placement presents another set of challenges for the birth family as parents, siblings, and other family members begin to adapt to a home life without the child and the child begins to settle into new routines in the foster family home.

Agency practices reflecting what Plumer (1992) termed "total transfer" reflect the view that parental "failure" results in "losing" their child. "When a child leaves one placement for another, too often he is required to sever all relationships with his old placement—he is 'totally transferred' to the new location" (p. 201). Changing family relationships are misunderstood as severance of family ties. Such practices ignore the reality that "children never lose their basic conviction that their biological mothers are their real mothers and no one can substitute for them" (Meyer, 1985, p. 256).

Given the instability of some foster care placements, encouraging this type of family substitution can place the child in a peculiarly vulnerable situation. One former foster resident commented, "The only security you have got when you are in care is that that is given to you from the people above. Where you happen to live and the bed you sleep in isn't your bed, because if you move from there somebody else will have it. Nothing is ever completely yours, other than perhaps a few possessions that you have got" (Kahan, 1979, p. 52).

The practice of "total transfer" exacerbates fears of parents, especially a dread that once their children have been removed, they will never return to the family home (Hubbell, 1981; Horejesi, Craig, & Pablo, 1992). Having themselves experienced difficulties with the child welfare agency, or having heard of difficulties others experienced, parents worry that even their best efforts to improve will not be recognized or considered sufficient for reunification. They also fear losing their child's affection and respect to the foster parents.

Worker facilitation of family readjustments is based on an understanding of the impact of the child's removal on the birth family. A study of foster family care in Sheffield, England (Fisher, Marsh, & Phillips, 1986) described changes in the parenting role. The research found parents relatively unconcerned with losses during the early stages of placement. Instead, they concentrated on decision making with regard to the best possible care for their children and on insuring that their children were in "good hands." Parents felt they had come to placement only after repeated efforts to manage the child at home had failed. (This was true even for abusive parents.) While workers saw removal of the child as a major loss of parental responsibility, parents perceived their role as changing but undiminished in importance. They hoped that placement would be a positive step in helping the child and struggled to communicate to the worker about ways they felt this could be accomplished. (See also Packman, 1986.)

Additional work needs to be done to articulate the complex changes in birth family life that can occur after a child moves to a foster home (Bullock, Little, & Millham, 1993). How does removal affect the family's definition of itself and its responsibilities to members? How are family roles reallocated? What is the reaction of siblings to this move? Do they perceive parents as less able to protect children and to prevent outsiders from taking them away? Does this result in diminished parental authority with children who remain at home? What is the response of extended family members? Do they ally with parents, feeling that the entire family has been invaded, or do they blame the birth parents and withdraw their support? Because the worker's ability to facilitate reunification is dependent on an understanding of these factors, they must be explored with the family.

Parents are especially in need of the worker's recognition and support for their investment in their children, their struggle to maintain valid parenting roles, and their love for their offspring. These provide positive indicators of parental motivation to work toward the child's return. The worker can reflect with parents on the difficulty and great pain that accompany alternations in family dynamics and parenting functions. Parents in Packman's (1986) study valued workers who had a "human and informal" approach, who were good listeners, who could be honest and direct, and who could provide tangible assistance along with more intangible kinds of support.

The J Case

It is difficult for the worker to discover the full impact of Timothy's removal from his family's home. The family appears to be very isolated, and it is not clear that any of the relatives even know about this situation. Mr. J has fought with many of his immediate relatives and no longer speaks to them; Mrs. J has had limited contact with the two sisters who live in the area.

Mrs. J appears to be the family member who misses Timothy most. However, she is largely inarticulate about her feelings and needs, so she does not speak of this to the worker. Because Mr. J refuses to say much to agency personnel, it is difficult to tell how he reacts to Timothy's leaving. It is some months later that the worker begins to understand that Timothy often stood up for his mother against his father, trying to serve as her "protector." With him gone, Mrs. J is even more frightened than ever.

Timothy's leaving has not diffused the tense and angry atmosphere in the J home; instead, Mr. J's anger is now more intensely directed at the remaining children. None of them have stood up to their father the way Timothy used to do. Mr. J has become more verbally abusive with Monica lately. Joey has also begun bullying his younger siblings more than he did when Timothy was at home.

The worker realizes she does not have a clear picture of the relationship Timothy had with his siblings before he left home. They have not asked to call him in his new foster home, and they have not asked how he is doing when the worker meets with the family. However, Monica and Marsha manage to be present whenever Timothy's foster care worker comes to visit, "listening in" on anything she says about him.

Initial Readjustments for the Children

So many changes accompany the move, that the early period after placement is often one in which both the foster family and the child feel relieved at having simply survived (Stahl, 1990). For the children, making a successful transition requires that they begin to fit into the foster family, to be socialized in its mores and daily customs. Learning the rules of social intercourse and becoming comfortable with them is a process that Fanshel and Shinn (1978) labeled "embedment." Patterns of eating, sleeping, and completing the day's tasks, means of communicating, problem solving, and parental discipline may be at variance with those learned in the birth family home. Differences between these two home environments can exacerbate children's uncertainty:

> In general, people find a sense of security in familiarity and sameness. Even in cases of severe child abuse, most children would rather remain with their abusing parents than move to a physically safe, but strange environment. . . . In such cases where involuntary life changes may occur, losing the emotional or psychological security that comes from being in a familiar and predictable environment is more fearsome and stressful than the occasional physical pain. (Norton, 1981, p. 157)

Differences in family patterns may be especially noticeable when the child moves from a family living with chronic poverty to a home where finances and employment are more stable, as many children in foster care have to do.

This is a transitional period, a time in which children live physically in the foster home but psychologically in the home they left behind. The children live in one home and love in another. The children struggle with what is, for them, an unusual situation—having two families at the same time. The stresses of adaptation they face are much the same as those for children whose parents are undergoing divorce. Eventually, they must arrive at some level of contentment with and acceptance of their dual family status and must learn that they can care about and be cared for by two different sets of parents simultaneously (Meyer, 1985; Humphrey & Humphrey, 1988; Fahlberg, 1991; Steinhauer, 1991).

The social worker helps children begin this adjustment by letting them know as clearly as possible what is going to happen next, by helping them anticipate some of their fears and discomforts, and by helping them feel some sense, however limited, of control over their lives. The worker establishes continuity by making regular visits to the children in their foster homes.

Foster parent recognition that ambivalence and loyalty conflicts are normal aspects of foster child adjustment and tolerance for their expression can help them through this initial period. For example, allowing children freedom to decide whether to call them "mom" and "dad" reflects a respect for them and their birth parents and an understanding that adjustment is a complex process that cannot be hurried.

The J Case

Timothy came to his foster placement expressing a great deal of belligerence toward his new foster father. He had not had an opportunity to meet Rod prior to his placement and felt strongly that his own desire to return home had been ignored. On the first day of placement (and repeatedly during the following weeks), he told Rod that he did not want to stay in his home, that he was only biding his time until he could leave, and that he had no intention of cooperating in meeting day-to-day living needs. He refused to make his bed, to clear the supper dishes, or to fold his laundry.

Rod initially tried to handle these issues by showing Timothy that he was a supportive person who wanted to get to know him. Although he tried not to show this to Timothy, he was pained by his foster son's rejection. As the days passed, he realized he was becoming increasingly angry at Timothy, and he called the worker and other foster parents to discuss what he should do. The worker helped him understand the grief and fear that underlay Timothy's behavior. He was counseled to tell Timothy that this was a very upsetting, frightening, and sad time, being away from his home. He decided to tell Timothy that he was not interested in "replacing" his parents. However, he also had to become clearer and firmer with Timothy about his chores and to use realistic consequences whenever Timothy chose not to participate.

The situation was made more difficult for both Timothy and Rod by the agency's lack of clarity about when Timothy could visit with his parents. Timothy thought that the worker was keeping him away from his family for no good reason. He refused to hear the worker's explanation that it was taking some time to make safe arrangements with his father. Timothy avowed that he did not need anyone to keep him safe—that he could take care of that himself. Rod vacillated between feeling sad that Timothy's family could not be more supportive of him and feeling angry at his parents, wondering whether he could ever like "those people."

Surprisingly to everyone, Timothy made a fairly easy adjustment to his new school. Being away from old associates seemed to help him develop some tentative friendships with less troubled peers. He did a minimal amount of studying but managed to maintain his grades above failing. He seemed to use school and studying as a means of escape from all the complex issues involving his family and his new home.

During this early period, Rod and Timothy both feel unsettled, frightened, and unsure of how to treat one another. The worker has reassured each of them about the normalcy of these feelings. It has helped Rod to realize that he and Timothy share many of the same concerns. Each of them wishes, however, that this unsettled time were over.

Relationship with the Child Welfare Agency

At the time of placement, questions of responsibility and authority arise for the birth parents and for the children. What is the changing nature of the children's influence on what subsequently happens to them? What changes occur in the extent of power parents hold over the lives of their children?

Transfer of custody of the child from the parent to the child welfare agency provides a visible indicator of parents' diminished authority. It is to be expected that parents will feel threatened by this process. They may feel the agency has "stolen" their child. For parents who have struggled with poverty or other chronic problems, all social service agencies may be seen as unsupportive, invasive, and dangerous.

It is more difficult for the foster care worker than for the home-based worker to envision a collaborative role with the birth family. Believing "as a fundamental tenet that the genesis of child care problems lies in family relationships rather than in the intrinsic qualities of individuals" (Fisher, Marsh, & Phillips, 1986, p. 48), the worker in substitute care tends to believe it is the attitudes and actions of parents that created the need for placement. Parents, in contrast, are more likely to consider the child's impact on the family as causative (Maluccio, 1985).

Both inequities in relative power and differences in attitudes and assumptions can create a divisive wedge between workers and parents. In an effort to reach out to the parents and overcome these differences, workers are advised to "spell out, at an early stage in negotiations, their own ultimate legal powers and responsibilities for children's welfare, rather than producing them like an unpleasant rabbit out of a hat once all their efforts to help in other ways have failed" (Packman, 1986, p. 205). Workers also rely on client empowerment strategies, a means of helping parents "regain some power and control" (Maluccio, Fein, & Olmstead, 1986, p. 146). This involves the worker's active efforts to recognize, maintain, and build parent involvement in and responsibility for the child's life.

In his study of child placement decisions, Packman (1986) found that approximately two-thirds of the parents who were interviewed "reckoned that the social workers had shared their own perceptions of the 'problem,' at least in part, and they had responded to some, if not all of what the parents wanted" (p. 129). The remaining one-third were "conspicuously dissatisfied," however, "feeling their problems had been wholly misunderstood, that decisions had been taken right out of their hands, and that the action that had (or had not) been taken was against their wishes" (p. 129).

Collaboration building presents a challenge to the parents as well, as they try to establish a trusting, workable partnership with the agency. Fisher, Marsh, and Phillips (1986) explained that parents do this, in part, by trying to convince the worker that their perceptions of the child's problems and needs are legitimate. Furthermore, they "must lay a claim to recognition of these important issues from the worker without generating antipathy and without giving the impression of total helplessness" (p. 44).

For children, both the research and clinical literature suggest that placement generates a "profound sense of powerlessness" (National Commission on Children, 1991, p. 283), "a sense of being unaware and uninformed about the actions of significant adults in their lives (including the social worker) and particularly about the formal mechanisms by which decisions were taken" (Fisher, Marsh, & Phillips, 1986, p. 69). (See also Aldgate, Stein, & Carey, 1989.) Fahlberg (1991) described feelings of chronic anxiety that result when children see both themselves and their parents as having no control over the situation. These children may feel as if they have been kidnapped or snatched. Their perception of parents as trustworthy, powerful individuals is diminished. People outside the family seem to have more power than family members. Indeed, every time there is a power-based move, at some level the importance of any and all family ties is diminished. (p. 166)

In a service delivery system where children's control over their lives is severely restricted, there are clear limitations to the workers' ability to overcome these fears and alter these perceptions. To the extent that workers are genuinely interested in the children and carefully listen to their views and concerns, this feeling of alienation can be somewhat mitigated. When workers and birth parents actually work together to resolve problems and plan for the children's futures, the children's belief in parental authority can be at least somewhat restored.

Developing Permanency Plans

Responsible placement requires that parents be helped to plan and try to carry out the necessary changes that can ultimately permit their children to return home or find permanent placement elsewhere. Work toward concrete placement outcomes begins at the time the child first goes into care (Rosenberg, 1991).

Case planning is now required by PL 96-272 for all children in federally supported or state-supervised foster family homes. The record for each child must include a "plan for providing services to the parents, child, and foster parents to improve conditions in the parents' home and facilitate the return of the child to the home, or into a permanent placement" (U.S. House of Representatives Committee on Ways and Means, 1992, p. 886). *Systematic case planning* is defined as the identification of the specific changes the family must make in order for the child to return home, the setting of time limits for achieving these changes (which are established by the Adoption and Safe Families Act), and work that must be done to bring about such changes, including help and support the agency must provide the parents in this process (Wiltse & Gambrill, 1974). Guidelines for planning procedures are carefully spelled out by several authors (Stein & Gambrill, 1976; Pike et al., 1977; Jones & Biesecker, 1980; Steinhauer, 1991; Triseliotis, Sellick, & Short, 1995).

Maluccio and Simm (1989) delineated six essential characteristics of effective case planning. They include "mutuality; explicitness; honesty; realism; flexibility; responsiveness" (p. 105). During a series of meetings with parents, the worker develops a contract that clearly spells out expectations. Written contracts as a part of written case plans are required by PL 96-272. The more specific, concrete, and behaviorally oriented the language of the contract, the greater the likelihood that it will be understood, accepted, and achieved (Hubbell, 1981). Explicit contracts prevent "aimless drifting or jolting from crisis to crisis without any real sense of direction" (Steinhauer, 1991). In order to be effective, parents and workers must work together to formulate the contract. Once drawn up, it should be open to periodic renegotiation.

Contracts include expectations for changes in parental behavior or family circumstances that must be made before the child can be returned. In addition, the contract must specify expectations for the maintenance of parental involvement with the child. Contracts specify not only what the client will do, but also what the worker is obligated to do to help the client—agencies that will be contacted, the number of appointments the worker will make with the client, resources the worker will provide, and procedures the client can use in order to arrange for visits. Contracts list objectives in specific measurable terms (CWLA, 1995).

In contracting with parents, the consequences of breaking the agreement need to be spelled out, since failure to work toward change can result in permanent loss of a child. Contracts can provide the explicit evidence needed to support a petition to the court for the termination of parental rights (Pike et al., 1977). Thus one supposedly prime condition of good contracting—that it be honestly entered into without coercion—is at variance with another aspect of contracting when it is undertaken with parents who have children in foster care.

Here workers are faced with implementing multiple roles as helpers, facilitators, and supporters of clients in planning for family changes and as evaluators of the outcomes of such efforts. The obligation to clients is to make clear these different responsibilities. "We will work together so that you are no longer alcoholic, or drug addicted, or abusively rejecting of your child, but if within [some specified period of time] the situation has not changed, we will recommend to the court the termination of your parental rights." Service programs involved in such unwelcome dilemmas express confidence that clients can distinguish between a "threat and a clear explanation of realistic alternatives" and that parents respond to such frankness (Pike et al., 1977, p. 43).

Despite its necessity, agencies do not always engage parents in the planning process. Parents who do not play a substantial role in planning may not even be aware of the foster care worker's objectives.

> Most of the natural parents we interviewed were virtually ignorant of the details of their plans or had been so at the beginning of the placement. Nine of the thirteen families said that they either did not know the requirements for unification when their children began foster care or were unclear about them. (Hubbell, 1981 p. 88)

Reanalyzing the data from Shyne and Schroeder's (1978) national study of child welfare services, Olsen (1982) discovered that more than half the families had no social service plans and that Native American families were least likely to be provided with them. Thoburn (1980) documented a similar situation in Britain. She found that fewer than half the families in her study had any kind of explicit service contract with the worker (p. 87). However, Yoshikami's (1984) more recent assessment indicated that public child welfare agencies are now complying more fully with PL 96-272 case-planning requirements:

> In all five states agency policy required the use of written plans for foster care (including reunification) cases. There were written case plans for 90 percent or more of the cases in 14 of the 18 agencies; this was true of all agencies in three of the five states. In a large majority of the local agencies, supervisors reported that most case plans met agency standards and were developed jointly with parents. (p. 71)

Research conducted by the National Black Child Development Institute (1989) found more than 80 percent of foster care cases in four of the five cities surveyed had at least one family service plan in the record (p. 67).

Defining workable goals can prove difficult when the worker is dealing with the "massive disability" (Fanshel, 1982, p. 8) and "relatively severe and enduring problems" (Cautley, 1980, p. 47) of some birth parents. Motivational difficulties must also be anticipated. Evaluating a New York City placement prevention project, Halper and Jones (1984) commented, "Although they would verbally contract for services they often did not perform the tasks they had agreed to" (p. 15). Poor reading and writing skills, illiteracy, and unfamiliarity with the use of written materials may be obstacles to effective use of written contracts with clients.

The timing of the development of case plans is of considerable importance. Early development of a plan and intensive work with families is crucial for positive case outcome because they are associated with earlier exit from foster care, less time in care, and greater likelihood the child will return to the birth family home (Weiner & Weiner, 1990; Steinhauer, 1991; Plumer, 1992). Gibson, Tracy, and DeBord (1984) studied variables affecting length of stay in foster care. An analysis of forty-three children in foster care showed that "intensive and very frequent contacts between agency and family at the very beginning of placement may be necessary to affect the return of the child as quickly as possible" (p. 145). However, once the child has been placed in foster care, there is a tendency for the worker to feel "There now. He's out of that terrible situation. Now I can relax" (Steinhauer, 1991, p. 127) and to put off this essential work with the birth family.

The J Case

Although sometimes the child welfare agency works with the child and parents to develop a contract, in this case the worker decided to meet only with Mr. and Mrs. J. Because Mr. J continued to express such hostility toward Timothy—blaming him for the agency's involvement—the worker felt that holding meetings with the entire family was not yet appropriate. In fact, developing a working contract with this couple was exceedingly difficult for the worker. Because she could get so little useful cooperation from the parents, she felt she was forced to impose intervention goals on the family, even though she knew that collaborative development of goals would have been far more productive.

The worker's primary concern was to try to help the family work toward protecting Timothy from abuse and having him return home. Initially, she developed a written contract that stated that a goal for Timothy's return had to involve a commitment from Mr. J to use other types of less dangerous discipline with him. The worker explained that a failure to achieve this goal might result in Timothy's not being able to return home. To address this issue, the worker was referring Mr. and Mrs. J to a local agency that was skilled in working with abusive parents. The contract stated that the couple must satisfactorily complete treatment in this program in order to have their son returned.

Mr. J's response was to insist that he had not "abused" Timothy but disciplined him properly for repeated disobedience and for trying to interfere with his proper role as a father. He argued that no program was going to prevent him from having the right to properly discipline his son. He said it was Timothy who had to change and no one else. Mrs. J said she would like to have Timothy home and that she "supposed he would have to behave better" in order to do so. She said she wanted to see Timothy soon and wanted to know how to arrange that. Mr. J said Timothy was not going to come into his house until he apologized for causing all these problems. The worker recognized their perspectives and concerns but reiterated the substance of the agency's contract.

Neither parent could describe any of their own behaviors that needed changing. Neither parent offered any other suggestions for goals to be achieved. At the end of the meeting, the worker did not know if the parents would actually contact the treatment program for an appointment. The worker realized that developing a really useful contract was going to take some time with this family. A three-month review date was set.

Questions for Discussion and Debate

1. If you were the foster care worker for a child just placed in care whose parents seemed preoccupied and disinterested, how would this affect you? How would you find out whether these parents are grieving for their lost child or disengaged and uncaring?

2. How would you go about trying to get these parents to maintain relationships with their child?

3. If you were a parent whose child was in placement because you had severe mental health problems and needed intensive treatment, what kinds of dilemmas would you face in trying to convince the foster care worker that you wanted to continue to parent your child?

4. A grandmother is serving as a kinship placement for her grandchild whose mother is receiving treatment for cocaine addiction. This child was neglected by her mother prior to her placement. How should her grandmother explain the need for placement to the child?

5. How could the child welfare system go about creating a better sense of empowerment for foster children and their parents?

7

Ongoing Intervention with Birth Parents and Their Children

The foster care worker is responsible for providing services to birth parents and their children throughout each child's stay in care. In this chapter, we deal with two central and related concerns of the family—continuing to deal with the losses that occur as a consequence of placement, and repairing and maintaining a vital sense of connection and caring between parents and their children.

Loss and the Foster Child

Once children begin to settle into their foster homes, it is frequently assumed that grief issues have been resolved and that they have no immediate relevance to children's lives. However children, like adults, require much time and patient attention to these issues if they are going to be fully dealt with. Problematic behavior may be indicative of grieving (Jewett, 1982; Garon, Mandell, & Walker, 1984). During the protest stage, acting out behaviors, projection of blame onto others, and sudden angry outbursts are common. Children sometimes become "neighborhood nuisances" or "classroom clowns" (Terr, 1990). Anger may be expressed in a variety of ways and may be directed at the self or at others. Although the child may make numerous appeals for help in overcoming negative, unacceptable behaviors, there is also an almost ritualistic rejection of this help throughout the entire protest stage (Norton, 1981; Levine, 1990).

During the stage of despair, the child may make few demands on the new environment. Activities may appear disorganized and the child unmotivated, depressed, or overwhelmed (Terr, 1990). "There is marked regression as the child withdraws, no longer wanting to relate to individuals that make up the present external world" (Norton, 1981, p. 157). "At school, peer relationships may improve, but simultaneously academic work may deteriorate" (Stahl, 1990, p. 39).

Although children vary greatly in the amount of time they need to pass through each of these phases, for many, the more extreme responses are short-lived. With appropriate assistance from the birth and foster families and from the worker, most children will eventually come to terms with the reality of the separation and begin to function more adaptively.

There are, however, some children for whom progress is much slower. Preoccupied with their loss, these children divert much of their energy to the internal work of mourning; however, these efforts do not result in movement toward resolution. As a consequence, other important developmental tasks—growth in cognitive and academic abilities, emergence of more sophisticated interpersonal skills—receive much less attention than they should. Stuck in "incomplete mourning," these children have difficulty perceiving caretakers in a realistic and balanced light. Instead, they tend to idealize lost parents, focusing exclusively on positive qualities they remember or wish had been characteristic. At the same time, current caretakers, seen as "bad" parents, become targets of scorn and rejection (Schachter, 1989; Rosenberg, 1991; Steinhauer, 1991; Kates, Johnson, Rader, & Strieder, 1991; Palmer, 1995). A few children become "permanently detached," unable to reinvest energy in current intimate relationships. Feelings of extreme isolation and despair are reflected in the memories of one such child:

> As a tiny child in the children's Home (he left when he was 6) he recalled "I used to spend half my time in the toilet actually, standing on the seat looking out of the window at the cars going by to the local. I used to go up there when I had a problem or something. I'd go up looking all gloomy and come down smiling. I used to like being on my own. I still do when I have a problem to sort out. Some people don't need people to talk to. I used to talk to a big elephant once when I had a problem—I used to tell my troubles to that. I used to punch it when I had a few problems, and that was one of my personal toys." (Kahan, 1979, p. 48)

When the child left this home, the elephant remained behind. "Persistent, diffuse rage," chronic depression, excessive dependency, low self-esteem, and antisocial or asocial behavior are problems these children may struggle with (Bayless, 1990; Steinhauer, 1991, pp. 35–37).

The child's ability to successfully complete the stages of grieving is affected by a number of factors:

> The more vulnerable the child prior to the loss of the parent—either because of organic liability, difficult temperament, past deprivation or parental discord, previous separations, insecure attachment (especially those remaining incompletely resolved) or because of a highly strained and/or ambivalent relationship to the parent who was lost—the less likely the child is to mourn successfully even under optimal conditions. (Steinhauer, 1991, p. 40)

This describes the experiences of many foster children, who have had multiple unresolved losses prior to this placement (Wolfelt, 1991). It is not unusual for a child to have moved to the homes of relatives or friends, to have had multiple or changing caretakers in their own homes, or to come from families experiencing marital separation or divorce before coming into care. A study of 104 children going into their first placement (Kliman, Schaeffer, & Friedman, 1982) found 58 percent had already experienced "notable separations." Steinhauer (1991) pointed out that the nature of the loss and the reasons for it are less clear for foster children than for children whose loved ones are deceased. "Genealogical bewilderment," an inability to create a coherent picture of one's past life, is not an uncommon outcome of such difficulties (Aldgate, Stein, & Carey, 1989; Siu & Hogan, 1989; Palmer, 1990; see also Rice & McFadden, 1988).

> Every time somebody went out of my life, a bit of me was there, left behind too. Probably why I look back so much was because I wanted those bits, I wanted to feel a whole person again. Even now I suppose I don't really feel a whole person, I feel as though there's something people have got that I haven't, something indefinable, something I cannot place. (Kahan, 1979, p. 46)

Foster children may face further dilemmas in resolving loss issues because of their prior experiences with abuse or neglect. When loss has emerged out of intimate relationships characterized by mistrust, when caretakers have been dangerous and threatening, or when revealing one's true feelings has placed one in great jeopardy, successful movement toward a sense of stable connectedness to safe, reliable, and nurturing parenting figures may be severely compromised (Steinhauer, 1991).

Helping the Children Deal with Their Losses

The tasks of helping foster children work through loss issues and confront attachment concerns are both complex and necessary ones. Working on these concerns helps insure the child's healthy development in a wide variety of areas and facilitates positive adaptation to the foster home as well. In order to do this, the children will need help in recognizing and understanding the facts of separation, the lessons learned about relationships in the birth family home, and feelings of sadness, anger, and yearning connected with the wish to return to that home (Kliman, Schaeffer, & Friedman, 1982; Bondy, Davis, Hagen, Spiritos, & Winnick, 1990; Land, 1990; Folaron, 1993). They will need to explore ways the move to foster care has changed their relationships with birth parents and to understand the aspects of those relationships that remain consistent. Children will need further help in putting these facts and feelings together to create some coherent and realistic understanding of their lives. The birth family's pivotal role in this process is discussed in the next section. The family's work is complemented by efforts of the foster parents and foster family workers.

By offering children a substitute home, loving care, and concern, foster family members challenge the children to begin confronting grief issues and reexamining attachment concerns. While it might be difficult for foster parents to accept the responsibility of helping children through this process, this is an essential and relevant task for caretakers who, after the children's parents, must serve as models of reliable, nurturing parenting (Wald, Carlsmith, & Leiderman, 1988; Fein, 1991). Foster parents do this by repeatedly demonstrating their trustworthiness to the children and by tolerating the expression of deep rage and powerful sadness. Foster parents are readily perceived as birth parents' competitors, and they offer convenient targets for children's rage (Steinhauer, 1991). They must help children manage expression of such feelings while recognizing their purpose (Kliman, Schaeffer, & Friedman, 1982; Fahlberg, 1991). This is accompanied by efforts to create a history of positive interactions with the children, an especially important but difficult task with children

> who do not believe that they deserve to have good things happen to them. They are likely to convince adults that they are undeserving of love, affection, and positive gratification rather than vice versa. (Fahlberg, 1991, p. 288)

Pasztor and Leighton (1993) offered a resource manual for foster parents to guide them in this work.

By providing services to both children and birth families, the foster care worker can serve as another source of continuity—helping to link past, present, and future in some kind of meaningful way (Laird, 1981). Particularly in situations in which the children's contacts with birth family members are intermittent and unpredictable, the worker may become the only resource the children and foster parents can turn to for ongoing information about the whereabouts and well-being of birth family members (Kahan, 1979; Shulman, 1980; Hubbell, 1981; Colon, 1981; CWLA, 1995). Children may even need to be reassured that family members are still alive.

In order to help children with grief work, workers, like foster parents, must convince the children that they are caring, trustworthy, and reliable human beings (Three Feathers Associates, 1989). Fanshel, Finch, and Grundy's (1990) study of foster care reported that 90 percent of the troubled children in the Casey Family Program thought the social worker cared about them, 83 percent found the worker easy to talk to, and 70 percent believed they could depend on the worker for help with their problems (pp. 95–96; see also Johnson, Yoken, & Voss, 1995).

Research examining the extent to which social workers keep children informed of family affairs has produced mixed results. Meier's (1962) and Hubbell's (1981) studies indicated that most of the children interviewed understood why they were in placement and the changes in their families that had to be made in order for them to be returned. Thorpe's (1980) results, based on responses of 121 children in long-term care, are not so positive:

> A disturbing 22 per cent of children had no, or very little, understanding of their background and present situation, the majority had some but inadequate understanding, and only 26 per cent, i.e., a quarter, had what can be called a good understanding. In fact, three children were not even aware that they were fostered.

As would be expected, the extent of understanding increased with age, but at all ages a majority of children have limited knowledge and understanding. (p. 94)

Stein and Carey's (1986) research found adolescents who were placed when very young had little background information about their past. "They admitted to gaps in memory which were like missing parts of their lives and spoke of partial revelations about their past as being very disturbing" (p. 33). In Fanshel, Finch, and Grundy's (1990) research, 41 percent of the children said that the workers had not given them information about their birth families (p. 95).

As Jolowicz (1946) pointed out many years ago, it is not easy for the worker to embrace a responsibility for helping children with grief work, to face their deep pain and rage. While "child welfare workers, foster caregivers, and clinicians naturally view the abusive or chaotic conditions that precipitated placement as the primary threat to the child's survival," the children in care experience placement itself as the major threat (Kates, Johnson, Rader, & Strieder, 1991, p. 584). In an effort to avoid dealing with these powerful feelings, foster care workers may "fail to recognize or appreciate the significance of behavioural signs of the child's mourning" or "may collude in and help the diversion of the mourning process by distracting or cheering up the child" (Steinhauer, 1991, p. 145; see also Palmer, 1990, 1995).

High caseloads and frequent turnover make it difficult for some workers to play a significant role as a source of continuity. One former client commented that her social workers "all disappeared and somebody new came and it was a new story, from the beginning. I got sick of telling my life story over and over again and not getting anywhere" (Kahan, 1979, p. 126). Kates, Johnson, Rader, and Strieder (1991) argued that coordinated efforts among service providers and integration of services to children and their parents are necessities for helping children understand the complex relationships among the various agencies and individuals responsible for their care and, ultimately, in helping them successfully struggle with the question "Whose child am I?" (See also Molin, 1988.)

A treatment tool that explicitly focuses children's attention on issues of identity and continuity is the Life Book. Working together with the children, foster care workers, foster parents, and birth family members construct a life history that is both realistic and meaningful to the children (Project CRAFT, 1980; Thorpe, 1980; Beste & Richardson, 1981; Backhaus, 1984; Maluccio, Fein, & Olmstead, 1986; Bondy, Davis, Hagen, Spiritos, & Winnick, 1990; Fahlberg, 1991; Holody & Maher, 1996). Using words, pictures, and drawings that are pasted in the pages of a book, the children are helped to explore significant life events and the reasons why changes in their living situation had to be made.

An 11-year-old boy started sessions insisting he had never been a baby. The Life Book provided him with pictures of himself as an infant and toddler, and he realized that his initial perception was not true. His caseworker believed that seeing himself well cared for in these pictures helped him to realize that his birth parents did value him, even if he could not stay with them. (Backhaus, 1984, p. 554)

Children may need to work at constructing the Life Book intermittently, with opportunities to take time off to consolidate ideas and reflect on feelings or simply to rest from the difficult work of mourning. Children who are more resistant to recognizing and sharing feelings may benefit from more persistent encouragement to continue work on their Life Book, however (Steinhauer, 1991). Maluccio and his colleagues (1986) commented that adolescent interest in constructing a Life Book is "unpredictable."

Group meetings for foster children also provide a useful mechanism for sharing questions and concerns about being in foster care and for exploring the relationship between foster- and birth-family experiences (Palmer, 1990). Groups have proven particularly useful for preadolescents and teenagers, and they have also been successfully used with former foster care clients who are now adults (Kahan, 1979). Palmer (1990) recommended coleaders for these groups so that quieter or more disruptive children can receive individualized attention.

The J Case

Early in the placement, the worker decided that Timothy would be needing some individual treatment, primarily to help him handle his belligerence, which was bothering his foster father, his teachers, and peers in his new school. During the early months of placement, he has been, at best, a distant and uncommunicative child and, at worst, openly hostile. While his negativity mostly took the form of verbal abuse, he had also, in the past, had some physical altercations with peers.

The treatment worker began exploring with Timothy his views of his behavior and the "trouble" it caused. However, Timothy had great difficulty doing more than blaming others for his problems. When the worker suggested that this is what his dad also did, Timothy exploded, screaming that Mr. J was not his "dad" and that he was not like Mr. J at all. The worker realized that he needed to step back from Timothy's behavior and, instead, help him express his feelings. He soon found that Timothy's rage covered a deep sadness and panic. Timothy missed his mother and siblings and was fearful that he would never see them again. He was very concerned for his mom's safety, especially since he could not be home to "help" her. He worried that his siblings might be hurt by Mr. J. He was also afraid of his own anger and worried that, perhaps, he too would become more violent.

Timothy was too frightened to openly voice these feelings and retreated into silence whenever the worker tried to explore them. However, he could more readily use drawing and writing in a journal to approach them.

Slowly the worker began to help Timothy acknowledge these feelings and recognize how realistic they were. The worker realized that Timothy would need a great deal of help in letting adults assume some of the burden of responsibility he felt toward his family.

Maintaining Attachments between Birth Parents and Their Children

For any child, attachment experiences with birth family members serve as the basis on which all subsequent relationships are built. Despite disruption and adversity, family ties are central. This has been documented across a number of studies. When Fanshel (1982) asked workers to assess the intensity of children's relationships to their natural family, 20 percent were described as having a deep or close attachment (p. 251). However, when the children were asked to complete a sentence about "the person I love best," 51 percent described a birth parent; only 9 percent described a foster parent. When asked to choose the person whom they would live with if they could, 37 percent chose the birth family; 7 percent chose the foster family (p. 463). In Wald, Carlsmith, and Leiderman's (1988) research, seven of the thirteen children still in care after two years wanted to live with one or another of their parents, and two wished they could live with both their birth and foster families (p. 138). Poulin (1992) examined attachment of one-hundred children who were two or older and were in long-term care. Although they had been foster children for an average of 7.4 years, 29 percent still had a strong relationship with biological family members (p. 74). (See also Walsh & Walsh, 1990; Bullock, Little, & Millham, 1993.)

In the child welfare literature, discussion of parent-child attachment tends to be confused with parental visitation (Grigsby, 1994). "Thus, the fact that a parent attends visits is often taken as a sign of a strong bond between the parent and child and overrated in the agency's and judge's efforts to effect reunification" (Loar, 1998, p. 42). However, attachment and visitation are not equivalent. Attachment has to do with the overall quality of and sense of closeness in the parent-child bond (Lamb, Thompson, Gardner, & Charnov, 1985). An assessment of attachment would include an examination of whether the child appears to feel secure with and trusting of the parent. Is the parent someone the child can turn to for comfort and guidance in time of need? Is the parent a "secure base" from which the child can venture out to explore in the world? Does the child appear to be anxious and ambivalent or to be evasive and seek to avoid the parent in situations of stress and uncertainty? Experiences with parental abuse or neglect have clear impact on the child's attachment. Of particular importance for the child's long-term adjustment is what he or she, as a result of being maltreated, has come to believe about the connections among trust, safety, and intimacy (Crittenden, 1988).

Visitation is a vehicle whereby positive connections to the parent and other family members—when they already exist—can be facilitated:

> Regularly scheduled visits are valuable, as a means of helping the child maintain his or her sense of connectedness and identity with the biological family. Even when children cannot live with their biological parents, they continue to belong to them. . . . Regardless of the outcome (of care), their sense of roots and heritage

should be theirs to keep. This identity is best preserved when regularly scheduled visits are planned and encouraged. (Maluccio, Fein, & Olmstead, 1986, p. 164)

(See also Hess & Proch, 1988; Aldgate, Maluccio, & Reeves, 1989; Kates, Johnson, Rader, & Strieder, 1991; Poulin, 1992; Grigsby, 1994). However, parents may visit children to whom they are insecurely attached or for whom they have few positive feelings. Moreover, when problems with attachment are evident prior to the child's coming into care, visits, by themselves, will not rectify the difficulty. Active guidance from the worker will be needed, both during visits and through other types of intervention, to help birth parents work to build stronger, more responsive ties to their children.

The Impact of Visitation

The literature describes a connection between the extent and regularity of visits and positive outcomes for children. (Note, however, that the link between visitation and attachment has not been systematically studied. Instead, visitation is assumed to indicate a positive attachment.) Regular, frequent visits are linked to better adaptation while in care and better adjustment after leaving placement (Weinstein, 1960; Holman, 1973; Sherman, Newman, & Shyne, 1973; Thorpe, 1980; Fanshel, 1975; Davis, 1989; Maluccio, 1991; Plumer, 1992).

Some evidence suggests that children who are visited regularly have a more positive sense of well-being and better overall developmental adjustment than those who are not (Proch & Howard, 1986; Hess, 1987; Hess & Proch, 1988; Weiner & Weiner, 1990). Thorpe (1980) explained that:

> children who were in contact with their natural parents seemed reassured that they were loved, rather than rejected. They understood that the reasons for their being in care were not because they were bad, unlovable, or "no-good"; as a result they could tolerate the "difference" implicit in being a foster child. (p. 95)

However, two studies (Festinger, 1983; Rowe, Cain, Hundleby, & Keane, 1984), exploring the impact of long-term care on children, did not find an association between well-being and parent visitation. Research conducted by Cantos, Gries, and Slis (1997) uncovered a complex relationship among visitation, adaptation in the foster home, and children's problems:

> Visiting may minimize the amount of externalizing behaviors exhibited by these children, but the extent of internalizing behaviors exhibited may depend on the degree of adjustment the children have made in their placement. Children who are visited regularly may be less angry than those who are not visited or those who are visited irregularly. When these children are happy with their family foster home placement, visiting may also increase their dysphoria and anxiety, although not to clinical levels. (p. 325)

Regular visits are also associated with a better overall adjustment to the foster home (Fanshel & Shinn, 1978). There appears to be a connection between the child's ability to trust in and accept foster parents and the opportunity to maintain ties to the birth family (Tiddy, 1986; Fanshel, Finch, & Grundy, 1990). Children who are visited appear to move more effectively through the mourning process (Steinhauer, 1991), and they have a more realistic and balanced view of birth parents (Hess & Proch, 1988; Rosenberg, 1991). Visitation can reduce isolation between parents and children so that they do not "consolidate their alienation from and their scapegoating of each other" (Steinhauer, 1991, p. 141). During visits, children can have enjoyable contact with people they care about (Hardin, 1983; Hess & Proch, 1988). Even in instances in which children have not met with their birth parents for long periods, reestablishing contact may prove to be beneficial (Davidson, 1980, p. 50; Tiddy, 1986).

Visitation appears to be linked to shorter stays in care. Reanalyzing data from Shyne and Schroeder's (1978) national survey of social services to children, Mech (1985) reported that children who had had no visits within a three-month period ultimately remained in care almost one year longer, on the average, than those who received at least some visits during that time. The more often the child was visited, the shorter the stay in care tended to be. (See also Fanshel, 1975, 1982; Gibson, Tracy, & DeBord, 1984; Lawder, Poulin, & Andrews, 1985; Katz, 1990; Benedict & White, 1991; McMurtry & Lie, 1992; Bullock, Little, & Millham, 1993; Barth, Courtney, Berrick, & Albert, 1994; Davis & Ellis-MacLeod, 1994; Cantos, Gries, & Slis, 1997.) A two-year follow-up study of children in care in New York City (Fanshel, 1982), however, did not uncover a link between visitation and discharge (p. 97).

Visitation may also be tied to the type of placement after discharge (Proch & Howard, 1986). In an analysis of Connecticut data, Simms and Bolden (1991) found that 41 percent of children who had regular visits returned home within the study year; only 8 percent of children without such visits were reunified. (See also Lawder, Poulin, & Andrews, 1985; Davis, English, & Landsverk, 1995.)

Despite its potential value for children, visitation occurs infrequently for or is unavailable to substantial numbers of foster care clients (Hess, 1987). Studying children who had been in care for a year or more, Fanshel (1982) discovered that almost half had no contact with adult relatives (p. 26). Among children in the Casey Family Program in Montana, Walsh and Walsh (1990) noted that 59 percent had no contact with their mothers and 84 percent had not seen their fathers (p. 45). Exploring visitation of seventy Connecticut preschoolers, Simms and Bolden (1991) found 37 percent had had no opportunity to meet with their parents. However, Kufeldt, Armstrong, and Dorosh (1989), studying 101 children aged nine to sixteen, reported that only 14 percent had no family contact (p. 360). (See also Fanshel & Shinn, 1972; Rowe, Cain, Hundleby, & Keane, 1984; Colton, 1988; Grigsby, 1994; Cantos, Gries, & Slis, 1997.)

Among the forty children asked to evaluate parent contacts by Kufeldt, Armstrong, and Dorosh (1995), two-thirds were satisfied with the number of their visits, while the remainder wanted more. The authors went on to comment:

although there is some correlation between the actual frequency of visits and satisfaction with amount of visiting, there are children in each of the three categories of visiting (i.e., weekly, two weeks to one month, less than monthly) who would like to have additional visits with their parents. (p. 704)

Longer stays in care appear to be associated with more attenuated visiting. Following the foster care history of thirteen children, Wald, Carlsmith, and Leiderman (1988) indicated that most of the mothers visited early in their children's placement; however, after one year, "four parents now saw their children regularly"; after two years, only two parents did so (p. 86). Among one hundred older children in care two or more years, Poulin (1992) found 42 percent had never been visited by relatives; an additional 15 percent had had no visits within the last year (p. 74). For children in care three or more years, Rowe, Cain, Hundleby, and Keane (1984) reported that only 21 percent "had even casual contact with a parent during the previous year" (p. 95). Assessing children in care five years or longer, Festinger (1983) found that more than half (57 percent) had few or sporadic contacts with parents or other relatives, and an additional 15 percent had had no recent visits. In this study, "sporadic" contacts included "few contacts over the span of several years" (p. 74).

Visitation frequency may be associated with the reasons for initial placement of the child in care. Thorpe (1980) found that placement because mothers were physically incapacitated had the strongest association with regular parent contact; children placed because they were disturbed were visited next most frequently; abused or neglected children were least likely to see their parents while in care (p. 67).

Developing Visitation Plans

Visitation may take place at the foster care agency or child welfare agency, in the foster home, or in the birth parent's home. While many agencies establish relatively rigid visitation rules for parents (such as "all visitation must take place monthly in the office"), permanency for the child is better facilitated if the plan varies depending upon the needs of the children and families (Proch & Howard, 1986). Visits at the birth family home are most "normative," providing children with opportunities to see their old toys and bedrooms and to remain in contact with friends and neighbors (Kufeldt, Armstrong, & Dorosh, 1989). However, home visits may also jeopardize children's safety and require the most time and effort on the part of the child welfare worker to consistently monitor. Visits to the child in the foster home can help children integrate their experiences with birth and foster families and can be used to help the birth parents develop better parenting skills. However, foster parents must be willing to play a facilitative role, and the child welfare worker may have to be available to help the foster and birth families work through any problems that arise. Least normative but most easily supervised are visits at the child welfare agency. This is a typical visitation arrangement in many agencies, particularly early in the placement process (Proch & Howard, 1986; but see Simms & Bolden, 1991). When visits must be made in this setting, efforts to make the environment appealing, to provide toys and other activities for the children, and to insure the family some privacy are important (Hess & Proch, 1988).

Visitation should be scheduled so that there is sufficient time for family members to overcome their initial discomfort with one another. Blumenthal and Weinberg (1984) recommend starting with weekly visits of at least two hours duration. To maintain attachments with younger children, visits may need to be scheduled even more frequently. Steinhauer (1991) recommended daily visits with youngsters younger than two and thrice-weekly visits for those between two and four years old (p. 176). As the birth parents begin to work on parenting issues and the worker determines that the child is not endangered, visits may be scheduled for longer periods (Hess & Proch, 1988). Overnight and weekend visits allow the child and birth parents to maintain a realistic picture of the stresses and problems that resulted in placement (Maluccio, Fein, & Olmstead, 1986; Stein, 1987). Visits are often increased when reunification is imminent (Hess, 1988).

Visitation plans should encompass contacts with the child's siblings and with other individuals who are important to the child (Hegar, 1988; Davis, 1989; Hess, Mintun, Moelhman, & Pitts, 1992; Poulin, 1992). Examining the experiences of children in long-term care, Rowe, Cain, Hundleby, and Keane (1984) noted, "A continuing contact with grandparents appears to be almost wholly beneficial." In some states, noncustodial parents and grandparents may have a legal right to visitation (Carrieri, 1992). Birth parents may also need financial help with the costs of transportation to and from visits.

Because unpredictable or irregular visits can create anxiety and feelings of rejection in the child, the foster care worker strives to help parents develop a plan for regular visitation (Holman, 1973, p. 201; Festinger, 1983). Predictable visiting is considered an important sign of parental capability, responsibility, and concern for the child. Development of a concrete visitation schedule is important, since "if there is a schedule, parents tend to keep it, especially if they were involved in making the schedule" (Hess & Proch, 1988, p. 8; see also Proch & Howard, 1986). The researchers also "strongly discourage" use of open-ended arrangements in which the parents call to request visits, since this tends to result in irregular patterns of contact.

Regular visiting is reinforced when the foster care worker uses praise and approval for parents who fulfill their commitments in this way. When a regular schedule of visits is maintained, the parents might be sent a letter of commendation, whereas failure to visit might prompt a phone call or special delivery letter from the agency as a reminder. Parental investment is also reinforced when parents are routinely notified about and included in major events in their children's lives. Parents should be contacted about school reports, medical problems, and the like. Failure to apprise them of these matters is a common source of parental dissatisfaction (Jenkins & Norman, 1975; Thoburn, 1980; Hubbell, 1981).

Simms and Bolden (1991) and Hess, Mintun, Moelhman, and Pitts (1992) described programs that make innovative use of visitation to help parents work on critical childrearing issues and to move the family toward permanency goals.

Maintaining Visits

Parental Challenges.   Meetings between parents and their children evoke powerful emotions. Anger, guilt, confusion, fear, and discouragement may be mixed with pleasure, excitement, and satisfaction (Fisher, Marsh, & Phillips, 1986; Kufeldt, Armstrong, & Dorosh, 1989; Steinhauer, 1991). Children who are angry and frightened about the placement may attempt to "punish" their parents by misbehaving or by trying to make them feel guilty. Children may beg parents to take them home and become enraged or very sad when parents cannot comply. Birth mothers realize that visits are upsetting experiences, both for themselves and their children (Jenkins & Norman, 1975). Few parents enjoy visiting, and some find it a painful ordeal. "It reminds them of their failures and inadequacies. Each visit tells parents that while they are not capable of caring for their children, someone else is" (Hess & Proch, 1988, p. 5). Thoburn (1980) found that it is not difficulties parents encounter with foster families but with their own feelings, engendered by the realization they cannot adequately care for their children, that can make contact so difficult. When either the children or their parents decide that facing one another is too painful, visits may be canceled (Davidson, 1980). Because of its importance for helping families, there is a need for more detailed study of the feelings and perceptions of parents and children during this process (Hess, 1987).

There may be difficulties in establishing comfortable visiting regimes when parents "are disorganized and have standards and schedules for the child who visits at home that are different from those of the foster family; miss appointments without calling, arrive late, and return the child late" (White, 1981, p. 467). Research by Hess, Mintun, Moelhman, and Pitts (1992) found "no-shows averaged 25% . . . primarily because of parents' transportation problems and ambivalence about visiting, foster parents' scheduling and transportation problems and ambivalence about visiting, and children's illnesses" (p. 86). (See also Kufeldt, Armstrong, & Dorosh, 1989.)

Parents may behave inappropriately during visits, although serious problems with parents are infrequent. Fanshel (1982) found that among children who were not in the process of being freed for adoption, approximately one in ten of the parents had created some type of disturbance, one in ten had attempted to visit while intoxicated or addicted, and almost 9 percent had exhibited bizarre or otherwise seriously inappropriate behavior (p. 51). However, half of the mothers had never had any of these problems.

Caretaking inadequacies may also become evident during visits (Blumenthal & Weinberg, 1984; Plumer, 1992). One in ten of the parents in Fanshel's study were described as relating very poorly to their children, and an additional one-third were considered marginal. Only one in three appeared to know how to make the visit an enjoyable experience for the children (p. 55). Considering both the frequency of contact and parental effectiveness, Fanshel (1982) estimated that one in four was performing as a responsible parent (p. 44). Teenage mothers in Kliman, Schaeffer, and Friedman's (1982) study:

> generally . . . had little understanding of what to expect from the infants and attributed negative motives to them when the babies cried or did not respond as desired. Often there was growing impatience with the infants as visiting sessions progressed. On several occasions, mothers asked to have their visits terminated early because they became too frustrated by their inability to stop the babies from crying or because they were jealous when the babies responded to other people. (p. 209)

Loar (1998) described childrearing capabilities that birth parents may not have, even though most visitation plans assume they:

- know how to play with their child, and that a safe site is all that is required for a visiting plan;
- know how to talk politely with their child, and that verbal abuse is related to stress;
- know how to use toys to play together with their child;
- know how to enjoy their child's company. (p. 47)

She added, "These overestimations of parental capacity prevent the formulation of realistic visiting plans, which should include the teaching of fundamental interpersonal skills necessary not only for constructive visits but also for safe and realistic reunification" (p. 47).

Occasionally, problems between birth parents and their children during visiting are so severe that the worker seeks to restrict or delay contact with the children. Parents who cannot control their own behavior or that of their children to create a minimally safe environment may need specific help with these issues before visits can recommence (Maluccio, Fein, & Olmstead, 1986; Rosenberg, 1991). Children sometimes become extremely upset as a result of visiting. When their distress cannot be "tolerated or contained," visiting may have to be diminished or delayed (Steinhauer, 1991, p. 181). Older children may refuse to visit their parents. When counseling does not alter this decision, the worker may decide that forcing the child to see parents is counterproductive (Aldgate, Maluccio, & Reeves, 1989).

The J Case

The treatment worker was eventually able to convince the foster care worker that visits between Timothy and his family be considered.

The foster care worker was reluctant because she feared for Timothy's safety if he were in a tense situation with his father. It was decided that visits should begin in the child welfare agency office on a monthly basis. Mr. J sometimes came with his wife and some of the children; these visits were uncomfortable, since he voiced repeated criticism of Timothy, and the worker was unable to deflect him from this. Visits with Mrs. J alone were also explored, but these were frequently sabotaged by Mr. J, who would not let his wife come. Because the family did not notify the agency that they were not coming, Timothy was often let down and deeply hurt when they did not arrive.

For this family, Timothy's phone calls were an increasingly important means of contact. Mrs. J seemed better able to manage contacts when her husband was not at home, and Timothy could often talk on the phone with other family members, even when he was present. Although Mr. J usually made the family cut short these calls, they were a more reliable way for Timothy to manage contact.

Sometimes these contacts went well, but at other times they left him frustrated, more deeply enraged at Mr. J and more frightened about his mother's welfare. However, the calls and visits provided a valuable "reality check"; the treatment worker could use these experiences to help Timothy explore what it would be like to go back to his home.

Foster Parent Responsibilities.   Ideally the developing relationship between foster and biological parents becomes one of mutual cooperation toward achieving what is best for the children, with each recognizing and accepting the different responsibilities and the different contributions of the other toward the children's welfare (Maluccio, Fein, & Olmstead, 1986). However, some degree of tension, discomfort, and competitiveness are a natural part of this relationship. Frequently coming from different worlds, foster parents and biological parents may have little in common—except for the child, around whom they compete (McFadden, 1980; Murphy, 1981; Steinhauer, 1991). More than thirty years ago, Weinstein (1960) recognized:

> The foster mother may define the status of the natural mother as inferior in the relationship. She may be unwilling to entertain suggestions made by the natural mother on the ground that she is inadequate by virtue of the child's being in placement. . . . The natural mother . . . may see her position as the child's natural parent as entitling her to the right of unlimited critical review of the foster mother's actions. Such conflicting definitions of the situation may lead to open hostility. (p. 13)

Birth parents sometimes complain that foster parents intrude on their visits with their children and make significant decisions about their children without consulting them. Competition from foster parents may be overt. During a family visit, a foster mother asked the child, "Did you show Mary (the natural mother) what Mommie bought you when we shopped yesterday?" (Murphy, 1981, p. 435). Birth parents may also feel that they may never be able to give their children the material goods easily available in the foster home. Imprisoned or institutionalized parents may fear their child will forget them (Beckerman, 1989). Approximately one in ten of the parents surveyed by Jenkins and Norman (1975) felt foster parents did things to make visiting particularly difficult (p. 67).

Foster parents may find it difficult to understand how children who have been harmed by birth parents can still feel strong affection for them. When the children continue to miss their parents, foster parents may interpret this as personal rejection or as a comment on the adequacy of their care. "It is easy to see why foster parents, who, day after day, week after week, have to put up with frustrating and disruptive behavior while doing their best for a difficult child, might resent that child's seeming to care more for the idealized natural parents than for them" (Steinhauer, 1991, p. 160). Interviewing new foster parents, Cautley (1980) found many highly critical—especially of the birth mother. Uninformed foster parents interpreted the child's "early upsets" when visiting as "events to be avoided," rather than a normal part of the adaptation process (p. 263).

Visitation can raise issues for kinship caretakers that are equally potent. Caring for their grandchildren means, for some grandparents, that they must recognize their children's (and perhaps their own) deficiencies:

> They feel that they can no longer trust their adult sons and daughters, and they often wonder whether they are to blame for their children's behaviors. Having "failed" as parents with their own children, they question what they can improve this time, and wonder if they will "fail" a second time around. They also wonder how to counter the continuing negative influences of their children on their grandchildren. (Poe, 1999, p. 7)

Loneliness and isolation, lack of financial support, and fears about their children's and grandchildren's welfare can compound these worries and negatively affect interactions when parents visit their children.

Kin appear to make a more concerted effort at collaboration with birth parents than non-kin do. A study comparing the role perceptions of kin and non-kin foster parents in the Casey Family Program (Pecora, LeProhn, & Narsuti, 1999) found kin take on greater responsibilities as "birth family facilitators." Kin were more likely to believe they should help arrange visits (55 percent versus 24 percent), supervise these visits (63 percent versus 16 percent), and arrange contacts with siblings (66 percent versus 40 percent). Kin were also more likely to feel they were responsible for keeping parents informed about the child's welfare and helping their foster child "deal with future relationships with members of his or her birth family" (p. 168).

The social worker carries a central responsibility in assisting foster parents in coming to terms with their obligations with regard to the children's birth families (Murphy, 1981; Blumenthal & Weinberg, 1984; Steinhauer, 1991). Foster parents can be helped to see that they do not assume sole parenting responsibility but always share it. This relationship is facilitated by creating many opportunities for birth and foster families with one another. With caseworker assistance, early mistrust, hostility, and fear can gradually give way to a more facilitative role, and in some instances to the growth of close supportive relationships between the two families (Cautley, 1980; Lee & Park, 1980; McFadden, 1980; Thoburn, 1980; Davies

& Bland, 1981; Felker, 1981; Ryan, McFadden, & Warren, 1981; Meezan & Shireman, 1985; Hess, 1988; Aldgate, Stein, & Carey, 1989; Davis, 1989; Smith, 1991). A study in northwest England found "a number of the foster parents interviewed had clearly been instrumental in helping foster children to maintain relations with their natural families" (Colton, 1988, p. 83).

Although foster parents can play such a vital role in assisting birth families in this way, many are not allowed an opportunity to do so or are provided with insufficient assistance in becoming effective supports for birth parents (Shulman, 1980; Hubbell, 1981; Fanshel, 1982).

> Little or no attempt appeared to have been made by agencies to ensure that foster carers had the training, skills, or knowledge of child care research to provide a framework for understanding and managing parental access. (Waterhouse, 1992, p. 44)

The J Case

Early in the placement, Rod tended to stay out of any planning or preparation for Timothy's visits with his family. The foster care worker had to repeatedly explore with him his dislike of Timothy's parents. Rod continued to blame them for the pain they had caused Timothy; he felt that this bright and potentially happy child had been deeply harmed by their actions. Gradually he was helped to see that it was not his role to be angry on Timothy's behalf. Instead he had to be a supportive person to Timothy, who would have to work through his own feelings about Timothy's birth parents. On those occasions when Timothy returned from visits deeply upset, Rod's anger would return.

In an effort to facilitate interactions between Rod and the Js, the worker asked Rod to begin transporting Timothy to his visits at the agency. This was arranged after consultation with the Js, who said they did not mind if Rod did this. The worker introduced Rod to the Js and always stayed to chat with the foster father and parents for a few minutes before taking Rod out of the room. Although Mr. J ignored him, Mrs. J and the other children did talk with him. He was surprised to find his picture of this family gradually changing, and the meetings gave him a better understanding of Timothy's strong sense of caring for his family.

This arrangement had an unexpected benefit for the Js as well. Mrs. J shared with the foster care worker her sense of relief in meeting Rod and finding out how "nice" and responsible he was. She, too, appreciated having a real person to associate with the notion of "Timothy's foster parent." Mr. J, while continuing to be highly critical of the entire arrangement, did not interfere, and the worker suspected that he, too, liked seeing the real person with whom Timothy was living.

Responsibilities of Worker and Agency. "Arranging and supporting visits are two of the most difficult and time-consuming aspects of caseworkers' work with children in placement" (Hess & Proch, 1988, p. 4). Studying the activities of workers in the Casey Family Program, Staff and Fein (1991) found that 30 percent of their time "involved coordinating, implementing, and discussing family visits" (p. 338). (See also Holman, 1973.) Studies of case plans conducted by Proch and Howard (1986) and the National Black Child Development Institute (1989) indicated that visitation plans were routinely included.

Once visits have stopped, for whatever reason, they are very difficult to renew, so the foster care worker's regular review of visitation plans is an important impetus for regular parent-child contact. Assessing the records of 256 children in care in Illinois, Proch and Howard (1986) concluded:

> Most parents who were scheduled to visit did so, and most visited in compliance with the schedule specified in the case plan. . . . This clearly suggests that a way to increase the frequency of visits is to schedule them to occur more frequently. (p. 180)

(See also George, 1970; Gruber, 1973; Thorpe, 1980.)

Because establishment of regular, reliable parent-child contacts requires active, often intensive effort on the part of the foster care practitioner, the worker's attitudes about visitation are especially important (Fisher, Marsh, & Phillips, 1986; Hess, 1987; Aldgate, Maluccio, & Reeves, 1989; Hess, Mintun, Moelhman, & Pitts, 1992; Palmer, 1995). Does the worker perceive visits as essential vehicles for building family relationships, or are they seen as having vague or inconsequential meaning for the child? Steinhauer (1991) concluded, "Having lost respect for the natural parents, [many workers] fail to recognize their continuing importance to the child in care" (p. 162). However, Kufeldt, Armstrong, and Dorosh (1989) found that most parents and children see the worker as actively supporting contacts between them (p. 362).

Of equal importance is the worker's understanding of the various, sometimes complex reasons for visitation failures. Unsuccessful visits can be perceived as a signal that the family is in need of additional help, as a sign of bad parenting, or as evidence that parents have failed to earn the right to see their children (Hess, 1988). Given the nature of the barriers parents must sometimes overcome in maintaining contact with their children, it is unwise to use visitation, by itself, as an indicator of parental interest (White, 1981). On occasions, workers have canceled visits in an effort to punish birth parents or children for inappropriate behavior or for failing to meet expectations. However, it is recommended that visits never be used in this way (Blumenthal & Weinberg, 1984; Hess & Proch, 1988).

In an effort to maintain foster homes for children, workers sometimes attempt to pacify angry foster parents by making increasingly restrictive visitation decisions (Holman, 1980; Rowe, 1980; Cox & Cox, 1984; Steinhauer, 1991). Rowe, Cain, Hundleby, and Keane (1984) suggested the situation is even more complex, that the worker, parents, and foster family can collude in creating visitation breakdown:

> We were frequently dismayed and sometimes angered by the way in which social workers so often failed to provide the necessary support and encouragement to

maintain visiting. Sometimes they actually seemed to set up "no win" situations for natural parents, first discouraging visits "to let the children settle" and later saying that after such a long gap renewed visiting would be upsetting. But . . . ambivalence towards visiting seemed to be a prevalent attitude in natural parents and foster children as well as in social workers and foster parents. Everyone seems to draw back from the pain and potential conflict involved. (pp. 99–100)

(See also Hubbell, 1981.) Hess (1988) described "workers feeling helpless, emotionally drained, anxious, abused, angry, and uncomfortable while making decisions about or assisting with visits" (p. 321). The workers' need for ongoing training, supervision, and support is evident from these findings.

Visitation frequency may be determined by agency policy rather than the therapeutic needs of family members. Hubbell (1981) found that in one state parents were not allowed to visit more than once a month; all visits were arranged at the child welfare office, unless the child's return home was imminent, in which case parents were allowed to visit with their children in their own home (p. 105; see also Pelton, 1989). Agencies have also created more restricted visiting policies because some individuals have performed poorly, thereby punishing the many for the mistakes of the few. In many instances, evolution of the requirement that all visits must take place at the agency grows out of one or two particularly troublesome experiences with foster family-based or home-based visiting (Blumenthal & Weinberg, 1984).

While workers tend to see visitation scheduling as an administrative decision to be made without input from families, parents usually assume they will be asked to make the schedules (Fisher, Marsh, & Phillips, 1986). Packman (1986) noted that, for parents, "anger and confusion at the time of the child's removal were not easily forgotten and were frequently rekindled by the bewildering and seemingly arbitrary way in which subsequent plans were developed and fresh decisions taken" (p. 184).

A study of visitation practices in five major U.S. cities (National Black Child Development Institute, 1989) found considerable variation from community to community. While 75 percent of children in New York had been visited at least once, only 36 percent of those in Seattle and 37 percent in Miami had ever been visited (p. 78). A nationwide study of 103 voluntary placement agencies (Proch & Hess, 1987) also documented widespread variations. Approximately one-fifth of the agencies had no specific visitation policies; only 38 percent of those with policies specified a minimum frequency for visits.

The J Case

Timothy's foster care worker found herself in the midst of controversy when she first suggested that he should be allowed to visit in his home. Some of the workers in her agency felt that this jeopardized Timothy's safety, especially since Mr. J had not yet recognized

continued

his mistreatment as abusive. They worried that Mr. J could easily erupt during one of these visits, and Timothy would again be harmed. These colleagues talked about the "hidden" impact of marital violence on children and worried about Timothy's ability to effectively manage his own angry feelings. They concluded that Mr. J was such a "bad example" that Timothy ought not to be in contact with him unless he entered a treatment program for abusive husbands.

Other of her colleagues emphasized the fact that Timothy was no longer a young child and that his persistent insistence on seeing his family at home had to be respected. They argued that as long as Timothy could be trusted to call for help if he needed it, the visits should be tried on an experimental basis.

Still other workers felt that it was the bond between Timothy and his mother that had to be acknowledged. They pointed out his persistent need to be in touch with her. They wondered whether visits couldn't be arranged with just Mrs. J in some neutral place away from Timothy's home.

In the absence of any clear agency policy with regard to this decision, the worker and her supervisor had to make their own initial plans. They talked about their continued responsibility to keep Timothy safe and to change any plans that jeopardized his welfare. However, because the worker and Rod felt Timothy would contact them if he needed help, it was decided to begin home visits on an experimental basis. The benefits for Timothy in seeing his siblings and friends were also important considerations.

The worker and supervisor decided that Timothy's parents would have to agree with and actively support this plan and to be told about agency concerns for Timothy's well-being. Mr. J would have to agree that he could not physically discipline Timothy during visits. The supervisor told the worker that this plan should be a written one, and a copy be given to Timothy and the Js. The initial visits were to be scheduled for one hour. Although it took another month of discussion with the Js, both parents eventually supported this plan.

Questions for Discussion and Debate

1. As Timothy's foster care worker, how would you try to explain to him why he could not go on home visits?

2. How would you use visitation as a means to assess the attachment between parents and their children? How would you use visits to help strengthen these attachments?

3. If you were responsible for establishing an agency policy with regard to "missing" visits (i.e., parents arranging visits with their children and then not showing up), what type of policy would you establish?

4. Should a foster child remain with a foster parent who continues to strongly dislike the child's parents, even after he or she has had extensive counseling from the foster care worker?

8

Ongoing Intervention Work
Moving toward Permanency

Much of what is done in the work with families during the middle phases of care reflects themes that emerged early in the placement—themes of loss and grieving, connecting and caring. Parents and children must also deal with issues that emerge in their new living situation. For the children, this involves ongoing adjustment in the foster home. For the children's families, this involves ongoing adaptation with the children absent from the home. Of special importance for parents is work on their own child care abilities, so that insufficiencies can be remedied and the family prepared for the children's return. Finally, parents and children must continue their involvement in negotiating with the agency and in planning for their future together.

One new theme receives considerable attention during this phase of placement; this involves attention to more chronic personal and interpersonal problems. Children may need assistance in overcoming the effects of severe mistreatment, deprivation, and attachment instability. Some children also need help with serious emotional or behavioral problems or with medical or academic difficulties during this time. Parents, too, may need help with complex problems that interfere with their ability to parent adequately. These may include severe family stress, marital instability or spousal abuse, mental health problems, drug or alcohol addiction, medical difficulties, or difficulties in the criminal justice arena.

The foster family worker and the foster parents provide direct help to families in dealing with these concerns. In addition, the worker coordinates for the family services that are provided by outside agencies—public assistance and housing programs, mental health clinics and inpatient facilities, drug and alcohol treatment programs, family therapy programs, agencies specializing in work with batterers and battered women, probation and parole services, and so forth.

Changing Foster Family Dynamics: Helping Children's Integration into the Foster Family

Children in the middle phase of adjustment to foster family care are doing a great deal of learning about day-to-day functioning of the foster family and the roles, expectations, and sanctions operative in the foster home. They are also working to gradually develop a sense of belonging in that home. Settling into the foster home plunges children into a set of seemingly contradictory dilemmas: (1) to become a part of the family with whom they live but to remain an important member of their birth families and (2) to identify themselves as children who belong in their foster homes but to realize that they have a place that is different from that of other children who live there permanently. A goal of intervention with these children is to help them move from conflict, tension, and pain around these issues toward a sense of integration and a vision of themselves as unique and welcome members of the foster family (Allen, 1992).

Considering the extensive adjustment that foster children must make with this move, it is not surprising that a number of them engage in troublesome and obstructive behavior early in their placement (Hampson & Tavormina, 1980). Although some go through an initial "honeymoon" period (Stahl, 1990), others begin the struggle to adapt almost immediately. This is a testing period, during which the children probe parental limits and challenge parental control. If separation symbolizes rejection, then rejection is something these children have actually experienced and are fearful of encountering again. Testing can reflect their plea for reassurance that they are wanted in this home.

While misbehavior among foster children may have varied causes, for some it represents a misguided attempt to resolve another dilemma inherent in the foster child role:

> If foster parents actually are "good," the children are torn between rejecting the biological parent or parents and being "good," or rejecting the foster caregiver and being "bad." Because of their attachment to their biological parents or denial of negative characteristics of those parents and their fear or mistrust of other persons, foster children may choose to be "bad." (Kates, Johnson, Rader, & Strieder, 1991, p. 587)

When "getting close" symbolizes abandonment of birth parents to the child, resistant, acting out behavior appears to the children to allow them to live in the substitute home but to remain attached only to the birth family. Some of these children, on the point of making positive progress in foster care, will consistently "mess up," giving caretakers a "'stiff arm,' keeping them at a safe, familiar distance" (Delaney, 1998, p. 64). (See also Timberlake & Verdieck, 1987; Stahl, 1990; Rosenberg, 1991.) A comparative study of children in foster and residential care (Colton, 1988) found foster children more likely to be described as "cheeky, abusive or disobedient towards their caretakers" (p. 150). While more than half (55.2 percent) of foster parents described children in their care in this way, only 29.4

percent of residential workers did so. Only 48 percent of the foster children were well liked by their foster parents. Wald and his colleagues (1988) documented children's resistance to perceiving themselves as full-fledged members of their foster families. Even after two years in care, only half of the children saw their foster parents as "psychological caretakers" (p. 137). (See also Palmer, 1990.) Children of substance-abusing mothers may be particularly vulnerable in this regard (Kliman, Schaeffer, & Friedman, 1982).

The need to come to terms with their dual family status is recognized by foster children themselves. One child in care explained,

> You may feel as if your foster parents are trying to take the place of your real parents, but after you have been there for a while you will realize that they are not trying to take the place of your birth parents, they are really there to give you love and support. (Virginia Youth Advisory Council, 1994, p. 8)

In Colton's (1988) study, "foster children spoke enthusiastically . . . about the sense of security and belonging derived from being part of a family" (p. 145). (See also Fanshel, 1989.) The foster care worker and foster parents collaborate in their support of the children as they make this change (Kates, Johnson, Rader, & Strieder, 1991).

Molin (1988) found that most latency age children understand the concept of being a foster child. Occupying this status can bring with it a sense of shame in being different, a perception that one is not as good as "real" family members. "Many foster children feel more humiliated and ashamed about being in foster care than they do about having been abused by their parent" (Gries, 1990, p. 71; see also Norton, 1981; Rowe, Cain, Hundleby, & Keane, 1984; Steinhauer, 1991). Fearing criticism or ostracism, they may be reluctant to let peers know about the situation (Fisher, Marsh, & Phillips, 1986). These children can be helped to explore the negative beliefs about themselves underlying such attitudes, thus freeing them to turn more easily to foster family members and friends for needed support. Children's needs for privacy about their personal lives can also be validated. Some children benefit from development of a "cover story"—answers to intrusive questions that protect them from unwanted exposure.

Living with these ambivalent children poses special challenges for foster parents who must find ways to invite foster children into their family, even in instances in which the children voice consistent rejection of this invitation (Gries, 1990; Massinga & Perry, 1994).

> Many foster parents are under the illusion that the child will come into their home and immediately begin to form a "normal" parent/child-like relationship. They rarely expect that the foster child will call them "Mom" or "Dad," but foster parents often expect children to be somewhat affectionate, listen to the rules, and be a part of the family. They recognize that new foster children require some time to develop a relationship, but they often expect that a fairly substantial relationship will develop within a month or two after the child comes into foster care. They usually believe that this relationship will be similar to the relationship they have

with their own children, though possibly not as intense. Thus it is a rude awakening for them to discover that the foster child remains somewhat aloof and uninvolved in family activities and continues to act more like a boarder than a child within the family. Even when foster parents do everything they can to nurture a warm parent/child relationship, foster children may remain relatively isolated from the family. (Stahl, 1990, pp. 90–91)

(See also Colton, 1988; Mansfield, 1993.) In the face of the child's reluctance, there is a need for "gentle persistence to build a relationship with the child" (Fahlberg, 1991, p. 163; see also Schachter, 1989). "Claiming" behaviors are actions that emphasize the child's participation as a member of the family group. Foster parents claim children when they provide them with information about family history and rituals, seek similar information about life in the children's birth families, and try to integrate rituals that are familiar to the children into their own family activities. They welcome children into the family circle when they have them participate in important family holidays and events (Fahlberg, 1991, pp. 58–59; Blome, Pasztor, & Leighton, 1993).

In helping children adjust to their home, foster parents face another responsibility, that of guiding the family through the many changes incumbent in adding a new member to the household. To some extent, children's adjustment depends upon their "goodness of fit" with their foster parent (Doelling & Johnson, 1990). The more compatibility there is between the children's temperamental qualities and behavior and those parents prefer or can tolerate, the greater the likelihood that the children will settle well into the home. However, a great deal of adjustment is dependent on the types of mutual compromises and alterations that occur on the part of both the foster children and their foster families after placement. This is an unfolding process in which children and family members work together to eventually find some kind of comfortable level of adaptation to one another. Development here is much like that found in reconstituted families (Kates, Johnson, Rader, & Strieder, 1991). Family members must struggle through an early period of role confusion, feelings of dislocation, and unease about the loss of clear family boundaries (Cautley, 1980; Shulman, 1980; Euster, Ward, & Varner, 1982; Colton, 1988; Siu & Hogan, 1989; Stein, 1991).

The usual dilemmas inherent in adding a new member to the family are often exacerbated for foster families because the children come from birth families whose values, expectations, and experiences may be vastly different. "One of the most common complaints foster parents make is that a child's behavior is unlike anything they have ever encountered in children they have previously raised" (Stahl, 1990, p. 85). While parents are attempting to introduce the child to a family system in which trust, fairness, and respect are valued qualities, the children may be equally insistent on inducing their foster families to function in a system characterized by mistrust, a "win/lose" mentality, and beliefs in individual unworthiness (Kliman, Schaeffer, & Friedman, 1982; Fahlberg, 1991). This is evidenced in the conflicts between foster children and other children in the home. Foster children may be perceived as being a "bad influence" on these children (Colton,

1988); they may be disliked by other children because of their inability to play fairly, their need to always win (or fail), or their tendency to disrupt play activities (Stahl, 1990). Disparate values and beliefs will also influence patterns of social control in the family. Because ordinary disciplinary techniques used with children rely on children's feelings of positive regard for their parents and require them to have "reasonable feelings of self worth" (Fahlberg, 1991, p. 290), they may not work effectively with foster children. Fahlberg (1991) singles out distancing techniques (sending the child to time out in his or her room, for example) and withholding of affection as particularly inappropriate for some foster children.

During this process of adaptation and change, foster parents are especially vulnerable to feelings of inadequacy:

> There is nothing more destructive to the successful foster home placement than the foster parents' growing sense of futility and powerlessness. With the child who stubbornly reenacts, foster parents often feel increasing levels of impotence and uselessness. They do not experience any parental sense of satisfaction and worth, any sense that their involvement with the child is accomplishing anything. (Delaney, 1998, p. 47)

When parents are trying to deal with an unresponsive or highly ambivalent child, the worker might conclude that the source of the problem lies within the foster family. However, foster parents may be coping as well as they can in a difficult situation; they should not be blamed by the worker or labeled as "failures." Instead, they need understanding and guidance in working through these issues (Reeves, 1980; Shulman, 1980; Levine, 1988; Mansfield, 1993; Delaney, 1998).

The early period of placement poses especially high risks. In her meticulous study of the changes that occur in new foster families, Cautley (1980) discovered that, over time, early concerns about potential family disruption gradually give way to an emphasis on the children's progress and, finally, by eighteen months to a level of acceptance of their own role, with all of its ups and downs (p. 244; see also Berridge & Cleaver, 1987). However, the foster child's passage into adolescence may catapult the family into a new period of vulnerability (Levine, 1988).

Foster parents may be especially in need of help from the worker in sorting out their reactions, determining which stem from difficulties with the child and which result from their own unrealistic expectations and needs. The worker helps by visiting the foster home regularly to discuss the child's adjustment and the family's reaction to the child. Acting as adviser/teacher, counselor, and source of psychological support, the worker allays anxiety and provides reassurance when it is needed. The worker is also a significant resource for information and guidance when the foster parents must seek assistance with medical, educational, or emotional difficulties that arise in the course of living with and helping a particular child. Cautley (1980) noted that information must be given to parents when and as they need it, since they cannot fully understand the meaning of this adaptation process and its attendant difficulties until they reach and work through each particular stage. Training materials have been developed to assist parents and workers with this task (Blome, Pasztor, & Leighton, 1993).

A Canadian study (Shulman, 1980) presented mixed findings with regard to the availability of such support from workers. Sixty percent of the foster parents in the study said the worker had often discussed the child with them, and 83 percent of this group felt that the worker had been helpful. However, only 30 percent believed that such discussion contributed to their developing a more positive relationship with the child.

A final task for foster parents in helping the children become members of their families is to come eventually to accept these children "as they are," with all of their positive qualities and strengths, with all of their special difficulties and needs. The goal here is not only to recognize the children's characteristics but also to celebrate them, to value the children's uniqueness and individuality, and to realize how the children's special qualities are valuable as well as challenging for the family.

This may be particularly difficult in instances in which foster children are deeply troubled or unattached. "The child who cannot resolve separation trauma and adjust to the foster household is especially susceptible to being labeled 'bad' or 'disturbed'" (Kates, Johnson, Rader, & Strieder, 1991, p. 589). Foster parents tend eventually to turn away from such children in frustration and rage. "Even experienced foster parents may be appalled, somewhat disoriented, and mortified by the depth of their negative reactions to the child" (Delaney, 1998, p. 36). The foster care worker plays an especially important role with such parents, helping them to express their feelings appropriately, understand the origins of their powerful reactions, and eventually come to terms with the reality of the children's impact on their lives. Cautley (1980) commented:

> it became clear that some sort of return was needed to enable foster parents to continue. The occurrence of the year's anniversary appeared to prompt these new families to review the progress made and consider their investment of time and energy. The return could be an expression of affection from the child; or evidence that the child was improving. But if neither of these occurred, the social worker needed to provide the support, reassurance, and encouragement to the foster parents if they were to be expected to continue. (p. 244)

It is reassuring to find that, in the face of these many problems and dilemmas, most foster parents persevere. Research conducted by James Bell Associates (1993) noted that more than three-quarters of foster parents plan to continue this work in this future (p. 76). In addition, parents who have decided to stop fostering are more likely to cite agency-related problems or personal factors than they are to list difficulties with the child as primary reasons for quitting (p. 77).

Foster children attest to the value of foster parents who are welcoming, who work to integrate them into the family, and who value them for who they are (Rowe, Cain, Hundleby, & Keane, 1984; Steinhauer, 1991; Virginia Youth Advisory Council, 1994). Responding to a question about what the fostering experience was like, "C," a former foster child in the Casey Family Program, was one of many respondents to comment on this:

> Knowing that somebody was there when I was sick—someone who loved me for who I was. I don't know how to describe it—it's just a warm feeling. Tried to make it look like any other ordinary family. They treated me like one of their own children. (Fanshel, Finch, & Grundy, 1990, p. 182)

Data from a longitudinal study of children in foster family care (Fanshel, Finch, & Grundy, 1989, 1990) highlight the importance for children's life course development of their successful adjustment to the foster home. Some children begin well and have few difficulties during their stay in care: "a child who was friendly and well adjusted at entry adapted well to foster care and left the Casey program in good shape and prospered as an adult" (1989, p. 470; see also Rowe, Cain, Hundleby, & Keane, 1984; McDonald, Allen, Westerfelt, & Piliavin, 1993). However, for those children whose adaptation was initially poor, finding a means to enhance adjustment while in care was important:

> [W]hen a successful intervention occurred so that a child's oppositional behavior was overcome and the child led to a good adjustment, the effects of this good adjustment to foster care continued to a better condition at exit and greater financial security and conventional success in living as an independent adult free of antisocial behavioral tendencies. (pp. 470–471)

The ability to become an integrated member of the foster family is linked to better overall functioning of the foster family (Walsh & Walsh, 1990) and reduces "bouncing," the transferring of children from foster home to foster home (Kliman, Schaeffer, & Friedman, 1982; Doelling & Johnson, 1990; Walsh & Walsh, 1990).

Available data indicate that most children eventually come to some sense of resolution about their dual family status, although they continue to experience some discomfort and discontinuity. Studying children in the New York foster care system, Fanshel (1982) reported that social workers rated approximately half as at peace with their current family arrangements. Although a substantial number had some degree of anxiety about their relative standing with their birth and foster families, few were highly disturbed about this issue. Seven percent of the six- to nine-year-olds and 10 percent of those ten to thirteen were very concerned (p. 258). Assessing the reactions of 121 children in long-term foster care, Thorpe (1980) discovered that three out of four felt comfortable in their foster family home and wanted to remain there. However, "despite the extent of expected permanence, concern with their security of tenure in the foster home nevertheless coloured the interview responses of several of the children" (p. 91). One of these children, Lynn (14 years old), explained:

> I don't think you should have to be extra specially obedient but you don't like saying things to foster parents that you might later regret. I argue because I like to stick up for what I believe in, but I think sometimes foster children are frightened to do this. They are afraid of being sent back. (p. 91)

(See also Gardner, 1996.)

Kliman and his colleagues (1982) documented the utility of short-term interventions with children early in the placement to facilitate the adaptation process. (See also Bondy, Davis, Hagen, Spiritos, & Winnick, 1990.) Their program also included interventions for foster and birth parents, providing information about the adjustment process, opportunities for emotional support, and assistance in problem solving when issues and problems arose.

The J Case

Timothy continued for many months to maintain his distance from Rod and rarely let down his guard. Over these months, Rod came to realize that his own positive experiences with close relationships made him deeply frustrated with the little Timothy was able to give to him. He found it difficult to grasp how a child could turn down love and caring when it was offered to him. He wondered sometimes if he should not be a foster parent and found himself complaining to his friends about this very difficult role.

Gradually Rod came to understand Timothy's perspective on their relationship and to realize that Timothy deeply feared that closeness to Rod meant disloyalty to his family. He learned from the worker that Timothy's mother repeatedly begged him not to "forget" her and that Timothy interpreted this as a request to remain attached only to her. He tried to remind himself that Timothy felt he should be at home to protect his mother and feared that becoming settled and happy in the foster home would somehow make him responsible for his mother's lack of safety and, perhaps, even for her death. However, it was difficult to remember these things in the face of yet another rejection or hostile attack from Timothy.

Rod found he periodically made most progress with Timothy when he reminded the boy that he was not trying to take the place of his parents and that he was interested in helping Timothy do whatever he felt he wanted to do with his family, so long as it was safe. When Timothy had been in his home for nine months, Rod's mother commented on how settled Timothy was, how happy he was looking. This made Rod realize how much progress they had made during this time. Rod recognized that he had begun to give up his naive intentions to "save" Timothy, and he realized that Timothy no longer saw him as an "enemy." They were beginning to build a relationship of some trust, and Timothy even let Rod act in a nurturing way sometimes.

Rod now began to think about how he could help Timothy with his future and to accept the fact that Timothy had never given up on his intention to return home. He wondered how he could help this boy take care of himself and achieve his own life goals.

Changing Birth Family Dynamics: Working to Achieve Effective Parenting

The primary objective of parent intervention during placement is to work to improve caretaking behavior so that children can receive minimally sufficient care in the home, they are no longer endangered, and the family has improved resources to address ongoing and future problems that might arise. When such improvement does not occur within a reasonable period of time, the worker documents the types of "reasonable efforts" that have been undertaken and helps the parents consider other, more permanent arrangements than long-term foster family care (Maluccio, 1985; Stein & Comstock, 1987; Hess & Folaron, 1991).

Although difficulties with childrearing skills are often linked to—and affected by—a range of other life problems, in this section we will focus on the worker's efforts to help remediate problems in the parenting arena. In the face of other serious personal crises, child welfare workers (and parents) sometimes lose sight of the need to redress inadequacies in childrearing that led to placement. However, it is understood that improving the quality of parenting may be dependent on the parents' obtaining help for drug or alcohol abuse, finding a steady income and safe place to live, obtaining assistance with complex mental health problems, or resolving issues of spousal violence (CWLA, 1991a; Lie & McMurtry, 1991; Steinhauer, 1991). The worker's efforts to help parents address these other major stresses are discussed in the next section of this chapter.

In broad outline, intervention approaches to improve parenting when children are in care are similar to those generally used with parents whose children remain in the home. However, the childrearing problems found in the former group are usually more serious, more complex, and more intractable than those found among maltreating parents whose children are not in care. Service delivery is further complicated by the need to help parents improve child care skills in the absence of the child. Parents have to learn about and practice skills "as if" the child were present, and special arrangements have to be made to integrate this learning with ongoing behavior. In addition, there is a greater sense of failure among these families, since they have been judged incapable of raising their children to the extent that the children must be removed. This experience, in turn, can make them feel more vulnerable and more resistant to working on the problems that led to separation (Stein & Comstock, 1987; Steinhauer, 1991; Zamosky, Sparks, Hatt, & Sharman, 1993). These factors suggest a need for much longer-term intervention than is required by families whose children remain at home (Maluccio, Warsh, & Pine, 1993; Lewis, 1994).

Parenting problems in many families reflect difficulties in two general areas of caretaking—one having to do with discipline and control, and the other involving structure and predictability (Thoburn, 1980; Hardin, 1983; Maluccio, Fein, & Olmsted, 1986). Other basic parenting skills, such as the ability to play, may also be lacking. These insufficiencies are intensified when the general family context is one of repeated disruptions, disorganization, and intense conflict (Weiner & Weiner, 1990; Steinhauer, 1991). In his research on families using care in England, Packman (1986) commented, "The fluidity of family structures and the speed with which they fragment and re-form is striking" (p. 204; see also Weiner & Weiner, 1990). Wald, Carlsmith, and Leiderman (1988) described substantial family conflict in sixteen of the nineteen families they studied, and they believed such conflict to be more damaging to the child than specific incidents of mistreatment (p. 196). Packman's (1986) study uncovered 47 percent of the families in which "there was thought to be acute stress and danger of actual breakdown (fragile), or where chronic marital discord was perceived (poor)" (p. 35). Excessive disruption and conflict contribute, in turn, to the family's social isolation, which is more prevalent among those with children in care than among families whose children remain in the home (Thoburn, 1980; Wald, Carlsmith, & Leiderman, 1988).

Steinhauer (1991) offered a tool for evaluating parenting capacity that describes three distinct levels:

> Group A. The child's development is not, and never has been, seriously at risk. . . .
>
> Group B. The child's current adjustment shows serious problems, although, until recently, the parenting and development seemed adequate. With prompt and adequate intervention, the prognosis for these parents once again meeting their child's needs so that development can again proceed is reasonable. . . .
>
> Group C. The child's development and adjustment have chronically been significantly impaired. The parents have long been unable to meet their children's developmental needs, and there is little to suggest this will change significantly, even given realistically available intervention. (pp. 101–102)

Group C parents may be struggling with severe psychiatric illness that substantially compromises their child care capabilities. Alternative caretakers for the children who do not have serious mental health problems may not be available. The family's history frequently gives evidence of numerous unsuccessful attempts to help the parents change, failure of the parents to assume responsibility for such change, and severe social isolation (pp. 102–103). Prognosis for Group C parents is guarded.

In addition to deficiencies in concrete parenting skills, many mothers and fathers who have children in care give evidence of disordered attachment relationships with their children. These parents have been described as emotionally rejecting or unavailable, extremely hostile toward their children, ambivalent about caring for them, or alienated from them (Fanshel, 1982; Maluccio, Fein, & Olmsted, 1986; Hess & Proch, 1988; Wald, Carlsmith, & Leiderman, 1988; Weiner & Weiner, 1990; Steinhauer, 1991), or not "fully prepared, ready, or interested in the parenting role" (Hess & Folaron, 1991). Frequently there is a history of severe deprivation, repeated separations, and impaired attachment in the parent's own early years. One-quarter of the parents in Packman's (1986) study thought their early childhood was "sad or dreadful" (p. 118). The problems these parents bring to treatment pose a substantial challenge for intervention agents.

To help families remediate multifaceted difficulties requires the use of multidimensional services. "Since these are usually parents who have weak or defective ego structures and who are very needy themselves, they can best be helped through a total therapeutic approach involving ego-building procedures and aid with immediate practical problems as well as with their emotional difficulties" (Maluccio, 1981, p. 22; see also National Black Child Developmental Institute, 1989). In her manual for judges outlining reasonable efforts that might be needed to help these families, Debra Ratterman (1987) listed more than a dozen specific parenting services, ranging from day care and parent aides to various kinds of individual, group, and family interventions (pp. 5–6).

Services designed to improve parenting capability must be provided in a timely fashion, as soon as possible after the child is placed in care. This is particularly important for the foster care worker to monitor, since the worker, thinking that the child is now safe, may not challenge the parents to get further help, and the parents, who are being asked to participate in (and perhaps fail at) yet another treatment intervention, may resist taking concrete steps in this regard. Steinhauer (1991) pointed out that it is important to work intensively with parents after placement, since removal of the child "risks even further disruption of an already disturbed family equilibrium" (p. 141; see also Lewis, 1994).

Effective help to improve parenting capacity must provide the parents opportunities to practice particular skills with their children (Wald, Carlsmith, & Leiderman, 1988; Boutilier & Rehm, 1993) and to develop a more effective and supportive relationship with them (Folaron, 1993). Hess and Proch (1988) described effective use of visitation time for this purpose. Interventions to improve parenting must also take into account the various family members who play an ongoing role in the children's lives. Too often both the child welfare agency and parent education programs focus exclusively on mothers, while fathers, aunts, or grandmothers, who may have already assumed or may be capable of assuming collaborative or coparenting roles, are ignored. These coparents may also be in need of assistance to enhance their own caretaking skills (Fisher, Marsh, & Phillips, 1986; Packman, 1986; Walsh & Walsh, 1990; Kahkonen, 1997).

Strengthening the parenting capabilities of collaborative or alternative caretakers is especially critical in cases where these caretakers play a well-established role in family life. A neglecting mother may, for example, have a long-term relationship with a supportive male who carries out many child care activities in the family. However, because he has no legally recognized relationship to the children, the child welfare agency may have ignored his involvement and dealt exclusively with the children's mother. Attention to parenting deficits is even more imperative in instances where coparents have actually mistreated the children. In cases where husbands have abused both their wives and their children, it is not uncommon for the agency to consider the women their sole clients. It has been common practice to insist that these mothers either leave their abusers, taking the children with them, or eject the abusers from the home. Mothers are charged with this responsibility even in situations where it is unfeasible or dangerous for them to comply. Meanwhile, the abusive father has not been challenged by the agency to change his abusive behavior. Effective work toward reunification with such families is dependent on the agency's efforts to help both caretakers, not just the mother, develop adequate child care skills (Hess, Folaron, & Jefferson, 1992).

Like families served by home-based programs, these families may benefit from individual, family, or group services. In recent years, most focused efforts to enhance parenting capacity have used a group format. "Group work can be an excellent means of countering the problems of isolation, of lack of familial and community supports, and of lack of information about the foster care system and their legal rights" (Carbino, 1983, pp. 16–17. See also Murphy, 1981; Hess & Williams, 1982; Blumenthal & Weinberg, 1984; Maluccio, Fein, & Olmsted, 1986; Davis, 1989; Levin, 1992; Boutilier & Rehm, 1993.).

Schatz and Bane (1991) described one model for group intervention with parents that includes a strong family advocacy component. This approach incorporates "training in personal and family decision-making," assertiveness training, and help with resource development as essential services (p. 672). Another model, using a self-help format, is described by Tunnard (1989), who noted "The common function of the groups is the moral support in times of stress that members give each other" (p. 223).

The National Black Child Development Institute's (1989) study of child welfare services for African American children in five major cities found that 39 percent had parent education and four percent had parent support group counseling included in their case plans (p. 60). More recent research (Davis, English, & Landsverk, 1995) found 83 percent of parents were to be offered such services (p. 50). Based on their research, Wald, Carlsmith, and Leiderman (1988) concluded that many families could also benefit from family therapy, particularly when parent-child conflict was evident. (See also Maluccio, 1985.) However, the National Black Child Development Institute's study found family services included in only 16 percent of the case plans (p. 60).

Foster parents play a pivotal role in helping families move toward successful reunification (Fein & Staff, 1991). They directly assist birth parents by working with them as a team to resolve difficulties with childrearing, by modeling appropriate caretaking behaviors, and by educating them about childrearing issues (Maluccio, Fein, & Olmstead, 1986; Lowe, 1991; Michaud, 1992; Sellick, 1992). A foster parent's comments on the value of this work with birth families:

> I felt very good about this (getting the birth mother to the child's parent-teacher conference) because I had accomplished the goal I wanted to accomplish, and that's to save this family. The day that child came into my home I said, "The kid is going to go home. I know that's going to be the court order. My responsibility is to make sure that he does not return into care." What I know now will happen. She will be able to call me when she needs help when he goes home. And he will have a friend to talk to when he doesn't know what else to do. That is a success story to me, and it works. (Hess & Hicks, 1979, pp. 161, 170)

Hess and Proch (1988) described characteristics of foster parents that enhance their capacity to do this work: valuation of the child's relationship with birth parents, the ability to limit their own relationship with the child, flexibility, the capacity to handle stress, and willingness to intervene as needed and to seek help when needed (pp. 50–52).

Despite understandable tendencies to be protective of children and to feel negative about parents, many of whom have harmed their children, evidence indicates that most foster care workers are fond of the parents with whom they work and that they do believe children can eventually return home (Hubbell,

1981). The worker's efforts may be directed at helping parents obtain services from other agencies or may include provision of services directly to the family. In helping remediate child care problems, the worker serves as an advocate, service coordinator, and resource developer (Fein & Staff, 1993). This type of intervention "requires skill in making complex professional judgments, including assessing risk; balancing conflicting needs, requests, and expectations; dealing with constantly changing plans; and managing others' and one's own intense emotional reactions" (Hess, Mintun, Moelhman, & Pitts, 1992, p. 85; see also Werrbach, 1993). High turnover, lack of adequate experience or preparation for these tasks, and personal problems handling emotionally turbulent and highly unpredictable relationships may interfere with or prevent the worker from effectively helping parents with their problems (Thoburn, 1980; Van Gelder & Brandt, 1988; Hess & Folaron, 1991; Steinhauer, 1991; Massinga & Perry, 1994). Studying families for whom reunification efforts had failed, Hess, Folaron, and Jefferson (1992) discovered that 73 percent had five or more workers during the course of their child's stay in care (p. 307).

Many parents recognize that they must change their behavior or circumstances in order to have their children returned and that they may require some help in accomplishing this (Packman, 1986). Several studies indicate that they appreciate the contributions made by foster care workers to this end. Most parents in Hubbell's (1981) survey "spoke positively of their caseworker" (p. 112). Only one of the 20 parents Thoburn (1980) interviewed claimed to be dissatisfied with the social worker (p. 112). In their longitudinal study of the reactions of mothers to the placement process, Jenkins and Norman (1975) found that, as a group they rated social worker interest, understanding, and communicative efforts as at least somewhat helpful (p. 64). "Several parents said that agency sessions in which parents met with workers and were helped to understand their problems, or in which workers counsel parents, were extremely useful" (p. 78). Surveying families served by eighteen child-welfare agencies in five states, Yoshikami (1984) also found them generally appreciative of the help they received. Parents considered practical services that got results and were provided by "an understanding service provider" as especially meaningful (p. 89).

Studies from other countries (Packman, 1986; Weiner & Weiner, 1990), however, find parents are frequently frustrated and concerned that workers seem unable to provide ways to help them resolve their problems. Fisher, Marsh, and Phillips (1986) found "just a few families who were outstandingly positive about their field social worker" (p. 111). What distinguished these workers from less effective helpers was their ability to take the parents' concerns and needs as seriously as those of the children. These cases were also

> notable for the convergence of social worker and family understanding of the family's situation: the social worker could describe the family's views in similar ways to the family's own descriptions, and the families were better able to describe the role of the social worker, commenting on his or her openness and reliability of approach. (pp. 111–112)

The J Case

Working on parenting issues continued to be challenging with this family, since Mr. J continued to deny that he had been abusive of Timothy, and Mrs. J continued to be too frightened to disagree with him or to reveal her own abuse. Initially the couple was referred for parent education classes; however, this was ineffective, since Mr. J sabotaged the teachers and incited other parents to "stand by" their disciplinary approaches. The worker then proposed a revision of the family service plan, outlining a plan that Mr. J attend a group for batterers and Mrs. J a group for battered women. Mr. J became enraged over this proposal, insisting that he was never a "batterer" and that no one was going to make him go to any such program. After much negotiation with the Js, the worker found they would agree to go to a local agency serving maltreating families. Mr. J would go into a "men's" group, and Mrs. J into a "mothers'" group. Since many of the men in his group were also batterers, some of the issues that needed to be addressed could be discussed there. The family service plan was revised so that Mr. and Mrs. J had to successfully complete these groups in order to request that Timothy be returned.

Eventually, therapists for these groups were able to help the parents define a set of "rules" that Timothy would have to agree to live by if he were to return home, but it remained unclear whether Mr. J actually wanted the boy to return. The rules continued to reflect Mr. J's insistence on maintaining control of the family. However, they provided a starting point for discussions between Timothy and his parents to explore what it would be like if he were allowed to return.

The foster care worker also struggled to establish a clear expectation that Mr. J could not physically discipline Timothy. At times he appeared to remember that the agency could seek prosecution of him for injuring the boy; at other times such a threat only incited him to further claims that he could do "whatever was necessary" as a parent. This issue was also addressed in group, and the men there did help Mr. J acknowledge that he might be a "little too hard" on the boy sometimes. However, his progress in this regard was minimal.

Mrs. J's group worker attempted to draw her out about her parenting goals and issues. Although Mrs. J began to admit that her husband hurt her sometimes, she was still unwilling to see this as unacceptable; the worker discovered that Mrs. J was convinced that her husband would react violently if his parenting prerogative were interfered with. Mrs. J saw herself as a cook and cleaner in the home, but not as a person of authority there.

The worker was very worried about the very limited progress this couple was making. She began to wonder about potential mistreatment of other children in the family but could find no clear evidence to pursue an investigation concerning their welfare.

Working on Long-Standing Issues and Special Problems

While many of the problems faced by children in foster family care are "normal," growing out of typical developmental needs and exacerbated by the challenges of adjusting to a new family situation, some children in care face particular difficulties. Problems may arise in the social-psychological, medical, or academic arenas. Birth parents may also struggle with the challenges that underlay insufficient parenting. Again it is not uncommon to find that emotional, economic, medical, and behavioral problems intertwine in the lives of individual family members. The impact of these problems on provision of services is explored next.

Foster Children's Special Needs

Severe Emotional Problems. As discussed in Chapter 5, severe emotional problems in foster children can have many origins. For some children, problems develop while living in relatively supportive and caring families; for others, it is the problematic nature of their family life that creates maladaptive patterns. As a result of chaotic family experiences, some children become "severely attachment disordered," reacting to life circumstances by cutting themselves off from reliance on others for nurturing, protection, or support. These are children who "cannot live in anyone else's family and who cannot live on their own" (Wells, 1991, p. 8). A foster parent writes:

> Most of the time we knew them, the children were frightened and desperate. They hated their lives, hated themselves, and hated those who created them. They were stuck between the intense desire to have a close and loving relationship with somebody and the inability to trust, to bond, or to really feel. . . . We witnessed them survive the emotional demands placed on them by manipulating, by seducing, by pretending, but above all, by not feeling. They had survived this way since they were aware of wanting to survive. (Mansfield, 1993, pp. x–xi)

Delaney (1998) reported that problems for these children fall into seven broad categories: "sadism/violence; disordered eating; counterfeit emotionality; compulsive lying and kleptomania; sexual obsessions; passive/aggression; and defective conscience" (p. 69). (See also James, 1989; Fahlberg, 1991; Steinhauer, 1991; Delaney & Kunstal, 1993.) Others described these children as "traumatized." In the face of chronic abuse from which they are unable to escape, their normal defenses become "overwhelmed and disorganized" (Herman, 1992, p. 34); they become hypervigilant and hyperaroused, stuck in "frozen watchfulness." These children resort to extreme measures in an attempt to control their anxiety, warding off feelings of terror and panic by blocking, distorting, or dissociating themselves from certain thoughts, feelings, and memories (James, 1989). They may play and replay segments of the trauma without recognition, relief, or resolution (Terr, 1990). A few will develop multiple personalities. Self-awareness, self-evaluation, and the ability to grow and change may be severely compromised for these youngsters.

The child welfare literature states that increasing numbers of foster children are affected by emotional disorders (Vasaly, 1978; Kamerman & Kahn, 1990; Klee, Soman, & Halfon, 1992; Davis & Ellis-MacLeod, 1994; Courtney, 1995; Altshuler & Gleeson, 1999). However, it is difficult to obtain precise estimates of changes in the size of this group over time. Appendix 8.1 summarizes recent research in this area. One of the few efforts to involve a carefully developed control group and standardized measures (Hulsey, 1989) concluded that foster children exhibit more serious problems. Data from California foster parents (Barth, Courtney, Berrick, & Albert, 1994) indicated that "at almost every age, children in foster family care had total scores that were more than 1 standard deviation above the mean compared to a national sample of children" (p. 246). Using data gleaned from records as well as from direct assessment of 1,165 children in care, Davis, English, and Landsverk (1995) also described wide-ranging difficulties. Case files indicated 12 percent were developmentally delayed and 10 percent had severe behavior problems (p. 43). Further assessment of a subsample of the children indicated that a full 50 percent "scored in the problematic range on the Vineland Adaptive Functioning Scale" (p. 44), while, among younger children, Denver Developmental screening indicated 70 percent were in difficulty. While McIntyre and Keesler (1986) concluded that "children in foster care are almost nine times more likely than home-reared children to manifest psychopathology" (p. 30), other studies (Fox & Arcuri, 1980; Kliman, Schaeffer, & Friedman, 1982; Kavaler & Swire, 1983) found no evidence that the level of psychopathology is greater than that of nonplaced children from similar socioeconomic backgrounds.

Evidence suggests that foster parents who are kin tend to see the children in their care as easier to handle than non-kin parents do (Gebel, 1996; Brooks, 1999). Children in kinship homes do not show evidence of additional behavior or emotional problems, when compared to those in nonrelative homes (Inglehart, 1994; Benedict, Zuravin, & Stallings, 1996).

Wide variations in measures, sample composition and use of control groups make comparisons among the studies in Appendix 8.1 risky. Further complicating such research is the need to differentiate between more long-standing psychological impairment and transitory adjustment problems caused by the move into care and the need to adapt to a new living environment (Zimmerman, 1988; Kates, Johnson, Rader, & Strieder, 1991). Charles and Matheson (1991) also reminded us that difficulties may not be evident at the time of placement but may emerge during the course of care; longitudinal studies of this issue, similar to those undertaken by Fanshel and his colleagues (1990), Wald, Carlsmith, and Leiderman (1988), and by Benedict, Zuravin, and Stallings (1996) will, therefore, be needed.

Therapeutic intervention has been recommended for children in care as a preventive measure (Kliman, Schaeffer, & Friedman, 1982; Davis, 1989; Schneiderman, Connors, Fribourg, Gries, & Gonzales, 1989). However, it is especially necessary for those who have been affected by abuse or neglect (Gries, 1990), for children exhibiting posttraumatic stress reactions (Terr, 1990), for those who have mental health problems related to exposure to drug or alcohol abuse (Flynn, 1990; CWLA, 1992a), for those with severe attachment disorders (Steinhauer, 1991; Delaney, 1998), and for otherwise severely behaviorally or emotionally disordered youngsters (Simms, Freundlich, Battistelli, & Kaufman, 1999). Bondy, Davis, Hagen, Spiritos, and Winnick (1990) estimated that 41 percent of the children coming into care in New York City were in need of some type of "developmental and supportive services" (p. 32). Children in federally funded foster care settings are entitled to such services under the Early and Periodic Screening, Diagnosis and Treatment (EPSDT) program (National Black Child Development Institute, 1989). "Compliance with these requirements, however has generally been poor" (Simms, Freundlich, Battistelli, & Kaufman, 1999, p. 170), and proposed changes in the medicaid program makes the future of this program uncertain.

There is some indication that provision of therapeutic services to children in need of such intervention helps deter development of chronic problems in the foster home, helps minimize movement of the child from one foster home to another, and has positive impact on the child's overall adjustment after leaving care (Kliman, Schaeffer, & Friedman, 1982; Fanshel, Finch, & Grundy, 1990; Weiner & Weiner, 1990; Landsverk, 1996). Individual treatment, family therapy, or support group services may be of help to the child in care; these services are most typically provided by outside agencies with whom the child welfare agency contracts to offer treatment.

Evidence suggests the need for therapeutic services far outdistances the response. "Numerous commentators have noted that a shortage of community-based services and coordination across agencies has left this population significantly underserved" (Davis & Ellis-MacLeod, 1994, p. 137). "Both current and former foster parents cited counseling as their greatest service need" (James Bell Associates, 1993, p. 88). Evaluating children placed in foster homes under the auspices of private child placement agencies in California, Fitzharris (1985) found that 15 percent were in individual treatment, 12 percent received group counseling, and less than 10 percent experienced family-based interventions (p. 121). Studying the case records of African American children in care in five major cities across the United States, the National Black Child Development Institute (1989) reported that 15 percent obtained individual interventions from a child welfare agency, 12 percent obtained such services from other sources, and 9 percent were in family therapy (p. 63). A Washington state study (cited in Simms, Freundlich, Battistelli, & Kaufman, 1999), comparing foster children with others whose families received AFDC, found they had "significantly greater utilization of mental health care services (25% vs. 7%)" (p. 172).

An intensive examination of 13 children in care (Wald, Carlsmith, & Leiderman, 1988) revealed "a very sad picture. . . . Unless the child exhibits significant behavioral problems, most agencies do not evaluate the child's academic or social development" (p. 192). Studying the records of a random sample of 194 children in care in Jackson County, Missouri, Mushlin, Levitt, and Anderson (1986) disclosed that 20 percent of the children had "physical, emotional or intellectual problems" for which they received no services (p. 146). Barth, Courtney, Berrick, and Albert (1994) found "little or no relationship . . . between the child's disturbance and the number of social work services provided by the agency" (p. 247). Dugger (1992) stated that more than one-third of the children transferred from foster care to an inpatient mental health facility were not receiving outpatient services at the time of the move.

Foster care workers appear to have insufficient knowledge about the causes of children's behavior problems and the potential impact of therapeutic interventions on them (Molin, 1988; Wald, Carlsmith, & Leiderman, 1988; Fanshel, Finch, & Grundy, 1989; Simms, Freundlich, Battistelli, & Kaufman, 1999). This may be due to the complex nature of the task. Does a child's difficulty arise because the foster family is responding poorly, or does it arise out of the child's previous experiences? Which types of problems might dissipate after the child is settled in the foster home, and which will not? What types of issues are amenable to treatment, and what kinds of interventions will be most helpful for various types of problems? Answering these questions requires a fairly sophisticated knowledge of child development and child psychopathology, family dynamics, and family dysfunction—a level of ability a foster care worker may not have attained. Because it is this worker who must recognize that a problem exists and must mobilize resources to respond to it, the lack of such capability will prevent some children from receiving needed help.

Foster and birth families play pivotal roles in supporting the need for therapeutic interventions for children in care. However, they, like the worker, may lack the skill or preparation to recognize the nature or origins of problems encountered in their day-to-day interactions with their foster children. Without foster parent support, it may be difficult to arrange for therapeutic sessions, to insure that the child attends them regularly, or to obtain sufficient involvement in the therapeutic program from the foster family (Molin, 1988; National Abandoned Infants Resource Center, 1996). Helping the child obtain these services may also place additional financial and other burdens on the foster family (James Bell Associates, 1993). Birth parents may also resist recognizing the need for treatment out of personal concerns about disclosing sensitive family issues and fear that the information obtained may prevent or delay the child's return home.

Developmental and Academic Difficulties.   In addition to (and sometimes because of) emotional disabilities, substantial numbers of foster children have special developmental and academic needs (Rowe, Cain, Hundleby, & Keane, 1984; Richardson, West, Day, & Stuart, 1989; Goerge, Voorhis, Grant, Casey, & Robinson, 1992; McDonald, Allen, Westerfelt, & Piliavin, 1993; Dubowitz & Sawyer, 1994; Festinger, 1994; Sawyer & Dubowitz, 1994). Research conducted in Ohio estimated that "20% of all children in out-of-home care are mentally retarded or developmentally disabled" (Richardson, West, Day, & Stuart, 1989, p. 607), and Minnesota data suggested that 40 percent of all children receiving child welfare services were delayed. Wald, Carlsmith, and Leiderman (1988) found "substantial social and academic deficits" among abused children in care (p. 55). Fanshel, Finch, and Grundy's study of children in regular and specialized foster homes (1990) revealed that one in four had school problems at the time of placement, one in three had difficulties functioning in a normal school setting, and three in ten had not achieved the expected grade level for their age. Fifty-two percent of these children "could not apply themselves, being restless and being unable to pay attention in class" (p. 214). One in three children in Barth, Courtney, Berrick, and Albert's (1994) survey "had either repeated a grade or were enrolled in special education classes" (p. 245). In Davis, English, and Landsverk's (1995) examination of child welfare records, 10 percent of the children in care were described as having school problems, and 6 percent were considered learning disabled. The authors consider these figures "an underestimate of the true prevalence" (p. 44). Studies in England (Packman, 1986; Colton, 1988) replicate these findings. However, Kliman, Schaeffer, and Friedman's (1982) research on children entering care for the first time concluded that overall academic performance of the children was "average" (p. 122). (See also Altshuler & Gleeson, 1999.)

In part, these academic difficulties stem from problems in social relations, so that interactions with peers and teachers are maladaptive or strained. In part, these result from the children's preoccupation with personal issues, so that their capacity to attend to learning tasks and to maintain that attention are compromised. Language delays, inability to engage in abstract thinking, impulsivity, low frustration tolerance, and difficulties in attentiveness are typical (Fahlberg, 1991; Steinhauer, 1991; Davis & Ellis-MacLeod, 1994). Children with Fetal Alcohol Syndrome may also have "extreme difficulty with abstractions like time and space, cause and effect, and generalizing from one situation to another" (Streissguth, Aase, Clarren, Randels, LaDue, & Smith, 1991, p. 1966).

The effectiveness of foster care agencies in helping children and foster parents address these academic problems is unknown.

Medical Needs.   Foster children may also have unmet medical and dental needs.

> Children entering care have unusually poor health compared with their peers from similar social and ethnic backgrounds who live at home. . . . Many of these children have suffered physical injuries as a result of abuse, and most have experienced some form of physical and/or emotional neglect prior to placement. Not unexpectedly, chronic medical conditions and mental health disorders are extremely common, as are birth defects and physical growth disorders. (Simms, Freundlich, Battistelli, & Kaufman, 1999, pp. 171–172)

Pediatric evaluations of 308 infants and young children whose families received child welfare services in the Philadelphia area (Silver, DiLorenzo, Zukoski, Ross, Amster, & Schlegel, 1999) revealed that one in five were underimmunized, 43 percent had an "acute medical illness," and 60 percent had chronic medical problems (p. 156). These children have chronic health problems at a rate "two to four times as high" as the rate for the general population of children (Davis & Ellis-MacLeod, 1994, p. 135). (See also Altshuler & Gleeson, 1999.)

"Crack-babies" have been entering the foster care system in record numbers, particularly in communities hardest hit by the drug epidemic (National Black Child Development Institute, 1989, 1991; Besharov, 1990; Curtis & McCullough, 1993; Albert, 1994; Barth, Courtney, Berrick, & Albert, 1994). "An HHS office of the Inspector General (OIG) 1989 survey of 12 cities found that 30 to 50 percent of drug-exposed infants enter foster care. New York City has reported a 268 percent increase in referrals of drug-exposed infants to the child welfare system from 1986 to 1989" (U.S. House of Representatives Committee on Ways & Means, 1992, p.

900). Among a sample of 1,165 children age twelve or younger who were going into care, Davis, English, and Landsverk (1995) found 15 percent who were substance addicted at birth (p. 43). The responsibility for caring for these children has fallen disproportionately on the shoulders of kin caretakers (Gleeson, 1999; Wilson, 1999).

Coping with a baby's drug withdrawal or with fetal alcohol syndrome can present special challenges to foster families and foster care workers (Olson, Burgess, & Streissguth, 1993). A study of infants placed in foster care (McNichol, 1999) found "the infants with verified drug exposure had a higher incidence of asthma and small size, and a higher incidence of eating, sleeping, and early behavior problems" (p. 189).

Because intravenous drug use is a primary factor in adult exposure to the AIDS virus, drug-exposed children are also at risk for developing AIDS. An unknown but growing number of children in foster care are affected by this epidemic—either because their parents have the virus and are unable to care for them or because they, themselves, are infected (Lockhart & Wodarski, 1989; Taylor-Brown, 1991; Davis & Ellis-MacLeod, 1994; Merkel-Holguin, 1996). "Health officials estimate that 25 to 33 percent of infants born with AIDS will be cared for by someone other than their biologic mothers" (Melina, 1987). HIV infection is also believed to be a growing problem for adolescents, although most are not identified as infected until adulthood (CWLA, 1993). Young children who test positive for the HIV virus have an uncertain future. While some of them will go on to develop AIDS and to die within a few years, others (approximately 70 percent) will serorevert to HIV negative status (Miller & Carlton, 1988; Leeds, 1993). Children who are HIV positive "may be completely asymptomatic; may suffer growth and developmental retardation; and may suffer damaged skin, brain, heart, kidneys, and other organs, but they may never develop AIDS" (Lockart & Wodarski, 1989, p. 216).

Even the stress of managing the medical needs of children who are exposed to AIDS or drugs can be intense for foster parents. In interviews with 15 families caring for HIV-positive children, Carten and Fennoy (1997) found seven families who were "making three or more visits each month to health care professionals, even though the disease process in these children primarily reflected absent to mild symptoms" (p. 117). Coordinating educational and child care resources and obtaining adequate financial supports add considerably to the foster family's load (CWLA, 1987).

In its 1995 Standards, the Child Welfare League of America recommended, "Comprehensive medical, dental, developmental, and educational assessments should be arranged within 30 days of placement in family foster care" (p. 58). (See also Schor, 1987.) When serious medical problems are uncovered, foster parents will benefit from special training in dealing with these problems (Burry, 1999) and from additional "support and respite services" (Carten & Fennoy, 1997, p. 122). Kinship caretakers may be especially in need of such assistance (Berrick, Needell, & Barth, 1999).

Interagency efforts to enhance collaboration and planning to meet foster children's health care needs have also proven highly beneficial for both the children and their foster families. "Deficiencies in access to appropriate services are systemic, due to a lack of coordination among service providers responsible for the children's health welfare" (Silver, DiLorenzo, Zukoski, Ross, Amster, & Schlegel, 1999, p. 151; see also National Commission on Children, 1991, p. 287). Evidence suggests that access problems are more pervasive among African American children in care than for those who are Caucasian (Benedict, White, Stallings, & Cornely, 1989). Silver and her colleagues described one effort to address this deficiency, the Starting Young Program, a "follow-up diagnostic and referral service exclusively for children who are receiving services through the Philadelphia Department of Human Services" (p. 153). Another program in Syracuse provides a "comprehensive, multidisciplinary clinic for children in out-of-home care involving pediatrics, child psychology, nursing, child development, and child welfare" (Blatt, Saletsky, Meguid, Church, O'Hara, Haller-Peck, & Anderson, 1997, p. 331). (See also Combs-Orme, Chernoff, & Kager, 1991; Klee, Soman, & Halfon, 1992.)

Discrepancies in service provision are found for children placed with kin when compared to those placed with non-kin. Among children in kinship placements in Baltimore, Dubowitz, Feigelman, Harrington, Starr, Zuravin, and Sawyer (1994) found "substantial" health problems that had not been recognized or treated (p. 91); 44 percent of the children had not been given even minimal dental care. According to Dubowitz and his colleagues, "the number of unidentified and untreated health problems and the lack of basic health information point to serious shortcomings in the child welfare and health care systems" (p. 102) for this group.

The J Case

Timothy's treatment therapist continues to work with him, not only on problems of immediate concern but also on more embedded problems that stand in the way of his healthy development. For Timothy, long-standing problems center around his use of aggression in interpersonal relationships with both peers and adults. Although he can do well academically, he has missed many days of school because he has been suspended for fighting. These problematic behaviors are, of course, tied to his family experiences. After observing his father and stepfather use aggressive approaches to control family members, Timothy practices using these techniques. They appear to him to offer a way to feel less powerless, more "in control" of others and of his future. He is also confused about the need to be aggressive in order to be "manly."

While Timothy has many issues and questions about intimate relationships, he does not appear to be "attachment disordered." He has been able to develop close, trusting relationships with some members of his family and sees these ties as predictable. However, he is confused about his own level of responsibility for maintaining the welfare of family members and is unsure of the extent to which parents can be relied on for security and protection. These concerns are being addressed in therapy.

Birth Parents' Special Needs

Mental Health and Addiction Problems.   For parents whose children are in care, long-standing difficulties most often have to do with economic hardship (unemployment, lack of usable housing, homelessness, etc.), drug and alcohol abuse (most notably cocaine addiction), and mental illness. In its survey of African American families receiving foster care services, the National Black Child Developmental Institute (1989) found housing was inadequate for 30 percent of the families, and 11 percent were homeless. Studying children in foster care with the Casey Family Program in Montana, Walsh and Walsh (1990) found that 25 percent had mothers who were hospitalized or institutionalized. Packman's (1986) research in England described 30 percent of the mothers as having some type of mental disorder. Kliman, Schaeffer, and Friedman's (1982) study and Benedict and White's (1991) research on children coming into care for the first time found approximately one in three mothers had a mental health problem and one in five with a history of drug or alcohol abuse. Nine of the thirteen mothers in Wald, Carlsmith, and Leiderman's (1988) research had "continued severe" difficulties with mental, alcohol, or drug-related problems.

Emotional difficulties of abusing and neglecting parents may range from mild to severe; the parent may be depressed, psychotic, or have conduct disorders. For many of these mothers and fathers, it is not the mental illness itself but other family circumstances and problems that combine with parental limitations to increase vulnerability for the child. The impact of maternal depression on parenting is complex, according to Goodman, Radke-Yarrou, and Teti (1993), "depending on the specific qualities of the mother's illness, the 'person' characteristics of the mother, the contexts of risk or protection in which mother and child are embedded, and characteristics of the child" (p. 11). Constantino (1993) pointed out that the presence of "one healthy parent" can, in some families, insure that the child has adequate nurturing and can function well. (See also Steinhauer, 1991.) This suggests the need for careful evaluation of parent-child relationships and extensive assessment of family resources and supports in order to provide effective services for mentally ill parents when their children are in care. Whitman, Graves, and Accardo (1989) and Tymchuk (1992) drew similar conclusions with regard to families in which parents are retarded.

The drug abuse "epidemic" has touched the lives of many, if not most children coming into care, and drug involvement influences the course and outcome of care. In its research on parental drug abuse, the National Black Child Development Institute (1991) noted that continued misuse of drugs prevented the child's return home for 63 percent of the families whose children were still in placement by the end of the study (p. 37). Katz's (1990) description of an intervention program for parents with "chronic, severe dysfunctions" whose children had been removed found that drug or alcohol abuse was a major cause of referral for 71 percent.

Kliman, Schaeffer, and Friedman (1982) described the complex array of life problems that make reunification difficult for many of these families:

> Despite their initial willingness to cooperate as a group, these mothers faced formidable obstacles in their attempts to establish a secure home for themselves and their children. Their employment prospects were bleak. Few had the resources or opportunities to avoid the social milieus which helped stimulate their original addictions. For many, enlisting the aid of the biological fathers on behalf of the children, where they were known, carried the danger of increasing the mothers' vulnerability to recurrence of addiction. (p. 211)

Because of these challenges, Ritter (1995) noted, workers are "especially hesitant to terminate supervision in the cases of substance-abusing parents in the absence of detoxification and extensive follow-up treatment" (p. 475). When one parent in these families is addicted, the burden is on the remaining parent to take major responsibility for child care; when both parents are drug-involved, the family's difficulties are compounded (Burns & Burns, 1988). Societal attitudes suggesting that drug-abusing parents are to be condemned for their addictions have placed added burdens on these families (CWLA, 1992a; Franck, 1996):

> Thus, child placement and reunification decisions are all too often based on the number of "clean" or "dirty" urine screens reported for a given parent rather than a comprehensive assessment of risk factors, strengths, and supports available for the care and nurturing of children. (Azzi-Lessing & Olsen, 1996, pp. 16–17)

Visitation and reunification planning are also impacted by these problems. Visits may have to be more closely monitored to prevent the child's exposure to further abuse or neglect. Stress induced by visits may be difficult for the vulnerable parent to manage (Hess & Proch, 1988). In addition,

> The recovery process from crack cocaine addiction is a difficult one, typically involving one or more relapse episodes. When a parent is addicted, the complicated processes of setting up an intervention to leverage treatment, and working toward reunification through relapse and recovery, often do not fit into clearly established permanency time frames. (National Foster Care Resource Center, 1992, p. 3)

The child welfare agency may urge reunification at a point when the parent is in the midst of recovery but may not yet be ready to manage the challenges of parenting or to withstand temptations to reabuse (Staff & Fein, 1991).

The Child Welfare League of America (1992a) described an "ideal service mix" that includes the following:

> perinatal case-managed services, developmental follow-up for the children, extensive family support services, AOD education, intervention or treatment services, transportation, child care, parenting training, outreach, aftercare, HIV counseling/testing, family planning counseling, nutritional services for women and their young children, and mental health services. (p. 27)

There is a particular need for intervention programs adapted to the needs of women and for residential programs that involve women and their children in treatment (CWLA, 1992a). Because of the widespread nature of this problem, parents needing drug treatment services may find them unavailable or be placed on long waiting lists. One study found that only 60 percent of the parents needing such help had been referred for assistance (National Black Child Development Institute, 1991). This research calls for better service coordination and training for child welfare workers in order to help these families.

Medical Needs.   Chaotic life-styles, drug addiction, poverty, unhappiness, and uncertainty should all be expected to take their toll on birth parents, affecting not only their mental but also their physical functioning. Virtually no attention has been paid to the medical needs of birth parents who have children in foster family care.

"Aids is the leading cause of death among adults age 25 to 44 in the United States. . . . As of December 1996, 85,500 women of childbearing age (13 to 44) were reported as having AIDS" (Wiener, Battles, & Heilman, 1998, p. 116). The fatal course of this disease, which is accompanied by the emergence of complex medical problems, suggests that assessment of infected parents involve a comprehensive understanding of their medical condition and an evaluation of its impact on their emotional and social functioning. Parents may need assistance with housing; financial support; nutrition; medical services; educational, counseling, and support group services; service coordination and referral; and hospice care (CWLA, 1991b; Merkel-Holguin, 1996).

The J Case

For Mr. and Mrs. Jelico, long-standing issues involve a history of abusive experiences for each partner. Both Mr. and Mrs. J grew up in homes where mistreatment was prevalent; both had families in which their mothers were beaten by their fathers. Mrs. J was also mistreated by Timothy's father, who died after being shot in an argument with a friend. It is difficult for both of these individuals to envision relationships that do not have as a central component the need to control or be controlled. Mrs. J has also had previous bouts with severe depression, although she has not been hospitalized for this for the past three years. Being hospitalized for this disorder appears to be one way in which she has protected herself when her abusive partners become exceptionally dangerous. Mr. J has had periodic problems with heavy drinking,

and this has been tied to his excessive abusiveness. Although he says he now drinks "about once a week," both parents insist he has not been "bad drunk" since Timothy went into care.

Programs that help adults address these concerns are individualized. They require that each partner seek treatment or support in order to address mental health, substance abuse, or battering problems. Mr. J is not willing to seek treatment around these issues at this time. However, he has continued to attend his "men's" group. The group leaders feel he has made some modest progress in understanding his rage and its impact on Timothy.

Mrs. J also finds it difficult to explore these problems in therapy. She continues to attend her "mothers'" group but continues to refuse to seek help from a program for battered women. She has had a psychological evaluation, and her therapist, while finding her depressed, feels she is functioning at a marginal level and does not recommend that she receive medication at this time.

Mrs. J claims that Mr. J has been "treating her better" over the past several months, and her group workers suspect that the agency's presence in this family's life has had a dampening effect on his aggressiveness.

She has been able to move toward more clearly acknowledging that she is being abused, and she has been able to discuss making a safety plan for herself and her children, should Mr. J become abusive again. However, substantial movement beyond this point has not occurred. Her group workers feel she is not strong enough yet to insist that Mr. J change his behavior and that she may not be able to adequately protect herself or her children in case of further abuse.

Planning for the Future: Working toward Permanency Goals

While case planning at the beginning of placement outlines the overall goals to be achieved with the family, the middle phase of placement finds the worker and family concerned with working through this plan. Effective implementation of case planning requires that services offered to the family be appropriate, accessible, and carefully coordinated; that the worker be able to articulate clear links between services offered and outcomes expected; that permanency planning decisions be made in a timely manner; and that agency policies and practice support the complex tasks that must be undertaken at this time. The goal here, as in all stages of foster care service, is to move the family toward a permanency outcome that is reasonable, fair, and appropriate for the child's needs (Seltzer & Bloksberg, 1987).

Describing the nature of services that are adequate to meet the needs of children and their parents, Ratterman (1987) stated, "The first criteria is the relevance of the services: there should be a match between the family problem and the services offered" (p. 10). Services should be adapted to the seriousness, chronicity, and perceived reversibility of parenting problems (Glasser, 1983). Quantity and quality of effort are equally important:

> the agency should ensure that the family receives quality services. For example, if services are contracted for outside the public agency, the agency should determine whether the selected service provider is well-qualified to meet the family's needs. Quality also relates to the caseworker's skills, which are developed through education and experience, compassion and commitment. Second, the agency case plan should ensure that sufficient services are identified and allocated to meet the needs of the family. . . . The services must also be at an intensity level that will enhance the family's potential for achieving success. (Ratterman, 1987, p. 11)

(See also Maluccio, 1985; Stein, 1987; Herring, 1992; Maluccio, Warsh, & Pine, 1993.) Designing appropriate services requires that the agency be clear about the exact nature of parenting problems that need to be rectified, since misunderstanding of these difficulties can derail the entire intervention process (Seaberg, 1986).

Effective planning with and on behalf of families requires a process of systematic decision making (Steinhauer, 1991) that involves ongoing case assessment, goal development, monitoring, service coordination, and revision of goals and activities as needed (CWLA, 1990; Herring, 1992; Massinga & Perry, 1994). With the parents, the worker develops a list of specific steps that must be taken to achieve permanency for the child and a timetable for decision making with regard to the child's future (Hess & Folaron, 1991). To facilitate this process, workers must carefully think through the connection between individual case activities and overall goals for the child and family (Humphrey & Humphrey, 1988; Fein & Staff, 1991).

The objective of such assistance is to provide "services and supports to facilitate family reunification and to maintain safe, healthy relationships, or to make decisions about alternative living arrangements intended to be safe, nurturing and permanent" (CWLA, 1991a, p. 38). Some agencies initially work toward reunification goals and then explore alternative outcomes (adoption, emancipation, long-term foster care) only if efforts to reunite the child and parents fail (Hess & Folaron, 1991); however, a number of experts in the field (Kliman, Schaeffer, & Friedman, 1982; Katz, 1990, 1999; Hess & Folaron, 1991; Allen, 1992; Hess, Folaron, & Jefferson, 1992) now recommend that all reasonable outcomes be reviewed with the family from the beginning of placement. This provides the parents with a more realistic picture of future possibilities and prevents the participants from assuming any outcome other than reunification indicates "failure."

The child's role in this decision-making process is important but is frequently overlooked during this stage of intervention (Maluccio, Fein, & Olmsted, 1986; Aldgate, Stein, & Carey, 1989; CWLA, 1991a). Bullock, Little, and Millham (1993) found reunification is facilitated when children "have participated in decisions about their future and in the departure process" (p. 36). However, interviews with 1,100 children in Illinois (Wilson & Conroy, 1999) led the researchers to conclude that "their input is not considered when the issue of permanency is debated" (p. 63). While older children in some states may be invited to participate in periodic case reviews, a study of younger children (twelve or younger) found that only 4 percent had done so (Davis, English, & Landsverk, 1995, p. 119). In fact, lack of participation in decision making is a problem for others besides the foster child:

> The bad news is that there is little evidence that caseworkers significantly involve biological parents, kinship caregivers, children, and other members of the kinship network in the planning and decision-making process. Permanency plans appear to be made primarily by child welfare caseworkers, their supervisors, and other service providers rather than by the persons who will have to live with the consequences of these decisions. (Gleeson, O'Donnell, & Bonecutter, 1997, p. 818)

The worker's responsibility goes beyond encouraging such participation. Even when children or their parents are uncertain or ambivalent about their wishes, it is important to help them think through permanency questions (Folaron, 1993). In order to avoid slipping "into the role of unilateral decision-maker by default," Gries (1991) argued, the worker must offer "as much time as may be necessary for the child to clarify and to resolve his competing feelings, and to thereby arrive at a more meaningful position regarding his future" (p. 92).

Service coordination can present problems for the worker as well as the family. One study (National Black Child Development Institute, 1989) noted that parents working toward reunification may be referred to five or more social service agencies for assistance. The study concluded:

> [A]ny services received by the parent will be delivered in fragmented and uncoordinated bits and pieces. While several social service agencies or organizations may be providing services to the same client, no one agency will assume the responsibility for managing or coordinating the services provided. (p. 61)

(See also Fisher, Marsh, & Phillips, 1986; Hess, Folaron, & Jefferson, 1992.)

The child welfare worker, who should carry central responsibility for service coordination, may not be active enough with individual families to carry out this task. Yoshikami's 1984 study of eighteen agencies in five states found that 27 percent did not see their workers every month (p. 92). While 87 percent of the children in the Casey Family Program (Fanshel, Finch, & Grundy, 1990) reported the worker visited regularly and kept in touch, research at one public child welfare agency (Mushlin, Levitt, & Anderson, 1986) found three-quarters of agency records gave no indication that the children had been visited within the past year. Large caseloads, a perennial problem in public child welfare, prevent the foster care worker from providing all families with sufficient attention, forcing the worker to respond to crises (Blumenthal, 1983; Blumenthal & Weinberg, 1984) or to invest in more responsive and cooperative parents, since more limited efforts are likely to help them achieve family reintegration (Fanshel, 1982).

An important aspect of systematic decision making is the responsibility to make timely decisions with regard to the children's future (Maluccio, Fein, & Olmsted, 1986; Usher, Gibbs, & Wildfire, 1995). In this arena the parents' needs may be in direct conflict with the needs of their children (Wald, 1994). Because longer placements increase both the amount of time children stay in limbo and the likelihood of multiple placements, it is in the children's best interest that decisions with regard to the future be made as rapidly as possible (Steinhauer, 1991; Solnit, Nordhaus, & Lord, 1992; Cahn & Johnson, 1993; Weisz, 1994). However, from the parents' point of view, more time may be needed to address complex child care difficulties, to stabilize recovery from drug or alcohol abuse or other personal problems, or to gain access to parent education services after incarceration or institutionalization (Kinnie & Hardin, 1983; Beckerman, 1989; Staff & Fein, 1991; Azzi-Lessing & Olsen, 1996). A 1994 survey of child welfare administrators (Berrick & Lawrence-Karski, 1995, p. 9) found them evenly divided on the question of whether permanency planning time limits for drug-abusing families should be shortened or lengthened.

The need for timely case resolutions challenges the worker to make very difficult decisions and come up with clear, well-supported recommendations; there is a tendency to put off this task until some indefinite point in the future (Cahn & Johnson, 1993; Dugger, 1992). Agency policies and procedures sometimes unnecessarily prolong this process. Hubbell (1981) noted that some states mandate that workers may not terminate parental rights so long as parents are making sincere efforts to improve their parenting abilities, even when these efforts are "hopeless" (p. 136). In some communities, child welfare workers appear to believe that every parent "deserves" to have a chance to have his or her child returned, even in instances where the worker believes the parent incapable of providing a sufficient level of care (Hess & Folaron, 1991; Allen, 1992). Baker and Vick (1995) noted that "while twenty-four state statutes detail a minimum time in foster care (usually between six months and one year before parental rights can be terminated), only Montana has a maximum time in placement after which termination must occur" (p. 64).

Sometimes the difficulty lies in the lack of any clear agency policy to guide the worker's decisions. For example, a 1997 CWLA survey revealed that "only six of the 38 responding states reported having policies that focus specifically on children with incarcerated parents" (Seymour, 1998, p. 476).

Coming to these decisions further requires that the worker grapple with the fact that not all parents are capable of sufficient change within a reasonable period of time (Glasser, 1983; Steinhauer, 1991; Pierce, 1992; Cahn & Johnson, 1993; Maluccio, Warsh, & Pine, 1993). There are parents whose vulnerabilities suggest the need to move toward finding some other type of permanent home for the child. Although "only four [out of 13] of the biological parents of the foster children received extensive services, owing in part to limited availability of such services" in Wald, Carlsmith, and Leiderman's (1988) research, the "high mobility and lack of interest evidenced by the majority of biological parents made service delivery impossible in most cases" (p. 79). Examining the experiences of families in which children were subsequently returned to parental care, Festinger (1994) noted that 61.2 percent "did not want, or refused, at least one of the suggested services" (p. 41). In a study of birth families who had children in care in New York (Fanshel, 1982), more than half were depicted as somewhat or very resistant to seeing the worker, almost half missed appointments, and almost a third were late for them. In addition, among those keeping appointments, "sizeable groups were rated as being unable to discuss personal problems (52.3%), to be defensive about themselves (59.1%) or to be excessively dependent (51.3%)" (p. 151).

The difficult task of the child welfare workers is to struggle to make permanency decisions with the child's family while preventing the child from remaining for years in limbo. Linda Katz and Chris Robinson (1991) designed a planning tool to be used for younger children in care who have no potential caretakers available other than their maltreating parents. Use of this tool facilitates timely decision making by suggesting situations in which planning for potential reunification or termination of parental rights should be done concurrently. The following types of families are affected:

> *Group I:* These are families in which the child has been exposed to considerable danger or parental problems are extreme and long-standing. Examples include parents who have "killed or seriously harmed another child" and those with severe mental illnesses that have not previously responded to treatment. Other permanency options should always be explored for this group.

> *Group II:* This group includes families in which there are "strong contra-indicators for family reunification" (p. 349) and prognosis for change is guarded. Included here are families in which there has been a pattern of repeated abuse or neglect and evidence of chronic drug or alcohol abuse or marital violence. The greater the number of these vulnerabilities in the family, the likelier it is that the worker should pursue other permanency options along with reunification.

(See also Ratterman, 1993.) Permanency planning initiatives like those in Washington and Idaho (Katz, 1990), Michigan (Herring, 1992, 1993), and Kentucky (Farley, 1993) demonstrated that timely decisions can be made, even with the most complex and "intractable" cases. However, Tatara (1994) worried that the recent decrease in substitute care exit rates suggests a "decline in the child welfare system's effectiveness in helping to achieve permanency" (p. 136).

Parents who are unavailable to the child, on either a temporary or long-term basis, present another type of challenge to a child welfare system concerned about "drift." Collecting data from a stratified random sample of children, Bush and Goldman (1982) discovered that one-third had parents who were deceased or whose whereabouts were unknown. Over half of the subjects in Fanshel's (1982) study of foster care "were rated as devoid of any relationship with parents (37.7%) or as having families totally out of the picture (13.9%)" (p. 251). Olsen (1982) described 160,000 children in care without a "principal child-caring person." These included one in four of the white children, one in three who were Hispanic, and 40 percent of those who were African American (p. 576). (See also Rowe, Cain, Hundleby, & Keane, 1984.)

Parents who are incarcerated may be unavailable to their children in a different way. Although they may wish to maintain close family ties, correctional system policies or practical difficulties may prevent them from seeing their children regularly or from taking any responsibility for their care. It is estimated that "seven percent of mothers currently in jail have children in out-of-home care" (Katz, 1998, p. 498). Foster care workers may find it difficult to collect even the most basic essential information about these parents, such as the length of their sentences (Seymour, 1998). These factors place barriers in the way of effective permanency planning:

> Given the cumbersome aspects of maintaining contact with the mother, determining the date when a mother will be released from prison, assuring that the necessary rehabilitation and discharge planning will have occurred, and developing documentation of what is in a child's "best interests," formulation of a convincing plan for reunification becomes increasingly difficult or even impossible. (Beckerman, 1998, p. 517)

Parents who are infected with the AIDS virus face permanency planning challenges of yet another kind. These parents know that they must reckon with a future in which they will be increasingly unable to care for their children. However, looking to the future means facing the reality of their own demise. Perceived as too morbid or too frightening, this is experienced by many parents as a task to be avoided. Many of these parents also struggle with a fear that they will lose control of their children to strangers (Mason, 1998; Taylor-Brown, Teeter, Blackburn, Oinen, & Wedderburn, 1998).

Even this brief review of permanency planning tasks suggests the highly complex nature of the problems to be addressed and the responsibilities to be undertaken in helping families plan for the future:

> We are dealing with a 'hard-core' group of families where much effort is needed even to locate or visit, and much more to influence parents regarding the return of their biological offspring. Yet the process of releasing such children from severely decompensated families, not for foster care but for adoption, is extremely arduous. (Kliman, Schaeffer, & Friedman, 1982, pp. 223–224)

(See also Staff & Fein, 1991.) Instead of relying on the efforts of a single worker, the difficulty of this work strongly suggests the need to use a team approach for planning and decision making (Gries, 1990; Massinga & Perry, 1994; CWLA, 1995).

At the most basic level, effective implementation of case plans requires that services needed by families actually be provided to them. In 1982, Lindsey reported that encouraging parent-child contact, when accompanied by interventions designed to enhance parent skills, was effective in reunifying a large number of families in the Alameda Project. Whereas one-third of control group children returned to their birth home after placement, almost two-thirds of Project children did so; while more than half of control group children eventually experienced long-term care, only one in five Project children did so (p. 493).

Unfortunately, historical evidence (Maas & Engler, 1959; Fanshel & Maas, 1962; Stone, 1969; George, 1970) as well as more contemporary studies (Fanshel, 1981, 1982; Hubbell, 1981; Maluccio, 1981; Yoshikami, 1984; Besharov, 1986; Sosin, 1987; Weiner & Weiner, 1990; Hartman, 1993; Tatara, 1994) describe little direct rehabilitative programming offered to biological parents whose children are in care. While Thoburn's (1980) study reported three-quarters of the families received assistance from other agencies (p. 74), Turner's (1984) research uncovered a much lower rate of service utilization. "It is noteworthy that community services were infrequently rendered to parents or children, either while the children were in care or following their return home" (p. 502). Festinger's (1994) study of families reunified with their children described 66 percent of caretakers who had needed parent training while only 54 percent received it; 13 percent continued to have a need for such services at the point of discharge (p. 39). In *Out-of-Home Care: An Agenda for the Nineties* (1990), the Child Welfare League of America concluded that the "system of services for children and families . . . is most often better described as a nonsystem" (p. 13) and added, "Services that do exist often become inappropriately used due to the absence or unavailability of other more appropriate ones" (p. 13).

These findings suggest serious challenges to permanency planning efforts. When relevant, useful "reasonable" efforts to help parents address the problems that resulted in placement are not undertaken, agencies fail to carry out their most essential responsibility to families, and children, their parents, and the agencies themselves suffer as a result.

The J Case

Timothy has been in his foster home for eleven months, and a review of the family's move toward permanency must now be undertaken. The original plan for this family focused on a goal of having Timothy return home after Timothy's father had received services and curbed his abusive behavior. A secondary goal was to have Timothy's mother receive help so that she would no longer be abused and she could more effectively protect her children in the home. Services were also to be provided to Timothy to help him deal with some behavioral problems and to sort out the impact of his family's problems on his outlook and behavior.

The community in which the Js live did not have a program specifically designed for Mr. J—a service for battering husbands who also abuse their children. However, the "men's" group he attended at the local treatment agency did have a number of men in it who were abusive toward their spouses, so these joint issues could be addressed. The treatment providers recognize that change for men with these types of problems is frequently a long-term affair. They did not feel

that Mr. J made sufficient progress in recognizing and controlling his abuse, although he did make some changes with regard to these issues. He now recognizes that others will consider his discipline excessive and that agencies will intervene on behalf of his children if he were to harm his children again. He remains very aggressive and controlling in his home, however. Mrs. J has also cooperated in attending her treatment group and has made minimal progress. However, she is not in a position to actively protect Timothy from his stepfather's aggression.

Timothy has made substantial progress in therapy over the past several months. He has come to recognize the ways he tries to help his mother at home and has come to see that, while he is sometimes aggressive, that does not make him "just like" Mr. J. He now sees that he can control his own behavior, although sometimes that will not be easy to do. He is doing substantially better in school and has settled in well in the Tedesco foster home.

Timothy has persistently insisted that he wants to return home throughout his

continued

placement, and his mother has been equally persistent in her request that he return. Neither Timothy nor his mother have been willing to consider other possible permanency outcomes. Timothy continued to threaten to run away if it appeared to him that he was being moved toward any other option; in fact, he ran away on two occasions when he felt he was needed at home. The lack of appropriate extended family resources as alternative living arrangements made placement with other kin an untenable option.

Mr. J has recently admitted that he would "allow" Timothy to return. He has not been excessively aggressive toward Timothy during home visits, even on the four occasions when these visits were lengthened to two days. Timothy appears to be willing to seek help from others if Mr. J should become abusive; he knows there are several people he can contact if the need arises. He has recognized that Mr. J does not have the right to abuse him and that he needs to have plans for staying away from or extricating himself from unsafe situations at home.

Because this family has made some progress toward creating stability and safety for its children, the child welfare worker will recommend to the courts that Timothy be returned home. The worker will recommend that in-home services be provided for a transition period of at least six months to insure that these gains can be maintained. The worker will also recommend that Timothy and his parents remain in the treatment programs which they now attend and that the agency retain custody of Timothy until it can be determined that he is functioning adequately at home.

Questions for Discussion and Debate

1. You are a foster care worker and you receive a call from an upset foster parent who reports to you that Samantha, a nine-year-old foster child who has been in her home for four months, refuses to go to school, do her homework, or take a bath. When the foster mother insists, Samantha screams, "You are not my mother. You're just doing this for the money like the rest of them. You all just take kids in and kick them out anyway. You're not telling ME what to do!" What would you advise this foster mother to do about the situation?

2. What do you see as some of the important issues that need to be addressed with a local public school when a child who has a history of academic and behavioral problems moves into a new foster home? Should the child welfare worker or the foster parent contact the school about this child? Why?

3. You have been assigned to a permanency planning task force in your child welfare agency. You must come up with guidelines for permanency planning for children whose parents are in prison. What kinds of guidelines would you develop?

4. Did the child welfare agency make the right permanency recommendation for Timothy? Why or why not?

APPENDIX 8.1   Chronic Emotional and Behavioral Problems in Foster Children, Recent Studies

Study	Characteristics of Sample	Program	Measures	Behavioral/Emotional Problems
Frank (1980) p. 258	50 children in care 5+ years			More than 90% had neuroses, borderline personality disorder, or psychoses; 11% runaways
Thorpe (1980) p. 87	121 children aged 5–17 in current home 1+ years		Rutter Behavior Scale completed by foster parents	39% seriously disturbed
Kliman, Schaeffer, & Friedman (1982) pp. 124, 174	First time placements of 104 children 12 or younger; evaluations of 31 children aged 5–10 years old	Referrals from Westchester County DSS	Caseworker and researcher evaluations; Bender Gestault Protocols	55% of children aged 5–10 had scores suggestive of emotional disturbance; no differences from scores of children from similar SES backgrounds
Kavaler & Swire (1983) p. 87	668 children in care, 1973–1974	8 New York City agencies	Pediatric and psychological evaluations	10% severe, 25% marked, 35% moderate degree of emotional symptoms
Rowe, Cain, Hundleby, & Keane (1984) pp. 79, 82	21 children aged 10–11 in care 3+ years; compared with normative group from Isle of Wight	Five local authorities in England	Interviews with foster parents, children, and workers	*Behavior* *Study* *Control* Eating problem 19% 21% Sleeping problem 24% 18% Lying 19% 11% Temper tantrums 33% 18% Enuresis 19% 5% Lack of concentration 38% 21% Destructive 24% 4% Stealing 33% 3% 30% judged "disturbed"

continued

Study	Characteristics of Sample	Program	Measures	Behavioral/Emotional Problems			
				Behavior	*Foster Home*	*Group Home*	*Shelter*
Fitzharris (1985) pp. 100–101	140 children in foster care compared with those in other facilities	Private agencies throughout California	Agency staff completed forms	Impulsive	30%	35%	<1%
				Delayed social competence	23%	14%	<1%
				Aggression toward people	19%	30%	2%
				Fearfulness	16%	8%	<1%
				Runaway	14%	36%	6%
				Misdemeanors	13%	17%	<1%
				Substance abuse	12%	23%	<1%
				Sexual acting out	9%	15%	<1%
				Extreme dependency	8%	11%	<1%
				Hyperactivity	8%	10%	<1%
				Passive-aggressive	6%	11%	<1%
McIntyre & Keesler (1986) pp. 300–301	158 children 4–18 in care (includes group care and institutions)	Regular care, Eastern Tennessee	Child Behavior Checklist on one child completed by foster parents	49% "manifested psychological disorders"; difficulties across a wide spectrum of internalizing and externalizing patterns			
Packman (1986) pp. 41–42	361 children being "seriously considered for care" (includes institutional care); 161 admitted and 200 served in home over one-year period	2 administrative areas, south of England	Interviews with workers and parents, case record reviews	For 57%, concern expressed by worker for one or more aspects of behavior;			
				Disobedient or disruptive			46%
				Verbal or physical aggression			31%
				Delinquency			28%
				Runaway			15%

Study	Characteristics of Sample	Program	Measures	Behavioral/Emotional Problems
Colton (1988) pp. 148–149	29 older children in "special" foster homes compared to 34 in Children's Homes	2 local authorities northwest England	Instruments completed by foster parents, residential staff; direct observation	*Problem* — *Foster* / *Residential* Absconded — 21% / 38% Physically violent — 3% / 12% Otherwise aggressive — 13% / 15%
Wald, Carlsmith, & Leiderman (1988) pp. 60–61	13 white abused children aged 5–10; control group of abused children still at home; comparison group of children from local schools	Children in care in Alameda and Santa Clara Counties, CA	Interviews with caretakers, child, teachers, and social workers	Abused children had more problems and more combinations of problems than those in foster care *Problem* — *Home* / *Foster* / *Comparison Group* Vandalism — 28% / 8% / 5% Fire Setting — 17% / 8% / 5% Stealing — 22% / 8% / 5%
Hulsey & White (1989) p. 507	65 abused children 4–8 years old in care 3+ months; control group from well child clinic	In regular foster care	Achenbach CBC completed by foster parents	Foster children's scores 10.7 points higher on CBC
Fanshel, Finch, & Grundy (1990) pp. 59–60	585 children	Regular and specialized foster care, Casey Family Program	Researchers' data collection tools and agency records	35% posed substantial difficulty for foster parents in first year 39% posed moderate difficulty 28% posed slight difficulty 6% posed no difficulty 66% moody or depressed 13% bizarre behavior

continued

Study	Characteristics of Sample	Program	Measures	Behavioral/Emotional Problems
Walsh & Walsh (1990) p. 44	51 children at high risk for emotional problems	Casey Family Program	Agency records and worker ratings	Passive-aggressive 39% Aggressive or violent 25% Acting out 18% Withdrawn, moody 14% (Importance of these factors for child's success in program validated in two subsequent studies at different program sites)
Lie & McMurtry (1991) p. 114	110 children placed for abuse, in care 6+ months; controls were in care for other reasons	Regular foster care, Maricopa County, Arizona	Agency records	*Problem* *Abused* *Nonabused* Behavior problems 28% 39% Emotional problems 26% 29% Runaway before placement 10% 12%
English, Kovidov-Giles, & Plocke (1994) p. 149	Random sample of 500 youth 16 or older in care 6+ months	Washington state	Case file	25% had problems with emotional disturbance
Inglehart (1994) pp. 163–164	152 randomly selected youth 16 or older in foster care	Los Angeles County	Caretaker	22% had "mental health problems serious enough to require attention when planning for his/her situation after foster care"

9

Ongoing Work with Foster Families

To participate effectively as members of the professional foster care team, foster parents must be knowledgeable about the foster care system, the impact of mistreatment on children, and children's reactions to placement. In addition, they must feel free to communicate about their ideas and experiences with other team members. Finally, they need to feel that their contributions are of value to their team and that their input will be helpful to the children and families they serve. Agency efforts to enhance their knowledge, to recognize their status, and to support them in their role are considered in this chapter.

Enhancing Expertise

Expertise of foster parents grows out of their own personal experiences with foster children, dialogue with the foster care worker and other foster parents, and more formal group training provided by the agency. Agreement concerning the need for such training is widespread (Ryan, Warren, & McFadden, 1979; Hubbell, 1981; Euster, Ward, & Varner, 1982; Aldgate, Maluccio, & Reeves, 1989; Kamerman & Kahn, 1990; National Commission on Children, 1991; Chamberlain, Moreland, & Reid, 1992; CWLA, 1995).

Hampson (1985) reported that group training that is provided after children have been placed has greater impact than preservice training efforts. In the face of limited interest in fostering in most communities, training becomes a critical tool for preparing those who are selected for the arduous task of caring for today's foster children (Hampson, 1985). The Child Welfare League of America, in its *Blueprint for Fostering Infants, Children, and Youths in the 1990s* (1991), recommended that action be taken to

> Amend Title IV-B to require mandatory preservice and inservice training for foster parents. Such training shall: (1) be based on nationally recognized training

models; (2) include, at a minimum, joint training with family foster care social workers; (3) include interdisciplinary training related to such issues as HIV infection, chemical dependency, and accessing special education, health care, and mental health for children and youths in foster care; (4) be culturally responsive; and (5) provide foster parents with support for transportation and child care costs incurred while participating in training. (p. 83)

Some states have already moved to mandate training for all foster parents serving child welfare families (Whitmore, 1991).

Training groups are not universally available to foster parents, however. A 1987 study in the San Francisco area found only 46 percent of foster parents reported having been trained and provided with support groups (cited in Pasztor & Wynne, 1995). The James Bell Associates study (1993) found that training was not mandated in two of the nine states surveyed, although some individual counties in these states decided to institute their own programs. More worrisome were results obtained using a random sample of 194 children who had entered foster care in Jackson County, Missouri. "Fewer than 3% of the foster parents had received any foster parent training" (Mushlin, Levitt, & Anderson, 1986, p. 147).

Training is provided to kinship caretakers less frequently than to foster parents caring for unrelated children. In Berrick, Barth, and Needell's (1994) California research, 76 percent of non-kin foster parents received training, but only 13 percent of kin did so. Data from another study indicated workers frequently waived training requirements for kin. This resulted in an average of 9.97 hours of preparation for non-kin but only 1.55 hours for kin (Lewis & Fraser, 1987).

Trainers agree that effective adult learning requires that the concerns and needs of members be specifically addressed and the knowledge they already have be respected (Sellick, 1992). Sometimes group meetings are directed only to foster mothers, but more frequently they are designed for both foster parents. Although the groups often start with didactic instructional material, they usually move to a more informal pattern in which content for discussion is decided on or influenced by participants. Hampson (1985) concluded that a focused skill-building approach is more useful than a more unstructured discussion group format.

In-service training typically offers foster parents the opportunity to learn behavior management skills; to better understand the nature of attachment, separation, and loss; to explore cultural, racial, and ethnic issues; and to examine particular problems such as drug dependency (Sellick, 1992; Child Welfare Institute, 1993; Burry, 1999). Data recently collected from foster parents suggests they are especially in need of further education about child sexual abuse (James Bell Associates, 1993). Jackson (1999) described a training curriculum specifically developed for kinship foster parents.

Sellick (1992) described the impact of such training on participants:

As for evaluation, most found positive results such as greater confidence, an increased ability to prevent or deal with difficult behavior, and longer service from trained foster carers. Several studies found that both attendance and performance were improved by payments such as attendance allowances and baby sitting and traveling expenses, as well as by foster carers being previously consulted about course content. (p. 32)

Group effectiveness is also dependent on the level of preparation and skill that the leader provides and, to some extent, the degree of commitment that participants bring with them. Assessing the overall quality of six different eight-week programs, Engel (1983) considered only half of them to be of "good quality" (more than half the sessions characterized by good attendance, good participation, and meaningful subject matter) (p. 205). In some instances, skilled group leaders produced these results; in others, foster parent mistrust of the agency's motives or anger toward the agency turned meetings into unproductive gripe sessions.

Concrete Assistance

In addition to insuring that foster parents have sufficient knowledge to care adequately for children, the foster care agency provides financial resources that help compensate the parent for costs of child care. Children's eligibility for welfare benefits is carried with them when they are removed from their own family and placed in substitute care. These payments are then made to the foster home. For children ineligible for this type of support, the agency can make payments out of general child welfare funds. The agency also takes care of medical and dental treatment; it provides glasses, orthopedic appliances, and prescription medicine; it pays for psychological testing and psychotherapy when these are needed by the child.

There is widespread agreement that financial compensation is insufficient to cover the costs foster families incur in caring for children in their homes. A survey of Wisconsin agencies found only 50 percent fully reimbursed foster parents for their expenses (cited in Pasztor & Wynne, 1995). In 1992, the average subsidy for a child of two was $311 a month, for a child of nine was $332, and for a sixteen-year-old was $385 (U.S. House of Representatives Committee on Ways & Means, 1993, p. 895). However, in 1991, the U.S. Department of Agriculture estimated that the basic cost of caring for a child was $475 (James Bell Associates, 1993). This disparity suggests foster parents "actually subsidize the child welfare system to an almost incalculable degree through the donation of their time and out-of-pocket expenses" (Pasztor & Wynne, 1995, p. 4. See also Cully, Healy, Settles, & Van Name, 1977; Thomas et al., 1977). Foster parents typically use their own funds to pay for extra clothing, recreational activities, toys, personal grooming needs, and school expenses.

States differ in their average payment to foster parents. While Alabama paid $234 a month in 1992, Connecticut paid $572 and Alaska $621 (U.S. House of Representatives Committee on Ways & Means, 1993). Similar variations are found in Britain (Sellick, 1992). Payment rates are typically higher to treatment foster homes and for children whose special needs make unusual demands on the foster parent's time and energy (Kamerman & Kahn, 1990; Pasztor & Wynne, 1995). The North American Council on Adoptable Children (NACAC) reported that, in 1990, the average daily rate was $8–$15 for children in general and $15–$30 for those needing specialized care (cited in U.S. House of Representatives Committee on Ways & Means, 1993, p. 895).

Questions about adequacy of compensation arise out of recognition of the desperate need for additional homes for children at this time. There is a concern about matching competing sources of income for the foster parents (Steinhauer, 1991; Sellick, 1992; Pasztor & Wynne, 1995). The idea here is that the parent should have the opportunity to choose to foster rather than working at another job, especially when the family income is insufficient. A research study of 458 foster families (Fein, Maluccio, & Kluger, 1990; Fein, 1991) found one in five of all the families and almost half of the single parent families had incomes below $10,000.

Increased compensation is associated with better retention of foster homes. Campbell and Downs (1987), studying 1,094 families, found that higher board rates were an inducement, positively affecting the parents' decision to become foster caregivers. Interestingly, the extent of payment was not associated with the number of children the parents decided to foster. Chamberlain, Moreland, and Reid (1992) conducted an experimental test of the impact of a $70 monthly supplement on fostering practice. One group of parents received the extra payment and additional intensive supportive services from the worker; a second group received only the enhanced payment; the control group received the usual board rate and worker services. While 10 and 14 percent of the first two groups dropped out of the program, 26 percent of the control group parents decided to leave. Groups one and two were less likely to have children in their care run away, move to another foster home, or go into residential care (29 percent did so as compared to 53 percent of control group families). There was greater improvement in children's behavioral problems in the experimental groups. (See also Jaffee & Kline, 1970.)

Compensation is not only a fiscal concern but also a reflection of the family's status with the agency. Providing sufficient remuneration helps foster parents feel better respected and empowered. Chamberlain, Moreland, and Reid (1992) commented:

> we have the strong impression that the positive benefits of participation in the study went beyond the monetary benefits supplied by the payments for the assessments or the additional monthly stipends. Foster parents expressed satisfaction, accomplishment, and appreciation for being seen as experts or professional people who were contributing to a greater good (working on a project to improve foster care). The payments for their time and efforts seemed to contribute clearly to their sense of being valued. (p. 400)

Research conducted by Sellick (1992) in England echoed this theme. "Adequate payments efficiently paid, realistic rates for retainers, and swift compensation for damage seem to lead to job satisfaction and respect for the agency and its staff"

(p. 90). (See also Aldgate, Maluccio, & Reeves, 1989; Walsh & Walsh, 1990; Smith, 1991; James Bell Associates, 1993.)

Besides paying foster families a monthly fee that helps cover food, shelter, and other general expenses, there are recommendations that parents be given additional assistance to cover unusual clothing needs (since some children come into care with no clothing at all), day care, transportation (since some children have many medical, educational, or court-related appointments), and respite care (Pasztor, Shannon, & Buck, 1989; CWLA, 1991a; Sellick, 1992; ARCH, 1994; Pasztor & Wynne, 1995). The Child Welfare League of America (1991a) considers that "adequate" compensation may also "include, but not be limited to, health insurance, retirement/Social Security benefits, and a professional service fee above the monthly cost [of] reimbursement payment" (p. 82). Some foster families are routinely provided with this type of support, but too often receiving extra financial help is based on the parents' knowing how to request it or the worker's willingness to offer it (James Bell Associates, 1993).

In Britain, foster parents may also be paid a retainer fee to cover their ongoing expense while waiting to have a child placed in their home (Sellick, 1992). The Child Welfare League of America (1991) recommended national study of the true costs foster parents incur in their work.

Evidence indicates that many kin caretakers are in desperate need of financial support for raising their foster children. In a California study (Berrick, Barth, & Needell, 1994), the gross income of kin foster parents was $32,000 but of non-kin parents was $51,000. A study in an urban county in the southeastern part of the country (Gebel, 1996) found 60 percent of kin but 10 percent of non-kin parents living on incomes of less than $10,000. (See also Dubowitz, Feigelman, & Zuravin, 1993; McLean & Thomas, 1996.) While most child welfare administrators believe kin homes need financial and other supports equivalent to those given non-kin homes (Berrick & Lawrence-Karski, 1995), this clearly is not happening (Hegar & Scannapieco, 1999). The more limited financial resources kin bring to fostering makes this lack of support especially troubling.

Providing for Recognition and Input

Consideration of the current status of foster parents raises questions that go far beyond compensation matters. The notion that foster parents function as team members has meaning only if these mothers and fathers have sufficient input into and clear influence on team decision making. Foster parents ask that their special expertise be acknowledged:

> Foster parents . . . are developing and extending their sense of responsibility in this caring process, demanding an input into the decision-making process surrounding the children they care for. They will not be treated simply as a depository for children. (Reeves, 1980, p. 125)

(See also Horowitz, 1983; Lowe, 1991; Pasztor & Wynne, 1995.) However, there is a serious question whether they are respected in this way (James Bell Associates, 1993; Triseliotis, Sellick, & Short, 1995). One foster parent commented:

> We don't get heard and I think it's because we have no status. I think we're treated badly by society as a whole. We're not given the credibility, the status that we deserve. . . . It makes me think we need to get a university degree and letters behind our names so we can say something and somebody will listen. That is a very frustrating part about being a foster parent. That when you say something you're not believed. (Sellick, 1992, p. 67)

A foster parent's ability to influence the course of a child's care is curtailed by state laws and regulations and by the courts. Although foster parents sometimes have a right to be heard in court, especially in circumstances where the foster child has resided with them for a long period of time, this still does not give them the right to have their opinions or goals considered. Birth parents and the child welfare agency have far more standing with the court (Stein, 1991).

Governmental regulations define "acceptable" foster parent characteristics and place constraints on foster parent behavior. These rules may determine whether a family's income or the size of their bedrooms makes them ineligible to become foster carers. Although all parents are accountable in a general way to society, there are no formal channels that periodically take a measure of their performance. However, foster parents are accountable in this way, and the yearly relicensing is the procedure by which such accounting is explicitly made. Specific actions of these parents may also be curtailed. An instructional pamphlet for foster parents points out, "Disciplining a child must be done with kindness and understanding. Corporal punishment, which includes striking, whipping, slapping, or any other form of discipline that inflicts the child with physical pain, is prohibited. *Don't forget that prohibited means not allowed.* Disobeying the regulations is cause for cancellation of the foster home license." (See also CWLA, 1995.) Avoiding any use of physical means to control the child is not an approach that many foster parents would embrace if given free choice in the matter. Effective and permissible means of disciplining have become common discussion topics in foster parent group and agency training sessions (Hampson & Tavormina, 1980; Felker, 1981).

Further constraints are placed on foster families by the child welfare agency. Applicants have no "right" to be studied or approved as foster homes. Foster parents are obligated to discuss the child's behavioral difficulties with the agency, and they are not free to pursue various remedial services for the child without the worker's approval.

Foster parents are well aware of the impact of these limitations on their role:

> If there's something wrong with my [birth] child I can seek help but there's only so much you are allowed to do with a child that is not yours. And it's frustrating

when you know that something is happening, something is wrong and you can't do anything and the people who are supposed to be doing something are not taking you seriously at all. (Sellick, 1992, p. 65)

(See also Shulman, 1980.) Frequently, the family must obtain agency approval in order to change sleeping arrangements or to take the child out of state on a vacation trip.

The decision as to whether the child remains or goes rests with the agency. Removal of a child from the biological parents' home can be effected only after due process of law. Removal of the foster child from the foster-family home can be undertaken merely on the basis of the agency's decision (Steinhauer, 1991). Carrieri (1991) asserted:

foster parents have sought virtually every conceivable way to either stay the removal of the child from their home pending administrative review or to circumvent the administrative procedures entirely by seeking court review of the agency's decision to remove the child. At every turn, the foster parents have been denied in these attempts. (p. 285)

Because the foster parents' relationship with the child has such limited legal protection, their valuation of this relationship must of necessity make them anxious and desirous of pleasing—and sometimes even of placating—the agency. Parents may fear the foster child will be taken away if they challenge agency decisions or insist on greater participation in decision making (Steinhauer, 1991). One parent in Sellick's (1992) study commented, "People don't make a fuss. There are a lot of foster carers who don't make waves because they won't be allowed to have any more children" (p. 62). These concerns can impel foster parents to remain silent about problems they are having with a child, sometimes until it is too late for the agency to help alleviate them (Fisher, Marsh, & Phillips, 1986; Cohen & Westhues, 1990).

The highly circumscribed status of foster families is most clearly suggested by data on foster parent participation in formal planning efforts on behalf of children (meetings to develop or implement case plans, case reviews, etc.). Research evidence indicates that while, in theory, foster parents have the "right" to make contributions to such planning (CWLA, 1995, p. 99), in reality they are rarely invited to participate (Taber & Proch, 1988; Simms & Bolden, 1991). A study of almost 2,000 current and former foster parents (James Bell Associates, 1993) found only half had attended informal meetings with staff, and approximately one in four had gone to court hearings. While most states participating in the study left it up to the worker to notify foster parents of upcoming hearings, counties in two states "indicated that while foster parents were routinely notified, they might not actually be allowed to attend the hearing" (p. 93). Steinhauer (1991) asserted, "in many agencies, foster parents are rarely or minimally considered, let alone consulted, around decisions that involve them as much as they do the child" (p. 191). (See also Edelstein, 1981.) Foster parents also complain that they are not given basic, essential information about the children in their care (Horowitz, 1983; Sellick, 1992).

Additional restraints on foster parents grow out of their relationship with the foster care worker. Foster parents recognize important differences among workers—some consider them valuable participants in the child's care, while others largely ignore their input (McFadden, 1990). In Sellick's research, "a working relationship was valued where there was a real sense of partnership between worker and carer with each making a contribution that was valued and recognized by the other" (p. 63). The respect that underlies this type of relationship also provided the basis for the foster parents to work through any conflicts that arose with the worker. In Rosenblum's (1977) study, foster parents responded positively to the fact that the worker had a "good understanding of a child or a child's problems," that "the worker treated them with respect and/or like fully capable adults and/or *not* like clients" (p. 57). (See also Berrick, Barth, & Needell, 1994; Triseliotis, Sellick, & Short, 1995.)

Foster parents more frequently ask for support and sanction than for instruction or advice. What they want, and keenly appreciate, is a worker who listens with empathy, sympathy, and interest, and who gives them the commendation of the agency for their efforts. Foster parents want and respond warmly to the worker's availability, interest, concern, and willingness to discuss their problems with them in a joint effort to find possible solutions. Compared with the foster parent, the worker has greater experience with foster care, a wider perspective on foster care, and a structured, problem-solving approach to child-care problems. These are helpful even if the worker may lack ready, easy answers to the particular questions raised (CWLA, 1991a; Sellick, 1992).

Unworkable partnerships develop because of worker inaccessibility, lack of worker respect, or practice "characterized by delay, incompetence, or ignorance" (Sellick, 1992, p. 64). Foster parents have cited "poor communication with the foster care worker" and the worker's "insensitivity" to parental needs as primary reasons for deciding to cease being foster parents (James Bell Associates, 1993, p. 76; see also Hampson & Tavormina, 1980). Parents claimed these factors had greater impact on their decision to leave than particular difficulties with a child or other personal concerns.

Kin foster parents are far more likely to find themselves in infrequent contact with foster care workers than their non-kin counterparts (CWLA, 1994). In Dubowitz, Feigelman, and Zuravin's (1993) Baltimore study of kinship care, "twenty-nine percent of the caregivers had not contacted the caseworker at all in the year preceding the evaluation" (p. 160). In Inglehart's (1994) Los Angeles County study, "kinship care children did not receive the same level of monitoring or supervision as the foster family minors" (p. 118). Although this might be interpreted as respect for the privacy of kinship families (Takas, 1993), it can also be interpreted as abandonment, particularly when it occurs with families who are overburdened with responsibilities but have meager resources and supports.

The influence foster parents have with the foster care worker is complicated by the worker's obligation to join with a foster parent to plan for the child's future while serving as "supervisor" for that same parent, making sure that the child is treated well and that the foster parent carries out the case plan that has been developed (Sellick, 1992; Triseliotis, Sellick, & Short, 1995). To handle such complex situations, workers need specific training that targets their relationship-building skills with foster families (James Bell Associates, 1993). Too often workers must obtain these skills through trial-and-error efforts on the job.

Many agencies assume that it is foster mothers—not fathers—who are the primary providers of foster family care. Treatment of foster parents thereby reflects general treatment of women and mothers in our society.

> To work for (with ? under ?) a child welfare agency, to be paid a pittance, to be asked to parent a child whom no one else is able to parent, to try to love that child and to lose him or her when loving has been achieved, to be supervised by a 22-year-old social worker, to have to deal with school teachers, police, courts, medical appointments, angry biological parents, and the impact of all this upon one's own family—that is the lot and life of a typical foster mother in America. (Meyer, 1985, p. 252)

Foster fathers may be the parents who provide first indications when trouble is developing in the family (Weinstein, 1960; Rowe, Cain, Hundleby, & Keane, 1984). The foster father is often less hesitant about speaking up. Cautley (1980), for example, found fathers less enthusiastic about and more critical of agency policies and of worker behavior (p. 245).

In summary, effective participation in case planning with full participation of all team members appears to be an ideal goal to be striven for rather than a reality in many foster care programs at this time. Aldgate, Maluccio, and Reeves (1989) pointed out:

> [W]e have to examine honestly and openly the power relationships in the partnership between foster parents and social workers. Foster parents are currently junior partners in the child care system. This does not prevent them from working successfully within this limitation if roles and activities are scrupulously delineated. But, in the end, if foster parents are to reach their optimal potential, a partnership of equality is the ultimate aim. (p. 30)

Offering Support

In order to cope with demanding children on a day-to-day basis, foster parents require support and understanding from others as well as opportunities for "time off" or "respite." One agency has offered these services to families using the "foster extended family" model. The agency recruited and trained neighbors, friends, and extended family members who agreed to make themselves available to the foster family when assistance in child care tasks was needed or when the parents needed temporary relief from child care. Providing this type of support helped the families more successfully care for the young, multiply severely handicapped children who were placed in their homes (Barsh, Moore, & Hamerlynck, 1983). (See also Engel, 1983.) Goldstein, Gabay, and Switzer (1981), describing a successful foster care program for children who were severely emotionally impaired and had previously been placed in mental hospitals, noted that families may also need to have available to them more intensive backup services. Some of these very disturbed children required emergency hospitalization, and plans were made ahead of time with the family for such an eventuality.

Planned support to foster parents can be provided in a variety of ways (Sellick, 1992): most typically in individual sessions with the worker, through the use of foster parent "buddies" (Pasztor, Shannon, & Buck, 1989; James Bell Associates, 1993), and in specially designed support groups. These groups may be led by the worker, coled by a worker and foster parent, or run directly by the foster parents themselves. Providing support group services has been shown to be helpful to participants (Carten, 1990; Steinhauer, 1991; Sellick, 1992).

Foster parents have also developed their own associations which function independently of child-serving agencies (Sellick, 1992; Pasztor and Wynne, 1995). Since the First National Conference of Foster Parents met in Chicago in 1971, statewide and local foster parent associations have been formed in many communities across the country. The National Foster Parent Association has played an active advocacy role since the early 1970s, although withdrawal of federal funding has weakened the impact of this group to some extent (Pasztor, 1985, p. 203).

Kinship caretakers have also been active in creating their own supportive environments. Scannapieco (1999) noted:

> Relatives in and out of the formal child welfare system have joined together to give one another the support they feel they cannot obtain elsewhere. Kinship care support groups have been created through grassroots efforts from relative caregivers, private and public agencies, and churches. (p. 79)

Concluding Note

Although foster parents find themselves central players in a very complex system, with unclear authority and excessive responsibility, the difficulty of this situation is not reflected in their assessment of foster care workers. Recent research (Berrick, Barth, & Needell, 1994) echoes the findings of an earlier study (Rowe, Cain, Hundleby, & Keane, 1984) that "there was a sense of considerable loyalty to the department and the general level of satisfaction seemed remarkably high" (Rowe, Cain, Hundleby, & Keane, 1984, p. 167). (See also Rosenblum, 1977; Shulman, 1980.)

The J Case

Rod has had a positive experience with Timothy's foster care worker. He has found her knowledgeable, accessible, and responsive to problems as they arise. However, he does not support the long-range plan for Timothy's return to his home. He is worried not only about the boy's safety but about his mental health as well. He feels that Timothy struggles mightily to manage all of his conflicting emotions and needs and that return to an unhappy and abusive environment will bring with it losses in school achievement, peer relationships, and personal happiness.

As he gains experience as a foster parent, Rod feels increasingly frustrated with his inability to inform or participate in planning for Timothy. He has not been invited to any permanency planning sessions or to the court hearings where these plans are finalized. He has to trust that the child welfare worker will communicate his concerns but fears she might not do so when she disagrees with his ideas. He wonders why a foster parent, who knows this child most directly, does not play a more central role in helping him toward his future. Rod realizes that he will have to deal with these feelings if he is going to continue to foster children after Timothy goes home.

Rod has found foster parent training helpful, but he has especially appreciated the support of other foster parents. He joined the local foster parent association and tries to attend their meetings regularly. Timothy goes with him and has an opportunity to meet other foster children who are his own age. Rod feels that some of the parents he has met at these meetings have been of special importance to him, serving as a source of information and support in times of crisis. They have also taught him a great deal about the functioning of the child welfare agency and have given him useful tips for managing his relationship with Timothy's workers.

Questions for Discussion and Debate

1. If you were establishing your own foster care agency, how would you envision the role of foster parents vis a vis your agency?
2. You find in your agency that many kinship caretakers have not been visited by their foster care workers. What factors do you need to consider before deciding that workers must visit these families regularly?
3. What do you see as the major differences between a group session focusing on "effective discipline" set up for birth families and a group session on the same topic set up for grandmothers caring for their grandchildren?
4. In an era of fiscal conservatism and managed care, how could better funding be developed for compensating foster parents for their expenses?

10

Leaving the Foster Care System

For most children, leaving foster family care is a period of major transition, a time of change as full of upheaval and strong emotions as the initial placement was (CWLA, 1995). This transition is part of a larger process of change that begins well before the child is physically removed from the foster home and that goes on well after the child goes on to a new location (Fisher, Marsh, & Phillips, 1986). Bullock and his colleagues (1993) used the term *care career* to suggest the interconnected nature of this experience. Use of the term *leave-taking* rather than *termination* or *outcome* is meant as a reminder that this move in no way suggests that the child's or family's problems have been fully resolved or that they are in need of no further services or supports (Packman, 1986; Bullock, Little, & Millham, 1993).

Options

Most commonly, children go on to one of the following settings:

1. They return to the home of birth family members. Commonly referred to as "reunification," this is the preferred leave-taking choice for children.
2. They become emancipated. Also called "independent living," this move places older children in relatively autonomous living situations, ones in which they are expected to move toward more mature self-care and to become self-supporting.
3. They move to a new permanent home, most often after their birth parents' rights have been terminated and they have been placed in an adoptive setting.

These moves are considered most desirable because they can contribute to the child's sense of family connectedness and stability over time.

Two other types of transitions are seen as less desirable but optimal for some children:

4. They are placed in a more restricted, more treatment-oriented setting, such as a mental hospital or residential care.
5. They remain in foster care on a planned long-term basis. This can occur when the child's ties to his or her birth and foster families are strong but circumstances in the birth family are such that the child cannot safely return to that home.

Two other moves are seen as undesirable because they may further jeopardize the child's attachments and sense of stability. To the parties involved, these moves indicate a failure of commitment and responsibility. However, Staff and Fein (1991) reminded us that even these transitions might be the best choice for a child at a particular point in his or her care career:

6. They are moved from one foster home to another, most often because the foster parents feel they cannot handle the child or out of the agency's concerns about foster parent inadequacies.
7. They move back into foster care after reunification. Here, too, it may be the child's or family's problems that precipitate this transition.

(See also Hess, Folaron, & Jefferson, 1992.)

In this chapter, we present the numbers of children who move from foster family care into these various settings and the length of time it takes them to make this change. Chapter 11 will consider in more detail the family circumstances of children experiencing one or another type of transition. For each type of move, whether it involves reunification, emancipation, or a change in foster homes, effective service delivery continues to address themes that were present throughout the placement: helping the child and the birth and foster families respond to losses and strengthen attachments; helping them deal with new family dynamics caused by changing family membership; helping the child and birth parents continue to work on vulnerabilities that threaten child safety and family viability; and assisting all parties involved in the change to more effectively define their concerns and plan for their various futures.

Outcomes

Appendixes 10.1 and 10.2 summarize available information on the types of placement settings in which foster children find themselves over a period of time. Appendix 10.1 describes placement circumstances for entire groups of children in care. These data suggest that the majority of children do eventually leave care. Approximately two out of three children move on to one or another type of new placement, while one-third remain in foster care, either because their families are still working toward reunification or because long-term care is considered the most viable plan for them. Appendix 10.2, which describes placements for children moving out of care, indicates that by far the largest number move on to the homes of their parents or other relatives. (See also Little, Leitch, & Bullock, 1995.) Adoption, emancipation, and long-term care choices are made for few children. The enormous variability in outcome from region to region and from one study population to another suggests a critical need for further study in this area (Davis & Ellis-MacLeod, 1994).

In what was to become a major catalyst for change in the child welfare field, Maas and Engler's 1959 study drew attention to the unexpectedly long time many children spent in foster family care. The authors were especially concerned about children who were "drifting," spending years away from home with no clear move toward any permanency option. Cross-sectional studies assess length of stay by measuring the amount of time spent by a representative group of children already in care (Fanshel & Grundy, 1975; Hargrave, Shireman, & Connor, 1975; Vasaly, 1978; Rowe, 1980; State of California, 1981; Fanshel, 1982; Becker & Austin, 1983; Gershenson, 1983; Lawder, Poulin, & Andrews, 1985; National Black Child Development Institute, 1989; Festinger, 1994). An essential difficulty with such studies is that they exaggerate the impact of the backlog of all the children who, over the years, have been unable to move out of foster care and underestimate the number of children who stay in care for only a few weeks or months. Longitudinal studies, which follow a group of children through their care careers, provide a more accurate estimate of length of stay (Jenkins, 1967; Fanshel & Shinn, 1978). Valid estimates are also provided by studies that use sophisticated predictive tools such as "event history analysis," an estimate of "the probability that an individual will experience an event or make a transition" at one point in time or during a particular time interval (Barth, Courtney, Berrick, & Albert, 1994, p. 91; Goerge, Wulczyn, & Harden, 1994). Appendix 10.3 reflects use of these methodologies to evaluate the length of children's foster care careers.

These data show a remarkable similarity in findings across widely different samples. It is reassuring to find that approximately half the children leave within the first half year after placement and that they are leaving care at a faster rate than in the past. "We have a foster care system that is far harder to get into and somewhat easier to leave than it was in the 1980s" (Barth, Courtney, Berrick, & Albert, 1994, p. 261). In an analysis of VCIS data, Tatara (1993) found the median length of time children stay in substitute care dropped from nine months in 1985 to seven months in 1989 (p. 79). Unfortunately, there are also a number of children who do not go home or move on to other permanent placements but who remain in foster family care for a substantial part of their childhood. This may be a particular problem for young children. In a Michigan study of infants placed in care, Schwartz, Ortega, Guo, & Fishman (1994) found less than three-quarters had achieved permanent homes after four years of care; the average length of stay for these children was 2.3 years (pp. 410–411).

In a survey of children in care in twelve counties across six states, Smollar (N.D.) found three groups for whom short-term foster care was typically used:

Group 1: Adolescents placed in foster care because of their own behavior problems;

Group 2: Child maltreatment victims whose parents (1) deny that the maltreatment occurred, (2) refuse to cooperate with the child welfare agency in effecting changes, and/or (3) are unable to prevent the maltreatment from occurring;

Group 3: Children who are placed . . . because their parents are unable to care for them for a limited period of time due to illness, incarceration, temporary homelessness, or family emergency. (p. x)

For the second group of children, the agency used foster care as a temporary safety measure during the investigation period.

Examining the foster care careers of more than a thousand Illinois children, Goerge (1990) described an association between the length of time a child is in care and the number of moves he or she experiences. Children returning home after one placement were in care approximately ten weeks. Those returning home after two placements stayed in care approximately 30 weeks, while those in three placements remained in care for 40 or more weeks (p. 432).

There is a link between the duration of a child's foster care career and the child's age, with younger children spending longer periods of time in care (Kliman, Schaeffer, & Friedman, 1982; Seaberg & Tolley, 1986; Wulczyn, Goerge, & Harden, 1993; Schwartz, Ortega, Guo, & Fishman, 1994; Goerge, Wulczyn, & Harden, 1996). Wulczyn's (1994) analysis of New York data suggested that the situation is changing most rapidly for the very young. While one in four infants left care in that city within 90 days in 1985, only 11 percent did so by 1989. Half of the infants who went into care in 1984 were still in care two years later (pp. 170–171). Analyses of California (Barth, Courtney, Berrick, & Albert, 1994) and Michigan (Weisz, 1994) data found similar trends. However, Benedict and White's (1991) study of Maryland children entering care for the first time found no link between age and time in care.

Data collected over the last twenty-five years indicate that African American, Hispanic, and Native American children remain in the foster care system for longer periods than other children do (Tizard & Joseph, 1970; Fanshel & Shinn, 1972; Olsen, 1982; Jenkins et al., 1983; Finch & Fanshel, 1985; Mech, 1985; Maluccio & Fein, 1989; Wulczyn, Goerge, & Harden, 1993; Barth, Courtney, Needell, & Jonson-Reid, 1994; Courtney, Barth, Berrick, Brooks, Needell, & Park, 1996). Analysis of data collected from twelve states between 1984 and 1990 led Tatara (1994) to conclude:

An analysis of the data . . . clearly shows that the substitute care exit rates among minority children were substantially lower than the rates among white children throughout this period. Particularly, the exit rates of black children consistently lagged far behind the rates of white children. (p. 8)

In McMurtry and Lie's (1992) study, African American children spent three years in care, on the average, while white and Hispanic children were in care for two and a half years (p. 44). Analyzing national data collected in 1977, Seaberg and Tolley (1986) found that a child's age and race explained 40 percent of the variance in duration of care. (A study of children conducted by Benedict, White, and Stallings [1987], once again in Maryland, found no link between the child's race and length of care, however.)

Placement with kin results in longer stays in care. Using a sample of 600 California foster families, Berrick, Barth, and Needell (1994) found the average length of stay for non-kin homes was 2.3 years but for kin homes was 3.3 years. For 58 percent of children living with kin, the family's expectation was that they would stay until adulthood; this was true for only 38 percent of non-kin foster children (pp. 45, 56. See also Goerge, 1990; Benedict & White, 1991; Wulczyn & Goerge, 1992; Dubowitz, Feigelman, & Zuravin, 1993; Goerge, Wulczyn, & Harden, 1994; Gleeson, O'Donnell, & Bonecutter, 1997; Berrick, Needell, Barth, & Jonson-Reid, 1998). A study conducted in Erie County, New York (Link, 1996) found that children discharged from kinship care had been living with their relatives for 4.7 years. A New York City survey noted that "infants with a placement in a relative's home remained in foster care 1,366 days longer than children without such a placement" (Wulczyn, 1994, pp. 175–176). However, studies done in Baltimore (Benedict, Zuravin, & Stallings, 1996), in Los Angeles County (Inglehart, 1994) and at the Casey Family Program (LeProhn & Pecora, 1994) suggested no differences in the total time in care between kin and non-kin placements. Because children who are not Caucasian are more likely to be placed with kin, correlations between race and length of stay may be confounded with kinship care's effect.

There is evidence of wide disparity in children's tenure in care from agency to agency and state to state. Black children in Houston entering care for the first time had an average stay of seven months; in New York it was 15 months (National Black Child Development Institute, 1989). Smollar's (N.D.) survey found that the proportion of those staying 90 days or less ranged from 28 percent to 67 percent in the twelve counties studied. Goerge, Wulczyn, and Harden's (1996) analysis of a decade of data collected from five states described the median stay in care in Texas as less than nine months; in California it was a year and a half; in New York two years; and in Illinois, almost three years (p. 21). (See also Davis, English, & Landsverk, 1995.) There are also variations between urban and rural areas; with the length of stay substantially greater in some major cities (Goerge, Wulczyn, & Harden, 1996). Perhaps these data measure the extent to which these major metropolitan areas are overwhelmed by the burgeoning need for care. More detailed analyses of the reasons for these differences might provide useful insights for improving service delivery.

Not surprisingly, family circumstances are associated with the length of the child's tenure in care. Research by Benedict and White (1991) and McMurtry and Lie (1992) found that children with disabilities were slower to leave care, while sexually abused children left at a faster pace than children who were abused in other ways. Parental substance abuse is an important contributor to children's longer stays in care (Maluccio & Fein, 1989; Benedict & White, 1991; National Black Child Development Institute, 1991; CWLA, 1992a). As we have previously noted, parental involvement with the child, most often assessed through evaluation of visitation patterns, is associated with more rapid exit from care.

There is some recognition in the child welfare field that while shorter stays in care are financially appealing, they are not necessarily reflective of the best interests of all children. McDonald, Allen, Westerfelt, and Piliavin (1993), in reviewing a number of studies on adult outcome, found that those in care for longer periods were functioning more effectively as adults, especially if their placement was in a "normal, stable foster family setting" (p. 125). Their findings remind us that what the child is moving toward must be weighed against what he or she is leaving in determining what is most important for the child. (See also Walsh & Walsh, 1990; Weiner & Weiner, 1990; Bullock, Little, & Millham, 1993.)

APPENDIX 10.1 *Placement Options for All Children in Foster Care*

Source	Characteristics of Sample	Reunited	Adopted	Emancipated	Still in Care	Other
Stein, Gambrill, & Wiltse (1978) p. 56	Alameda Project outcomes N=157 (C G N=158)	36% (25%)**	22% (11%)**	—	42% (64%)	—
State of California (1981) p. 34	Demonstration Project in 2 counties N=188 (C G N=224)*	39% (41%)**	—	—	61% (59%)**	—
Lahti & Dvorak (1981) p. 54	Oregon Project N=509	26% to parents; 3% to relatives	36%	—	36%	—
Lahti (1982) p. 559	Oregon Project children under 12 in care 1+ years N=259 (C G N=233)	26% (24%)**	40% (21%)**	—	34% (55%)**	—
Fanshel (1982) p. 293	Children in New York, in care 1+ years N=372	5%	7%	—	81%	7%
Becker & Austin (1983) p. 2	Children in Wisconsin during 2 years N=10,428	33–40% to parents, 6% to relatives	12–13%	7%	33%	—
Yoshikami (1984) p. 115	Children in 18 sites in 5 states N=299	29%	—	—	63%	8%
Lawder, Poulin, & Andrews (1985) p. 14	Children's Aid Society of Pa. over 1 year N=185	62%	16%	—	18%	5%

APPENDIX 10.1 *Continued*

Source	Characteristics of Sample	Reunited	Adopted	Emanci-pated	Still in Care	Other
Wald, Carlsmith, & Leiderman (1988) p. 98	13 children in Casey Program; followed for two years	15% to parents; 31% to relatives	8%	—	46%	—
Goerge (1990) p. 432	1,196 Illinois children who went into first placement	33% after 1 placement; 13% after 2 placements; 5% after 3 placements	—	Expected for 10%	Approximately 30%	—
Lie & McMurtry (1991) p. 116	110 sexually abused children in care 6+ months in Arizona	35% to parents; 2% to relatives	2%	4%	33% in care; 14% in long-term care	10%
McMurtry & Lie (1992) p. 44	775 Arizona children	29% to parents	9%	—	34% in care; 5% in planned long-term care	—
Barth, Courtney, Needell, & Johnson-Reid (1994) p. 19	7,709 California children in first placement with nonrelatives; followed 4 years	54%	9%	—	22%	—
Davis, English, & Landsverk (1995) p. 121	1,165 California & Washington children under 13	66%	14%	—	15%	4% guardian-ship

*C G = Control Group

**Control group data are indicated in parentheses.

APPENDIX 10.2   *Placement Options for Children Leaving Foster Care*

Source	Characteristics of Sample	Reunified	Adopted	Emanci-pated	Long-Term Care	Other
Hubbell (1981) p. 58	Data from 1 state	56% to parents; 12% to relatives	12%	7%	—	13%
Gershenson (1983) p. 22	VCIS data from 29 states N=45,133	42% to parents; 7% to relatives	12%	9%	—	28%
Fein et al. (1983) p. 501	Connecticut children under 14 in care 30+ days N=726	73% to parents; 7% to relatives	16%	—	6%	—
National Black Child Development Institute (1989) p. 81	401 Black children from 5 major cities	55% to parents (50–77%)*; 23% to relatives (5–31%)*	7% (0–13%)*	4% (0–16%)*	—	8% guardi-anship
Tatara (1993) pp. 71–72	1989 VCIS from 25 states; children in substitute care N=136,518	63% to parents or relatives	8%	7%	—	22%
Courtney (1994) p. 88	8,748 California children in care for first time followed 3+ years	79% to parents; 4% to relatives	3%	1%	—	12%

*Data in parentheses describe the range of outcomes for various cities.

APPENDIX 10.3   *Recent Estimates of Length of Time in Care*

Source	Characteristics of Sample	Short-Stay Children	Long-Stay Children
Benedict & White (1991) pp. 49–50	689 children in care for first time	51% 6 months or less	42% 13 months or more
McMurtry & Lie (1992) p. 43	775 Arizona children in care between 1979 and 1984	Approximately 50% leave care within 6 months	—
Tatara (1993) p. 116	1989 VCIS data from 23 states; all children in substitute care	22% 6 months or less	40% 2 years or more
Wulczyn, Goerge, & Harden (1993) p. 23	Data collected between 1988–1992 in 5 states	20–30% 3 months or less	20–40% 3 years or more
Barth, Courtney, Berrick, & Albert (1994) p. 26	California data collected since 1988	30% 7 weeks or less	50% 2 1/2 years or more
Davis, English, & Landsverk (1995) p. 113	1,165 California & Washington children under age 13	46% 6 months or less	42% 13 months or more
English & Clark (1996) p. 6	77,000 Washington children in care over a 10-year period	64% 6 months or less	18% 2 years or more
U.S. Children's Bureau (3/12/99)	AFCAR data for children in care	17% less than 6 months	51% 2 years or more

11

Transitions Out of Care

In this chapter, foster care practice that facilitates effective leave-taking is considered. Returning the child to the birth family home, moving the adolescent into some type of self-support situation, leaving the child in long-term care, placement in other types of substitute care, and adoption will be discussed. In addition, moving the child from one foster home to another will be examined.

Returning Home

Children who are reunified with their parents have the shortest tenure of all children in care (Lawder, Poulin, & Andrews, 1985; Link, 1996). Goerge (1994), studying Illinois children, found that those who went home spent 51 weeks in care on the average, while other children spent 152 weeks. The probability of reunification is greatest during the first few weeks after placement and decreases as time in care goes on (Goerge, 1990; Barth, Courtney, Berrick, & Albert, 1994). Infants and children of color tend to return to parental homes at slower rates than those who are older or Caucasian (Olsen, 1982; Lawder, Poulin, & Andrews, 1985; Mech, 1985; Barth, Courtney, Berrick, & Albert, 1994; Davis, English, & Landsverk, 1995). Following the care careers of California children for four years, Barth, Courtney, Needell, and Jonson-Reid (1994) reported that 39 percent of those placed as infants but more than half of older children were eventually reunified (p. 19.1). Forty percent of the African American children, 59 percent of Caucasians, and 62 percent of Hispanics in this sample went home (p. 21).

Returning children home does not comprise a single event but a series of decisions made with and on behalf of the family. Reunification may be said to "begin" at the point where worker and family start to seriously discuss the child's possible return, proceeds to actual physical placement of the child, and continues through a subsequent period of family readjustment (Plumer, 1992; Bullock, Little, & Millham, 1993).

For the worker, "one of the major challenges in family reunification practice is working with family members to assess whether and when they are ready to be reunited" (Maluccio, Warsh, & Pine, 1993, p. 14). What is involved here is a balancing of the children's need for family connectedness with the parents' abilities to provide proper care, an assessment of potential risks to children's safety weighted against consideration of the parents' desire to have their children reintegrated into the family. As with most child welfare decisions, the outcome is rarely unambiguous; most children are returned to families who have clear strengths but who must also deal with continuing vulnerabilities.

In many instances, events related to a child's return home are in line with the intent of foster care: the child's mother and father have progressed sufficiently in overcoming parenting difficulties, the parents have worked on personal problems that interfered with effective childrearing, and the child has made gains in care that permit a safe return home (Stein, Gambrill, & Wiltse, 1978; Fanshel, 1982). Children who come into care because of physical illness of a parent or because of situational stress are more likely to return home than those who are neglected, abused, or abandoned, or who have parents who abuse drugs (Fanshel, 1975; Jenkins & Norman, 1975; Kliman, Schaeffer, & Friedman, 1982; Lawder, Poulin, & Andrews, 1985; National Black Child Development Institute, 1991). Kliman, Schaeffer, & Friedman (1982), for example, found only one of twenty-three mentally ill mothers was able to resume care of her child after seventeen months of placement (p. 205).

However, a certain number of families, despite little or no improvement in parental functioning, have their child returned (Turner, 1986; Hess, Folaron, & Jefferson, 1992). This can occur because of persistent pressure from family members to have the child back (Thoburn, 1980; Kliman, Schaeffer, & Friedman, 1982; Yoshikami, 1984; Fisher, Marsh, Phillips, & Sainsbury, 1986; Farmer & Parker, 1991). Reunification can also occur because the agency can no longer use the child's foster home but is having great difficulty finding a suitable replacement; at times, it occurs as a result of the sheer length of time the child has been in care (Fanshel, Finch, & Grundy, 1990; Fein & Staff, 1993; Bullock, Little, & Millham, 1993; Jones, 1993). In a detailed study of twenty-four families, Bullock and his colleagues (1993) found "reunion is more likely to be negotiated informally between relatives and offspring even in defiance of social work decisions" (p. 76).

Although there is a tendency to concentrate on the positive impact on the family of returning the child home, even to sometimes picture it as a "rapturous experience, the stuff of which made many good 'B' movies" (Fisher, Marsh, & Phillips, 1986; Bullock, Little, & Millham, 1993), this change point in the life of the family naturally brings with it renewal of old fears and uncertainties, remembrance of old pain, worry about the future, and much upheaval (Rzepnicki, 1987; Plumer, 1992; Fein & Staff, 1993; Maluccio, Warsh, & Pine, 1993). This, like other major transitions in children's lives, "is likely to lead to regression and developmental interruption" (Fahlberg, 1991, p. 199).

When children yearn to return home, what they remember is "a static view of the situation as they had once known it" (Bullock, Little, & Millham, 1993,

p. 152). Children develop strategies to "reoccupy lost territory," fantasizing about the way they will return with their possessions to take back the place they held in the family when they left. It comes as a considerable shock for some to discover that this is not a realistic expectation for reunion. Among the 247 children who had been in care for less than six months in Bullock and his colleagues' study, one in five returned to a differently configured family. (See also Farmer & Parker, 1991; Folaron, 1993.) Many children also find themselves living in different housing in new neighborhoods and going to new schools.

For most families, the process of reunification follows a pattern that parallels the process of adjustment found among children entering care. A period of bewilderment and uncertainty is followed by a honeymoon period, typified by feelings of elation and warm welcome. Quarrels signal the end of this stage and a move toward more normalized relations (Bullock, Little, & Millham, 1993; Zamosky, Sparks, Hatt, & Sharman, 1993). Frequently, families need help to understand this process and to anticipate common problems of readjustment (Project CRAFT, 1980; Lahti & Dvorak, 1981; Zamosky, Sparks, Hatt, & Sharman, 1993).

In an English study of family reunification, Farmer and Parker (1991) evaluated the outcome as positive or adequate for 79 percent of the children and unsatisfactory or detrimental for 19 percent (p. 29). For families where maltreatment has occurred, there is an ongoing need for supportive services, since reunification is associated with some likelihood of reabuse (Solnit, Nordhaus, & Lord, 1992; Davis, English, & Landsverk, 1995). Reabuse rates ranging from 13 to 55 percent have been reported (Barth & Berry, 1987).

Yet reabuse is not the only post-reunification problem to occur. Some children return to homes in which other parenting deficiencies, serious family disorganization, intense stress, and violence continue to be evident (Rzepnicki, 1987; Wald, Carlsmith, & Leiderman, 1988; Simms & Bolden, 1991; Fein & Staff, 1993; Festinger, 1994). In Bullock, Little, and Millham's (1993) study, three-fifths of the children who had been in care for six months to two years returned to homes where the "relationships between mother and child was [not] warm, accepting and affectionate" (p. 74). Some returns occurring after more than two years of placement were "fraught with conflict and some occur[red] in the absence of any alternative for the young person; living with an abusing father can be better than the shelter of a cardboard box" (p. 77). Reunification under these conditions is particularly worrisome since, in at least one study, it was families who did not receive supportive services while the child was in care who were more likely to have the child subsequently returned home (Davis, English, & Landsverk, 1995, pp. 65–66).

Reunifying a child under such circumstances may challenge the developmental progress the child had been making while in foster family care. "Studies consistently show that children who are returned home have inferior measureable developmental outcomes" (Barth & Berry, 1987, p. 77). The overall adjustment of these children is also poorer. Weiner and Weiner (1990), examining the experiences of Israeli children in care, described one group who were placed in infancy because of parental physical or mental health problems. Although these children were the healthiest and best developed while in placement, after return:

> their language was often unclear, their energy level was low, and their abilities to organize their thinking and respond to intellectual challenges were lower than the other groups. When asked to describe what pleased them, they often could not respond. (p. 72)

A second group of children, returned after spending much of their childhood in placement, "were more likely than most other groups to have learning, behavioral and emotional problems" (p. 76). Declines in academic performance are also found among these children (Kliman, Schaeffer, & Friedman, 1982; Wald, Carlsmith, & Leiderman, 1988; Davis, English, & Landsverk, 1995).

There is further need to help individual family members whose vulnerabilities were evident prior to or during the placement. Studying foster care in San Diego County, Davis, English, and Landsverk (1995) found that children with a diagnosed mental illness, severe behavioral problems, and school problems were overrepresented among those who were reunified (p. 61). Festinger's (1994) study of children returned to their families found "nearly one-third of the children (32.9%) were considered to have one or more moderate or severe problems at the time they were discharged home" (p. 26). Children who return home with a great deal of unresolved rage can prove especially challenging for the birth family and can overwhelm one that is already fragile or disorganized (Folaron, 1993).

Birth parents, too, continue to need assistance with personal difficulties (Fein et al., 1983). Berrick, Needell, Barth, and Jonson-Reid's (1998) study of infants in care noted many ongoing problems:

> It is arguable whether the families who "succeed" in the child welfare system, by achieving the goal of having their children returned home and remain at home for at least two years would generally be labeled so by the public at large. Over one-third of the mothers were still using drugs when their children were returned to their care, 55 percent had continued mental health problems, 21 percent had engaged in more criminal behavior during their children's absence, and 36 percent had new or continuing housing problems. Even if the mothers were viewed as successful by virtue of sufficiently meeting the requirements of their case plans, the likelihood that their infants would thrive under such circumstances and become part of a "succeeding generation" is slim. (p. 115)

(See also Kliman, Schaeffer, & Friedman, 1982; CWLA, 1992a.)

Reunification Services

Well-designed, appropriate, and intensive services, provided over a sufficient period of time after the child's return, can help families successfully navigate through the reunification period (Block & Libowitz, 1983; Weiner & Weiner, 1990; CWLA, 1991a, 1992a, 1995; Hess, Folaron, & Jefferson, 1992; Plumer, 1992; Fein &

Staff, 1993; Davis & Ellis-MacLeod, 1994; Davis, English, & Landsverk, 1995). There is now widespread recognition of the need for such services and some evidence of efforts to make them more consistently available (Simms & Bolden, 1991; Boutilier & Rehm, 1993; Maluccio, Warsh, & Pine, 1993). The U.S. Children's Bureau recently funded a series of Family Reunification Demonstration Projects that achieved a 75 percent success rate, reducing the length of time children spent in care and lessening the likelihood they would reenter care (Rzepnicki, 1987; Terpstra & McFadden, 1993; Smollar, N.D.). However, the many vulnerabilities of families and the high cost of these services suggest the need for them will continue to outstrip availability (Fein & Maluccio, 1992; Tatara, 1994; Wulczyn, 1994).

Like programs that help parents while children are in care, aftercare services often fail to reach out to and nurture supportive efforts by the extended family or by foster parents. Extended family members may play a critical role by offering child care and direct help to parents who are overwhelmed by immediate needs and crises (Bullock, Little, & Millham, 1993). Foster parents play a similar role for some families. "Many parents who have successfully reunited with their children credit foster parents who were available to help with problems, give advice, or 'just be there when I needed someone'" (Folaron, 1993, p. 150. See also Maluccio, Kriegert, & Pine, 1990; Bullock, Little, & Millham, 1993; CWLA, 1995).

Because foster parents may believe that they are not permitted to maintain ties with a child leaving placement, they need to have agency assurances that such support is appropriate and useful. A survey of families whose foster homes had been closed in Alaska (Baring-Gould et al., 1983) disclosed that 69 percent had never been informed of the child's subsequent adjustment, and 74 percent were not encouraged to stay in touch with the child (p. 57). Hubbell (1981) described the experiences of parents who had cared for seven foster children:

> They have not tried to contact any of the children. They admit that they were "kind of afraid to. We'd love to know what's happening but how would the parents feel? If one of our foster kids goes on to another foster home and we contacted him, it might interfere with the new relationship. One of our (former foster) children called once and the (new) foster parents didn't like it." (pp. 122–123)

Foster parents like these remain an untapped resource for birth families.

Foster Parents' Separation Work

While birth parents work to make a new place for their children in the family, foster families must grieve the loss of a cherished family member (Takas & Warner, 1992; Mansfield, 1993). Siu and Hogan (1989) described this as a crisis of "dismemberment" (p. 342). The support of the foster care worker is crucial in this process, particularly if the agency hopes to place another child in the foster home; however, many agencies fail to recognize this need (Sellick, 1992). Some workers believe that foster parents "are not entitled to feel sad or angry since relinquishing the child is part of the job or since the child's best interests, not their own, are what matter" (Steinhauer, 1991, p. 192). Failure to recognize the foster family's right to mourn this loss can create problems in future work with the family and can contribute to the foster parents' decision to terminate their contract with the agency.

For kinship caretakers, the child's return to birth parents can also evoke grief responses. At the very least, the role of kin in the child's day-to-day life will be changing. Grandmothers and aunts, who may have been caring for these children for some considerable period of time, may be anxious and worried about their care and ambivalent about the advisability of the move itself. All of these factors can make grief work more difficult for them. The supportive services of foster care workers can be particularly helpful during this transition. "Because of the feelings involved in possible shifts in relationships among the triad, the worker's skills in this phase are important" (Jackson, 1999, p. 109). The goals here are to recognize the losses and concerns of all parties while helping family members offer one another as much support as possible.

Replacement after Reunification

Considering the range of ongoing problems and challenges faced by reunified families, it should come as no surprise that, for a certain number of them, the child's return is not a stable option, and placement is, once again, a necessity. Recognition of the importance of this issue can be traced as far back as 1913, when the Boston Children's Aid Society expressed concern (Pelton, 1989). Appendix 11.1 summarizes recent estimates of the extent to which children are replaced in care.

While these data suggest the most likely outcome for children is to remain with their families after return, anywhere from 15 to 30 percent will eventually go back into care. "Sooner or later," according to Maluccio, Warsh, and Pine (1993), "a substantial proportion of children who are returned to their families reenter some form of out-of-home placement or another helping system, such as juvenile justice or mental health" (p. 3). Since replacement can occur after some time in the home, studies that follow children for longer periods tend to report higher replacement rates.

We have already pointed out that reunification stability is linked to the provision of relevant, good quality services to the family after the child's return. Other family characteristics and circumstances are also linked to reentry. Children are more vulnerable to replacement when they are infants, African American, and from poorer families (Courtney, 1995.) Reentering children are more likely to be those who are difficult to live with. This includes children with mental or developmental disabilities and those with severe behavior problems (Rzepnicki, 1987; Davis, English, & Landsverk, 1993). Some studies suggest that children who recidivate tend to have been in substitute care for a longer time before being reunified (Lahti & Dvorak, 1981), while other research indicates that it is short-stay children who are most vulnerable to return (Davis, English, & Landsverk, 1995; Berrick, Needell, Barth, & Jonson-Reid, 1998).

Bullock and his colleagues (1993) found that there are actually four different groups of returning children. "Short-Term Breakdowns" are children who had initially been in care for only a brief period of time. For the majority of this group, a second family reunification resulted in placement stability. "Oscillators" were initially in placement for short (less than six months) or intermediate time periods (seven to twenty-four months). No particular family characteristics distinguished this group. "All they seem to have in common is their failure to settle" (p. 92). The third and fourth groups were primarily comprised of teenagers. "Adolescents Seeking Independence" were in care for at least six months. Perceptions among family members that the teenager was well adjusted and well accepted were influential in determining stability of these reunifications. The final group, considered "Homeless and Skill-Less," came out of long-term foster care and comprised a "small group of adolescents who not only fail to find succor in the family home but who are also bereft of the social skills which enable them to survive alone" (p. 86).

In contrast to these findings, Festinger's (1994) follow-up study of 210 reunified families concluded that it was not children's qualities but parenting capacity that most strongly predicted reunification breakdown. "Particularly strong differences existed with respect to the caregivers' level of understanding of child development, quality of communication, consistency of discipline, and handling of conflict" (p. 66). In addition to parenting capability, the research found measures of social connectedness and social support to be significant. (See also Boutilier & Rehm, 1993.) Interestingly, in Festinger's research, the level of attachment between parent and child did not distinguish families who remained together from those who did not. However, research conducted by Hess, Folaron, and Jefferson (1992) suggested that "persistent ambivalence about the parental role and family reunification" contributes to reunification failure (p. 306). Studies have also linked parental mental illness, health problems, and difficulties with drug and alcohol abuse to the child's reentry into care (Turner, 1986; Hess, Folaron, & Jefferson, 1992).

One study (Berrick, Needell, Barth, & Jonson-Reid, 1998) concluded, "Children who were returned home from kinship care appeared to be less likely to reenter than were those who spent all or most of their first spell in nonkin care" (p. 68). However, further analysis of their data revealed that this was primarily true for children living with kin who had not received federal foster care subsidies (p. 69).

For those who return to care, reunification is a bittersweet experience. On the one hand, evidence indicates that these children benefit from reconnection with their siblings and extended family and from contact with neighbors and friends during the reunification period (Weiner & Weiner, 1990). At the same time, they view the return to placement as another failure on their own and their parents' parts, an inability to make this important relationship work. There is a further danger that, for these children, "separation, far from being an unwelcome incident in life's rich pattern, is likely to become the pattern itself" (Bullock, Little, & Millham, 1993, p. 148; see also Steinhauer, 1991). The desirability of making an effort to better understand the dynamics of such situations and to explore means of minimizing the likelihood of reentry is evident from these findings. (See also Courtney & Barth, 1996.)

The J Case

After spending eighteen months in foster family care, Timothy returned home to live with his family. This has been a challenging transition for him, but he has worked to maintain his grades in school and, thus far, has avoided serious altercations with his stepfather. However, there is frequent tension in the home, and Timothy is easily caught up in the struggle to protect his mother when his father becomes aggressive. It has not been easy for him to find a place with his siblings; verbal (and sometimes physical) fights have been common among the five children in the home.

Since Timothy's return, Mrs. J has periodically contacted the worker to talk through issues and to help her make decisions. The worker appreciates this link to the family and is happy to serve in this advisory role. Mrs. J has, for the first time, considered the possibility of leaving Mr. J, and the worker feels she might do so if he becomes dangerous once again.

The foster care worker recognizes that this may not be a long-term option for Timothy. She would not be surprised to find he has to leave home again at some point in his adolescence. She suspects that Timothy will be highly resistant to making a move back into foster family care and that, without his cooperation, such a move would not be feasible. He has maintained informal contact with Rod Tedesco, and Rod has offered him a place to stay if "things just get too hot at home." Rod and the worker hope Timothy will take advantage of this offer if needed.

Rod is currently considering accepting another foster child for placement.

Emancipation

Children are emancipated from the foster care system via one of three primary routes. Because some children have both the desire and the skills necessary to live on their own, the agency may decide to support such a plan, particularly if the youth is an older teenager. The second and perhaps the largest group of adolescents to be emancipated are those who reach an age at which the agency can no longer provide services for them. In most states this is the age of 18, although some now permit children to continue in care until they reach 21. While some youths in this group are ill-prepared to live on their own, no other options may be available for them in the child welfare system. A third group leave care on their own volition without the support or approval of the agency, but for a variety of reasons the agency decides not to insist that they return to care. These are considered "unplanned" emancipations. Some adolescents who repeatedly run away are found in this group.

One estimate of the need for emancipation services is based on the assumption that many, if not most, teens in care could benefit from some level of assistance in their growth toward greater autonomy. Drawing on VCIS data from 1989, Tatara (1993) described 41 percent of the children leaving care as 13 or older (p. 62). A study of children in care for two or more years in Connecticut (Kluger, Maluccio, & Fein, 1989) found that foster parents believed only one in three of the sixteen to twenty year olds were well prepared for independent living; social workers felt that half the youths were ready (p. 82). Caregivers of 431 youths in foster care in Washington state (English, Kouidou-Giles, & Plocke, 1994) thought 56 percent "could live independently" (p. 151). The Child Welfare League of America (1993) noted that "unfortunately, less than half of the youths discharged from out-of-home care receive assistance in developing specific skills that will enable them to live on their own" (p. 11).

Another estimate of service need focuses on teens who may be most cut off from adult guidance and support, those leaving care who are not planning to stay on with foster parents or return to their birth parents' homes. Tatara (1993) cited a figure of 7 percent (p. 71). Courtney and Barth (1996), considering California teens aged seventeen or older who had been in care for at least eighteen months, found 60 percent were in this situation. An additional nine percent had unknown plans because they had run away or "refused" service (p. 77). Fanshel, Finch, and Grundy (1990), studying children leaving the Casey Family Program (a foster care service for troubled children who were not likely to return home), found 37 percent were going to live on their own at age eighteen, 18 percent were going to do so at a younger age, and 4 percent had run away. Only 20 percent were returning to birth parents' homes (p. 72).

Teens in foster family care share with all adolescents the task of growing toward more mature adulthood. This includes the responsibility for greater self-support, for increasingly looking to peers for significant social ties, and, in our culture, for eventually living apart from parents (Lammert & Timberlake, 1986). However, the circumstances under which adolescents in care must address these tasks creates special burdens and stresses for them. Unlike most older youths living at home, teens in foster care do not have a major voice in determining how long they stay with their foster families. Instead, the child welfare agency and the courts hold this right. Children living with their birth families are not expected to "turn away" from them or to sever ties to them in young adulthood; many foster parents and the youths who live with them believe that this is required (Stein & Carey, 1986; Cook, 1988; Inglehart, 1995). Leaving the foster family home may also entail leaving friends, a neighborhood, and a community, and separating from the adults who have most strongly encouraged them to be productive at school and on the job (Project CRAFT, 1980; Zimmerman, 1982; Festinger, 1983; Maluccio & Fein, 1985a; Beyer, 1986). Ties to birth family members may be tenuous, leaving these youths feeling that they are completely alone and isolated in the world. The process of leaving foster family care also reactivates old separation issues for children who may have a substantial history of losses by the time they reach their teen years (Land, 1990).

Attachment and loss themes that have been evident throughout the child's stay are again highly salient at this time. Stein and Carey (1986) suggested the use of "interdependent" rather than "independent" living skills when considering programming for this group:

> The dominant 'independence' message of 'managing on your own' and 'coping by yourself' subtly negates the significance of *interdependence,* that is, young people giving as well as taking, getting on with other people and negotiating reality with the support of agencies, neighbours, friends and partners; the very important interpersonal and relationsip skills that our young people needed all the time, and which they often found so difficult. (p. 158)

(See also Downes, 1993.)

Helping these adolescents build social skills involves assistance in making decisions regarding contacts with birth and foster families, building new friendships, and enhancing their relationships with roommates and coworkers (Stein & Carey, 1986; Aldgate, Maluccio, & Reeves, 1989; Barth, 1989). Although birth family connections may have been tenuous or absent (Kluger, Maluccio, & Fein, 1989), many teens seek opportunities to reestablish or strengthen these connections during this time. Support and encouragement for this effort from foster parents and the foster care worker are vital (Bullock, Little, & Millham, 1993). "A trusted foster parent standing alongside an adolescent while he meets with his parents may lend strength to the process of reappraisal and renegotiation" (Downes, 1993, p. 74). Adolescents are particularly in need of adult guidance in sorting out expectations and dealing with the reality of birth family life, once contact with their parents has been made (Beyer, 1986). Adolescents may find their parents can be helpful in unexpected ways or that other members of their extended family can be supportive, even when birth parents cannot be (Carbino, 1990; U.S. House of Representatives Committee on Ways and Means, 1993).

A number of older teens in care have developed strong, nurturant ties to foster parents (Kluger, Maluccio, & Fein, 1989; McDonald, Allen, Westerfelt, & Piliavin, 1993). As they move into adult roles, the foster family can become a "family of resource" for them (Fahlberg, 1991). This involves a joint effort between the foster family and the youth to recognize and support their continued relationship, use of foster parents for advice and counseling, and reliance on the foster home as a safe haven in times of uncertainty or change (Land, 1990; Bullock, Little, & Millham, 1993; Downes, 1993).

Maintaining and strengthening ties to birth and foster families is linked to the development of greater effectiveness in general social skills. Bullock and his colleagues (1993) have found that teens who have highly conflicted and mistrustful relationships with adult caretakers also tend to have bereft or conflict-laden peer networks. Thus the strengthening of general social skills must be embedded in strengthened ties to significant adults.

Services to teens leaving care also encompass a group of "tangible life skills." Summarizing the results of a London study, Bullock and his colleagues (1993) captured the range of concerns here:

After leaving care, the young people proved very mobile. Only 20% stayed in the same place for two years. Most hated living alone and had all kinds of difficulties, from rows with neighbours to poor sleep or extreme fears. They left the lonely situations of flats or bedsits and moved quickly to group or shared situations. None undertook further education and all were fitful in employment. Former care-givers occasionally proved important sources of support, especially foster parents who were often seen as 'family.' Most young people, however, continued to be dependent on welfare agencies and viewed the decisions made about them as being largely out of their hands. (p. 33)

U.S. studies have also documented the limited educational attainment, poor job preparation, minimal work experience, and lack of self-support capabilities of many emancipated adolescents (Beyer, 1986; Cook, 1988; Kluger, Maluccio, & Fein, 1989; CWLA, 1993; U.S. House of Representatives Committee on Ways and Means, 1993). A 1992 Westat study, following youths for two to four years after leaving care, did not find improvement in employment or in self-support abilities during that time (Cook, 1994). Many young adults in the sample had periods when they were homeless. (See also Maluccio, Krieger, & Pine, 1990; McDonald, Allen, Westerfelt, & Piliavin, 1993.) Thus, help to enhance educational and occupational capabilities are practical components of any interdependent living service (ILS) (North, Mallabar, & Desrochers, 1988; Barth, 1989). Specific needs may also encompass learning to take responsibility for the tasks of day-to-day living, such as balancing a checkbook, cleaning, and shopping. Finding and maintaining suitable housing and making decisions about living alone or with others are also among areas of concern (Stein & Carey, 1986; Irvine, 1988; Brickman, Dey, & Cuthbert, 1991).

One study found 91 percent of adolescents leaving foster care were sexually active within a year of discharge (CWLA, 1993, p. 16). The 1992 Westat follow-up survey found 60 percent of young women leaving care had become pregnant (Cook, 1994, p. 222). Youths in aftercare are also highly vulnerable to infection from sexually transmitted diseases (CWLA, 1993). Preparation for emancipation needs to incorporate some training in this area. Helping emancipated adolescents grow toward maturity may also require some special services, such as treatment for drug and alcohol abuse, help for emotional difficulties, particularly depression, and assistance in meeting other health needs (Pine, Krieger, & Maluccio, 1990; CWLA, 1993; Cook, 1994; English, Kouidou-Giles, & Plocke, 1994; Inglehart, 1994).

Programming for emancipated youths has been enhanced by passage of PL 99-272, the Independent Living Initiative. This 1986 legislation established targeted ILS funding and specified that evaluation of youths' need for emancipation services be included in case plans. Youths in foster care who are sixteen to eighteen were initially eligible for services; subsequent passage of PL 101-508 allowed states to extend services up to the age of twenty-one (Hardin, 1987; CWLA, 1993). By 1992, estimates of potential recipients ranged from 65 in Wyoming to 18,000 in California (CLWA, 1993, pp. 31–33). All states and the District of Columbia now provide some ILS programming; for more than half, this legislation spurred the first statewide effort in this area (Allen, Bonner, & Greeman, 1988).

Interdependent living services may be offered to youth before they leave the foster family home ("pre-emancipation phase"), while they are in the process of leaving the home ("emancipation phase"), and after they go on to more self-sufficient housing ("post-emancipation phase" or "aftercare") (Irvine, 1988; Land, 1990). In the pre-emancipation phase, foster parents play a central role in helping youths to learn skills that support greater autonomy (Kluger, Maluccio, & Fein, 1989; Carten, 1990; Land, 1990; Downes, 1993). "Given the restricted time frame foster parents have to help youths in their homes, they must consciously set about teaching these young people skills many other youngsters have acquired by the same age" (Ryan, McFadden, Rice, & Warren, 1988, pp. 565–566). Agency training and supervision may be required for foster parents involved with this task.

During emancipation and aftercare phases, it is recommended that a variety of housing options, varying in intensity of adult supervision, be made available (Aldgate, Maluccio, & Reeves, 1989; Brickman, Dey, & Cuthbert, 1991). Examples include:

- placing the youth in an apartment with other youths, supervised by an adult caretaker who helps establish and monitor rules for day-to-day living
- placing the youth in a boarding-house type of situation, where he or she lives with a family; meals may be provided, but the youth is not seen as a family member
- helping the youth "match up" with other youths who are interested in shared housing
- providing financial subsidies to help pay the start-up costs of independent housing (Cook, 1988; Kroner, 1988; Meston, 1988; Sims, 1988; Barth, 1989)

(For descriptions of specific programs, see Pasztor, Clarren, Timberlake, & Bayless, 1986; Barth, 1989; Jones, 1989; Wedeven & Mavzerall, 1990; CWLA, 1993.)

ILS programs could be strengthened by expansion of aftercare services (Mech & Leonard, 1988). A CWLA (1993) survey of member agencies found only 16 percent offered such help, and the majority of these followed youths for only three to six months after discharge (p. 18). While many ILS programs focus on educational and occupational planning and housing needs, dialogue around sexual behavior and avoidance of alcohol or drugs are often overlooked. A study of more than 800 children who were eight or older and in care in Baltimore (Risley-Curtiss, 1997) found one in three who admitted being sexually active (p. 486). However, the CWLA survey found that, while 42 percent offered youths some type of health education, only 17 percent addressed sexuality issues; an even smaller number, 7 percent, offered drug education (p. 17). In another survey of state agencies, Polit, White, and Morton (1987) found only nine of forty-eight had some type of written policy on sex education and family planning services for children in foster family care. "Almost all states conceive of their role in this area as a reactive one," allowing for child welfare involvement "only after the agency had determined that the adolescent was sexually active, and in many cases only when the client had asked for information about family planning" (p. 21).

Emancipation programs are more likely to reflect tangible life skill training than social skill training (CWLA, 1993; Cook, 1994; Waldinger & Furman, 1994) and to focus more on outcomes (i.e., getting a GED or a job) than on maturational processes (i.e., moving into more equitable and responsible adult relationships). To establish programs that address relational issues in meaningful ways, agencies must grapple with a number of difficult questions. Among them are the following:

1. For ILS programs that have a limited amount of time to work with clients, what are realistic goals for improvement in relational abilities? For some children, services may be able to accomplish little beyond superficial adaptation.
2. How can ILS programs intervene effectively with teens whose attachment problems and relational deficits are deep-seated and long-standing? Many of these teens enter the program believing themselves to be failures and expecting others to fail them (Brickman, Dey, & Cuthbert, 1991; Bullock, Little, & Millham, 1993). Working to break down these barriers can pose a substantial challenge.
3. How can the agency find effective means to make work done in the program have impact on a teen's real-world relationships? To adequately address relational concerns, programming must be able to facilitate the building and maintaining of ties with family members and significant others in healthy and growth-producing ways for the adolescent (Carbino, 1990; Land, 1990; Inglehart, 1995). To do this, program staff may have to either bring those significant others into the agency or find ways to monitor progress made by participants when they are "out of sight" of program personnel.
4. How can program staff avoid the pitfall of considering themselves "substitute" attachment figures for adolescents? This is a particular challenge with teens who are alone and bereft (Taber & Proch, 1988) and longing for someone to take care of them. Careful supervision helps staff realize that offering themselves as attachment figures merely insures youths another major loss at the point of program completion.

Adoption

When children cannot return to their parents' home from foster family care, the child welfare worker seeks some other permanent family for them. This can involve, for the child, a move out of foster care and into the home of a new adoptive family. It can also involve a change in the foster parents' status so that they can become the child's permanent adoptive family. The latter type of adoption is the one that we will consider in this section of the chapter.

Because preference in adoption is given to individuals who already have a close relationship with the child, who give evidence of a capacity to parent effectively, and who are willing to make a commitment to carry out this role, child welfare workers are now more likely to consider whether kin and non-kin foster parents are equipped to take on this responsibility (Mica & Vosler, 1990). Pecora, Whittaker, and Maluccio (1992) described the benefits of such placements for the child:

> The advantages of fost-adoptions are the continuity of home life afforded the child, the retention of a familiar community, the ability for ongoing assessment of the placement, and the involvement of the child in the decision to adopt. Fost-adoptions can begin when the children are younger and more able to bond with a new family—even if custody battles stretch out in the courts over years. Adoptive parents who were previously foster parents are also reported to be more accepting of ongoing contact with the agency—especially when problems arise. (p. 382)

(See also Meezan & Shireman, 1985.)

Support for foster parent adoption by the agency has been termed "fost-adopt," or "legal risk," or "at risk" adoption (Mica & Vosler, 1990). The National Adoption Information Clearinghouse (Smith, 1995) estimated that foster parents become permanent parents to between 40 and 80 percent of children who are adopted through public agencies (p. 2). A national study of foster parents (James Bell Associates, 1993) found 31 percent of respondents had adopted and, of these, three-quarters had adopted foster children (p. 97).

In fact, this represents "a significant change in the attitude of social service professionals toward foster parents' becoming adoptive parents" (Derdeyn, 1990). In the past, foster parents were discouraged or forbidden to adopt because this was considered a conflict of interest; there was concern that genuine efforts to reunify children with their birth families would not be made if foster families were encouraged to make a permanent commitment to the children (Mica & Vosler, 1990; Pecora, Whittaker, & Maluccio, 1992; Meezan, 1994; Smith, 1995). Careful use of concurrent planning, which involves an intensive effort toward reunification while adoption possibilities are being explored, is one means whereby birth parent needs and rights can be respected during this process (Berrick, Needell, Barth, & Jonson-Reid, 1998).

Critics of foster parent adoption have warned that foster care applicants are not evaluated or screened at the same level of intensity that adoptive applicants are. They have further argued that extensive use of adoption will draw resources away from foster family care. However, data from the James Bell Associates (1993) survey disputed this claim, leading the authors to state: "it does not appear that adoption in and of itself is a deterrent to foster parent retention" (p. 97).

Meezan and Shireman (1985) conducted an evaluation of the Foster Parent Adoption Project in Chicago. The authors concluded:

> These findings seem to indicate that agencies that distinguish between short-term and long-term foster homes and that encourage long-term foster homes to think

about the possibility of adoption early in the placement should continue to do so, and that other agencies should adopt these practices. Many foster parents can identify themselves as potential adopters at intake, and agencies should capitalize on this ability. (p. 217)

A second study of older children conducted by Triseliotis and Hill (1990) found that adoption provided the children with a sense of "security and full belonging" (p. 114) not available to those in long-term foster care. Research has suggested that foster parent adoption is facilitated when children already have a close and positive relationship with their foster parents (Meezan & Shireman, 1985; Drotar & Stege, 1988) and where foster care workers provide consistent support for this effort (Meezan & Shireman, 1985). Interestingly, the Meezan and Shireman (1985) research also found that children who had ongoing contact with their birth families were more likely to eventually be adopted by their foster parents; decreasing birth family contact was more typical for children who remained in long-term foster family care.

While informal adoption by kin has a long history, particularly in the African American community (Sandven & Resnick, 1990), pursuing the goal of formal kinship adoption has not been a successful strategy for many children in this type of care. In the instances where it has been achieved, it has usually taken several years to accomplish (Link, 1996). In the 1991/1992 fiscal year, 27 percent of children placed for adoption by public agencies in California went to kin homes (Magruder, 1994). However, Barth, Courtney, and Needell (1994), following children in foster care over a four-year period beginning in 1988, found that 14 percent of those placed with non-kin but only 5 percent of those placed with kin had actually been adopted (pp. 6–7). Gleeson, O'Donnell, and Bonecutter (1997) examined 77 kinship care families participating in a demonstration project to enhance permanency in Chicago. While workers described two-thirds of the families as willing to consider adoption, active planning toward this goal was undertaken with only one-third of the cases during the two-year time span of the study (pp. 812–813). Flango and Flango (1995) indicated wide variability among the states in use of relative adoptions by public agencies. While Iowa, Rhode Island, and West Virginia had less than five percent of their public agency adoptions with kin in 1992, California, Michigan, and Hawaii made one-quarter of their adoptions in this way (p. 1029).

A number of studies describe kin as less interested in pursuing this type of permanency arrangement (Thornton, 1991; Berrick, Barth, & Needell, 1994; McLean & Thomas, 1996). "In many cases, the required termination of parental rights could strain relationships and set back hard-won gains" (Takas & Hegar, 1999, p. 59). Some kin caretakers worry that finalizing the placement would leave birth parents feeling abandoned and demoralized (Testa, Shook, Cohen, & Woods, 1996; Gleeson, O'Donnell, & Bonecutter, 1997); for other families, there is a desire to avoid unwanted conflict with birth parents.

At least one study (Testa, Shook, Cohen, & Woods, 1996) suggested that relatives may be more interested in becoming adoptive parents than was previously thought. Kin appear to feel it is more appropriate to consider this as an option when young children are placed in their care (Link, 1996; Testa, Shook, Cohen, & Woods, 1996). A special program designed to help children in kinship homes achieve a permanent outcome has been effective in enhancing placement stability and increasing the number of adoptions (Mills & Usher, 1996).

An alternative arrangement is to designate kin as the child's guardian. "Guardianship provides a means for kin to assume parental responsibility and authority without permanently severing parental rights" (CWLA, 1994, pp. 67–68). This would add a measure of stability to the placement but not force birth parents to abandon all responsibility for their children (Gleeson, 1995; Hornby, Zeller, & Karraker, 1996). The Adoption and Safe Families Act of 1997 talks about the use of permanent legal guardianship. Pennsylvania, for example, has amended its laws to make this option available. However, guardianship does not fully protect the rights of kin to care for children, and it does not give kin the opportunity to receive adoption subsidies (Takas, 1993; Gleeson, O'Donnell, & Bonecutter, 1997; Takas & Hegar, 1999).

Scannapieco and Hegar (1999) recommended development of a new legal status they term "kinship adoption." They explained:

> Kinship adoption could involve either or both of two key differences from traditional adoption:
>
> 1. relinquishment or termination of the parental rights of **one but not both** parents (as in stepparent adoption), and/or
> 2. relinquishment or termination of **some but not all** parental rights of both parents (similar to open adoption with enforceable postadoptive visitation). (p. 60, emphases in original)

They argued that such an arrangement would create legal security for the child and family but not remove all birth parent rights unless they were detrimental to the child.

Sometimes agency practices serve as a deterrent to adoptions by kin caretakers. A Chicago study revealed:

> The complicated, bureaucratic child welfare and juvenile court systems were also cited as frustrations and as obstacles to permanency for children in kinship care. Caseworkers described problems processing adoption subsidies in a timely manner. They stated that difficulties getting payment approval prevented access to specialized services for some children and biological parents. Long delays at juvenile court were also noted as frustrations for caseworkers. (Gleeson, O'Donnell, & Bonecutter, 1997, p. 817)

The need to address insufficiencies in the level of financial support to adoptive kin families is also noted in other studies (Meezan & Shireman, 1985; Magruder, 1994).

Moving into Other Types of Care

Because children may come into care with a variety of emotional and interpersonal problems, some of which may be severe, foster care workers will find that some of them are in need of services that are more intense, more therapeutic, and sometimes more restrictive than can be provided in regular foster care placements. Options that might be considered for such children include:

1. Placement in a group home setting, where the children can interact more intensively with peers and less intensively with adults. Group home placements may or may not offer intensive therapy as an integral aspect of services.
2. Placement in a residential treatment center for emotionally disturbed children. Here milieu therapy and intensive individual and group intervention are common aspects of service, and the child's emotional difficulties and interpersonal problems are a focal point for treatment.
3. Placement in a psychiatric hospital for severely emotionally disturbed children. Services offered by this type of facility are similar to those made available to children in residential treatment centers. The focal point for treatment is the severe psychiatric problems of the child, and funding is provided under mental health auspices. In recent years, the length of stay in this type of facility has been considerably shorter than that found among children in group or residential care.
4. Placement in a therapeutic foster home, where specially trained foster parents provide services and supports similar to those made available in residential care. However, the facility is more home-like, and the children interact with a much smaller number of peers than they would in the other types of placements (Shaw & Hipgrave, 1983; Stepleton, 1987; Hampson, 1988; Webb, 1988; Hawkins & Breiling, 1989; Foster Family-based Treatment Association, 1991).

(See also Kadushin & Martin, 1988; Cohen, 1992; Pecora, Whittaker, & Maluccio, 1992.)

The number of foster children who are moved into these types of facilities from foster family care is unknown, since no data on this change in care are routinely made available by child welfare agencies. In fact, we have no consistent national data at all about children receiving these services. The "most recent systematic and comprehensive census of children and youth in specifically group care settings" was conducted in 1981 (Pecora, Whittaker, & Maluccio, 1992, p. 408). It should be noted that a number of children who are in need of more intensive therapeutic services will eventually return to regular foster family care or will return to their parents' homes after completing treatment.

Long-Term Foster Care

In contrast to other permanency options, where the goal is to move the child into some other type of living arrangement, the choice of long-term foster care involves a decision to maintain the child in the child welfare system for an indefinite period. Steinhauer (1991) described various circumstances under which such care may be preferred:

- for the older child who has lived as much of his life as he can remember securely attached in a foster family . . . ;
- for the older and more disturbed foster child, where the risk of removing her from a foster family that can accept her in spite of her disturbance, and in whose care she is at least holding her own, is greater than that of preserving the present placement;
- for the child over the age of four who remains obviously attached to an ineffectual but loving parent . . . ;
- for the older child who remains intensely but anxiously attached to natural parents who are neglecting or abusive. (p. 229)

(See also Fein & Maluccio, 1992; CWLA, 1995.)

Efforts to estimate the number of children for whom this option has been chosen are hampered by the lack of consistent criteria for determining what makes a placement "long-term." While some researchers use two or more years in care as a benchmark (Fein, Maluccio, & Kluger, 1990), others refer to considerably longer time frames (Barth, Courtney, Needell, & Jonson-Reid, 1994; Rowe, Cain, Hundleby, & Keane, 1984); still others give no specific period of time (Blacher, 1994). California data collected by Barth and his colleagues (1994) found 22 percent of those in foster family care have been there for four or more years (p. 19). Poulin (1992) reported that 20 to 25 percent of children were "likely to remain in care for extended periods" (pp. 65–66), while in Los Angeles, a figure of 57 percent has been cited (Blacher, 1994, p. 96).

Children may remain in care for two distinctly different reasons:

1. They are in planned long-term care; remaining in their foster home is considered the best permanency option for them. Tatara (1993) reported that in 1989 this was the goal for 11.9 percent of children in care (p. 89).
2. They remain in care inadvertently, "drifting," with no clear permanency plan or with unworkable plans that cannot come to fruition. This may occur, for example, when the child's parent is unable to provide minimally adequate care, but no other permanency options have been explored (Maluccio, Fein, & Olmstead, 1986; Steinhauer, 1991; Tolfree, 1995).

Unfortunately, research in this area does not differentiate between these two groups, so no accurate estimate of their relative size is available. Children may also move from one category to the other, making estimation particularly challenging.

In part because children may stay in care for reasons that either contribute to permanency or serve to undermine it, there has been considerable discomfort in the field about long-term foster care's viability as a planning option. Concerns have been voiced about the "danger of multiple placements, the inadequacies of foster homes in providing a sense of permanence, and the loosening of ties with the biological family" (Maluccio, Fein, & Olmstead, 1986, p. 201). However, numerous studies (Lahti et al., 1978; Fanshel, 1979; Triseliotis, 1980; Rowe, Cain, Hundleby, & Keane, 1984; Fein, Maluccio, & Kluger, 1990; Thoburn, 1990) have suggested that for the majority of such children, stability and permanence have been achieved. Stability rates in these studies ranged from 70 to 95 percent.

These studies indicated that most of the children in extended care had a sense of permanence in their placements and had foster parents who expected them to stay on indefinitely:

> The children did not just live with their families, they became part of them. The importance that the youngsters themselves placed on being in a family can scarcely be over-emphasized and not one of those we interviewed would have preferred to be in residential care. They spoke of their foster parents with genuine affection and almost all were accepted by foster grandparents and other relatives. They were growing up as normal members of their neighborhoods and communities and after leaving care had a home base from which to start adult life. (Rowe, Cain, Hundleby, & Keane, 1984, p. 223)

Rowe and her colleagues (1984) noted that while almost half of the foster parents had considered having the child removed at one time or another, for many this was only a temporary consideration, and only a few placements actually were disrupted during the time of their assessment (p. 32).

Developmentally and academically, the children showed no unusual problems (Davis, English, & Landsverk, 1995). While many of them had no contact with birth families, those who did appeared to benefit from this connection when the relationship was a positive one (Fein, Maluccio, & Kluger, 1990, p. 30).

Despite these findings, there is a lingering concern that permanency might not be fully achieved (or could be jeopardized) by long-term care (Blacher, 1994); at least five states do not recognize this type of placement as a permanency option (Hornby, Zeller, & Karraker, 1996). As we have pointed out, foster parents have only limited decision-making power in the child welfare system, and it is possible for the agency to remove a child at any time, even in the face of strong objections from the child and foster parents (Carrieri, 1991; Stein, 1991). In its recently revised standards, the Child Welfare League of America (1995) directed agencies to consider petitioning the court "to order the permanent foster care of the child with a specific foster family. This legal action sustains the commitment to long-term foster care by all parties involved" (p. 82).

There is also some question as to why agencies have not more aggressively pursued foster parent adoption (Thoburn, 1990). The Fein et al. (1990) research found that parental rights had been terminated for two-thirds of the younger children and one in four of the teens, so that adoption was a viable legal option for them (p. 48). In some instances, foster parents fear the loss of resources and supports provided to foster children; however, avenues for maintaining such services may be available via adoption subsidies (Testa, Shook, Cohen, & Woods, 1996). "Open adoption," which allows the child the opportunity to maintain birth family contacts while enjoying a permanent home with the foster family, may also be a possibility for some of these children (Borgman, 1981; McLean & Thomas, 1996). Clearly more research is called for on this complex but important topic (Kluger, Maluccio, & Fein, 1989; Steinhauer, 1991; Link, 1996).

Losing Foster Homes

The most desirable placement is one that permits the child to remain in the same home during the entire period of time that the child needs care. However, children may be moved to a new foster home, sometimes because they run away or refuse to stay in their current home, at other times because the foster parents request that they be placed elsewhere, and, in some instances, because the agency decides that the foster parents are not adequate caretakers (Fahlberg, 1991).

Removal for any reason is considered potentially damaging to children because it can impose serious emotional burdens associated with separation and change. Every replacement involves new losses and reactivates previous rejection experiences. While not all children are deeply affected by a move, Berridge and Cleaver (1987) found that some "suffered profoundly" (pp. 162–163). A caseworker noted, "I think we're just beginning to realize that moving babies has an effect. Some kids are really damaged by being moved" (cited by Berrick, Needell, Barth, & Jonson-Reid, 1998, p. 131). Weiner and Weiner (1990) believed the impact of removal is greater for those whose birth parents have already been rejecting, while Fahlberg (1991) considered removals especially detrimental for preschool children. Exploring the factors that might explain why some Native American children who had gone through multiple moves had dealt with them in a positive way while others had not, Long (1983) concluded that children were less likely to be traumatized when "the transfer family was emotionally and geographically close to the original parent or parents, and the child did not perceive the transfer as a response to bad or troublesome behavior" (p. 122). On the other hand, children who were suddenly replaced or who were "dumped" on unwilling caretakers experienced more severe trauma and had much more difficulty with integration.

Multiple placements are of particular concern because they can teach a child that close relationships are unstable and unreliable and that intimacy is too risky and painful (Cox & Cox, 1985; Pelton, 1989; Fanshel, Finch, & Grundy, 1990). While many children eventually recover from such losses (Berridge & Cleaver, 1987), some do not (Weiner & Weiner, 1990). Frequent replacement makes it more likely that the child will manifest emotional, academic, and social problems and that subsequent placements will fail (Eisenberg, 1965; Kliman, Schaeffer, & Fried-man, 1982; Aldgate, Stein, & Carey, 1989; Fanshel, Finch, & Grundy, 1990). Surveying the literature on outcomes of foster family care, McDonald, Allen, Westerfelt, and Piliavin (1993) described wide-ranging and long-term implications:

> Living in fewer placements was found to be associated with better school achievement and more years of education . . . ; increased contacts with and feelings of closeness to foster families after discharge . . . ; less criminal activity . . . ; more informal social supports . . . ; increased life satisfaction . . . ; greater housing stability . . . ; self-support . . . ; and better caring for one's own children. (p. 124)

Birth parents, too, can suffer as a result of their child's replacement experiences. They may worry that the chaotic and changeable life circumstances in their own homes are now being replicated for their children in the foster home. When they are not informed of their children's whereabouts or apprised of the reasons for removal, birth parents can feel particularly isolated and ignored.

Foster home replacement can be equally traumatic for foster parents, heightening their sense of bewilderment, anger, guilt, and frustration (Berridge & Cleaver, 1987). The children's removal can leave them deeply unhappy with themselves, the children, and the foster care agency. Typically they have no agency support in dealing with such feelings. As a result, removals may remain as painful and unsettling reminders of failure for many years to come.

While any movement in foster care may be considered a "disruption," children in some communities routinely go into short-stay, temporary care and then go into longer-term care once it is established that family circumstances are serious enough to require intensive intervention before the child can be returned (Kliman, Schaeffer, & Friedman, 1982; Wald, Carlsmith, & Leiderman, 1988). As a result, some researchers consider one or two moves to be "normative."

On the other hand, there is widespread agreement that having several moves is highly detrimental to children. Fanshel, Finch, and Grundy (1990) documented the profound effects of large numbers of moves on older children. "The common theme of these results is that the deterioration associated with 9 additional placements may be great enough to destroy the viability of foster care as a means of caring for the child" (p. 76). Goerge (1990) found that children may find stability after two or even three placements; however, four or more moves indicated serious instability (p. 44). Proch and Taber (1987) suggested the need to study both the number and length of placements in order to discover meaningful patterns.

Appendix 11.2 describes movement in care within general populations of children, while Appendix 11.3 considers those children who, because of age or length of time in care, might be expected to experience more moves. Although there is wide variation in outcomes across studies, in general, the data in these tables indicate that approximately half of the children live in a single, stable foster home, while 20 to 30 percent go through three or more placements. Statewide and national surveys (Goerge, 1990; Tatara, 1993; Davis, English, & Landsverk, 1995) suggest that replacement rates have risen in recent years. According to Tatara (1993), the greatest increase may be in the number of children who live in two foster homes. While 19 percent had two placements in 1982, 27 percent were replaced once in 1989 (p. 109).

While children who have been in care for longer periods might be expected to show greater placement instability, the data in Appendix 11.3 show that their placement patterns resemble those of children who have been in care for shorter periods. This comparability reflects the fact that disruption is most likely to occur early in the placement process (Kliman, Schaeffer, & Friedman, 1982; Festinger, 1983; Stone & Stone, 1983; Berridge & Cleaver, 1987; Humphrey & Humphrey, 1988).

Factors Associated with Children's Moves

To reduce placement changes, there is a need to more fully understand the factors that precipitate them. While some studies (Fenyo, Knapp, & Baines, 1989; Kufeldt, Armstrong, & Dorosh, 1989) find older children more likely to experience disruption, others (Maluccio & Fein, 1989) consider very young children more vulnerable. Festinger's (1983) research pointed out the need to compare the experiences of boys and girls.

As we have already noted, children with emotional, relational, and behavioral difficulties create more stress for their foster families. It comes as no surprise, therefore, to find that such children are also more vulnerable to placement disruption. Some studies have established a link between attachment difficulties and movement of children while in care (Cautley, 1980; Stone & Stone, 1983; Walsh & Walsh, 1990). Children experiencing disruptions are also more likely to engage in a variety of antisocial behaviors, ranging from stealing, lying, and sexual acting out to fire setting and running away (Rosenblum, 1977; Humphrey & Humphrey, 1988; Goerge, 1990; Walsh & Walsh, 1990; Ryan, 1993). While some research has found passive aggressive behavior to be "one of the least tolerable aspects of foster child behavior" (Walsh & Walsh, 1990, p. 127), other research has pointed to "disobedience and threatened or actual aggression" as most problematic (Proch & Taber, 1987, p. 12; see also Fanshel & Shinn, 1978; Stone & Stone, 1983). Berridge and Cleaver's (1987) study found child-related difficulties cited for 20 percent of placement breakdowns (p. 63).

Problems stemming from the child's experiences in the birth family can impact on stability of foster care placements. However, "negative early experiences fade unless reinforced" (Rowe, Cain, Hundleby, & Keane, 1984, p. 86). When children from troubled families are placed with foster parents who are responsive and supportive, the impact of these earlier difficulties is attenuated. Perhaps this is why researchers have reported few links between birth parent characteristics and disruption. One possible exception to this pattern is an association observed between parental substance abuse and movement of the child while in foster care (Walsh & Walsh, 1990; CWLA, 1992a).

Foster parent characteristics, circumstances, and limitations can also contribute to placement failure; Berridge and Cleaver (1987) considered them responsible for 30 percent of foster care breakdowns (p. 63). While it is not common for placements to disrupt because foster parents engage in seriously unacceptable behavior (Carbino, 1989, 1992; McCurdy & Daro, 1993), replacement is more likely when foster parents are unskilled, inexperienced, and uncomfortable in working with the kinds of children who come into care (Stone & Stone, 1983; Fenyo, Knapp, & Baines, 1989; Walsh & Walsh, 1990). Learning to respond to these children appropriately and effectively often involves a complex and stressful process of trial-and-error learning that can leave foster parents frustrated, exhausted, and pessimistic about the usefulness of their efforts. Following the careers of sixty-four families who initially expressed interest in becoming foster parents, Soothill and Derbyshire (1982) analyzed the reasons why they subsequently withdrew. One group included parents whose experiences with foster children were incongruent with their expectations or who found caring for a particular child very painful. Describing three such families, who had cared for thirty-two children before abandoning their fostering role, the authors commented:

> It is distressing to record how these . . . [parents] could not cope with rather familiar situations in fostering, namely the notion of rehabilitation to the natural parents in two cases and the possibility of ridicule by neighbors in the other case. (p. 40)

The age of the foster parent appears to be another important factor, with older parents able to provide more stable homes (Humphrey & Humphrey, 1988).

Foster parents may be unable to continue caring for children because of unexpected changes in family circumstances. Increasing stress associated with marital problems or divorce, a serious illness or death of a family member, or the need to move to another state for employment-related reasons may convince parents that they can no longer take on this responsibility (Soothill & Derbyshire, 1982; Wald, Carlsmith, & Leiderman, 1988).

In many situations, however, it is not characteristics of the foster family or the child alone but the interplay among these individuals that eventuates in placement changes. Sometimes there is a mismatch between the temperamental characteristics and relational styles of the child and parents (Doelling & Johnson, 1990; Walsh & Walsh, 1990; Steinhauer, 1991). Fanshel (1966) noted:

> Many of the foster parents in this study showed a fairly broad range of behavior with the foster children placed with them. One kind of child could evoke a positive, nurturing kind of response; a child with different characteristics could bring forth almost rejecting behavior from the same foster parent. (p. 162)

These tensions may underlie "the struggle between children and caregivers over control—a struggle that becomes much more salient at adolescence—as central to understanding placement disruption" (Proch & Taber, 1987, p. 12). Conflict can also occur when the foster child and other children in the family are too close in age, creating excessive competition among them (Humphrey & Humphrey, 1988; Fenyo, Knapp, & Baines, 1989).

Berridge and Cleaver (1987) reminded us that the actual process of disruption does not revolve around a single incident, although a particular event may serve as a "last straw" and the immediate catalyst for change. Instead, movement grows out of a series of increasingly frustrating and debilitating interactions, usually over an extended period of time, that involve the child, foster family members, and agency personnel. (See also Walsh & Walsh, 1990.) Berridge and Cleaver considered interactive factors responsible for 37 percent of the breakdowns in their study (p. 63).

Services to Foster Families to Limit Replacement

Foster carers who receive appropriate education and training and who are supported by the agency throughout the placement process are more successful and less frustrated with their parenting responsibilities (Berridge & Cleaver, 1987; Steinhauer, 1991; Pasztor & Wynne, 1995). One study found "strong evidence . . . for the positive effect of increased stipends and enhanced training and support for foster parents on minimizing foster parent dropout" (Chamberlain, Moreland, & Reid, 1992, p. 399). This serves to highlight the importance of the foster care agency's role in preventing replacement (Berrick, Needell, Barth, & Jonson-Reid, 1998). Stone and Stone (1983) concluded "that the degree of contact, active rapport building, and energy expended by the caseworker may be the single most critical variable in determining the outcome of a foster placement" (p. 15). Baring-Gould et al. (1983) contacted former foster families in Alaska in an attempt to understand factors associated with the high rate of foster home closure in that state. They found that lack of social worker contact had significant bearing on the family's decision in one-quarter of the cases. Berridge and Cleaver (1987) found many foster parents "isolated from social work support" (p. 157) with workers having no idea that serious problems had been developing in the family. (See also Proch & Taber, 1987; Titterington, 1990; Pasztor & Wynne, 1995.) Worker turnover contributes directly to problems in this area (Pardeck, 1983). There is also a tendency to overload foster parents who have shown themselves capable of caring for difficult children; however, placing more and more of such children in the home can create unendurable stress and, eventually, produce disruption (Institute for the Study of Children and Families, Winter, 1990).

When replacement must be made, it should be planned with the participation of the social worker, child, parents, and foster parents. A precipitous removal made in the heat of crisis is to be avoided (Proch & Taber, 1987). Fahlberg (1991) wrote, "Ideally, the agreements between foster parents and agencies would state that adequate notice, for example ten days to two weeks, would have to be given by either side if there is to be a move" (p. 200). If possible, the worker should work toward the foster and birth parents' acceptance of the move, so that they can be more helpful to the child in this process.

"The manner with which a foster child leaves foster care is far more important than the way a child enters the world of foster care" (Fanshel, Finch, &
Grundy, 1990, p. 200, quoting a former foster child). Berridge and Cleaver (1987)
found that "social workers tended to underestimate the effects upon a child of a
fostering breakdown" (p. 164; see also Palmer, 1995). The worker must offer honest information about the move and the reasons for it, must help the child sort
through his or her feelings regarding the replacement and should help to interpret it in such a way that the child is less likely to perceive the experience as another personal failure (Fahlberg, 1991). Children who are allowed this type of
exploration are less likely to fail in subsequent placements (Levine, 1990).

Throughout replacement, the worker must be sensitive to the feelings of the
foster parents and must attempt to help them feel less anxious, less guilty, and
less threatened (Fahlberg, 1991). As Herstein (1957) said many years ago, the caseworker should "present the reasons for replacement in terms that would be both
realistic and within the boundaries of what the foster parents can emotionally and
objectively accept" (p. 24). For some, the worker can point out that this is a time
for rest and recuperation (National Foster Care Resource Center, Winter, 1990).
The worker can also encourage them to contact other foster families for support
and guidance.

Current data are not available to determine how often and to what extent
foster families and children are prepared for changes in this way.

Summary

Although we have described the various outcomes of the foster care experience as
discrete and somewhat different experiences, it is important to remember that the
"care careers" of children may involve two—or more—of these outcomes. It is not
an unusual occurrence to find children who leave foster family care for the first
time and return home to their birth families; when this reunion proves unworkable, they return to care, perhaps to new foster homes; when the agency realizes
the children's need for support is likely to be long-term, relatives may then be
contacted in the hopes of making placement with them permanent through adoption; in the end, however, these plans might not work out, and the children might
stay with kin for several years until adulthood, might move out and establish
their own homes, or might return again to the home of their birth families. To
fully understand the meaning of the foster care experience for children, it is the
overall pattern and types of their placement experiences that need to be understood.

Questions for Discussion and Debate

1. Does the fact that children who are reunified with their parents tend to show developmental losses mean that we should be reluctant to return them to their families?
2. How would you manage a situation in which a child is returned to a birth family who you feel is in need of reunification services, but the family does not take advantages of these services?
3. What would it be like for you as a foster care worker to explain to a foster family and birth family that a child needs to be placed in another, permanent adoptive home?
4. How would you develop a program for foster families that would help reduce the likelihood that children would have to be moved to different foster homes?

APPENDIX 11.1 *Replacement of Children after Reunification with Families*

Source	Characteristics of Sample	Replacement Rate
Yoshikami (1984)	5-state data	15%
Fisher, Marsh, & Phillips (1986)	Children 8 or younger in 3 service divisions, England	30% (13% readmitted twice)
Packman (1986) p. 164	161 children in 2 service divisions, England	22% of voluntary & 11% of involuntary placements
Goerge (1990) p. 433	1,196 Illinois children entering care for first time	One-third
Farmer & Parker (1991) p. 30	321 children in 4 local authorities in Britain followed at least 2 years	43% "broke down"
Lie & McMurtry (1991) p. 117	110 sexually abused children; control group of children placed for other reasons	24% of SA children 31% of control group (15% of control group readmitted twice)
Bullock, Little, & Millham (1993) p. 83	247 children in care 6 months or less in England	28%
Davis, English, & Landsverk (1993) p. 7	625 children from 3 counties	13% within 9 months
Barth, Courtney, Needell, & Jonson-Reid, (1994) p. 5	7,709 California children followed for 4 years	8% within 6 months 13% within 1 year 17% within 2 years
Festinger (1994) p. 49	210 New York children age 15 or less in care 60+ days	6% within 6 months 13% within 12 months
Courtney (1995) p. 233	6,831 California children in care for first time	19% within 3 years; over half of these within 8 months
Davis, English, & Landsverk (1995) p. 77	1,165 children from 2 counties	15–16% within 12 months
English & Clark (1996) p. 8	77,000 Washington children in care over 10 years	32%
Goerge, Wulczyn, & Harden (1996) p. 23	10 years of data from 5 states	18–28%

APPENDIX 11.2 *Foster Home Replacement Rates: General Foster Care Populations*

Source	Characteristics of Sample	Replacement Rates
Vasaly (1978) p. 56	Reanalysis of data from five states; various time spans; foster family care	40–57% 1 placement 21–27% 3+ placements
Shyne & Schroeder (1978) p. 118	National data; in care on specific date; foster family care	53% 1 placement 22% 3+ placements
Fanshel & Shinn (1978) p. 139	In care in New York; foster family care	41% 1 placement 28% 3+ placements
Hubbell (1981) p. 58	From 3 communities over 3-year period; foster family care	1.8 average placements over 3 1/2 years
State of California (1981) p. 101	Annual rates from three counties; foster family care	46% 1 placement 31% 3+ placements
Kliman, Schaeffer, & Friedman (1982) p. 84	From one county; in care over 17-month span; foster family care	At 6 months: 56% 1 placement At 12 months: 52% 1 placement At 17 months: 49% 1 placement 27% 3+ placements
Gershenson (1983) p. 21	VCIS data from 20 states; annual rates; substitute care	53% 1 placement 27% 3+ placements 7% 6+ placements
Becker & Austin (1983) p. 6	From one state; substitute care	57% 1 placement 20% 3+ placements
Stone & Stone (1983) p. 13	From 3 child welfare units; 64 consecutive cases; foster family care	49% removed prior to completion of agency plan
Fisher, Marsh, & Phillips (1986) p. 15	340 children younger than 9 in 3 service divisions in England	69% 1–2 placements 19% 3–4 placements 12% 5+ placements
Mushlin, Levitt, & Anderson (1986) p. 146	Kansas City sample	29% in 4 or more homes in less than 5 years
National Black Child Development Institute (1989) p. 84	401 Black children from 5 major cities	Mean number of placements was 2.2

continued

APPENDIX 11.2   *continued*

Source	Characteristics of Sample	Replacement Rates
Doelling & Johnson (1990) p. 592	51 children recruited from 7 Florida counties	22% moved within 4–6 months of placement
Goerge (1990) p. 433	1,196 Illinois children in first placement	About 40% will have 4+ placements
Benedict & White (1991) p. 491	689 children in care for first time	72% 1 placement 18% 2+ placements
Lie & McMurtry (1991) p. 115	110 children in care 6+ months for abuse; controls placed for other reasons	Among abused 84% had 2+ placements; mean was 4.8 Among controls 88% had 2+ placements; mean was 6.2
Widom (1991) p. 201	772 abused/neglected children followed 20 years via court records	50% 1 placement 16% 2 placements 12% 3–5 placements 4% 6+ placements
Tatara (1993) p. 108	National sample of children in substitute care in 1989	44% 1 placement 27% 2 placements 22% 3–5 placements 7% 6+ placements
Barth, Courtney, Needell, & Jonson-Reid (1994) pp. 3–4	7,709 California children in first placement with non-relatives; followed 4 years	Mean number of placements for those who left care was 1.5; for those still in care was 2.0
Goerge (1994) p. 212	851 Illinois children; randomly selected	24% 1 placement 25% 2 placements 15% 3 placements 11% 4 placements 25% 5+ placements
Davis, English, & Landsverk (1995) p. 88	1,165 California & Washington children under 13	41% 1 placement 37% 2 placements 12% 3 placements 5% 4 placements 4% 5+ placements

APPENDIX 11.3   *Foster Home Replacement Rates: Older and Long-Term Care Populations*

Source	Characteristics of Sample	Replacement Rates
Older Children		
Wald, Carlsmith, & Leiderman (1988) p. 84	13 white abused children aged 5–10 in care; followed 2 years	46% 1 placement 23% several placements but 2 main caretakers 31% 3+ placements
Kufeldt, Armstrong, & Dorosh (1989) p. 365	73 children aged 9–16 in foster care in Ontario	30% 1 placement 22% 2 placements 22% 3–4 placements 15% 5–7 placements 11% 8+ placements
In Care for Longer Periods		
Fanshel (1982) p. 231	New York data; in care at least one year; foster family care	64% 1 placement 13% 3+ placements
Festinger (1983) pp. 55–56	New York City data; in care 5+ years and now aged 18–21; foster family care	32% of boys 1–2 placements 40% of girls 1–2 placements 68% of boys 3+ placements 60% of girls 3+ placements
Berridge & Cleaver (1987) p. 56	372 children from 3 English agencies; in care 1+ years	10–20% placements broke down within 1 year 20–40% broke down within 3 years 30–50% broke down within 5 years
Maluccio & Fein (1989) p. 392	274 younger children (aged 2–11) & 504 older children (12–20) in care 2+ years, Connecticut	younger / older 1 placement 47% 55% 2 placements 20% 14% 3+ placements 33% 30%
English & Clark (1996)	10,000 Washington children in placement 1+ years, with non-kin	1 placement 30% 2 placements 26% 3 placements 44%

12

Diversity Issues in Foster Care Practice

In several of the preceding chapters, we have documented the differential experiences children have in foster family care, depending upon their racial or ethnic background, their social class or gender, or their sexual orientation. In this chapter, we focus on the ways that foster family agencies can respond more effectively to families from diverse backgrounds.

Developing adequate services for these families requires that family foster care personnel and programs do the following:

1. Develop a greater understanding of and respect for the unique cultural and social experiences of birth families.
2. Develop an understanding of the impact of oppression, realize the means families use to cope with such denigration, and work with them to more effectively meet children's needs.
3. Improve planning and develop more responsive programs that will better meet the particular needs of families from diverse backgrounds.

To address each of these issues at sufficient depth would require much study and many chapters—an effort that is clearly beyond the scope of this text. The significance of these issues for foster family care, however, indicates that they, at the least, need to be mentioned. Therefore, this chapter reflects an overview of concerns about diversity and oppression as they impact on the delivery of services to families needing foster family care.

Recapitulation of the Issues

In Chapter 2 we pointed out that African American children enter care at a more rapid rate but that they do not leave care as readily as Caucasian children do.

Hispanic and American Indian children are also found in care in ratios that exceed their numbers in the general population. (See also National Black Child Development Institute, 1990; Stehno, 1990; Barth, Courtney, Berrick, & Albert, 1994; Palmer & Cooke, 1996; Barth, 1997; Brown & Bailey-Etta, 1997.) This is not only a matter of race but also of economics, however, since disenfranchised groups of all types are overrepresented in foster family care.

Foster care poses special problems for those individuals who are growing up in a repressive social environment, one in which they must struggle with prejudice from an early age. African American, Hispanic, American Indian, Asian American children, girls, and children who are homosexual or who have homosexual parents are among the groups for whom discrimination poses challenges to healthy development and normative family functioning. Racism, sexism, and homophobia contribute to and confound experiences with poverty, downward social mobility, and exclusion from resources and supports that characterize many of the families who need to use substitute care services (Barth, Courtney, Berrick, & Albert, 1994). Having birth parents who are judged "insufficient" and "incapable" of providing adequate caretaking for their children only adds to feelings of social devaluation already experienced by these families (Anderson, 1998).

Enhancing Workers' Understanding of Diversity

The Child Welfare League of America (1991a) defines cultural competence as

> Acceptance and respect for ethnic and cultural differences; continuing self-assessment regarding culture with careful attention to the dynamics of difference; continuous expansion of cultural knowledge and resources; and a variety of adaptations to service models to better meet the needs of minority populations. (p. 128)

To some extent, problems in providing adequate services to individuals from nonmiddle-class and non-Caucasian cultures grow out of ignorance. "Child welfare workers [who] are predominantly white, female, young and limited in experience" (Hogan & Siu, 1988, p. 496), supervisors and program administrators may not have sufficient knowledge about gender inequity or about African American, Hispanic, Asian American, Native American, or gay and lesbian family and community life.

Because racial and ethnic communities are not monolithic or homogenous, learning about client experiences in these cultures requires attention to "cultural heterogeneity," the wide variations in beliefs, behaviors, and attitudes that can occur within a particular cultural group. Elaborating on this theme, English (1991) pointed out that African Americans may see themselves as "native-oriented/traditional" (rooted in their own group and family history), "bicultural/multicultural" (living in two or more distinct cultures), "acculturated/

assimilated" (living predominately in another culture), or "transitional/ marginal" ("suspended" between cultures) (pp. 23–24). Mass and Yap (1992) also commented:

> Americans of Asian/Pacific background represent a complex, pluralistic aggregate of national and cultural characteristics. They also represent a great diversity of nationalities, languages, and cultures; and within each group they vary according to socioeconomic background and degree of Americanization or acculturation. (p. 109)

Understanding particular cultural mores with regard to family life and interpersonal relationships is crucial for effective practice with individuals from a particular community or racial group. It has been suggested that social agencies do not have a clear appreciation of Native American parenting patterns, the involvement of siblings in the care of younger children, and the importance of the extended family in childrearing in Native American communities (Ishisaka, 1978; Three Feathers Associates, 1989). Delgado (1992) urged workers to understand the role of female-headed families in Hispanic communities. (See also Mortland & Egan, 1987; Porte & Torney-Purta, 1987; Phillips & Gonzales-Ramos, 1989; McInnis, 1991; Mills & Usher, 1996.) Mallon (1992) noted that workers are "completely unprepared" to understand the needs of gay and lesbian youth in care (p. 549).

Developing "cultural sensitivity" and "ethnic competence" requires persistent, extended commitment on the part of child welfare workers, their supervisors, and the administrators of agencies in which they practice.

> Social work educators as well as child welfare practitioners often assume that competence with racially, culturally, and ethnically distinct groups can be achieved through short-term—and often one-shot—workshops or classes. This assumption reflects a short-sighted, simplistic view of a complex process. Restructuring one's worldview and developing a sound base of knowledge and skills are long-term professional endeavors. (McPhatter, 1997, p. 259)

A major challenge involves learning to distinguish between "differentness" and "insufficiency." Stovall and Krieger (1990) noted that "cultural values and related goals are frequently misunderstood and maligned" (p. 147).

> Cultural stereotypes of African-American adults as "lazy or violent," children as "non-verbal and aggressive," and the community as a whole as "culturally deprived" or "culturally disadvantaged," present "helping stumbling blocks" to the social worker. (Prater, 1992)

(See also Walker, 1981.)

Despite the greater attention given diversity training in recent years (CWLA, 1990), evidence indicates that agencies have much additional work to do to adequately prepare workers in this area (James Bell Associates, 1993; Courtney, Barth, Berrick, Brooks, Needell, & Park, 1996).

Enhancing Workers' Abilities to Address the Impact of Oppression

A task related to but somewhat different from understanding diversity involves understanding the impact of living in an oppressive environment on children needing care and on their families. "Minorities in communities throughout North America experience institutional racism, discrimination, and prejudice that often result in economic, social, and psychological deprivation," wrote the Child Welfare League of America (1990, pp. 15–16). The far-reaching consequences of discrimination have been repeatedly documented and have sometimes resulted in the active exclusion of minority children from agencies serving Caucasians (Prater, 1992). Writing of the history of child placement in Chicago, Stehno (1988) noted:

> Although the 1964 Civil Rights Act resulted in somewhat easier access of black children to white agencies, ultimately the bars of racial discrimination were broken when, due to a burgeoning black population in Chicago in the 1960s and 1970s and a declining white population, private agencies needed to serve more black children in order to survive. (p. 498)

(See also Hogan & Siu, 1988; Matheson, 1996.)

In a study of mixed race children in placement, Folaron and Hess (1993) found that agencies as well as the children's parents treated many of them differently from the way they treated African American or Caucasian children. The researchers documented "the impact of racism on parents' attitudes about their children, the extended families' willingness to extend support to parents, and the children's self-concepts" (p. 116). Agencies tended to place them in Caucasian homes without consideration for the family's racial identity or the cultural composition of the foster family's neighborhood. (See also Barn, 1993, p. 68.)

Horejsi, Craig, and Pablo (1992) articulated the link between experiences with discrimination and distrust of placing agencies by Native Americans:

> Many of today's Native American parents have parents or grandparents who were "snatched" from the reservation and placed in foster care or sent off to boarding school. Consequently, there exists a genuine and deep-seated fear of government agencies that have the power to place children. This fear intensifies the parents' fight-or-flight reaction when faced with a CPS agency expressing a concern over the care of the children. (p. 335)

(See also Palmer & Cooke, 1996.) Phillips, McMullen, Sparks, and Ueberle (1997) noted ways in which "the settings in which sexual minority youths live—communities, schools, religious organizations, peer groups, and families—may all be hostile toward gay, lesbian, bisexual, and transgendered people" (p. 396).

Recognizing the importance of oppression in the lives of families involves an understanding of the ways individuals and families have found to cope with such denigration and a realization that these coping strategies can serve to strengthen or to undermine families—to foster or to impede children's healthy development.

> Practitioners must demonstrate a firm understanding of the dynamics of oppression, racism, sexism, classism, and other forms of discrimination that shadow and defame culturally different clients irreparably. It is also critical to understand the process by which clients internalize oppression, how that process is manifested, and how it compounds an already overburdened reality. (McPhatter, 1997, pp. 267–268)

Discriminatory experiences assault children's feelings of self-worth, devalue children's self-images, and challenge their sense of social competence and desire to learn and to achieve (Yancey, 1998). To survive and to grow in healthy ways, children must rely on their families and communities to develop means to protect themselves from such assaults and to counteract their effects. The challenge for the ethnically and culturally competent foster care worker is to understand the ways in which racially, ethnically, and socially diverse communities have found to "empower . . . children to cope with stressful life situations" (Gould, 1991, p. 74). These empowering strategies represent individual, family, and community strengths that can help counteract problems with identity confusion, poor self-worth, low achievement motivation, and manipulativeness that might otherwise emerge from growing up in an oppressive environment (Small, 1986; Williams, 1987; Carten, 1990; Stovall & Krieger, 1990; Horejsi, Craig, & Pablo, 1992).

Perhaps the most difficult task faced by the foster care worker with regard to racism is to decide to address the issue rather than to deny or avoid it. There is evidence that workers often fail to explore children's experiences with prejudice or to assess its impact on their functioning (Williams, 1987). Folaron and Hess (1993) found that agencies provided no help to mixed race children or their families with their unique issues. Studying fifty-three children of Afro-Caribbean origins in placement in England, Mennell (1986) found workers "put off" talking with the children about racial concerns and, in some cases, were in collusion with the child's caretakers "in allowing, even encouraging, children to grow up attempting to pass as white" (p. 126).

> Color, ethnicity, and culture cannot be blithely ignored in planning for these children. It will not go away and no matter how insulated the cocoon in which we protectively wrap them, in the end the butterfly emerges the predestined hue. (Williams, 1987, p. 215)

Moving toward, not away from, this reality is an important first step toward building a more effective practice with clients.

Adapting Agency Policies and Services

A third arena in which issues of diversity and devaluation must be dealt with concerns reassessment and realignment of foster care agency policies and practices so that families can be more effectively supported and discriminatory treatment minimized. In its recent policy statement on foster care and adoption, the National Association of Social Workers (1994) stated that "patterns of funding" for these services "should guarantee high-quality services to all children, regardless of their race, language, capabilities, religion, geographic location, or socioeconomic class" (p. 122). Developing more responsive services for children, their parents, and their foster families will be discussed in this section.

Meeting the Needs of Children from Diverse Backgrounds

We have previously noted the chronic problems with recruitment and retention of an adequate number of same-race foster homes for African American, Native American, and Hispanic children (James Bell Associates, 1993). Placing minority children in same-race foster homes makes available adult caretakers who are knowledgeable about their unique needs and capable of helping them confront racism and maintain their cultural identity (Three Feathers Associates, 1989; Carten, 1990; Barn, 1993; Palmer & Cooke, 1996). Porte and Torney-Purta (1987) found that Indo-Chinese youths placed in same-race homes had significantly lower depression scores and were more motivated academically than those placed in Caucasian foster homes (p. 540). An English study (Barn, 1993) found that children were visited much more frequently when they were placed in same-race foster homes than when they were placed transracially (p. 84).

Giving first consideration to such placements for Native American children is legislated by PL 95-608, the Indian Child Welfare Act of 1978, which mandates that every effort be made to maintain the child in his or her tribal community and that tribal courts retain authority to make decisions on behalf of community children (U.S. Dept. of Health and Human Services, 1982; see also Pecora, Whittaker, & Maluccio, 1992; Matheson, 1996). Approaches that can help increase the number of homes from racial and ethnic minority communities have included using more culturally sensitive recruitment practices, revising foster care standards to remove a middle-class bias, and providing more effective support to families once children are placed. The fact that African American foster parents are more likely to be single or to have fathers who do not work outside the home (Downs, 1986) suggests provision of more adequate support payments is an important consideration for many of them.

Although there is considerable ambivalence in the field about placement of non-Caucasian children in Caucasian foster homes (Pierce, 1992), the lack of a sufficient number of same-race foster homes means that this practice is likely to continue. A recent California study (Berrick, Barth, & Needell, 1994) found 48 percent of Caucasian foster parents were caring for children of color. Efforts to select Caucasian parents who are more attuned to the needs of children who are racially or culturally different, who live in diverse neighborhoods, and who are willing to help children maintain substantial ties to their communities can ameliorate some problems with these placements (Rowe, Cain, Hundleby, & Keane, 1984; Small, 1986; Wilson, 1987; Hogan & Siu, 1988; CWLA, 1995). Bilingual foster homes are needed for some of these children (Hogan & Siu, 1988; Delgado, 1992; Mass & Yap, 1992). Ongoing training for and supervision of these families are also critically important (Mortland & Egan, 1987; Stovall & Krieger, 1990; James Bell Associates, 1993; Schatz & Horejsi, 1996). For children who are not placed in their own ethnic community, explicit assistance in maintaining ties to that community is essential (Mennell, 1986; Small, 1986; Williams, 1987). Help in this effort can be provided by community mentors who can work with the foster parents and child to provide ongoing support (Stovall & Krieger, 1990).

Meeting the Needs of Birth Families

Adaptations in services offered to birth families must explicitly recognize the impact that class, gender, and racial bias have had on the emergence of their problems and on the kinds of efforts families have made to resolve these problems (Hauswald, 1987). The worker's understanding of cultural differences and examination of patterns of coping with prejudice also undergird the development of appropriate and relevant services for them. Horejsi, Craig, and Pablo (1992) recommended that Native American parents receive parent education services that include content on "spirituality, customs, traditions, and other cultural ways of their tribe" (p. 335). (See also Stovall & Krieger, 1990.)

The core providers of such services are the child welfare workers. Without adequate efforts to hire non-Caucasian personnel and to train and supervise all personnel in ethnically competent practice, agencies will continue to be unresponsive to and unaware of problems in this arena (Phillips & Gonzales-Ramos, 1989; Three Feathers Associates, 1989; Barn, 1993; Johnson, 1994). With well-prepared staff, agencies can develop more adequate and race-sensitive monitoring, assessment, and decision-making procedures for their clients.

Gender bias plays a role in the delivery of services to parents. Although fathers comprise half of the physically abusive and most of the sexually abusive parents in the child welfare system, intervention services are geared primarily to women (Folaron & Wagner, 1998). In fact, the term "parent" is often used synonymously with "mother" by service providers. This results in excessive responsibility for change being placed on women's shoulders while men are frequently not challenged—or helped. We have provided evidence elsewhere in this text of the need to remind foster care workers that male caretakers have an important impact on the lives of children and that they should not be ignored.

Serving Foster Families More Effectively

An assessment of service delivery in California (Berrick, Barth, & Needell, 1994) found African American foster parents received fewer services (an average of 2.08) than Caucasian foster parents (2.43 services), were less likely to have been visited by the foster care worker within the last month, and had less time with the worker, once they were contacted (p. 54). Kin are far more likely to be asked to provide care for children who are African American, Native American, or Hispanic than for children who are Caucasian. In Berrick, Barth, and Needell's (1994) California study, 43 percent of kinship care was provided by African American women, while almost two-thirds of non-kin care was provided by Caucasians (p. 45). In Illinois, 87 percent of the 26,500 children in formal kinship care in March, 1995, were placed in African American homes (Gleeson, 1996, p. 441; see also National Black Child Development Institute, 1989; Thornton, 1991; Dubowitz, Feigelman, & Zuravin, 1993; Walker, Zangrillo, & Smith, 1994; Gebel, 1996; McLean & Thomas, 1996; Pecora, LeProhn, & Nasuti, 1999). Use of kinship care is more prevalent in major urban areas than in more rural sections of the country (Testa, 1992).

The recent dramatic increase in reliance on kinship care throughout the United States has given rise to concerns about criteria used to decide whether a child should be placed with relatives. In some child welfare agencies, placement with relatives has been interpreted as a "mandatory" effort; as a result, workers have sometimes exercised less than adequate judgment in determining that a relative's home can provide sufficient warmth, stability, and security before making the placement (Johnson, 1994; Scannapieco & Hegar, 1996). At times, children have gone to the homes of grandparents who struggle with the same severe types of problems as the children's parents; yet the parental home is considered inadequate while the grandparent's home is felt to be an acceptable alternative. Grandparents may be denied financial support by the agency because of insufficiencies in their homes or in their own backgrounds; yet the children remain in their care (Gleeson & Craig, 1994).

Findings that kinship foster homes may be provided less adequate financial compensation and that they are less likely to receive necessary health or other types of professional services than non-kin homes raise questions concerning the ways in which kinship services are valued by and utilized in the child welfare system (Gleeson, 1995; Hornby, Zeller, & Karraker, 1996). Gleeson (1996) has expressed concern that "welfare reform and kinship care reform efforts not be used to once again justify refusing services to children and families of color" (p. 442). Scannapieco and Hegar (1999) wondered whether this is producing another "two-tiered and segregated system" of foster care (p. 8). If kin placements are used to enhance permanency and stability for children without jeopardizing reunification objectives, they serve the underlying goals of foster family care. However, if they are used to contain costs and curtail services but, in the process, place children in greater jeopardy and undermine reunification, policies regarding the use of kin homes should be called into serious question (Fein & Maluccio, 1992; Hegar, 1999). These are issues requiring considerable discussion and debate and the promulgation of more clear-cut policy and practice guidelines.

A Note on Data Collection

Planning to meet the needs of clients from diverse cultural and racial backgrounds must be based on adequate tracking of the numbers of minority children and families using care and an evaluation of their experiences with services and supports while in care (CWLA, 1990; Stovall & Krieger, 1990; Abramson, 1991). In this way, agencies can discover families who are routinely denied access to services or who are routed to services perceived to "belong" primarily to people of their race (Hogan & Siu, 1988). The availability of this type of data is critical for development of affirmative action initiatives to redress imbalances and insufficiencies (Fein, 1991). Ongoing monitoring of service delivery in this way can ultimately work to reduce the exceptionally long period of time children spend in care and result in more stable and usable permanency plans for them.

Questions for Discussion and Debate

1. What difference would it make in developing effective services and doing planning work to know that the Jelico family (used in the case examples throughout the text) was African American instead of Caucasian? What difference would it make if this family were Native American?
2. What difference would it make in planning and delivering services if Rod Tedesco were Caucasian and Timothy were Native American?
3. If you were developing a parenting program for families with children in foster family care, what adjustments would you have to make in order to include fathers in the program?
4. How would you prepare yourself to work with Ms. R, a new client whose children have been placed in foster care? This woman is a 35-year-old lesbian who is addicted to alcohol.

13

Evaluation of Foster Family Services

Assessment of the impact of care involves a number of important considerations, some having to do with the functioning of the foster care system, and others dealing with the effects of care on the children and their families. "Intermediate" goals of foster family care focus on delivery of services and the experiences of children while in care, while "ultimate" goals concern contributions to permanency and to the child's development after leaving care. Achievement of intermediate goals assumes positive answers to questions like the following (Humphrey & Humphrey, 1988; CWLA, 1991a; Zill & Coiro, 1992):

1. Are children provided with stable homes while in care?
2. Are children placed in loving homes where they can feel wanted, cared about, comfortable, and relatively satisfied?
3. Does the foster care system promote healthy development and encourage productivity and achievement to the best of the children's abilities?
4. Does the foster care system treat children in ways that help remediate serious social, emotional, and cognitive difficulties they may have had at the time of placement?
5. Are children safe while in care? Are they provided foster homes where they are not inappropriately punished or abused?
6. Does the foster care system facilitate attachments between children and birth families and provide adequate, relevant, and appropriate services to and supports for birth parents?

Questions reflecting on achievement of ultimate goals include the following:

1. Does the foster care experience contribute to children's achievement of permanent, stable homes within a reasonable period of time?

2. Does the foster care experience have long-range impact on children that results in healthy functioning in adulthood?

In this text, a number of these areas have already been discussed. In order to create a broad picture of the overall impact of care, these findings will be briefly reviewed, while the larger part of this chapter will be devoted to questions that have not, as yet, been addressed. Because concerns about long-term and short-term impact may be interpreted somewhat differently when children are living with kin as compared to non-kin, data on the impact of kinship care services will be provided, where available. Since the complex nature of these questions would require a separate text to address them adequately, what follows is only a summary of findings on the impact of care.

Although a "foster care system" includes a public child welfare agency with its administration and foster care staff, foster parents, and, often, collateral services provided by outside agencies, studies evaluating the impact of care tend to present results "in toto." The relative contribution of one aspect of service or another to this outcome is usually not examined. Despite this, results tend to be interpreted in ways that suggest it is primarily the foster parents (and sometimes the foster care workers) who produce them. Impact research also tends to look at outcomes for foster children but not for their parents, except when specific programs directed only at parents are being considered. We found, for example, that research exploring the effects of visitation concentrates on the child in care but does not consider visitation's impact on the remainder of the birth family. The studies reviewed next reflect these biases.

As we have already documented, foster parents do not, in many cases, take into their homes children who are functioning well in the world, who expect caretakers to be responsive and nurturing, or who have not been repeatedly hurt or traumatized. Determining the effectiveness of foster care must involve a realistic consideration of expectations for change in these children as a result of placement and the use of baseline data to anchor these expectations in the reality of the child's (and family's) circumstances at the start of care. Research that does not include such baseline data must be considered descriptive but not evaluative of the impact of care on clients.

Achieving Intermediate Goals

Stability

When one considers the unpredictable environment in which many children lived prior to placement and the fact that 15 to 30 percent of those who are reunified with their parents will return to care, concerns for creating stability for children while they are in care become paramount. Data presented earlier in this text (in Chapter 11) suggest that there are two distinct groups of foster children, each having different experiences with regard to placement stability. For approximately two out of three children in care, there is considerable predictability; they will live in one or two foster homes over their care careers. The remaining children will move at least three times. While the complex emotional and behavioral problems of some of these children contribute to this instability, multiple moves can only exacerbate their difficulties. For this group, stability will not be achieved.

Data from several sources indicate that kinship placements are more settled than those of non-kin (Dubowitz, Feigelman, & Zuravin, 1993; Berrick, Barth, & Needell, 1994; Inglehart, 1994; Hegar & Scannapieco, 1995; Ritter, 1995). In a Baltimore study, Benedict, Zuravin, and Stallings (1996) report 43 percent of children in kin homes had only one placement; this was true of only 15 percent of children living with non-kin (p. 534). Children in kinship homes are also less likely to have to change their schools when entering placement (Barth, Courtney, Berrick, & Albert, 1994).

Attachments

There is evidence across a number of studies of considerable warmth, caring, and connectedness between children and their foster families. (See Chapter 8.) Highly functioning foster parents, rated by caseworkers in the Casey Family Program, were those with "emotional strength, comfort with themselves, openness, and tolerance" (Walsh & Walsh, 1990, p. 72). The foster mother's ability to provide love and acceptance was also a significant factor in this study. Fifteen percent of parents were rated excellent on this dimension, two-thirds were considered average, and 15 percent were doing poorly. Foster parents in Kufeldt, Armstrong, and Dorosh's (1995) study were evaluated on seven dimensions: task accomplishment, role performance, communication, affective expression, affective involvement, control, and values and norms. On a summary measure, 93 percent were rated normal or better. The only problematic ratings were in the area of affective involvement, where some 35 percent had difficulties.

Direct observation of interactions in foster homes and in residential settings (Colton, 1988) revealed that foster parents spent almost half their time doing "social child care" rather than administrative or supervisory work. Foster parents were warmer and less critical of the children, spent more time being approving and supportive, and created an environment in which children initiated far more interactions than in residential care. Interviews with the children revealed a greater sense of belonging and security in the home environments. In-person interviews with more than 1,000 children in care in Illinois (Wilson & Conroy, 1999) affirmed these results. "Children living in family foster care were more likely to say they were 'loved' and 'safe' as compared to their counterparts living in group care arrangements" (p. 60).

Data collected from children themselves indicate that they recognize the importance of a sense of connectedness to foster families and that they value it when it occurs. Interviews with 95 children between the ages of 11 and 14 (Johnson, Yoken, & Voss, 1995) revealed "all but seven children felt that their foster parents were trying hard to help them fit into the foster homes" (p. 965), and almost three-quarters said they got along well with them. Fanshel, Finch, and Grundy's (1990) research found a "vast majority" of children believed they were "treated kindly and accepted as family members" (p. 92). (See also Rowe, Cain, Hundleby, & Keane, 1984; Wald, Carlsmith, & Leiderman, 1988; Steinhauer, 1991; Berrick, Needell, Barth, & Jonson-Reid, 1998.) Those living with kin in Wilson and Conroy's study (1999) felt this sense of connection most strongly, with 94 percent saying they were "always loved," as compared with 82 percent of those in nonrelative homes (p. 60).

This sense of attachment is found among young adults who were in care as well. Reviewing a number of studies, McDonald, Allen, Westerfelt, and Piliavin (1993) concluded, "Foster families apparently provide a great deal of affiliation for former foster children in their early adult years" (p. 116). Most "graduates" of foster care were still in contact with their former foster parents, and 12 to 35 percent still lived with them. (See also English, Kouidou-Giles, & Plocke, 1994.)

Despite these findings, there is a lingering concern about the extent to which foster children feel they are full members of the families with whom they live (Thorpe, 1980; Fanshel, 1982; Maluccio, Fein, & Olmstead, 1986; Triseliotis & Hill, 1990; Gardner, 1996). Wald and his colleagues (1988) also raised questions concerning the means whereby foster care programs facilitate attachments. In their research, "to a large degree, it was a matter of luck for a child to end up in a home with strongly committed parents" (p. 135).

With regard to enhancing the child's sense of birth family connectedness, there is little research evidence regarding the specific role that non-kin foster carers play. However, kinship placements have been shown to help maintain and even strengthen these bonds. This type of "fostering does not mean the child is abandoned; rather, the child, who is valued, becomes part of a larger system of shared responsibility for the welfare of family and friends" (Kilbride & Kilbride, 1994, p. 313). Opportunities for visits with birth parents appear to be more readily available in these homes (Dubowitz, Feigelman, & Zuravin, 1993; Scannapieco & Hegar, 1994; Pecora, LeProhn, & Narsuti, 1999). One study (Berrick, Barth, & Needell, 1994) reported contacts with birth parents among 81 percent of kin homes as compared to 58 percent of non-kin homes. Contacts were also more frequent, occurring at least monthly in 56 percent of kin homes but only 32 percent of those of non-kin. A second study (LeProhn & Pecora, 1994) found children placed with kin saw their parents eight to nine times more often than those in other placements. In the Berrick et al. research, visiting in kin homes was also more likely to be informal and "family like" and to be arranged by the child's parents rather than the agency.

Broader questions do remain, however, with regard to impact of kin placements on the family as a whole. Solnit, Nordhaus, and Lord (1992) summarized the issues here:

> The desirable complication is the creation of the rich continuity of the extended family. The undesirable complication is that any conflict or ambivalence in the relationship between the adoptive/foster and biological parents is much more difficult to resolve or contain when kinship is involved. (p. 130)

(See also Fahlberg, 1991; CWLA, 1995.) Difficulties can arise, for example, when kin caretakers do not feel as free to plan for or voice opinions about the child's future as non-kin caretakers may. For birth parents who are already isolated and alienated from their kinship network, placement of their children with kin may exacerbate these problems (Lewis & Fraser, 1987). Complex questions also arise with regard to maintenance of autonomy, privacy, and confidentiality for individual family members and for the family as a whole (Takas, 1993; Gleeson, 1995; Merkel-Holguin, 1996).

In summary, research to date suggests that, although closeness may be an issue for some children, most develop some level of attachment to their foster families. Children living with kin appear to maintain stronger connections with birth parents than those living with non-kin. Evaluation of the depth and meaning of these connections awaits more detailed study.

Productivity and Achievement

The very limited evidence in this area suggests that, as a group, children placed in foster families show improved cognitive and academic performance (Kent, 1976; Fanshel & Shinn, 1978; Kliman, Schaeffer, & Friedman, 1982), although outcomes are not consistent across studies (Altshuler & Gleeson, 1999). Colton's (1988) research found truancy diminished after children went into care. One study (Fanshel, 1982) found most foster parents provided sufficient intellectual stimulation for the children in their care.

Reducing Serious Problems

In Chapter 3 we documented the array of behavioral, cognitive, and emotional problems that many children in foster family care struggle with. Altshuler and Gleeson (1999) have reviewed research in this area, examining the impact of care on "child well being." They noted:

> The longitudinal and cross-sectional studies that assessed the prevalence of emotional disturbance through standardized instruments . . . generally concluded that significantly higher numbers of children in nonrelative foster care than in the normed population demonstrated clinical levels of emotional disturbance. (p. 139)

A difficulty in studying the foster family's role in alleviating these difficulties in children lies in trying to determine the extent to which this family environment can be expected to be responsible for meaningful change in the child. "Caring foster parents whose own family lives are built upon solid foundations can help heal psychic wounds in children, but they cannot perform as miracle workers" (Fanshel, Finch, & Grundy, 1989, p. 476). In light of evidence suggesting that the problems children bring with them, especially if severe, tend to stay with them and have a strong impact on the course of care and its outcome (Fanshel, Finch, & Grundy, 1990; Widom, 1991), one may envision two distinct groups of foster children: (1) those with less complex problems, who might be expected to respond positively in an adequate foster care environment, and (2) those with more complex problems, whose response is more unpredictable and for whom the foster care environment may not be able to effect substantial change. Findings in this area await further clarification of expected outcomes.

Safety

Few foster families have been found, via official investigation, to be abusive of the children in their care (McFadden & Ryan, 1986; Carbino, 1989, 1992; McCurdy & Daro, 1993). A 1982 study (Fanshel) found most parents provided appropriate discipline. Observations of foster parents and residential staff revealed that foster parents were far less likely to use "inappropriate/ineffective techniques of control" (Colton, 1988, p. 92). However, interviews with 106 children (Fanshel, Finch, & Grundy, 1990) found one in four who said they were severely physically punished while in their foster homes (p. 91).

Children in care appear to recognize and appreciate that their foster homes are safer than those of their birth families (Johnson, Yoken, & Voss, 1995; Wilson & Conroy, 1999). This may, in part, explain why foster children tend to become less physically violent once they have been placed (Colton, 1988).

Some limited evidence suggests that, although birth parents have more access to them, children's safety may not be compromised by kinship placements (Berrick, Barth, & Needell, 1994). However, parental visits are less likely to be supervised or monitored by the agency in such settings (Dubowitz, Feigelman, Harrington, Starr, Zuravin, & Sawyer, 1994), which leaves individual kinship caregivers with primary responsibility for child protection (Takas, 1993). Safety questions can also arise with regard to the kinship caretaker's own parenting style, and problems with excessively rigid or unstructured parenting can be far more difficult to change when multiple generations of a family engage in similar practices (Ritter, 1995).

General Evaluations

Global assessments of the impact of care on children suggest that, for most children, the experience is a positive one. Fanshel and Shinn's (1978) study of New York children found 77 to 84 percent of foster homes were rated as excellent or good in overall performance. Fanshel, Finch, and Grundy's (1990) examination of a population of more challenging children also concluded, "the placement experience was apparently beneficial, for the children left care in relatively good condition" (p. 82).

Talking with 73 older children from Ontario, Kufeldt, Armstrong, and Dorosh (1989) found 59 percent who felt their time in care was "definitely helpful" and 30 percent who thought it was "probably helpful" (p. 365). Evaluating foster children's level of satisfaction with themselves, their peers and school, Wald, Carlsmith, and Leiderman (1988) found them more content than maltreated children who remained in their birth homes but less satisfied than a control group of children who had not been abused or neglected (p. 123). (See also Kent, 1976.)

The limited available evidence suggests birth parents believe that their children receive adequate care in foster family settings. A comparative study of foster and residential care found one in three birth mothers and 8 percent of fathers had negative views of foster care; almost half the mothers and one-third of the fathers had positive feelings about foster care (Colton, 1988, p. 147). Birth mothers were more likely to have strong feelings about foster care (both positive and negative) than about residential treatment services, about which they tended to be more neutral. (See also Thoburn, 1980.)

Impact on the Child's Parents

Although some studies suggest that intensive and appropriate services to parents can help alleviate the problems that led to the need for care (Lewis, 1994), we have described chronic insufficiencies in these services. (See Chapter 8.) To the extent that these difficulties remain unrectified, the foster care system cannot be said to have met its short-term goals with regard to birth parents.

No research has, as yet, evaluated in depth the impact of foster placement on the child's family as a whole. Such a study would require decisions about the expected impact of care on the extended family. Should parents be "comfortable" with care? Should they be expected to approve of its use, to like it? Which other family members should be expected to benefit from the child's placement? Hopefully, future research will grapple with these questions.

Achieving Ultimate Goals

The larger and more long-term the goals to be considered, the more difficult it becomes to come to some clear conclusions about whether they have been accomplished. Researchers are obligated to make choices among several alternative meanings of goals and appropriate measures for them. Philosophical and political beliefs influence these decisions as well as the interpretation of results. Of necessity, then, discussion in this area must accept the tentativeness of findings and embrace disagreement about their meaning.

Permanency and Timeliness

To examine the question of foster care's role in insuring permanency for children, one must determine whether to use more behaviorally oriented measures (studying the number of moves made by the child, for example) or an experientially oriented approach (measuring the child's achievement of an internal sense of stability and predictability). To some researchers, a child's return home is a useful indicator of achieving permanency, while others believe that the parents' ability to provide a stable, safe environment after reunification needs to be explored.

Evaluation of the role of foster family care in achieving permanency also requires decisions about foster care's place in this process, about realistic expectations for an experience that comprises only one time-limited aspect of a child's life.

A review of behaviorally oriented outcomes suggests that, for a substantial group of children (perhaps one-third to one-half), return to their family is achieved and, for many, it is achieved within a relatively brief period of time. (See Chapter 10.) However, permanency options for the children who remain in care are more clouded and preferable goals are less clear-cut. For some one-quarter to one-third of them, foster placement that continues for some years seems to be the outcome. For some children, returning home involves a return to chaos and unpredictability (Bullock, Little, & Millham, 1993), while for others, remaining in care results in having a long-term stable home that offers support into adulthood (McDonald, Allen, Westerfelt, & Piliavin, 1993). Relatively few children achieve permanency via adoption or emancipation.

Children living with kin stay in care far longer than those placed in non-kin homes. A number of these children will not leave care before they reach the age of majority (National Foster Care Resource Center, 1992; Hornby, Zeller, & Karraker, 1996; Link, 1996; Terpstra & McFadden, 1993). In California, Barth, Courtney, Needell, and Jonson-Reid (1994) found that after four years in care, only 45 percent of the children had been reunified. However, this same study found reunification from kin homes to be more stable, once it did occur.

Some consider this a serious problem and attribute it, at least in part, to insufficiencies in child welfare policy, noting that workers are not as active or persistent in their efforts to help birth parents work through their problems when their children are living with relatives (Fein & Maluccio, 1992; Courtney, 1995). In its recent publication on kinship care, the Child Welfare League of America (1994) pressed workers to make "reasonable efforts to reunite children with their birth parents" (p. 65). The goal here is to bring kinship care practice more in line with guidelines established for nonrelative care.

Others appear to be less concerned about longer stays with kin, arguing that this type of care is actually a "form of extended family preservation" (Berrick, Barth, & Needell, 1994, p. 59; see also Gleeson, 1995; Scannapieco & Hegar, 1994). They urge agencies to broaden their definition of "family" to bring kin in as active support systems even before children are placed (Ritter, 1995; Hornby, Zeller, & Karraker, 1996).

Long-Term Development

Research on adult outcomes for those who have lived in foster care suffers from a lack of baseline data, making it impossible in most studies to determine the extent to which results were influenced by the characteristics of the children and their families at the beginning of care. The research is further limited in that, in the lives of most people, a number of interdependent factors influence current functioning; however, these studies do not take any factors other than foster care placement into account. These shortcomings suggest that findings of these studies should be considered descriptive rather than explanatory, that they provide a picture of children who have left care but cannot be used to argue that foster placement "produced" adult outcomes, whether positive or negative.

Research on adult functioning has tended to describe three broad areas:

- performance in basic adult roles, which includes such items as completing one's education, finding and keeping a job, and maintaining a residence
- performance in socio/emotional arenas, which includes developing and maintaining adult relationships, parenting, using social supports, finding life satisfying, and measures of moderate or severe emotional difficulties
- performing in socially acceptable ways, which includes staying out of trouble with the law, not abusing alcohol or drugs, and so forth

A recently completed survey of the literature (McDonald, Allen, Westerfelt, & Piliavin, 1993) examined adult outcomes in each of these areas. (Note, however, that many of the studies they reviewed described children placed in any type of substitute care; children going into residential and group programs might be expected to be doing more poorly in later years than those in foster family care.) Results of their analyses will be complemented by other recent studies that were not included in their survey.

Role Performance.   McDonald and associates (1993) found that 15 to 56 percent of former foster care residents had not completed high school (p. 110; see also English, Kouidou-Giles, & Plocke, 1994). Stein and Carey's (1986) survey of forty-five young adults found their academic attainment "extremely low." "There was little interest in school or school subjects, and many saw exams as pointless and education as a whole a 'waste of time'" (p. 45). Fanshel, Finch, and Grundy's (1990) study noted "two thirds expressed regrets about school achievement" (p. 99). Limited academic skills were tied, in turn, to occupational limitations. Although most former foster children were employed (McDonald et al., 1993, p. 66), jobs were "precarious." Stein and Carey noted that jobs and job plans were "ever-changing" (p. 93). Approximately one in four former foster children relied on public funds for economic support. (See also Cook & Sedlak, 1995; Benedict, Zuravin, & Stallings, 1996.) How the occupational performance of foster care graduates compares to that of their birth parents is unclear.

Research with adults from Baltimore's foster care system (Zuravin, Benedict, & Stallings, 1999) uncovered greater difficulties for those who had spent their care careers with non-kin than for those who had spent at least half of their time in kin placements (p. 216).

There is also a great deal of housing mobility within this group. Fanshel, Finch, and Grundy (1990) contacted 106 individuals who had been out of care for seven years, on the average; two out of five had moved five or more times. Stein and Carey (1986), following young adults for two-and-a-half years, found 22 percent had moved at least four times. Given the young age of these subjects, it is unclear whether this represents an age-specific or more long-term pattern.

Zuravin, Benedict, and Stallings (1999) were very concerned in their study about the "magnitude" of their findings about homelessness. "Overall, former foster children are approximately five times more likely than their comparisons to have experienced at least one period of homelessness" (p. 216).

Socio/Emotional Performance.   The general mental health of former foster care recipients is poorer than that of the population in general (McDonald et al., 1993). Fanshel, Finch, and Grundy (1990) found one-third of their respondents were in poor spirits and felt strained and dissatisfied (p. 96). Interestingly, research conducted in 1952-1954 in Holland (Van Der Waals, 1960) noted similar results. One in three subjects in the Fanshel et al. study admitted problems with loneliness, as did 28 percent in Zimmerman's (1982) and 10 percent in Festinger's (1983) research. (See also Cook in Mech & Rycraft, 1995; Benedict, Zuravin, & Stallings, 1996.) Zuravin, Benedict, and Stallings (1999) found adults who had been in kin placements were more "socially isolated" than their non-kin counterparts (p. 217).

Socially Unacceptable Behavior

Studies tend to agree that alcohol and drug abuse and criminal behavior are found among former foster children at a level that exceeds that of the general population. Some 20 to 33 percent have admitted to problems with alcohol, while 13 to 30 percent have given evidence of difficulties with drugs (Stein & Carey, 1986; Barth & Berry, 1987; Fanshel, Finch, & Grundy, 1990; McDonald et al., 1993; Benedict, Zuravin, & Stallings, 1996). "For those males who were in placement, 22 to 33 percent were convicted of crimes; incarceration rates ranged from 14 to 22 percent" (McDonald et al., 1993, p. 113; see also Ferguson, 1966; Kraus, 1981). Criminal and substance abuse histories for birth parents were not cited in these studies. Benedict, Zuravin, and Stallings (1996) found that one in three adults with partners said they had been treated violently by that partner (p. 540). Barth and Berry (1987) described a West Virginia study that "found 19 percent of the sample's own children were or had been in foster care; this is an exceptionally high rate not found in other studies" (p. 80).

General Evaluations

Despite the prevalence of many life challenges, more global evaluations of their circumstances made by former foster children are fairly positive. Like Meier (1962), Festinger (1983) concluded that "generally . . . these young adults were managing their lives adequately and feeling quite satisfied with their physical, social, and psychological environments" (p. 133). Triseliotis (1980) investigated forty young adults who had had relatively stable, long-term foster care experiences. While 60 percent were coping well and were generally satisfied with their lives, 15 percent were "coping about half and half" (p. 153). The remainder, 25 percent, were doing poorly. Zimmerman's (1982) research on 109 adults in New

Orleans Parish found somewhat more than one-quarter functioning well, 39 percent functioning adequately, almost one-quarter with major dysfunction in one area, and 10 percent having serious difficulties in two or three areas (p. 88).

Outcomes and Other Factors

In one of the few studies to include characteristics of the child, the child's parents, and foster parents in a study of outcomes, Fanshel, Finch, and Grundy (1990) noted the significance of both family and child factors:

> There were associations that were not continuations of life course but rather suggest the intrusion of traumatic events. The physical abuse of a boy by his family and excessive turbulence in childhood living arrangements had significant associations with adult characteristics. (p. 106)

Boys who were physically abused were less likely to do well academically and more likely to subsequently use drugs and engage in serious criminal activity, especially burglary and armed robbery. Children coming out of chaotic home environments were more likely to be hostile and negative when entering the foster care program and to have problems managing such behavior throughout their stay. The importance of considering the child's gender is also suggested in this report. (See also Meier, 1962; Zimmerman, 1982.)

Fanshel and his colleagues pointed out the substantial impact of the foster home on the child's subsequent adjustment: "A reported abusive relationship was associated with negative adult outcomes. A positive relationship had positive outcomes" (p. 108). McDonald and others (1993) found that former foster children who had a long-term connection to their foster family did better educationally and academically, had fewer emotional or behavioral problems, and reported a stronger sense of well-being and life-satisfaction in later years. They added, "Benefits are maximized when the long-term placement is in a normal, stable foster family setting" (p. 125). (See also Theis & Van, 1924.)

Conclusion

These findings have led scholars in the field to voice cautious support for the idea that foster family care is of benefit to children. Widom (1991) found that "under certain circumstances, out-of-home placement experiences do not necessarily lead to negative effects" (p. 208). Fein (1991) concluded that "there is reason to believe that fostering can occur without detriment to the youngsters" (p. 579). Barth and Berry (1987) decided that children in care are not "doomed" but are still "shortchanged" (p. 80).

This review reveals the paucity of research with regard to foster family care's impact. For example, since 1985, we found fewer than a dozen published studies of foster care outcomes; most of these dealt with only limited aspects of the problem. Given the need for more persistent, detailed, and comprehensive assessment, directions for future research include the following:

- A more intensive analysis of the impact of foster family experiences on children's abilities to maintain healthy attachments. This research would be enriched by examination of all the relationships that children perceive as central in their lives.
- An effort to include data on all life domains of importance to healthy development. These include experiences with birth families and foster families and consideration of the children's characteristics as well as the social and economic environments in which they have lived.
- An examination of the children's changing perceptions of permanence as a result of foster care experiences (Maluccio & Fein, 1985a)
- Use of control groups and baseline data in all studies (Zill & Coiro, 1992; McDonald et al., 1993; Mech & Rycraft, 1995)
- Exploration of the "enormous range of individual needs and experiences" children and their families have in care rather than reporting summary data for whole samples (Little, Leitch, & Bullock, 1995, p. 671)
- Use of longitudinal data that follow children and track the integration of their learning over the course of their developmental careers, rather than segmenting their experiences (Mech & Rycraft, 1995)

14

Future Directions

Despite professional and governmental efforts to reduce the number of children in care, widespread use of this resource is likely to continue. Edmund Gordon recognized that foster family care meets a basic community need:

> It is in response to the social nature of human beings, and the functional necessity for family like groups for the nurturing of the young, that substitutions for family care have been developed. Such arrangements continue, and will do so, because the human condition requires their existence. It is to be remembered, in light of failures and abuses, that foster care arrangements serve important and essential social purposes. If foster care did not exist, all societies would find ways to invent it. (Jones, 1990, p. 179)

Moreover, it is clear that, at least in the foreseeable future, provision of foster family services will be seen as a responsibility of our federal, state, and local governments; this responsibility will continue to be tied to a mandate to care for maltreated and dependent children. When Halper and Jones completed their research on placement prevention in 1984, the conclusions they came to are still valid today:

> *The need for foster care will not wither away.* Good, strong, comprehensive foster care services will still be needed despite the growth of preventive services. The studies that have been done on preventive services, including the present one, indicate that the need for foster care is *reduced* but not eliminated through the use of the service. Some families are not capable of providing even minimally adequate care for their children; some families want to relinquish a child and should be permitted to do so; some families will need a brief period of placement; and some families will require a greater service investment to maintain them at an acceptable level of functioning than we will decide to afford. Preventive services will permit us to make some reduction in the incidence and duration of foster care *at the margins*; it will not supplant the need for foster care altogether. (p. 174, emphasis in original)

An attempt to articulate the components of "good, strong comprehensive foster care services" has been the primary purpose of this book. In this concluding chapter, we want to summarize what we have considered the most essential aspects of a well-managed and adequate foster care program.

Foster family programs will only work if we embrace the notion that this is a service provided to *families* by *families*—that at the core of foster family care is the notion that foster parents open their homes to children, that these children come from and remain connected to their own birth families, and that a primary goal for most of them is eventually to return them to these birth families. This task of providing loving care and "good" parenting to someone else's children is what makes foster parenting a unique and valuable child welfare service.

The J Case

Looking back on his experiences with Timothy, Rod Tedesco recognized that he had, for the first time in his life, become a parent. Throughout this experience, he was astonished to discover the range of emotions he had regarding his relationship with this child. He had expected to be able to maintain some sort of "professional distance"; he had assumed he would be able to see his involvement with Timothy as a "job" to do. But he quickly discovered that he really liked Timothy and cared about his welfare, that he felt responsible for him, and that he wanted Timothy to be happy living in his home. He struggled to understand the important family ties that made Timothy feel that such happiness would somehow be a betrayal of his mother's love. He found himself wishing Timothy could continue to live with him for the foreseeable future and was ashamed of his fantasies that Timothy would ask that Rod adopt him. He came to understand that the complex, intense, and conflicting feelings he was having reflected the essence of what he could give to Timothy as his foster parent—his attention, his caring, his involvement, his concern.

The process of becoming a family for someone else's child is an aspect of foster family care that is difficult to explain to foster care applicants, and their capacity to take on this challenge is difficult to evaluate. Out of the relationship between foster parents and foster children come many of the difficulties that make things go wrong; out of this relationship come many of the most valuable aspects of this service for children. The connections between foster and birth parents are also vital but sometimes difficult to establish. Providing services to develop and strengthen these unique family relationships is one of the most important and challenging tasks that foster care workers do. This, then, is one essential aspect of quality foster family care programming.

A second basic component of "good, strong" foster care services involves the provision of extensive, appropriate, and adequate preparation and support services for each group of actors in the foster care dialogue—the birth parents, their children, foster parents, and the foster care worker assigned to help them. Providing a "good home" for a child is a necessary but not sufficient condition for "good fostering" to occur. It is not enough to tell birth families to go and take care of their problems and come back for their children when they've straightened themselves out; it is not enough to tell foster parents to just "parent" the children in their care and everything will be all right; it is not enough to tell the foster children that they should just settle in and cooperate and all their problems will go away. Instead, each of these participants needs preparation for his or her tasks; foster parents and workers also need extensive training and supervision while carrying out their roles. Needed supports range from economic (enough money for birth families to live on, for example) to emotional (mental health services for foster children, for example) to social (opportunities for foster parents to meet together and exchange ideas, for example). Among the mandatory supports are those that grow out of the recognition of the unique role that cultural and racial factors play in service delivery. These are essential—not optional—aspects of effective foster care programming.

The J Case

The J family had two different foster care workers during Timothy's stay in care. These workers both had master's degrees in social work. At their agency ongoing training and intensive supervision were built into the program for all workers. The J family's workers realized how essential this preparation and support were. One of the workers had had to learn about marital violence, which he knew little about prior to meeting the Js. He had had to learn about attachment difficulties and to get some consultation to better understand why children can feel ambivalent in their attachments to foster parents. There were many weeks when he had to talk to his supervisor daily, particularly when Mr. J was being uncooperative or when Timothy was threatening to run away from the foster home. He remembered one especially hard time when Mr. J had physically threatened his wife while he was in a meeting with the couple; he had been fearful for her welfare and had not known what to do. He had had to return to the agency to talk the situation over with his supervisor, who had told him he had to take his cues from Mrs. J, since she was the person most threatened and most knowledgeable about how to handle this problem. He had found it difficult to see her as a resourceful person in this situation. Out of this experience, he came to ponder the meaning of a "strengths perspective" and spent a great deal of time clarifying what had happened in conversations with his colleagues at the agency.

He thought about what it must be like for a worker to be in a foster care agency that did not offer workers the type of preparation or supervision that he had. His friend was working in one of those types of agencies. He realized how much more effective and how much less frustrated he felt as a result of being in an environment that was rich in supportive resources for him.

A final essential component of "good, strong" foster care services is not provided by the worker or agency dealing with the family. Instead, it is offered by the broader community in which the family lives and the agency functions. Foster family care can only be effective when that community is able and willing to provide an array of social supports to all families—but particularly to the most vulnerable families that live there. Foster care services can only be effective when families also have ways to obtain safe, affordable housing; when they can obtain reliable means to feed their children and clothe them properly; when the community offers safe, accessible, and affordable places for them to live; when schools for their children offer a quality education and can be responsive to their children's special needs; and when the medical, mental health, and other services they need are within reach.

The J Case

Both Timothy and his parents are in need of assistance that goes far beyond the capacity of one particular social service agency to provide. Mr. and Mrs. J cannot stabilize their financial situation without periodic welfare funds or tailor-made job training programs responsive to their unique needs. Mr. J will not stop being abusive of his wife until the community in which he lives mobilizes to challenge this behavior and to provide protective services for Mrs. J. Their neighbors and extended family might be very helpful in this regard. He may need to be mandated by the criminal court to attend a program for batterers. Mrs. J will need to be offered confidential services for battered women that will not put her in further jeopardy. She may need psychiatric services when she has depressive episodes. Timothy is in need of specialized academic services to help improve his academic performance and to mediate his relationships with peers so that he does not get into fights at school. He has needed—and will continue to need—counseling to explore his relationship with his parents.

Foster family care cannot compensate for or substitute for these services if they are not available to the family. Without these additional supports, the program will probably fail in its goal to provide a safe and permanent family life for Timothy.

Frequently, public child welfare programs are required to function without these essential social supports. When the community does not embrace its responsibilities to families, the system cannot help but falter. Gleeson (1999) pointed out:

> The child welfare system has long been blamed for the failure to protect children and to ensure that children leave the foster care system for permanent homes in a short time period. For too long the child welfare system has accepted this responsibility and has pursued increased funding to assist in the pursuit of these goals; yet, the child welfare system has no ability to control the conditions of risk that increase the flow of children and families coming to the attention of the child welfare system. In effect, different parts of the child welfare system have been fighting with each other over problems they cannot solve. (p. 46)

Recognizing that foster family care is but one aspect of society's response to families in need, foster care workers need to be cognizant of the limitations of their role and the ways their tasks need to dovetail with those of many other community supports. When the neighbors will not act, when other social service agencies refuse to offer programming, and when the local and state governments refuse to provide funding for needed services, workers' mandate to act is compromised. Foster family services cannot act alone. The community's commitment to improve the lives of its hurting children and needy families is required.

References

Abramson, S. (1991). Use of court-appointed advocates to assist in permanency planning for minority children. *Child Welfare, 70*(4), 477–487.

Access to Respite Care & Help (ARCH). (1994, January). *Respite for foster parents* (ARCH Factsheet No. 32). Chapel Hill, NC: Author.

Albert, V. (1994). Explaining growth in the number of child abuse and neglect reports and growth in the foster care caseload. In R. Barth, J. D. Berrick, & N. Gilbert (Eds.), *Child welfare research review* (Vol. 1, pp. 218–249). New York: Columbia University Press.

Aldgate, J. (1987). Residential care: A reevaluation of a threatened resource. *Child and Youth Care Quarterly, 16*(1), 48–59.

Aldgate, J., Maluccio, A., & Reeves, C. (Eds.). (1989). *Adolescents in foster families.* Chicago: Lyceum Books.

Aldgate, J., Stein, M., & Carey, K. (1989). The contribution of young people and their families towards improving foster family care. In J. Aldgate, A. Maluccio, & C. Reeves (Eds.), *Adolescents in foster families* (pp. 61–76). Chicago: Lyceum Books.

Allen, M. (1992, Fall). Redefining family reunification. *The Prevention Report.* Iowa City, IA: National Resource Center on Family Based Services, The University of Iowa School of Social Work.

Allen, M., Brown, P., & Finlay, B. (1992). *Helping children by strengthening support programs.* Washington, DC: Children's Defense Fund.

Allen, M. L., Bonner, K., & Greeman, L. (1988). Federal legislative support for independent living. *Child Welfare, 67*(6), 515–527.

Altshuler, S., & Gleeson, J. (1999). Completing the evaluation triangle for the next century: Measuring child "well-being" in foster family care. *Child Welfare, 78*(1), 125–147.

American Humane Association. (1994, June). *Child Protection Leader.*

Anderson, K. (1998). A Canadian child welfare agency for urban natives: The clients speak. *Child Welfare, 77*(4), 441–460.

Armstrong, L. (1989). *Solomon says: A speakout on foster care.* New York: Pocket Books.

Asen, K., George, E., Piper, R., & Stevens, A. (1989). A systems approach to child abuse: Management and treatment issues. *Child Abuse and Neglect, 13,* 45–57.

Azzi-Lessing, L., & Olsen, L. (1996). Substance abuse-affected families in the child welfare system: New challenges, new alliances. *Social Work, 41*(1), 15–23.

Backhaus, K. A.(1984). Life books: Tool for working with children in placement. *Social Work, 29*(6), 551–554.

Baker, D., & Vick, C. (1995). *The child advocate's legal guide: Effective collaborative work to speed permanence for children in foster care.* St. Paul, MN: NACAC.

Baring-Gould, M. et al. (Fall, 1983). Why do foster homes close? *Arete 8*(2), 49–63.

Barn, R. (1993). *Black children in the public care system.* London: B. T. Batsford in association with British Agencies for Adoption and Fostering.

Barsh, E., Moore, J., & Hamerlynck, L. (1983). The foster extended family: A support network for handicapped foster children. *Child Welfare, 62,* 349–360.

Barth, R. (1989). Programs for interdependent living. In J. Aldgate, A. Maluccio, & C. Reeves (Eds.), *Adolescents in foster families* (pp. 122–138). Chicago: Lyceum Books.

Barth, R. (1995). *The Fedele F. & Iris M. Fauri Memorial Lecture Series on child welfare.* The University of Michigan, School of Social Work.

Barth, R. (1997). Effects of age and race on the odds of adoption versus remaining in long-term out-of-home care. *Child Welfare, 76*(2), 285–308.

Barth, R., Berrick, J. D., & Gilbert, N. (Eds.) (1994). *Child welfare research review* (Vol. 1). New York: Columbia University Press.

Barth, R., & Berry, M. (1987). Outcomes of child welfare services under permanency planning. *Social Service Review, 61,* 71–90.

Barth, R., Courtney, M., Berrick, J. D., & Albert, V. (1994). *From child abuse to permanency planning: Child welfare services and placement.* New York: Aldine De Gruyter.

Barth, R., Courtney, M., & Needell, B. (March 17, 1994). The odds of adoption vs. remaining in long-term foster care. Paper presented at Second Annual Child Welfare Conference, Washington, DC.

Barth, R., Courtney, M., Needell, B., & Jonson-Reid, M. (1994). *Performance indicators for child welfare services in California.* Berkeley, CA: Child Welfare Research Center.

Bath, H. I., & Haapala, D. A. (1993). Intensive family preservation services with abused and neglected children: An examination of group differences. *Child Abuse & Neglect, 17,* 213–225.

Bayless, L. (1990). *Assessing attachment, separation and loss.* Atlanta: Child Welfare Institute.

Becker, M., & Austin, S. (1983). *Alternate care case inventory.* Washington, DC: U.S. Department of Health and Human Services Administration for Children, Youth and Families.

Beckerman, A. (1989). Incarcerated mothers and their children in foster care: The dilemma of visitation. *Children and Youth Services Review, 11*(2), 175–183.

Beckerman, A. (1998). Charting a course: Meeting the challenge of permanency planning for children with incarcerated mothers. *Child Welfare 77*(5), 513–529.

Belsky, J., & Nezworski, T. (1988). *Clinical implications of attachment.* New York: Erlbaum.

Benedict, M., & White, R. (1991). Factors associated with foster care length of stay. *Child Welfare, 70*(1), 45–58.

Benedict, M., White, R., & Stallings, R. (1987). Race and length of stay in foster care. *Social Work Research and Abstracts, 23*(4), 23–26.

Benedict, M., White, R., Stallings, R., & Cornely, D. (1989). Racial differences in health care utilization among children in foster care. *Children and Youth Services Review, 11*(4), 285–297.

Benedict, M., Zuravin, S., & Stallings, R. (1996). Adult functioning of children who lived in kin versus nonrelative family foster homes. *Child Welfare, 75*(5), 529–549.

Berrick, J. D., Barth, R.; & Needell, B. (1994). A comparison of kinship foster homes and foster family homes: Implications for kinship foster care as family preservation. *Children and Youth Services Review, 16*(1/2), 33–63.

Berrick, J. D., & Lawrence-Karshi, R. (1995). Emerging issues in child welfare. *Public Welfare, 53*(4), 4–11.

Berrick, J. D., Needell, B., & Barth, R. (1999). Kin as a family and child welfare resource: The child welfare worker's perspective. In R. Hegar & M. Scannapieco (Eds.), *Kinship foster care: Policy, practice and research* (pp. 179–192). New York: Oxford University Press.

Berrick, J. D., Needell, B., Barth, R., & Johnson-Reid, M. (1998). *The tender years: Toward developmentally sensitive child welfare services for very young children.* New York: Oxford University Press.

Berridge, D., & Cleaver, H. (1987). *Foster home breakdown.* Oxford: Blackwell.

Berry, M. (1988). A review of parent training programs in child welfare. *Social Service Review, 62,* 302–323.

Besharov, D.(1986). The vulnerable social worker. *Children Today, 15*(5), 34–37.

Besharov, D. (1990). Crack children in foster care. *Children Today, 19*(4), 21–25, 35.

Beste, H., & Richardson R. (1981). Developing a life story book program for foster children. *Child Welfare, 60*(8), 529–534.

Beyer, M. (1986). Overcoming emotional obstacles to independence. *Children Today, 15*(5), 8–12.

Birmingham, J., Berry, M., & Bussey, M. (1996). Certification for child protective services staff members: The Texas initiative. *Child Welfare, 75*(6), 727–740.

Blacher, J. (1994). *When there's no place like home: Options for children living apart from their natural families.* Baltimore, MD: Paul H. Brookes.

Blatt et al. (1997). A comprehensive, multidisciplinary approach to providing health care for children in out-of-home care. *Child Welfare, 76*(2), 331–348.

Block, N. M., & Libowitz, A. (1983). *Recidivism in foster care.* New York: Child Welfare League of America.

Blome, W. W., Pasztor, E. M., & Leighton, M. (1993). *Homeworks #3: At-home training resources for foster parents and parents: Helping children and youths manage the placement.* Washington, DC: Child Welfare League of America.

Blumenthal, K. (1983). Making foster family care responsive. In B. G. McGowan & E. Meezan (Eds.), *Child welfare: Current dilemmas, future directions* (pp. 295–342). West Itasca, IL: F. E. Peacock.

Blumenthal, K., & Weinberg, A. (1984). *Establishing parent involvement in foster care.* New York: Child Welfare League of America.

Bolton, F., Morris, L., & MacEachron, A. (1989). *Males at risk: The other side of child sexual abuse.* Newbury Park, CA: Sage.

Bondy, D., Davis, D., Hagen, S., Spiritos, A., & Winnick, A. (1990). Mental health services for children in foster care. *Children Today, 19*(5), 28–32.

Borgman, R. (1981). Antecedents and consequences of parental rights: Termination for abused and neglected children. *Child Welfare, 60*(6), 391–404.

Boutilier, L., & Rehm, D. (1993). Family reunification practice in a community-based mental health center. In B. Pine, R. Warsh, & A. Maluccio (Eds.), *Together again: Family reunification in foster care* (pp. 51–66). Washington, DC: Child Welfare League of America.

Bowlby, J. (1969). *Attachment and loss* (Vol. 1). New York: Basic Books.

Bowlby, J. (1973). *Attachment and loss* (Vol. 2). New York: Basic Books.

Bowlby, J. (1988). *A secure base: Parent-child attachment and healthy human development.* New York: Basic Books.

Breitenstein, L. (1998). *Policy analysis of Pennsylvania's competency-based child welfare training and certification program.* Unpublished manuscript.

Bretherton, I. (1990). Communication patterns, internal working models, and the intergenerational transmission of attachment relationships. *Infant Mental Health Journal, 11*(3), 237–251.

Bretherton, I., & Waters, E. (1985). Attachment theory: Retrospect and prospect. *Growing Points Of Attachment Theory And Research: SRDC Monographs, 50*(1–2, Serial No. 209).

Brickman, A., Dey, S., & Cuthbert, P. (1991). A supervised independent-living orientation program for adolescents. *Child Welfare, 70*(1), 69–80.

Brodzinsky, D., & Schechter, M. (Eds.) (1990). *The psychology of adoption.* New York: Oxford University Press.

Brooks, D. (1999, Winter). Kinship care and substance-exposed children. *The Source, 9*(1), 1–2, 20–21.

Brown, A. W., & Bailey-Etta, B. (1997). An out-of-home care system in crisis: Implications for African American children in the child welfare system. *Child Welfare, 76*(1), 65–84.

Bryce, M., & Lloyd, J. (1981). *Treating families in the home: An alternative to placement.* Springfield, IL: Charles C. Thomas.

Bullock, R., Little, M., & Millham, S. (1993). *Going home: The return of children separated from their families.* Brooksfield, VT: Dartmouth.

Burns, W., & Burns, K. (1988). Parenting patterns in chemically dependent women. In I. Chasnoff (Ed.), *Drugs, alcohol, pregnancy, and parenting.* Boston: Kulwer Academic.

Burry, C. (1999). Evaluation of a training program for foster parents of infants with prenatal substance effects. *Child Welfare, 87*(1), 197–214.

Bush, M., & Goldman, H. (1982). The psychological parenting and permanency principles in child welfare: A reappraisal and critique. *American Journal of Orthopsychiatry, 52*(2), 223–235.

Cahn, K., & Johnson, P. (Eds.). (1993). *Children can't wait: Reducing delays in foster care.* Washington, DC: Child Welfare League of America.

Campbell, C., & Downs, S. W. (1987). The impact of economic incentive on foster parents. *Social Service Review, 61*, 599–609.

Cantos, A. L., Gries, L. T., and Slis, V. (1997). Behavioral correlates of parental visiting during family foster care. *Child Welfare, 76*(2), 309–330.

Carbino, R. (1983). Group work with natural parents in permanency planning. In S. Morris (Ed.), *The use of group services in permanency planning for children.* New York: Haworth Press.

Carbino, R. (Ed.). (1989). *Consequences of child abuse allegations for foster families: A report of a symposium.* Madison, WI: University of Wisconsin–Madison.

Carbino, R. (1990). Participation of biological families in preparation of adolescents for interdependent living. In A. Maluccio, R. Krieger, & B. Pine (Eds.), *Preparing adolescents for life after foster care: The central role of foster parents* (pp. 107–126). Washington, DC: Child Welfare League of America.

Carbino, R. (1992). Policy and practice for response to foster families when child abuse or neglect is reported. *Child Welfare, 71*(6), 497–512.

Carrieri, J. (1991). *Child custody, foster care, and adoptions.* New York: Lexington Books.

Carrieri, J. (Ed.) (1992). *Child abuse, neglect and the foster care system.* New York: Practicing Law Institute.

Carten, A. (1990). Building on the strengths of black foster families. In A. Maluccio, R. Krieger, & B. Pine (Eds.), *Preparing adolescents for life after foster care: The central role of foster parents* (pp. 127–146). Washington, DC: Child Welfare League of America.

Carten, A., & Fennoy, I. (1997). African American families and HIV/AIDS: Caring for surviving children. *Child Welfare, 76*(1), 107–126.

Cautley, P. W. (1980). *New foster parents: The first experience.* New York: Human Sciences Press.

Cautley, P. W., & Aldridge, M. (1975). Predicting success for new foster parents. *Social Work, 20*(1), 48–53.

Chamberlain, P., Moreland, S., & Reid, K. (1992). Enhanced services and stipends for foster parents: Effects on retention rates and outcomes for children. *Child Welfare, 71*(5), 387–401.

Charles, G., & Matheson, J. (1991). Suicide prevention and intervention with young people in foster care in Canada. *Child Welfare, 70*(2), 185–191.

Child Welfare Institute. (Spring, 1993). *Ideas in action,* 1–11.

Child Welfare League of America. (1990). *Out-of-home care: Agenda for the nineties.* Washington, DC: Author.

Child Welfare League of America. (1991a). *A blueprint for fostering infants, children, and youths in the 1990s.* Washington, DC: Author.

Child Welfare League of America. (1991b). *Meeting the challenge of HIV infection in foster family care.* Washington, DC: Author.

Child Welfare League of America. (1992a). *Children at the front: A different view of the war on alcohol and drugs.* Washington, DC: Author.

Child Welfare League of America. (1992b). *The youngest of the homeless II: A survey of boarder babies in selected hospitals in the United States.* Washington, DC: Author.

Child Welfare League of America. (1993). *Independent living services for youths in out-of-home care.* Washington, DC: Author.

Child Welfare League of America. (1994). *Kinship care: A natural bridge.* Washington, DC: Author.

Child Welfare League of America. (1995). *Standards of excellence for family foster care.* Washington, DC: Author.

Children's Defense Fund. (1978). *Children without homes.* Washington, DC: Author.

Children's Defense Fund. (1992). *The state of America's children.* Washington, DC: Author.

Cicchetti, D., Cummings, E., Greenberg, M., & Marvin, R. (1990). An organizational perspective on attachment beyond infancy: Implications for theory, measurement, and research. In M. Greenburg, D. Cicchetti, & E. Cummings (Eds.), *Attachment in the preschool years* (pp. 3–49). Chicago: University of Chicago Press.

Clement, P. F. (1979). Families and foster care: Philadelphia in the late nineteenth century. *Social Service Review, 53,* 406–420.

Cohen, J., & Westhues, A. (1990). *Well-functioning families for adoptive and foster children: A handbook for child welfare workers.* Toronto: University of Toronto Press.

Cohen, N. (Ed.). (1992). *Child welfare: A multicultural focus.* Boston: Allyn & Bacon.

Colon, F. (1981). Family ties and child placement. In P. A. Sinanoglu & A. N. Maluccio (Eds.), *Parents of children in placement: Perspectives and programs* (pp. 241–267). New York: Child Welfare League of America.

Colton, M. J. (1988). *Dimensions of substitute care: A comparative study of foster and residential care practice.* Brookfield, VT: Avebury.

Combs-Orme, T., Chernoff, R., & Kager, V. (1991). Utilization of health care by foster children: Application of a theoretical model. *Children and Youth Services Review, 13*(1/2), 113–129.

Constantino, J. (1993). Parents, mental illness, and the primary health care of infants and young children. *Zero to Three, 13*(5), 1–10.

Cook, R. (1988). Trends and needs in programming for independent living. *Child Welfare, 67*(6), 497–514.

Cook, R. (1994). Are we helping foster care youth prepare for their future? *Children and Youth Services Review, 16*(3/4), 213–229.

Cook, R., & Sedlak, A. (1995). National evaluation of independent living programs. In E. Mech, & J. Rycraft (Eds.), *Preparing foster youths for adult living: Proceedings of an invitational research conference* (pp. 19–26). Washington, DC: Child Welfare League of America.

Costin, L., Bell, C. J., & Downs, S. (1991). *Child welfare: Policies and practice* (4th ed.). White Plains, NY: Longman.

Courtney, M. (1994). Factors associated with entrance to group care. In R. Barth, J. D.

Berrick, & N. Gilbert (Eds.), *Child welfare research review* (Vol. 1, pp. 185–204). New York: Columbia University Press.

Courtney, M. (1995). The foster care crisis and welfare reform. *Public Welfare, 53*(3), 27–33.

Courtney, M., & Barth, R. (1996). Pathways of older adolescents out of foster care: Implications for independent living services. *Social Work, 41*(1), 75–84.

Courtney, M., Barth, R., Berrick, J. D., Brooks, D., Needell, R., & Park, L.(1996). Race and child welfare services: Past research and future directions. *Child Welfare, 75*(2), 99–138.

Cox, M. (1985). *Foster care: Current issues, policies and practices.* Norwood, NJ: Ablex.

Cox, M., & Cox, R. (1984). Foster care and public policy. *Journal of Family Issues, 5*(2), 182–199.

Coyne, A. (1986). Recruiting foster and adoptive families: A marketing strategy. *Children Today, 15*(5), 30–33.

Crittenden, P. (1988). Family and dyadic patterns of functioning in maltreating families. In K. Browne, C. Davies, & P. Stratton (Eds.), *Early prediction and prevention of child abuse* (pp. 161–189). Chichester, UK: Wiley.

Cully, J. D., Healy, D. F., Settles, B. H., & Van Name, J. (1977). Public payments for foster care. *Social Work, 22,* 219–233.

Curtis, P. A., & McCullough, C. (1993). The impact of alcohol and other drugs on the child welfare system. *Child Welfare, 72*(6), 533–542.

Dalgleish, L. I., & Drew, E. C. (1989). The relationship of child abuse indicators to the assessment of perceived risk and to the court's decision to separate. *Child Abuse and Neglect, 13,* 491–506.

Danzy, J., & Jackson, S. M. (1997). Family preservation and support services. *Child Welfare, 76*(1), 31–44.

Davids, L. (1968). *The foster father role.* Unpublished doctoral dissertation, New York University.

Davidson, C. (1994). Dependent children and their families: A historical survey of United States policies. In F. Jacobs & M. Davies (Eds.), *More than kissing babies: Current child and family policy in the United States* (pp. 65–90). Westport, CT: Auburn House.

Davidson, R. F. (1980). Restoring children to their families. In J. Triseliotis (Ed.), *New developments in foster care and adoption* (pp. 41–53). London: Routledge and Kegan Paul.

Davies, L. J., & Bland, D. C. (1981). The use of foster parents as role models for parents. In P. A. Sinanoglu & A. N. Maluccio (Eds.) *Parents of children in placement: Perspectives and programs* (pp. 415–422). New York: Child Welfare League of America.

Davis et al. (1984). Cluster homes: An alternative for troubled youths. *Children Today, 13,* 34–36.

Davis, I. (1989). Intervention with adolescents in foster family care and their families. In J. Aldgate, A. Maluccio, & C. Reeves (Eds.), *Adolescents in foster families.* (pp. 88–101). Chicago: Lyceum Books.

Davis, I., & Ellis-MacLeod, E. (1994). Temporary foster care: Separating and reunifying families. In J. Blacher (Ed.), *When there's no place like home: Options for children living apart from their natural families* (pp. 123–162). Baltimore, MD: Paul H. Brookes.

Davis, I., English, D., & Landsverk, J. (1993). *Going home—and returning to care.* San Diego: San Diego State University School of Social Work and Child and Family Research Group.

Davis, I., English, D., & Landsverk, J. (1995). *Outcomes of permanency planning for 1165 foster children.* San Diego: San Diego State University School of Social Work and Child and Family Research Group.

Delaney, R. (1998). *Fostering changes: Treating attachment disordered foster children.* Oklahoma City, OK: Wood 'N' Barnes.

Delaney, R., & Kunstal, F. R. (1993). *Troubled transplants: Unconventional strategies for helping disturbed foster and adoptive children.* Portland, ME: National Child Welfare Resource Center for Management and Administration.

Delgado, R. (1992). Generalist child welfare and Hispanic families. In N. Cohen (Ed.), *Child welfare: A multicultural focus* (pp. 130–156). Boston: Allyn & Bacon.

Derdeyn, A. (1990). Foster parent adoption: The legal framework. In D. Brodzinsky & M. Schechter (Eds.), *The psychology of adoption* (pp. 332–348). New York: Oxford University Press.

Dodson, D. (1983). Advocating at periodic review hearings. In M. Hardin & D. Dodson (Eds.), *Foster children in the courts* (pp. 86–127). Boston: Butterworth Legal Publishers.

Doelling, J. L., & Johnson, J. H. (1990). Predicting success in foster placement: The contribution of parent-child temperament characteristics. *American Journal of Orthopsychiatric, 60*(4), 585–593.

Downes, C. (1993). *Separation revisited: Adolescents in foster family care.* Brookfield, VT: Ashgate.

Downs, S. W. (1986). Black foster parents and agencies: Results of an eight state survey. *Children and Youth Services Review, 8*(3), 201–218.

Downs, S. W. (1990). Recruiting and retaining foster families of adolescents. In A. Maluccio, R. Krieger, & B. Pine (Eds.), *Preparing adolescents for life after foster care: The central role of foster parents* (pp. 19–34). Washington, DC: Child Welfare League of America.

Drotar, D., & Stege, E. (1988). Psychological testimony in foster parent adoption: A case report. *Journal of Clinical Child Psychology, 17*(2), 164–168.

Dubowitz, H., Feigelman, S., Harrington, D., Starr, R., Zuravin, S., & Sawyer, R. (1994). Children in kinship care: How do they fare? *Children and Youth Services Review, 16*(1/2), 85–106

Dubowitz, H., Feigelman, S., & Zuravin, S. (1993). A profile of kinship care. *Child Welfare, 72*(2), 153–169.

Dubowitz, H., & Sawyer, R. (1994). School behavior of children in kinship care. *Child Abuse & Neglect, 18*(11), 899–911.

Dugger, C. W. (1992, September 8). Troubled children flood ill-prepared care system. *New York Times Current Events Edition,* p. A1.

Early, B., & Hawkins, M. (1994). Opportunity and risks in emerging family policy: An analysis of family preservation legislation. *Children and Youth Services Review, 16*(5/6), 309–317.

Edelstein, S. (1981). When foster children leave: Helping foster parents to grieve. *Child Welfare, 60*(7), 467–474.

Eisenberg, L. (1965). Deprivation and foster care. *Journal of American Academy of Child Psychiatry, 4,* 243–248.

Emlen et al. (1977). *Overcoming barriers to planning for children in foster care.* Portland, OR: Portland State University, Regional Research Institute for Human Services.

Engel, J. M. (1983). The parent therapist program: A new approach to foster care of difficult adolescents. *Children and Youth Services Review, 5,* 195–207.

English, D., & Clark, T. (1996) *Report of Children in Foster and Group Care Placements in Washington State Between June 1985 and August 1995.* Unpublished manuscript.

English, D. J., Kouidou-Giles, S., & Plocke, M. (1994). Readiness for independence: A study of youth in foster care. *Children and Youth Services Review, 16*(3/4), 147–158.

English, R. (1991). Diversity of world views among African American families. In J. Everett, S. Chipungu, & B. Leashore (Eds.), *Child welfare: An Africentric perspective* (pp. 19–35). New Brunswick, NJ: Rutgers University Press.

Euster, S. D., Ward, V. P., & Varner, J. G. (1982). Adapting counseling techniques to foster parent training. *Child Welfare, 61*(6), 375–382.

Everett, J., Chipungu, S., & Leashore, B. (Eds.). (1991). *Child welfare: An Africentric perspective.* New Brunswick, NJ: Rutgers University Press.

Fahlberg, V. (1991). *A child's journey through placement.* Indianapolis, IN: Perspectives Press.

Fanshel, D. (1966). *Foster parenthood: A role analysis.* Minneapolis: University of Minnesota Press.

Fanshel, D. (1975). Parental failure and consequences for children: The drug abusing mother whose children are in foster care. *American Journal of Public Health, 65,* 604–612.

Fanshel, D. (1979). Preschoolers entering foster care in New York City: The need to stress plans for permanency. *Child Welfare, 58,* 67–87.

Fanshel, D. (1981). Decision-making under uncertainty: Foster care for abused or neglected children. *American Journal of Public Health, 71*(7), 685–686.

Fanshel, D. (1982). *On the road to permanency: An expanded data base for service to children in foster care.* New York: Child Welfare League of America.

Fanshel, D. (1992). Foster care as a two-tiered system. *Children and Youth Services Review, 14*(1/2), 49–60.

Fanshel, D., & Finch, S. (1985). Computerized information systems and the quest for permanency for children in foster care: Observations from the New York experience. In M. Cox & R. Cox (Eds.), *Foster care: Current issues, policies, and practices* (pp. 73–112). Norwood, NJ: Ablex.

Fanshel, D., Finch, S., & Grundy, J. (1989). Foster children in life-course perspective: The Casey family program experience. *Child Welfare, 68*(5), 467–478.

Fanshel, D., Finch, S., & Grundy, J. (1990). *Foster children in life course perspectives: The Casey family program experience.* New York: Columbia University Press.

Fanshel, D., & Grundy, J. (1975). *Computerized data for children in foster care: First analysis from a management information service in New York City.* New York: Child Welfare Information Service.

Fanshel, D., & Maas, H. (1962). Factorial dimensions of the characteristics of children in placements and their families. *Child Development, 33.*

Fanshel, D., & Shinn, E. B. (1972). *Dollars and sense in the foster care of children: A look at cost factors.* New York: Child Welfare League of America.

Fanshel, D., & Shinn, E. B. (1978). *Children in foster care: A longitudinal investigation.* New York: Columbia University Press.

Farley, B. (1993). Effective practices: Changing a system to change a child's life. In K. Cahn, & P. Johnson (Eds.), *Children can't wait: Reducing delays for children in foster care* (pp. 75–104). Washington, DC: Child Welfare League of America.

Farmer, E., & Parker, R. (1991). *Trials and tribulations: Returning children from local authority care to their families.* London: HMSO.

Fein, E. (1991). Issues in foster family care: Where do we stand? *American Journal of Orthopsychiatric, 61*(4), 578–583.

Fein et al. (1983). After foster care: Outcomes of permanency planning for children. *Child Welfare, 62*(6), 485–558.

Fein, E., & Maluccio, A. (1992). Permanency planning: Another remedy in jeopardy? *Social Service Review, 66,* 335–348.

Fein, E., Maluccio, A., & Kluger, M. (1990). *No more partings: An examination of long-term foster family care.* Washington, DC: Child Welfare League of America.

Fein, E., & Staff, L. (1993). Last best chance: Funding from a reunification services program. *Child Welfare, 72*(1), 25–40.

Felker, E. (1981). *Raising other people's kids.* Grand Rapids, MI: William B. Eerdmans.

Fenyo, A., Knapp, M., & Baines, B. (1989). Foster care breakdown: A study of a special teenager fostering scheme. In J. Hudson & B. Galaway (Eds.), *State as parent: International research perspectives on interventions with young persons* (pp. 315–329). Boston: Kluwer Academic.

Ferguson, T. (1966). *Children in care and after.* New York: Oxford University Press.

Festinger, T. B. (1974). Placement agreements with boarding homes: A survey. *Child Welfare, 53*(10), 643–652.

Festinger, T. B. (1975). The New York court review of children in foster care. *Child Welfare, 54,* 211–245.

Festinger, T. B. (1976). The impact of the New York court review of children in foster care. A follow up report. *Child Welfare, 55,* 516–544.

Festinger, T. B. (1983). *No one ever asked us: A postscript to foster care.* New York: Columbia University Press.

Festinger, T. B. (1994). *Returning to care, discharge and reentry in foster care.* Washington, DC: Child Welfare League of America.

Finch, S., & Fanshel, D. (1985). Testing the equality of discharge patterns in foster care. *Social Work Research and Abstracts, 21*(3), 3–10.

Fisher, M., Marsh, P., & Phillips, D. with Sainsbury, E. (1986). *In and out of care: The experiences of children, parents and social workers.* London: B. T. Batsford.

Fitzharris, T. (1985). *The foster children of California: Profiles of 10,000 children in residential care.* Sacramento, CA: Children's Services Foundation.

Flango, V., & Flango, C. (1995). Adoption statistics by state. *Child Welfare, 72*(3), 311–319.

Flynn, L. (1990). *Mental health services for children in foster care.* Atlanta, GA: Child Welfare Institute.

Focus on practice in permanency planning. (Fall, 1992). *Fostering Ideas, 7,* 3, 10.

Folaron, G. (1993). Preparing children for reunification. In B. Pine, R. Warsh, & A. Maluccio (Eds.), *Together again: Family reunification in foster care* (pp. 141–154). Washington, DC: Child Welfare League of America.

Folaron, G., & Hess, P. (1993). Placement considerations for children of mixed African American and Caucasian parentage. *Child Welfare, 72*(2), 123–125.

Folaron, G., & Wagner, M. (1998). Children in the child welfare system: An ecological approach. In R. Greene & M Watkins (Eds.), *Serving diverse constituencies: Applying the ecological perspective* (pp. 113–133). New York: Aldine De Gruyter.

Folks, H. (1902). *The care of the destitute, neglected, and delinquent children.* New York: The Macmillan Company.

Foster care up despite "permanency" efforts. (1993, July). *NASW News,* p. 9.

Foster Family-Based Treatment Association. (1991, Spring). FFTA standards for treatment foster care. *FFTA Newsletter, 2*(1).

Fox, M., & Arcuri, K. (1980). Cognitive and academic functioning in foster children. *Child Welfare, 59*(8), 491–496.

Franck, E. (1996). Prenatally drug-exposed children in out-of-home care: Are we looking at the whole picture? *Child Welfare, 75*(1), 19–34.

Frank, G. (1980). Treatment needs of children in foster care. *American Journal of Orthopsychiatric, 50*(2), 256–263.

Freud, A., Goldstein, J., & Solnit, A. (1973). *Beyond the best interests of the child.* New York: The Free Press.

Friedman et al. (1982). Length of time in foster care: A measure in need of analysis. *Social Work, 27*(6), 499–503.

Fullbright, M. (1988). Host homes: One alternative for troubled youth. *Children Today, 17*(5), 12–15.

Gardner, H. (1996). The concept of family: Perceptions of children in family foster care. *Child Welfare, 75*(2), 161–182.

Garon, R., Mandell, B., & Walker, J. (1984). Helping children cope with separation and divorce. *Foster Care Journal, 1*(6), 5–7.

Gebel, T. J. (1996). Kinship care and nonrelative family foster care: A comparison of caregiver attributes and attitudes. *Child Welfare, 75*(1), 5–18.

George, V. (1970). *Foster care: Theory and practice.* London: Kegan, Paul, Trench, Trubner & Co.

Gershenson, C. (1983). *Child welfare population characteristics and flow analysis: FY 1982.* Washington, DC: Administration for Children, Youth and Families.

Gibson, T. L., Tracy, G. S. & DeBord, M. S. (1984). An analysis of variables affecting length of stay in foster care. *Children and Youth Services Review, 6,* 135–145.

Gil, E. (1984). Foster parents: Set up to fail. *Child Abuse and Neglect, 8,* 121–123.

Glasser, M. (1983). Mental health consultation in long-term planning for foster children. In M. Hardin & D. Dodson (Eds.), *Foster children in the courts* (pp. 534–549). Boston: Butterworth Legal Publishers.

Glatz, J. C. (1998). *Fostering or adopting the troubled child: A guide for parents and professionals.* Brunswick, ME: Audenreed Press.

Gleeson, J. (1995). Kinship care and public child welfare: Challenges and opportunities. *Journal of Social Work Education, 31*(2), 182–193.

Gleeson, J. (1996). Kinship care as a child welfare service: The policy debate in an era of welfare reform. *Child Welfare, 75*(5), 419–449.

Gleeson, J. (1999). Kinship care as a child welfare service: Emerging policy issues and trends. In R. Hegar & M. Scannapieco (Eds.), *Kinship foster care: Policy, practice and research* (pp. 28–53). New York: Oxford University Press.

Gleeson, J., & Craig, L. C. (1994). Kinship care in child welfare: An analysis of states' policies. *Children and Youth Services Review, 16*(1/2), 7–31.

Gleeson, J., O'Donnell, J., & Bonecutter, F. J. (1997). Understanding the complexity of practice in kinship foster care. *Child Welfare, 76*(6), 801–826.

Glisson, C., & Hemmelgarn, A. (1998). The effects of organizational climate and interorganizational coordination on the quality and outcomes of children's services. *Child Abuse and Neglect, 22*(5), 401–421.

Goerge, R. (1990). The reunification process in substitute care. *Social Service Review, 64,* 422–457.

Goerge, R. (1994). The effect of public child welfare worker characteristics and turnover on discharge from foster care. In R. Barth, J. Berrick, & N. Gilbert (Eds.), *Child welfare research review: Volume 1* (pp. 205–217). New York: Columbia University Press.

Goerge, R., VanVoorhis, J., Grant, S., Casey, K., & Robinson, M. (1992). Special education experiences of foster children: An empirical study. *Child Welfare, 71*(5), 419–438.

Goerge, R., Wulczyn, F., & Harden, A. (1994). *Foster care dynamics 1983-1992: A report from the multistate foster care data archive.* Chicago: Chapin Hall Center for Children at the University of Chicago.

Goerge, R., Wulczyn, F., & Harden, A. (1996). New comparative insights into states and their foster children. *Public Welfare, 54*(3), 12–25.

Gold, N. (1998). Using participatory research to help promote the physical and mental health of female social workers in child welfare. *Child Welfare, 77*(6), 701–725.

Goldstein, H., Gabay, D., & Switzer, R. (1981). Fail safe foster family care: A mental hospital–child welfare agency program. *Child Welfare, 60*(9), 627–636.

Gomes-Schwartz, B., Horowitz, J., & Cardarelli, A. (1990). *Child sexual abuse: The initial effects.* Newbury Park, CA: Sage.

Goodman, S., Radke-Yarrou, M., & Teti, D. (April/May 1993). Maternal depression as a context for child rearing. *Zero to Three,* 10–16.

Gould, K. (1991). Limiting damage is not enough: A minority perspective on child welfare issues. In J. Everett, S. Chipungu, & B. Leashore. (Eds.), *Child welfare: An Africentric perspective* (pp. 58–84). New Brunswick, NJ: Rutgers University Press.

Greenspan, S., & Greenspan, N. (1985). *First feelings: Milestones in the emotional development of your baby and child.* New York: Penguin Books.

Gries, L. (1990). Decision-making in foster care: The child as the primary source of data. In J. Carrieri (Ed.), *Child abuse, neglect, and the foster care system* (pp. 73–114). New York: Practicing Law Institute.

Grigsby, R. K. (1994). Maintaining attachment relationships among children in foster care. *Families in Society, 75,* 269–276.

Gruber, A. R. (1973). *A study of children, their biological and foster parents.* Springfield, MA: Governor's Commission on Adoption & Foster Care.

Halper, G., & Jones, M. A. (1984). *Serving families at risk of dissolution: Public preventive services in New York City.* New York: Human Resources Administration.

Halpern, R. (1990). Fragile families: Fragile solutions: An essay review. *Social Service Review, 64,* 637–648.

Hampson, R. (1985). Foster parent training: Assessing its role in upgrading foster home care. In M. Cox & R. Cox (Eds.), *Foster care: Current issues, policies, and practices* (pp. 167–205). Norwood, NJ: Ablex.

Hampson, R. (1988). Special foster care for exceptional children: A review of programs and policies. *Children and Youth Services Review, 10*(1), 19–41.

Hampson, R. B., & Tavormina, J. B. (1980). Feedback from the experts: A study of foster mothers. *Social Work, 25,* 108–113.

Hansen, C. (1994). Making it work: The case for constitutional protection of foster children from abuse and neglect. In S. R. Humm, B. Ort, M. Anbari, W. Lader, & W. Biel (Eds.), *Child, parent, & state: Law and policy reader* (pp. 224–236). Philadelphia: Temple University Press.

Hardin, M. (1983). Setting limits on voluntary foster care. In M. Hardin & D. Dodson (Eds.), *Foster children in the courts* (pp. 70–85). Boston: Butterworth Legal Publishers.

Hardin, M. (1987). Preparing adolescents in foster care for independent living: Some issues in law and policy. *Children's Legal Rights Journal, 8*(3), 2–7.

Hargrave, V., Shireman, J., & Connor, P. (1975). *Where love and need are one.* Chicago: Illinois Department of Social Services.

Harling, D. (1981). Observation and assessment by foster parents. *Adoption and Fostering, 106*(4), 39–40.

Hart, H. H. (1884). Annual report. *Proceedings of the National Conference of Charities and Correction.* Boston: George H. Ellis.

Hartman, A. (1993). Introduction: Family reunification in context. In B. Pine, R. Warsh, & A. Maluccio (Eds.), *Together again: Family reunification in foster care* (pp. xv–xxii). Washington, DC: Child Welfare League of America.

Hauswald, L. (1987). External pressure/internal change: Child neglect on the Navajo reservation. In N. Scheper-Hughes (Ed.), *Child survival: Anthropological perspectives on the treatment and maltreatment of children* (pp. 145–164). Boston: D. Reidel.

Hawkins, R. P., & Breiling, J. (Eds.) (1989). *Therapeutic Foster Care: Critical Issues*. Washington, DC: Child Welfare League of America.

Hazel, N. (1981). Community placements for adolescents in the United Kingdom: Changes in policy and practice. *Children and Youth Services Review, 3,* 85–97.

Hazel, N., Schmedes, C., & Korshin, P.M. (1983). A case study in international cooperation. *British Journal of Social Work, 13*(6), 671–678.

Hegar, R. (1988). Sibling relationships and separations: Implications for child placement. *Social Service Review, 62,* 446–467.

Hegar, R. (1999). The cultural roots of kinship care. In R. Hegar & M. Scannapieco (Eds.), *Kinship foster care: Policy, practice and research* (pp. 17–27). New York: Oxford University Press.

Hegar, R., & Scannapieco, M. (1995). From family duty to family policy: The evolution of kinship care. *Child Welfare, 74*(1), 200–216.

Hegar, R., & Scannapieco, M. (Eds.). (1999). *Kinship foster care: Policy, practice and research.* New York: Oxford University Press.

Herman, J. (1992). *Trauma and recovery.* New York: Basic Books.

Herring, D. (Summer, 1992). Permanency planning as a force for reform of the child welfare system. *Levine's Newsletter, 7*(3), 5–8, 19.

Herring, D. (1993). The Michigan agency attorney project. In K. Cahn & P. Johnson (Eds.), *Children can't wait: Reducing delays for children in foster care* (pp. 13–38). Washington, DC: Child Welfare League of America.

Herstein, N. (1957). The replacement of children from foster homes. *Child Welfare, 36.*

Hess, P. (1987). Parental visiting of children in foster care: Current knowledge and research agenda. *Children and Youth Services Review, 9*(1), 29–50.

Hess, P. (1988). Case and context: Determinants of planned visit frequency in foster care. *Child Welfare, 67*(4), 311–326.

Hess, P., & Folaron, G. (1991). Ambivalence: A challenge to permanency for children. *Child Welfare, 70*(4), 403–424.

Hess, P., Folaron, G., & Jefferson, A. B. (1992). Effectiveness of family reunification services: An innovative evaluative model. *Social Work, 37*(4), 304–311.

Hess, P., & Hicks, J. (1979). Pulling together with the natural family. *Workshop Proceedings of the Tennessee Foster Care Association Annual Conference.*

Hess, P., Mintun, G., Moelhman, A., & Pitts, G. (1992). The family connection center: An innovative visiting program. *Child Welfare, 71*(1), 77–88.

Hess, P., & Proch, K. (1988). *Family visiting in out-of-home care: A guide to practice.* Washington, DC: Child Welfare League of America.

Hess, P., & Williams, L. (1982). Group orientation for parents of children in foster family care. *Child Welfare, 61*(7), 456–466.

Hessle, S. (1989). Families falling apart: A report from social services. *Child Welfare 68*(2), 209–213.

Hogan, P. T. & Siu, S-F. (1988) Minority Children and the Child Welfare System: An Historical Perspective. *Social Work, 33*(6), 493–497.

Holman, R. (1973). *Trading in children: A study of private fostering.* London, England: Routledge & Kegan Paul.

Holman, R. (1980). Exclusive and inclusive concepts of fostering. In J. Triseliotis (Ed.), *New developments in foster care and adoption* (pp. 69–84). London: Routledge and Kegan Paul.

Holody, R., & Maher, S. (1996). Using lifebooks with children in family foster care: A here-and-now process model. *Child Welfare, 75*(4), 321–335.

Horejsi, C., Craig, B. H. R., & Pablo, J. (1992). Reactions by Native American parents to child protection agencies: Cultural and community factors. *Child Welfare, 71*(4), 329–342.

Hornby, H., & Collins, M. (1981). Teenagers in foster care: The forgotten majority. *Children and Youth Services Review, 3,* 7–20.

Hornby, H., Zeller D., & Karraker, D. (1996). Kinship care in America: What outcomes should policy seek? *Child Welfare, 75*(5), 397–418.

Horowitz, H. (1983). The expanding role of foster parents: Access to case information and grievance procedures. In M. Hardin & D. Dodson (Eds.), *Foster children in the courts* (pp. 283–298). Boston: Butterworth Legal Publishers.

Howing, P., & Wodarski, J. (1992). Legal requisites for social workers in child abuse and neglect situations. *Social Work, 37*(4), 330–336.

Hubbell, R. (1981). *Foster care and families: Conflicting values and policies.* Philadelphia: Temple University Press.

Hulsey, T. C., & White, R. (1989). Family characteristics and measures of behavior in foster and nonfoster children. *American Journal of Orthopsychiatric, 59*(4), 502–509.

Humm, S. R., Ort, B., Anbari, M., Lader, W., & Biel, W. (Eds.). (1994). *Child, parent, & state: Law and policy reader.* Philadelphia: Temple University Press.

Humphrey, M., & Humphrey, H. (1988). *Families with a difference.* London: Routledge and Kegan Paul.

Inglehart, A. (1994). Kinship foster care: Placement, service and outcome issues. *Children and Youth Services Review, 16*(1/2), 107–121.

Inglehart, A. (1995). Readiness for independence: Comparison of foster care, kinship care, and non-foster care adolescents. *Children and Youth Services Review, 17*(3), 417–432.

Institute for Children and Poverty. (1993, August). *Homelessness: The foster care connection* (Volume 2, Issue 1). New York: Author.

Institute for the Study of Children and Families. (Winter, 1990). Quality placement for the 90's. *Fostering Ideas 4.* Ypsilanti, MI: Eastern Michigan University, 1–2, 6.

Irvine, J. (1988). Aftercare services. *Child Welfare, 67*(6), 587–594.

Ishisaka, H. (1978). American Indians and foster care: Cultural factors and separation. *Child Welfare, 57*(5), 299–307.

Jackson, D. D. (1986). A bittersweet trap. *Smithsonian, 17*(5), 94–103.

Jackson, S. (1999). Paradigm shift: Training staff to provide services to the kinship triad. In R. Hegar & M. Scannapieco (Eds.), *Kinship foster care: Policy, practice and research* (pp. 93–111). New York: Oxford University Press.

Jacobs, F., & Davies, M. (Eds.). (1994). *More than kissing babies: Current child and family policy in the United States.* Westport, CT: Auburn House.

Jacobsen, E., & Cockerum, J. (1976). As foster children see it. *Children Today, 5,* 32–36.

Jaffee, B., & Kline, D. (1970). *New payment pattern and the foster parent role.* New York: Child Welfare League of America.

James, B. (1989). *Treating traumatized children: New insights and creative interventions.* Lexington, MA: Lexington Books.

James Bell Associates. (1993). *The national survey of current and former foster parents* (DHHS, ACF, & ACYF No. 105-89-1602). Washington, DC: Author.

Janchill, Sr., M. P. (1983). Services for special populations of children. In B. McGowan & W. Meezan (Eds.), *Child welfare: Current dilemmas, future directions* (pp. 345–376). Itasca, IL: F. E. Peacock.

Jenkins, S. et al. (1983). Ethnic differentials in foster care placements. *Social Work Research and Abstracts, 19*(4), 41–45.

Jenkins, S. (1967). Filial deprivation in parents of children in foster care. *Children, 14*(1), 8–12.

Jenkins, S., & Diamond, B. (1985). Ethnicity and foster care: Census data as predictors of placement variables. *The American Journal of Orthopsychiatric, 55*(2), 267–276.

Jenkins, S., & Norman, E. (1975). *Beyond placement: Mothers' view of foster care.* New York: Columbia University Press.

Jewett, C. (1982). *Helping children cope with separation and loss.* Boston: Harvard Common Press.

Johnson, I. (1994). Kinship care. In D. Besharov & K. Hanson (Eds.), *When drug addicts have children: Reorienting child welfare's response* (pp. 221–228). Washington, DC: Child Welfare League of America.

Johnson, P., Day, P., & Cahn, K. (1993). Interagency collaboration: System improvements for planning permanence. In K. Cahn & P. Johnson (Eds.), *Children can't wait: Reducing delays for children in foster care* (pp. 105–128). Washington, DC: Child Welfare League of America.

Johnson, P., Yoken, C., & Voss, R. (1995). Family foster care placement: The child's perspective. *Child Welfare, 74*(5), 959–974.

Jolowicsz, A. (1946, November). *The hidden parent.* Paper presented at the New York State Conference on Social Welfare, New York.

Jones, E. P. (1990). *Where is home?: Living through foster care.* New York: Four Walls Eight Windows.

Jones, L. (1993). Decision making in child welfare: A critical review of the literature. *Child and Adolescent Social Work Journal, 10*(3), 241–262.

Jones, M. (1989). Crisis of the American orphanage, 1931–1940. *Social Service Review, 63,* 613–629.

Jones, M., & Biesecker, J. (1980). Training in permanency planning: Using what is known. *Child Welfare, 59*(8), 481–489.

Jones, M., Neuman, R., & Shyne, A. W. (1976). *A second chance for families: Evaluation of a program to reduce foster care.* New York: Child Welfare League of America.

Jordan, C. (1989). The guardian *ad litem*: Evaluation of citizen reviewers in foster care. *Children and Youth Services Review, 11*(4), 331–348.

Jordan, C., & Franklin, C. (1994). Have external review systems improved the quality of care for children? In E. Gambrill & T. J. Stein (Eds.), *Controversial issues in child welfare* (pp. 136–149). Boston: Allyn & Bacon.

Kadushin, A., & Martin, J. (1988). *Child welfare services* (4th ed.). New York: Macmillan.

Kahan, B. (1979). *Growing up in care: Ten people talking.* Oxford: Basil Blackwell.

Kahkonen, P. (1997). Troubles in Smurftown: Youth gangs and moral visions on Guam. *Child Welfare, 76*(3), 429–446.

Kamerman, S., & Kahn, A. J. (1990). Social services for children, youth and families in the United States. *Children and Youth Services, 12*(1/2).

Kates, W. G., Johnson, R. L., Rader, M. W., & Strieder, F. H. (1991). Whose child is this? Assessment and treatment of children in foster care. *American Journal of Orthopsychiatric, 61*(4), 584–591.

Katz, L. (1990). Effective permanency planning for children in foster care. *Social Work, 35*(3), 220–226.

Katz, L. (1999). Concurrent planning: Benefits and pitfalls. *Child Welfare, 78*(1), 71–87.

Katz, L., & Robinson, C. (1991). Foster care drift: A risk-assessment matrix. *Child Welfare, 70*(3), 347–358.

Katz, P. (1998). Supporting families and children of mothers in jail: An integrated child welfare and criminal justice strategy. *Child Welfare, 77*(5), 495–511.

Kavaler, F., & Swire, M. (1983). *Foster child health care.* Lexington, MA: Lexington Books.

Kent, J. (1976). A follow-up study of abused children. *Journal of Pediatric Psychology, 25–31.*

Kilbride, J., & Kilbride, P. (1994). Fostering in familial settings. In J. Blacher (Ed.), *When there's no place like home: Options for children living apart from their natural families* (pp. 301–328). Baltimore, MD: Paul H. Brookes.

Kinney, J., Haapala, D., & Booth, C. (1991). *Keeping families together: The homebuilders model.* New York: Aldine De Gruyter.

Kinnie, E., & Hardin, M. (1983). Psychological indications whether a neglected child should be removed or returned to parents. In M. Hardin & D. Dodson (Eds.), *Foster children in the courts* (pp. 518–533). Boston: Butterworth Legal Publishers.

Klee, L., Soman, L., & Halfon, N. (1992). Implementing critical health services for children in foster care. *Child Welfare, 71*(2), 99–111.

Kliman, G. W., Schaeffer, M., & Friedman, M. J. (Eds.). (1982). *Preventive mental health services for children entering foster home care: An assessment.* White Plains, NY: Center for Preventive Psychiatry.

Kluger, M., Maluccio, A., & Fein, E. (1989). Preparation of adolescents for life after foster care. In J. Aldgate, A. Maluccio, & C. Reeves (Eds.), *Adolescents in foster families* (pp. 77–87). Chicago: Lyceum Books.

Knitzer, J., & Olson, L. (1982). *Unclaimed children: The failure of public responsibility to children and adolescents in need of mental health services.* Washington, DC: Children's Defense Fund.

Kopels, S., & Rycraft, J. (1993). The U.S. Supreme Court rules on reasonable efforts: A blow to child advocacy. *Child Welfare, 72*(4), 397–406.

Kraus, J. (1981). Foster children grown up: Parameters of care and adult delinquency. *Children and Youth Services Review, 3,* 99–114.

Kroner, M. (1988). Living arrangement options for young people preparing for independent living. *Child Welfare, 67*(6), 547–561.

Kufeldt, K., Armstrong, J., & Dorosh, M. (1989). In care, In contact? in NATO Advanced Research Workshop on State Intervention on Behalf of Children and Youth, *The state as parent: International research perspectives on interventions with young persons* (pp. 355–368). Boston: Kluwer Academic.

Kufeldt, K., Armstrong, J., & Dorosh, M. (1995). How children in care view their own and their foster families: A research study. *Child Welfare, 74*(3), 695–716.

Lahti, J. (1982). A follow-up study of foster children in permanent placements. *Social Service Review, 56,* 556–571.

Lahti, J., & Dvorak, J. (1981). Coming home from foster care. In A. N. Maluccio & P. A. Sinanoglu (Eds.), *The challenge of partnership: Working with parents of children in foster care* (pp. 52–66). New York: Child Welfare League of America.

Lahti, J. et al. (1978). *A follow-up study of the Oregon Project.* Portland, OR: Regional Research Institute for Human Services, Portland State University.

Laird, J. (1981). An ecological approach to child welfare: Issues of family identity and continuity. In P. A. Sinanoglu & A. N. Maluccio (Eds.), *Parents of children in placement: Perspectives and programs* (pp. 97–126). New York: Child Welfare League of America.

Lamb, M., Thompson, R., Gardner, W., & Charnov, E. (1985). *Infant-mother attachment: The origins and developmental significance of individual differences in strange situation behavior.* Hillsdale, NJ: Lawrence Erlbaum Associates.

Lammert, M., & Timberlake, E. (1986). Termination of foster care for the older adolescent: Issues of emancipation and individuation. *Child and Adolescent Social Work Journal, 3*(1), 26–37.

Land, H. (1990). The coming-of-age in foster care. In A. Maluccio, R. Krieger, & B. Pine

(Eds.), *Preparing adolescents for life after foster care: The central role of foster parents* (pp. 35–52). Washington, DC: Child Welfare League of America.

Landsverk, J. (April 11, 1996). The mental health needs of children in foster care: A case of benign neglect? Summary of a forum on the findings from a cohort study of children in the child welfare system. Presentation sponsored by the University of Minnesota Center for Advanced Studies in Child Welfare. Mimeo.

Langsam, M. (1964). *Children west: Logmark.* Madison, WI: The State Historical Society of Wisconsin.

Lawder, E., Poulin, J., & Andrews, R. (1985). *185 foster children: Five years after placement.* Philadelphia: Children's Aid Society of Pennsylvania.

Lee, J., & Park, D. (1980). *Walk a mile in my shoes.* West Hartford, CT: New England Regional Child Welfare Training Center.

Leeds, S. (1993, November). *Medical and developmental profiles of 195 children born HIV-positive and placed in foster care families.* Yonkers, NY: Leaker and Watts Services.

LeProhn, N. S. (1994). The role of the kinship foster parent: A comparison of the role conceptions of relative and non-relative foster parents. *Children and Youth Services Review, 16*(1/2), 65–84.

LeProhn, N. S., & Pecora, P. J. (1994). *The Casey foster parent study: Research summary.* Seattle, WA: The Casey Family Program, Research Department.

Leung, P. (1996). Is the court-appointed special advocate program effective? A longitudinal analysis of time involvement and care outcomes. *Child Welfare, 75*(3), 269–285.

Levin, A. E. (1992). Groupwork with parents in the family foster care system: A powerful method of engagement. *Child Welfare, 71*(5), 457–476.

Levine, K. G. (1988). The placed child examines the quality of parental care. *Child Welfare, 67*(4), 301–310.

Levine, K. G. (1990). Time to mourn again. In A. Maluccio, R. Krieger, & B. Pine (Eds.), *Preparing adolescents for life after foster care: The central role of foster parents* (pp. 53–76). Washington, DC: Child Welfare League of America.

Lewis, R. (1994). Application and adaptation of intensive family preservation services to use for the reunification of foster children with their biological parents. *Children and Youth Services Review, 16*(1/2), 339–361.

Lewis, R., & Fraser, M. (1987). Blending informal and formal helping networks in foster care. *Children and Youth Services Review, 9*(3), 153–169.

Lie, G-Y., & McMurtry, S. (1991). Foster care for sexually abused children: A comparative study. *Child Abuse and Neglect, 15,* 111–121.

Lindsey, D. (1982). Achievements for children in foster care. *Social Work, 27,* 491–496.

Lindsey, D. (1992). Adequacy of income and the foster care placement decision: Using an odds ratio approach to examine client variables. *Social Work, 37*(3), 29–36.

Lindsey, E., & Wodarski, J. (1986). Foster family care review by judicial-citizen panels: An evaluation. *Child Welfare, 65,* 211–230.

Link, M. (1996). Permanency outcomes in kinship care: A study of children placed in kinship care in Erie County, New York. *Child Welfare, 75*(5), 509–528.

Little, M., Leitch, H., & Bullock, R. (1995). The care careers of long-stay children: The contributions of new theoretical approaches. *Children and Youth Services Review, 17*(5/6), 665–679.

Loar, L. (1998). Making visits work. *Child Welfare, 77*(1), 41–58.

Lockhart, L. L., & Wodarski, J. S. (1989). Facing the unknown: Children and adolescents with AIDS. *Social Work, 34*(3), 215–221.

Long, K. A. (1983). The experience of repeated and traumatic loss among Crow Indian children: Response patterns and intervention strategies. *American Journal of Orthopsychiatric, 53,* 116–126.

Lowe, M. (1991). The challenge of partnership: A national foster care charter in the United Kingdom. *Child Welfare, 70*(2), 151–156.

Luginbill, M., & Spiegler, A. (1989). Specialized foster family care. *Children Today, 18*(1), 5–9.

Maas, H., & Engler, R. (1959). *Children in need of parents.* New York: Columbia University Press.

Magruder, J. (1994). Characteristics of relative and non-relative adoptions by California public adoption agencies. *Children and Youth Services Review, 16*(1/2), 123–131.

Mallon, G. (1992). Gay and no place to go: Assessing the needs of gay and lesbian adolescents in out-of-home care settings. *Child Welfare, 71*(6), 547–556.

Maluccio, A. (1981). Casework with parents of children in foster care. In P. Sinanoglu & A. Maluccio (Eds.), *Parents of children in placement: Perspectives and programs* (pp. 15–31). New York: Child Welfare League of America.

Maluccio, A. (1985). Biological families and foster care: Initiatives and obstacles. In M. Cox, & R. Cox (Eds.), *Foster care: Current issues, policies, and practices* (pp. 147–166). Norwood, NJ: Ablex.

Maluccio, A. (1991). Response: Eagerly awaiting a child. *Child & Youth Care Forum, 20*(1), 23–25.

Maluccio, A., & Fein, E. (1983). Permanency planning: A redefinition. *Child Welfare, 62*(3), 195–201.

Maluccio, A., & Fein, E. (1985a). Growing up in foster care. *Children and Youth Services Review, 7,* 123–134.

Maluccio, A., & Fein, E. (1985b). Permanency planning revisited. In M. Cox & R. Cox (Eds.), *Foster care: Current issues, policies, and practices* (pp. 113–133). Norwood, NJ: Ablex.

Maluccio, A., & Fein, E. (1989). An examination of long term foster family care for children and youth. In J. Hudson & B. Galaway (Eds.), *State as parent: International research perspectives on interventions with young persons* (pp. 387–399). Boston: Kluwer Academic.

Maluccio, A., Fein, E., & Olmstead, K. (1986). *Permanency planning for children: Concepts and methods.* New York: Tavistock.

Maluccio, A., Krieger, R., & Pine, B. (Eds.). (1990). *Preparing adolescents for life after foster care: The central role of foster parents.* Washington, DC: Child Welfare League of America.

Maluccio, A., & Simm, M. (1989). The use of agreements in foster family placements. In J. Aldgate, A. Maluccio, & C. Reeves (Eds.), *Adolescents in foster families* (pp. 102–121). Chicago: Lyceum Books.

Maluccio, A., Warsh, R., & Pine, B. (1993). Family reunification: An overview. In B. Pine, R. Warsh, & A. Maluccio (Eds.), *Together again: Family reunification in foster care* (pp. 3–20). Washington, DC: Child Welfare League of America.

Mandell, B. (1973). *Where are the children?* Lexington, MA: Lexington Books.

Mannes, M. (1998). Promoting safe and stable families. Is it a renewed—or a new—Title IV-B, subpart 2? *Prevention Report, #1,* 2–4.

Mansfield, D. (1993). *Good bye, baby Venus.* Lanham, MD: University Press of America.

Mason, S. (1998). Custody planning with HIV-affected families: Considerations for child welfare workers. *Child Welfare, 77*(4), 161–177.

Mass, A. I., & Yap, J. (1992). Child welfare: Asian and Pacific Islander families. In N. Cohen (Ed.), *Child welfare: A multicultural focus* (pp. 107–129). Boston: Allyn & Bacon.

Massinga, R., & Perry, K. (1994). The Casey Family program: Factors in effective management of a long-term foster care organization. In J. Blacher (Ed.). *When there's no place like home: Options for children living apart from their natural families* (pp. 163–180). Baltimore, MD: Paul H. Brookes.

Matheson, L. (1996). The politics of the Indian Child Welfare Act. *Social Work, 41*(2), 232–235.

McCurdy, K., & Daro, D. (1993). *Current trends in child abuse reporting and fatalities: The results of the 1992 annual fifty state survey.* Chicago: The National Committee for Prevention of Child Abuse.

McDonald, T., Allen, R., Westerfelt, A., & Piliavin, I. (1993). What we know about the effects of foster care. *FOCUS, 14*(4), 22–34.

McFadden, E. J. (1980). *Working with natural families.* Ypsilanti, MI: Eastern Michigan University.

McFadden, E. J. (1985). Practice in foster care. In J. Laird & A. Hartman (Eds.), *A handbook of child welfare: Content, knowledge, and practice* (pp. 585–616). New York: The Free Press.

McFadden, E. (1990, Winter). Quality placement for the 90's. *Fostering Ideas, 4,* 1–2, 6.

McFadden, E. J., & Ryan, P. (August, 1986). Abuse in family foster homes: Characteristics of the vulnerable child. Paper presented at the Sixth International Congress on Child Abuse and Neglect. Sydney, Australia.

McInnis, K. (1991). Ethnic-sensitive work with Hmong refugee children. *Child Welfare, 70*(5), 571–580.

McIntyre, A., & Keesler, T. (1986). Psychological disorders among foster children. *Journal of Clinical Psychology, 15*(4), 297–303.

McLean, B., & Thomas, R. (1996). Informal and formal kinship care populations: A study in contrasts. *Child Welfare, 75*(5), 489–505.

McMurtry, S., & Lie, G-Y. (1992). Differential exit rates of minority children in foster care. *Social Work Research and Abstracts, 28*(1), 42–48.

McNichol, T. (1999). The impact of drug-exposed children on family foster care. *Child Welfare, 78*(1), 184–196.

McPhatter, A. (1997). Cultural competence in child welfare: What is it? How do we achieve it? What happens without it? *Child Welfare, 76*(1), 255–278.

Mech, E. (1985). Parental visiting and foster placement. *Child Welfare, 64*(1), 67–72.

Mech, E., & Leonard, E. (1988). Volunteers as resources in preparing foster adolescents for self-sufficiency. *Child Welfare, 67*(6), 595–608.

Mech, E., & Rycraft, J. (1995). *Preparing foster youths for adult living: Proceedings of an invitational research conference.* Washington, DC: Child Welfare League of America.

Meezan, W. (1994). Should foster parents be given first preference in adoption of their foster children? In E. Gambrill & T. J. Stein (Eds.), *Controversial issues in child welfare* (pp. 151–159). Boston: Allyn & Bacon.

Meezan, W., & Shireman, J. (1985). *Care and commitment: Foster parent adoption decisions.* Albany, NY: State University of New York Press.

Meier, E. C. (1962). *Former foster children as adult citizens.* Unpublished doctoral dissertation, Columbia University.

Melina, L. (May, 1987). Agencies face issues of placing babies with AIDS. *Adoptive child, 6*(5).

Melina, L. (1997). Clinton wants to double the number of children moved out of foster care by 2002. *Adopted Child, 16*(2), 1–4.

Melotte, C. J. (1979). The placement decision. *Adoption and Fostering, 95*(1), 56–62.

Mennell, M. (1986). The experience of Bradford Social Services Department. In S. Ahmed, J. Cheetham, & J. Small (Eds.), *Social work with black children and their families* (pp. 120–131). London: B. T. Batsford.

Meriwether, M. (1988). Child abuse reporting laws: Time for a change. In D. Besharov (Ed.), *Protecting children from abuse and neglect: Policy and practice* (pp. 9–46). Springfield, IL: Charles C. Thomas.

Merkel-Holguin, L. (1996). *Children who lose their parents to AIDS: Agency guidelines for kinship care and adoption placement.* Washington, DC: Child Welfare League of America.

Meston, J. (1988). Preparing young people in Canada for emancipation from child welfare care. *Child Welfare, 67*(6), 625–634.

Meyer, C. H. (1985). A feminist perspective on foster family care: A redefinition of the categories. *Child Welfare, 64*(3), 249–258.

Mica, M., & Vosler, N. (1990). Foster-adoptive programs in public social service agencies: Toward flexible family resources. *Child Welfare, 69*(5), 433–446.

Michaud, I. (1992). *Parenting partners: Foster parents as parent aids.* Iowa City, IA: National Resource Center on Family Based Services, The University of Iowa School of Social Work.

Miller, J., & Carlton, T. (1988). Children and AIDS: A need to rethink child welfare practice. *Social Work, 33*(6), 553–555.

Mills, C., & Ivery, C. (1991). A strategy for workload management in child protective practice. *Child Welfare, 70*(1), 35–44.

Mills, C., & Usher, D. (1996). A kinship care case management approach. *Child Welfare, 75*(5), 600–618.

Minuchin, P. (1990). *Training manual for foster parents based on an ecological perspective on foster care.* New York: Family Studies.

Minuchin, P. (1992, Fall). A systems approach to foster care. *The Prevention Report.* Iowa City, IA: National Resource Center on Family Based Services, The University of Iowa School of Social Work.

Molin, R. (1988). Treatment of children in foster care: Issues of collaboration. *Child Abuse and Neglect, 12,* 241–250.

Moore, B., Grandpre, M., & Scoll, B. (1988). Foster home recruitment: A market research approach to attracting and licensing applicants. *Child Welfare, 67*(2), 147–160.

Mordock, J. B. (1996). The road to survival revisited: Organizational adaptation to the managed care environment. *Child Welfare, 75*(3), 195–218.

Mortland, C., & Egan, M. (1987). Vietnamese youth in American foster care. *Social Work, 32*(3), 240–245.

Morton, E. S., & Grigsby, R. K. (Eds.). (1993). *Advancing family preservation practice.* Newbury Park, CA: Sage.

Murphy, D. A. (1981). A program for parents of children in foster family care. In P. A. Sinanoglu & A. N. Maluccio (Eds.), *Parents of children in placement: Perspectives and programs* (pp. 433–439). New York: Child Welfare League of America.

Musewicz, J. (1981). Failure of foster care: Federal statutory reform and the child's right to permanence. *Southern California Law Review, 54,* 633–765.

Mushlin, M., Levitt, L., & Anderson, L. (1986). Court ordered foster family care reform: A case study. *Child Welfare, 65*(2), 141–154.

Myers, M. (1989). Families on welfare: Foster children with special needs. *Children Today, 18*(4), 6–9, 129.

National Association of Social Workers. (1994). Social work speaks: Policy statement (3rd ed.). Washington, DC: NASW Press.

National Association of Social Workers. (1999, February). Shifting to managed care: Pluses, minuses in Kansas. *NASW News,* p. 5.

National Black Child Development Institute. (1989). *Who will care when parents can't? A study of black children in foster care.* Washington, DC: Author.

National Black Child Development Institute. (1990). *The status of African-American children: Twentieth anniversary report: 1970–1990.* Washington, DC: Author.

National Black Child Development Institute. (1991). *Parental drug abuse and African American children in foster care.* Washington, DC: Author.

National Black Child Development Institute. (1995). *Special issue: The status of African American children.* Washington, DC: Author.

National Commission for Children in Need of Parents. (1979). *Who knows? Who cares? Forgotten children in foster care.* New York: Author.

National Commission on Children. (1991). *Beyond rhetoric: A new American agenda for children and families.* Washington, DC: Author.

National Court Appointed Special Advocates Association. (1992). *Quality guardian ad litem representation for abused and neglected children.* Unpublished manuscript.

National Foster Care Resource Center. (Fall, 1992). Focus on practice in permanency planning. *Fostering Ideas, (7),* 3, 10.

National Resource Center for Family Centered Practice. (1998). Of practice improvement and reforming reforms. *The Prevention Report,(2),* 1–3.

Ney, P. G., Fung, T., & Wickett, A. R. (1994). The worst combinations of child abuse and neglect. *Child Abuse and Neglect, 18*(9), 705–714.

North, J., Mallabar, M., & Desrochers, R. (1988). Vocational preparation and employability development. *Child Welfare, 67*(6), 573–586.

Norton, F. (1981). Foster care and the helping professions. *Personnel and Guidance Journal 60*(3), 156–159.

Olsen, L. (1982). Services for minority children in out-of-home care. *Social Service Research, 56*(4), 573–585.

Olson, H., Burgess, D., & Streissguth, A. (1993). Fetal alcohol effects (FAE): A lifespan view with implications for early intervention. *Iceberg, 3*(3), 1, 3.

Packman, R. (1986). *Who needs care? Social work decisions about children.* Oxford: Basil Blackwell.

Palmer, D. (1981). Comparing home-finding methods. *Adoption and Fostering, 106*(4), 41–43.

Palmer, S. (1990). Group treatment of foster children to reduce separation conflicts associated with placement breakdown. *Child Welfare, 69*(3), 227–238.

Palmer, S. (1995). *Maintaining family ties: Inclusive practice in foster care.* Washington, DC: Child Welfare League of America.

Palmer, S., & Cooke, W. (1996). Understanding and countering racism with first nations children in out-of-home care. *Child Welfare, 75*(6), 709–726.

Pardeck, J. T. (1983). *The forgotten children: A study of the stability and continuity of foster care.* Lanham, MD: University Press of America.

Pasztor, E. M. (1985). Permanency planning and foster parenting: Implications for recruitment selection, training and retention. *Children and Youth Services Review, 7,* 191–205.

Pasztor, E. M., Clarren, J., Timberlake, E. M., & Bayless, L. (1986). Stepping out of foster care into independent living. *Children Today, 15*(2), 32–35.

Pasztor, E. M., & Leighton, M. (1993). *Homeworks #2: At home training resources for foster parents and adoptive parents: Helping children and youths develop positive attachments.* Washington, DC: Child Welfare League of America.

Pasztor, E. M., Shannon, D., & Buck, P. (1989). *A community approach to foster parent recruitment and retention.* Atlanta, GA: Child Welfare Institute.

Pasztor, E., & Wynne, S. (1995). *Foster parent retention and recruitment: The state of the art in practice and policy.* Washington, DC: Child Welfare League of America.

Pecora, P., LeProhn, N., & Nasuti, J. (1999). Role perceptions of kinship and other foster parents in family foster care. In R. Hegar & M. Scannapieco (Eds.), *Kinship foster care: Policy, practice and research* (pp. 155–178). New York: Oxford University Press.

Pecora, P., Whittaker, J., & Maluccio, A. (1992). *The child welfare challenge: Policy, practice and research.* New York: Aldine De Gruyter.

Pelton, L. (1989). *For reasons of poverty: A critical analysis of the public child welfare system in the United States.* New York: Praeger.

Petr, C., & Johnson, I. (1999). Privatization of foster care in Kansas: A cautionary tale. *Social Work, 44*(3), 263–267.

Phelps, D. (1989). Foster home recruitment and retention: A success story. *Children Today, 18*(2), 7–9.

Phillips et al. (1971). *Factors associated with placement decisions in child welfare.* New York: Child Welfare League of America.

Phillips, L., & Gonzales-Ramos, G. (1989). Clinical social work practice with minority families. In S. Ehrenkranz, E. Goldstein, L. Goodman, & J. Seinfeld (Eds.), *Clinical social work with maltreated children and their families: An introduction to practice* (pp. 128–148). New York: New York University Press.

Phillips, S., McMillen, C., Sparks, J., & Ueberle, M. (1997). Concrete strategies for sensitizing youth-serving agencies to the needs of gay, lesbian, and other sexual minority youths. *Child Welfare, 76*(3), 393–410.

Pierce, W. (1992). Adoption and other permanency consideration. *Children and Youth Services Review, 14*(1/2), 61–66.

Pike, V. et al. (1977). *Permanent planning for children in foster care.* Washington, DC: U.S. Department of Health, Education, and Welfare.

Pine, B., & Jacobs, M. (1989). The training of foster parents for work with adolescents. In J. Aldgate, A. Maluccio, & C. Reeves (Eds.), *Adolescents in foster families* (pp. 151–165). Chicago: Lyceum Books.

Pine, B., Krieger, R., & Maluccio, A. (1990). Preparing adolescents to leave foster family care: Guidelines for policy and program. In A. Maluccio, R. Krieger, & B. Pine (Eds.), *Preparing adolescents for life after foster care: The central role of foster parents* (pp. 77–90). Washington, DC: Child Welfare League of America.

Pine, B., Warsh, R., & Maluccio, A. (1993). *Together again: Family reunification in foster care.* Washington, DC: Child Welfare League of America.

Plumer, E. (1992). *When you place a child. . . .* Springfield, IL: Charles C. Thomas.

Poe, L. (1999, Winter). The Changing Family: Psycho-social needs of grandparents parenting a second shift. *The Source, 9*(1), 1–2, 20–21.

Poertner, J., & Press, A. (1990). Who best represents the interests of the child in court? *Child Welfare, 69*(6), 537–549.

Polit, D., White, C. W., & Morton, T. (1987). Sex education and family planning services for adolescents in foster care. *Family Planning Perspectives, 19*(1), 18–23.

Porte, Z., & Torney-Purta, J. (1987). Depression and academic achievement among Indochinese refugees unaccompanied by minors in ethnic and nonethnic placements. *American Journal of Orthopsychiatric, 57*(4), 536–547.

Portwood, S. G., & Reppucci, N. D. (1994). Intervention versus interference: The role of the courts in child placement. In J. Blacher (Ed.), *When there's no place like home: Options for children living apart from their natural families* (pp. 3–36). Baltimore, MD: Paul H. Brookes.

Poulin, J. (1992). Kin visiting and the biological attachment of long-term foster children. *Journal of Social Service Research, 15*(3/4), 65–79.

Prater, G. S. (1992). Child welfare and African American families. In N. Cohen (Ed.), *Child welfare: A multicultural focus* (pp. 84–106). Boston: Allyn & Bacon.

Proch, K., & Hess, P. (1987). Parent-child visiting policies of voluntary agencies. *Children and Youth Services Review, 9*(1), 17–28.

Proch, K., & Howard, J. (1986). Parental visiting of children in foster care. *Social Work, 31*(3), 178–181.

Proch, K., & Taber, M. (1987). Alienated adolescents in foster care. *Social Work Research and Abstracts, 23*(2), 9–13.

Project CRAFT. (1980). *Training in the adoption of children with special needs.* Ann Arbor, MI: University of Michigan School of Social Work.

Radinsky et al. (1963). Recruiting and serving foster parents. *Child Welfare, 42.*

Rapp, C. (1992). Effect of the availability of family support services on decisions about child placement. *Social Work Research and Abstracts, 18*(1), 21–27.

Ratterman, D. (1987). *Reasonable efforts: A manual for judges.* Washington, DC: American Bar Association.

Ratterman, D. (1993). Changing agency procedures. In K. Cahn, & P. Johnson (Eds.), *Children can't wait: Reducing delays for children in foster care* (pp. 39–74). Washington, DC: Child Welfare League of America.

Reeves, C. S. (1980). Foster care: A partnership of skill. In J. Triseliotis (Ed.), *New developments in foster care and adoption* (pp. 118–130). London: Routledge and Kegan Paul.

Rice, D., & McFadden, E. J. (1988). A forum for foster children. *Child Welfare, 67*(3), 231–243.

Richardson, M., West, M., Day, P., & Stuart, S. (1989). Children with developmental disabilities in the child welfare system: A national survey. *Child Welfare, 68*(6), 605–613.

Ricketts, W. (1991). *Lesbians and gay men as foster parents.* Portland, ME: National Child Welfare Resource Center.

Risley-Curtiss, C. (1997). Sexual activity and contraceptive use among children entering out-of-home care. *Child Welfare, 76*(2), 475–499.

Ritter, B. (1995). Children on the move: Placement patterns in children's protective services. *Families in Society, 76,* 468–477.

Roman, N., & Wolfe, P. (1997). The relationship between foster care and homelessness. *Public Welfare, 55*(1), 4–9.

Rosenberg, L. (1991). Psychological factors in separation and reunification: The needs of the child and of the family. *Children's Legal Rights Journal, 12*(1), 19–24.

Rosenblum, B. (1977). *Foster homes for adolescents.* Hamilton, Ontario: Children's Aid Society of Hamilton-Wentworth.

Rowe, D. C. (1976). Attitudes, social class and the quality of foster care. *Social Service Review, 50,* 506–514.

Rowe, J. (1980). Fostering in the 1970's and beyond. In J. Triseliotis (Ed.), *New developments in foster care and adoption* (pp. 54–68). London: Routledge and Kegan Paul.

Rowe, J., Cain, H., Hundleby, M., & Keane, A. (1984). *Long-term foster care.* New York: Martin's Press.

Runyan, P. et al. (1981). Determinants of foster care placement for the maltreated child. *American Journal of Public Health 71*(7), 706–710.

Russell, D. (1986). *The secret trauma: Incest in the lives of girls and women.* New York: Basic Books.

Ryan, K. (1993). Stemming the tide of foster care runaways: A due process perspective. *Catholic University Law Review, 42*(2), 271–311.

Ryan, P. (Fall, 1992). Professionalization of foster parents. *Fostering Ideas, 7,* 1, 20.

Ryan, P., McFadden, E., Rice, D., & Warren, B. (1988). The role of foster parents in helping young people develop emancipation skills. *Child Welfare, 67*(6), 563–572.

Ryan, P., McFadden, E. J., & Warren, B. (1981). Foster families: A resource for helping parents. In A. Maluccio & P. Sinanoglu (Eds.), *The challenge of partnership: Working with parents of children in foster care.* New York: Child Welfare League of America, 189–220.

Ryan, P., McFadden, E. J., & Wiencek, P. (1988, April). *Case Work Services in Preventing Abuse in Family Foster Care: Research Results.* Symposium conducted at the National Symposium on Child Victimization. Ypsilanti, MI.

Ryan, P., Warren, B., & McFadden, E. (1979). *Seventeen course outlines for foster parent training.* Ypsilanti, MI: Authors.

Rzepnicki, T. (1987). Recidivism of foster children returned to their own homes: A review and new directions for research. *Social Service Review, 61,* 56–70.

Salter, A. C. (1988). *Treating child sex offenders and victims: A practical guide.* Newbury Park, CA: Sage.

Sandven, K., & Resnick, M. (1990). Informal adoption among black mothers. *American Journal Orthopsychiatric, 60*(2), 210–224.

Sauber, M., & Jenkins, S. (1966). *Paths to child placement.* New York: Community Council of Greater New York.

Sawyer, R., & Dubowitz, H. (1994). School performance for children in kinship care. *Child Abuse and Neglect, 18*(7), 587–597.

Scannapieco, M. (1999). Kinship care in the public welfare system: A systematic review of the research. In R. Hegar & M. Scannapieco (Eds.), *Kinship foster care: Policy, practice and research* (pp. 141–154). New York: Oxford University Press.

Scannapieco, M., & Hegar, R. (1994). Kinship care: Two case management modes. *Child and Adolescent Social Work Journal, 11*(4), 315–324.

Scannapieco, M., & Hegar, R. (1996). A nontraditional assessment framework for formal kinship homes. *Child Welfare, 75*(5), 567–582.

Scannapieco, M., & Hegar, R. (1999). Kinship foster care in context. In R. Hegar & M. Scannapieco (Eds.), *Kinship foster care: Policy, practice and research.* New York: Oxford University Press, 1–13.

Scannapieco, M., & Jackson, S. (1996). Kinship care: The African American response to family conservation. *Social Work, 41*(2), 190–196.

Schachter, B. (1989). Out-of-home care: Family foster care and residential treatment. In S. Ehrenkranz, E. Goldstein, L. Goodman, & J. Seinfeld (Eds.), *Clinical social work with maltreated children and their families: An introduction to practice* (pp. 104–127). New York: New York University Press.

Schatz, M. S., & Bane, W. (1991). Empowering the parents of children in substitute care: A training model. *Child Welfare, 70*(6), 665–678.

Schatz, M. S., & Horejsi, C. (1996). The importance of religious tolerance: A module for educating foster parents. *Child Welfare, 75*(1), 73–86.

Schneiderman, M., Connors, M., Fribourg, A., Gries, L., & Gonzales, M. (1989). Mental health services for children in out-of-home care. *Child Welfare, 77*(1), 29–40.

Schor, E. (1987). A summary of a white paper on health care of children in foster care: Report of a colloquium on health care for children in foster homes. *Children's Legal Rights Journal, 8*(3), 16–22.

Schuerman, J. R., Rzepnicki, T. L., & Littell, J. H. (1994). *Putting families first: An experiment in family preservation.* Hawthorne, NY: Aldine De Gruyter.

Schwartz, I., Ortega, R., Guo, S., & Fishman, G. (1994). Infants in nonpermanent placement. *Social Service Review, 68,* 405–416.

Seaberg, J. R. (1986). "Reasonable efforts": Toward implementation in permanency planning. *Child Welfare, 75*(5), 469–479.

Seaberg, J. R. (1988). Child well-being scales: A critique. *Social Work Research and Abstracts, 24*(3), 9–15.

Seaberg, J. R., & Tolley, E. (1986). Predictors of length of stay in foster care. *Social Work Research and Abstracts, 22*(3), 11–17.

Sellick, C. (1992). *Supporting short-term foster careers.* Aldershot, England: Avebury.

Seltzer, M. M., & Bloksberg, L. M. (1987). Permanency planning and its effect on foster children: A review of the literature. *Social Work, 32*(1), 65–68.

Seymour, C. (1998). Children with parents in prison: Child welfare policy, program and practice issues. *Child Welfare, 77*(5), 469–493.

Shapiro, D. (1972). Agency investment in foster care: A study. *Social Work, 17*(3), 20–28.

Shaw, M. (1989). Thinking about assessment of foster parents. In J. Aldgate, A. Maluccio, & C. Reeves (Eds.), *Adolescents in foster families* (pp. 139–150). Chicago: Lyceum Books.

Shaw, M., & Hipgrave, T. (1983). *Specialist fostering.* London: Bradford Academic and Educational Ltd.

Sherman, E., Newman, R., & Shyne, A. (1973). *Children adrift in foster care: A study of alternative approaches.* New York: Child Welfare League of America.

Shulman, L. (1980). Social work practice with foster parents. *Canadian Journal of Social Work Education, 6,* 58–71.

Shyne, A. (1969). *The need for foster care.* New York: Child Welfare League of America.

Shyne, A., & Schroeder, A. W. (1978). *National study of social services to children and their families.* Rockville, MD: Westat.

Silver, J., DiLorenzo, P., Zukowski, M., Ross, P., Amster, B., & Schlegel, D. (1999). Starting young: Improving the health and developmental outcomes of infants and toddlers in the child welfare system. *Child Welfare, 78*(1), 148–165.

Sims, A. (1988). Independent living services for youths in foster care. *Social Work, 33*(6), 539–542.

Simms, M., & Bolden, B. (1991). The family reunification project: Facilitating regular contact among foster children, biological families, and foster families. *Child Welfare, 70*(6), 679–690.

Simms, M., Freundlich, M., Battistelli, E., & Kaufman, N. (1999). Delivering health care and mental health services to children in family foster care after welfare and health care reform. *Child Welfare, 78*(1), 166–183.

Siu, S-F., & Hogan, P. (1989). Common clinical themes in child welfare. *Social Work, 34*(4), 339–345.

Slingerland, W. H. (1919). *Child-placing in families.* New York: Russell Sage Foundation.

Small, J. (1986). Transracial placements: Conflicts and contradictions. In A. Ahmed, J. Cheetham, & J. Small (Eds.), *Social work with black children and their families* (pp. 81–99). London: B. T. Batsford.

Smith, B. (1991). Australian women and foster care: A feminist perspective. *Child Welfare, 70*(2), 175–184.

Smith, D. (1995). *Foster parent adoption: What professionals should know.* Rockville, MD: National Adoption Information Clearinghouse.

Smith, E. (1994). Bring back the orphanages? What policymakers of today can learn from the past. *Child Welfare, 74*(1), 115–142.

Smith, M. (1996). An exploratory survey of foster mother and caseworker attitudes about sibling placement. *Child Welfare, 75*(4), 357–375.

Smollar, J. *Presentation on short-term foster care.* Conducted by CSR Incorporated for the Administration on Children, Youth, and Families, Washington, DC.

Solnit, A., Nordhaus, B., & Lord, R. (1992). *When home is no haven: Child placement issues.* New Haven, CT: Yale University Press.

Soothill, K., & Derbyshire, M. (1981). Selecting foster parents. *Adoption and Fostering, 104*(2), 47–50.

Soothill, K., & Derbyshire, M. (1982). Retention of foster parents. *Adoption and Fostering, 6*(2), 38–43.

Sosin, M. (1987). Delivering services under permanency planning. *Social Service Review, 61,* 272–290.

Staff, I., & Fein, E. (1991). Reunification services: Issues in implementation. *Families in Society, 72,* 335–343.

Stahl, P. (1990). *Children on consignment: A handbook for parenting foster children and their special needs.* Lexington, MA: Lexington Books.

Starr, R., Dubowitz, H., Harrington, D., & Feigelman, S. (1999). Behavioral problems of teens in kinship care: Cross informant reports. In R. Hegar & M. Scannapieco (Eds.), *Kinship foster care: Policy, practice and research* (pp. 179–192). New York: Oxford University Press.

State of California. (1981) *Family Protection Act report.* Sacramento, CA: Author.

Stehno, S. (1988). Public responsibility for dependent black children: The advocacy of Edith Abbott and Sophonisba Breckinridge. *Social Service Review, 62,* 485–503.

Stehno, S. (1990). The elusive continuum of child welfare services: Implications for minority children and youths. *Child Welfare, 69*(6), 551–562.

Stein, M., & Carey, F. (1986). *Leaving care.* Oxford: B. Blackwell.

Stein, T. J. (1976). Early intervention in foster care. *Public Welfare, 34,* 39–44.

Stein, T. J. (1987). The vulnerability of child welfare agencies to class-action suits. *Social Service Review, 61,* 636–654.

Stein, T. J. (1991). *Child welfare and the law.* New York: Longman.

Stein, T. J., Callaghan, J., McGee, L., & Douglas, S. (1990). A caseload-weighting formula for child welfare services. *Child Welfare, 69*(1), 33–42.

Stein, T. J., & Comstock, G. (1987). *Reasonable efforts: A report on implementation by child welfare agencies in five states.* Washington, DC: National Legal Resource Center for Child Advocacy and Protection.

Stein, T. J., & Gambrill, E. (1976). *Decision making in foster care: A training manual.* Berkeley, CA: University Extension Publications.

Stein, T. J., Gambrill, E., & Wiltse, K. T. (1978). *Children in foster homes: Achieving continuity of care.* New York: Praeger.

Steinhauer, P. (1991). *The least detrimental alternative: A systematic guide to care planning and decision making for children in care.* Toronto: University of Toronto Press.

Stepleton, S. S. (1987). Specialized foster care: Families as treatment resources. *Children Today, 16*(2), 27–31.

Stone, H. D. (1969). *Reflections on foster care: A report of a national survey of attitudes and practices.* New York: Child Welfare League of America.

Stone, N., & Stone, S. (1983). The prediction of successful foster placement. *Social Casework, 64*(1), 11–17.

Stovall, B., & Krieger, R. (1990). Preparing minority foster adolescents for adulthood: The need for ethnic competence. In A. Maluccio, R. Krieger, & B. Pine (Eds.), *Preparing adolescents for life after foster care: The central role of foster parents* (pp. 147–162). Washington, DC: Child Welfare League of America.

Streissguth, A., Anse, J., Clarren, S., Randels, S., LaDue, R., & Smith, D. (1991). Fetal alcohol syndrome in adolescents and adults. *Journal of the American Medical Association,* *265*(15), 1961–1967.

Taber, M. A., & Proch, K. (1988). Parenting: An essential child welfare service. *Social Work,* *33*(1), 63–64.

Takas, M. (1993). *Kinship care and family preservation: A guide for states in legal and policy de-* *velopment.* Washington, DC: American Bar Association.

Takas, M., & Hegar, R. (1999). The case for kinship adoption laws. In R. Hegar & M. Scan- napieco (Eds.), *Kinship foster care: Policy, practice and research.* New York: Oxford Uni- versity Press, 54–67.

Takas, M., & Warner, E. (1992). *To love a child: A complete guide to adoption, foster parenting,* *and other ways to share your life with children.* Reading, MA: Addison-Wesley.

Tatara, T. (1993). *Characteristics of children in substitute and adoptive care: A statistical summary* *of the VCIS national child welfare data base.* Washington, DC: American Public Welfare Association.

Tatara, T. (1994). Some additional explanations for the recent rise in the U.S. child substi- tute care population: An analysis of national child care flow data and future research questions. In R. Barth, J. D. Berrick, & N. Gilbert (Eds.), *Child Welfare Research Review* (Vol. 1, pp. 126–145). New York: Columbia University Press.

Tatara, T. (1995, August). *U.S. child substitute care flow data for FY 1993 and trends in the state* *child substitute care populations* (VCIS Research Notes Vol. 11). Washington, DC: Ameri- can Public Welfare Association.

Tatara, T. (1996, June). *U.S. child substitute care flow data for FY 1994 and trends in the state* *child substitute care populations* (VCIS Research Notes Vol. 12). Washington, DC: Ameri- can Public Welfare Association.

Taylor-Brown, S. (1991). The impact of AIDS on foster care: A family-centered approach to services in the United States. *Child Welfare, 70*(2), 193–209.

Taylor-Brown, S., Teeter, J., Blackburn, E., Oinen, L., & Wedderburn, L. (1998). Parental loss due to HIV: Caring for children as a community issue—The Rochester, New York experience. *Child Welfare, 77*(2), 137–160.

Ten Broeck, E., & Barth, R. (1986). Learning the hard way: A pilot permanency planning program. *Child Welfare, 75*(3), 281–294.

Terpstra, J., & McFadden, E. (1993). Looking backward: Looking forward: New directions in foster care. Unpublished manuscript.

Terr, L. (1990). *Too scared to cry: Psychic trauma in childhood.* New York: Basic Books.

Testa, M. (1992). Conditions of risk for substitute care. *Children and Youth Services Review,* *14*(1/2), 27–36.

Testa, M., & Rolock, N. (1999). Professional foster care: A future worth pursuing? *Child* *Welfare, 78*(1), 108–124.

Testa, M., Shook, K., Cohen, L., & Woods, M., (1996). Permanency planning options for children in formal kinship care. *Child Welfare, 75*(5), 451–470.

Thies, S., & Van, S. (1924). *How Foster Children Turn Out.* New York State Charities Aid As- sociation.

Thoburn, J. (1980). *Captive clients: Social work with families of children home on trial.* London: Routledge and Kegan Paul.

Thoburn, J. (1990). *Success and failure in permanent family placement.* Brookfield, VT: Avebury.

Thomas et al. (1977). *Supply and demand for child foster family care in the southeast.* Athens, GA: Regional Institute of Social Welfare Research.

Thorpe, R. (1980). The experiences of children and parents living apart: Implications and guidelines for practice. In J. Triseliotis (Ed.), *New developments in foster care and adoption* (pp. 85–100). London: Routledge and Kegan Paul.

Thornton, J. (1991). Permanency planning for children in kinship foster homes. *Child Welfare, 70*(5), 593–601.

Three Feathers Associates. (1989). Case management and planning: Special article ICW: A status report. *Indian Child Welfare Digest: Model Practice Approaches* (February–March), 2–20.

Thurston, H. W. (1930). *The dependent child.* New York: Columbia University Press.

Tiddy, S. (1986). Creative cooperation: Involving biological parents in long-term foster care. *Child Welfare, 65*(1), 53–62.

Timberlake, E., & Verdieck, M. (1987). Psychosocial functioning of adolescents in foster care. *Social Casework, 68*(4), 214–222.

Tinney, M. A. (1985). Role perceptions in foster parent associations in British Columbia. *Child Welfare, 64*(1), 73–79.

Titterington, L. (1990). Foster care training: A comprehensive approach. *Child Welfare, 69*(2), 157–165.

Tizard, B., & Joseph, A. (1970). Today's foundlings. *New Society, 35*(418), 584–585.

Tolfree, D. (1995). *Roofs and roots: The care of separated children in the developing world.* Brookfield, VT: Ashgate.

Touliatos, J., & Lindhome, B. (1992). *Foster home evaluation.* St. Louis, MO: National Foster Parent Association.

Tourse, P., & Gundersen, L. (1988). Adopting and fostering children with AIDS: Policies in progress. *Children Today, 17*(3), 15–19.

Tower, C. C. (1996). *Understanding child abuse and neglect* (3rd ed.). Needham Heights, MA: Simon and Schuster.

Triseliotis, J. (1980). Growing up in foster care and after. In J. Triseliotis (Ed.), *New developments in foster care and adoption* (pp. 131–161). London: Routledge and Kegan Paul.

Triseliotis, J., & Hill, M. (1990). Constraining adoption, foster care, and residential rearing. In D. Brodzinsky & M. Schechter (Eds.), *The psychology of adoption* (pp. 107–120). New York: Oxford University Press.

Triseliotis, J., Sellick, C., & Short, R. (1995). *Foster care: Theory and practice.* London: B. T. Batsford.

Tunnard, J. (1989). Local self-help groups for families of children in public care. *Child Welfare, 68*(2), 221–227.

Turner, F. J. (1986). Theory in social work practice. In F. J. Turner (Ed.), *Social work treatment: Interlocking theoretical approaches* (3rd ed., pp. 1–18). New York: The Free Press.

Turner, J. (1984). Reuniting children in foster care with their biological parents. *Social Work 29*(6), 501–505.

Tymchuk, A. (1992). Predicting adequacy of parenting by people with mental retardation. *Child Abuse and Neglect, 16,* 165–178.

Tyson, A. (1997, August 15). Kansas pioneers a solution to child-welfare woes. *Christian Science Monitor,* p. 1.

U.S. Children's Bureau. (1998). Foster care and adoption statistics current reports [On-line]. Available: http://www.acf.dhhs.gov/programs/cb/stats/afcars/index.htm

U.S. Children's Bureau. (March 12, 1999). Foster care and adoption statistics current reports [On-line]. Available: http://www.acf.dhhs. gov/programs/cb/stats/afcars/index.htm

U.S. Department of Health and Human Services. (1982). *Child welfare training: Education for social work practice with American Indian families.* Washington, DC: Author.

U.S. House of Representatives Committee on Ways and Means. (1992). *Overview of entitlement programs: 1992 green book: Background material and data on programs within the jurisdiction of the Committee on Ways and Means.* Washington, DC: Author.

U.S. House of Representatives Committee on Ways and Means. (1993). *Overview of entitlement programs: 1993 green book: Background material and data on programs within the jurisdiction of the Committee on Ways and Means.* Washington, DC: Author.

Usher, C. L., Gibbs, D. A., & Wildfire, J. B. (1995). A framework for planning, implementing, and evaluating child welfare reforms. *Child Welfare, 74*(4), 859–876.

Van Der Waals, P. (1960). Former foster children reflect on their childhood. *Children, 7.*

Van Gelder, L., & Brandt, P. (1988, March). How foster care is failing our children. *McCall's,* Gruner and Jahr.

Van Pagée, R., Van Miltenburg, W., & Pasztor, E. (1991). The international transfer of foster parent selection and preparation technology: The example of the Netherlands and the United States. *Child Welfare, 70*(2), 219–227.

Vasaly, S. M. (1978). *Foster care in five states: A synthesis and analysis of studies from Arizona, California, Iowa, Massachusetts, and Vermont.* Washington, DC: U.S. Department of Health, Education & Welfare.

Vidal, C. (1988). Godparenting among Hispanic Americans. *Child Welfare, 67*(5), 453–459.

Vinokur-Kaplan, D. (1987). Where do they go from here? A national follow-up of child welfare trainees. *Child Welfare, 66*(5), 411–421.

Vinokur-Kaplan, D. (1991). Job satisfaction among social workers in public and voluntary child welfare agencies. *Child Welfare, 70*(1), 81–91.

Virginia Youth Advisory Council. (March, 1994). Youths in foster care speaking out to make a difference. *VA-YAC Newsletter.*

Vissing, Y., Straus, M., Gelles, R., and Harrop, J. (1991). Verbal aggression by parents and psychosocial problems of children. *Child Abuse and Neglect, 15,* 223–238.

Wald, M. (1988). *Protecting abused and neglected children.* Stanford, CA: Stanford University Press.

Wald, M. (1994). Termination of parental rights. In D. Besharov & K. Hanson (Eds.), *When drug addicts have children: Reorienting child welfare's response* (pp. 195–210). Washington, DC: Child Welfare League of America.

Wald, M., Carlsmith, J. M., & Leiderman, P. M. (1988). *Protecting abused and neglected children.* Stanford, CA: Stanford University Press.

Waldinger, G., & Furman, W. (1994). Two models of preparing foster youths for emancipation. *Children and Youth Services Review, 16*(3/4), 201–212.

Walker, C., Zangrillo, P., & Smith, J. (1994). Parental drug abuse and African American children in foster care. In R. Barth, J. D. Berrick, & N. Gilbert (Eds.), *Child Welfare Research Review* (Vol. 1, pp. 109–125). New York: Columbia University Press.

Walker, F. (1981). Cultural and ethnic issues in working with black families in the child welfare system. In P. Sinanoglu & A. Maluccio (Eds.), *Parents of children in placement: Perspectives and programs* (pp. 133–148). New York: Child Welfare League of America.

Walsh, J., & Walsh, R. (1990). *Quality care for tough kids: Studies of the maintenance of subsidized foster placements in the Casey Family program.* Washington, DC: Child Welfare League of America.

Wares, D. M., Dobrec, A., Rosenthal, J. A., & Wedel, K. R. (1992). Job satisfaction, practice skills, and supervisory skills of administrators of Indian child welfare programs. *Child Welfare, 71*(5), 405–418.

Waterhouse. (1992). How foster carers view contact. *Adoption and Fostering, 16*(2), 43–47.

Webb, D. (1988). Specialized foster care as an alternative therapeutic out-of-home placement model. *Journal of Clinical Child Psychology, 17*(1), 34–43.

Wedeven, T., & Mavzerall, H. (1990). Independent-living programs: Avenues to competence. In A. Maluccio, R. Krieger, & B. Pine (Eds.), *Preparing adolescents for life after foster care: The central role of foster parents* (pp. 91–106). Washington, DC: Child Welfare League of America.

Weiner, A., & Weiner, E. (1990). *Expanding the options in child care placement: Israel's dependent children in care from infancy to adulthood.* Lanham, MD: University Press of America.

Weinstein, E. (1960). *The self-image of the foster child.* New York: Russell Sage Foundation.

Weisz, V. (1994). Consequences of placement for children who are abused. In J. Blacher (Ed.), *When there's no place like home: Options for children living apart from their natural families* (pp. 63–100). Baltimore, MD: Paul H. Brookes.

Wells, K. (1991). Eagerly awaiting a home: Severely emotionally disturbed youth lost in our systems of care: A personal reflection. *Child & Youth Care Forum, 20*(1), 7–17.

Wells, K., & Biegel, D. (1990). Intensive family preservation services: A research agenda for the 1990s. Intensive Family Preservation Services Research Conference, Cleveland, OH.

Werner, E. (1994). Commentary: A social policy perspective. In J. Blacher (Ed.), *When there's no place like home: Options for children living apart from their natural families* (pp. 329–344). Baltimore, MD: Paul H. Brookes.

Werrbach, G. B. (1993). The family reunification role-play. *Child Welfare, 72*(6), 555–568.

Wert, E. S., Fein, E., & Haller, W. (1986). Children in placement (CIP): A model for citizen-judicial review. *Child Welfare, 65*(2), 199–201.

What you always wanted to discuss about foster care but didn't have the time or the chance to bring up: Conversations No. 1. (1971). New York, NY: Child Welfare League of America.

White, M. S. (1981). Promoting parent-child visiting in foster care: Continuing involvement within a permanency framework. In P. A. Sinanoglu & A. N. Maluccio (Eds.), *Parents of children in placement: Perspectives and programs* (pp. 461–475). New York: Child Welfare League of America.

White, P. (1994). Courting disaster: Permanency planning for children. *Juvenile Justice,* 15–20.

Whitman, B., Graves, B., & Accardo, P. (1989). Training in parenting skills for adults with mental retardation. *Social Work, 34*(5), 431–434.

Whitmore, J. (1991). Mobilizing training resources for rural foster parents, adoptive parents, and applicants in Oregon, U.S.A. *Child Welfare, 70*(2), 211–218.

Widom, C. S. (1991). The role of placement experiences in mediating the criminal consequences of early childhood victimization. *American Journal of Orthopsychiatric, 61*(2), 195–209.

Wiehe, V. (1983). Foster mothers: Are they unique? *Psychological Reports, 53,* 1215–1218.

Wiener, L., Battles, H., & Heilman, N. (1998). Factors associated with parents' decision to disclose their HIV diagnosis to their children. *Child Welfare, 77*(2), 115–136.

Williams, B. (1987). Looking for Linda: Identity in black and white. *Child Welfare, 66*(3), 207–216.

Williams, C. J. (1972). Helping parents to help the children in placement. *Child Welfare, 51,* 297–303

Wilson, A. (1987). *Mixed race children.* London: Allen & Unwin.

Wilson, D. (1999). Kinship care in family-serving agencies. In R. Hegar & M. Scannapieco (Eds.), *Kinship foster care: Policy, practice and research* (pp. 179–192). New York: Oxford University Press.

Wilson, L., & Conroy, J. (1999). Satisfaction of children in out-of-home care. *Child Welfare, 78*(1), 53–69.

Wiltse, K. T. (1985). Foster care: An Overview. In J. Laird & A. Hartman (Eds.), *A handbook of child welfare: Content, knowledge and practice* (pp. 565–584). New York: The Free Press.

Wiltse, K. T., & Gambrill, E. D. (1974). Foster care, 1973: A reappraisal. *Public Welfare, 32.*

Wolfelt, A. (1991, January). Central reconciliation needs of mourning in the bereaved child. *Bereavement Magazine,* 38–39.

Woodworth, R. (1996). You're not alone . . . You're one in a million. *Child Welfare, 75*(5), 619–635.

Wulczyn, F. (1991). Caseload dynamics and foster care recruiting. *Social Service Review, 65,* 133–156.

Wulczyn, F. (1994). Status at birth and infant foster care placement in New York City. In R. Barth, J. D. Berrick, & N. Gilbert (Eds.), *Child Welfare Research Review* (Vol. 1, pp. 146–184). New York: Columbia University Press.

Wulczyn, F., & Goerge, R. (1992). Foster care in New York and Illinois: The challenge of rapid change. *Social Service Review, 66,* 278–294.

Wulczyn, F., Goerge, R., & Harden, A. (1993). *The multi-state foster care data archive year one results: Foster care dynamics in five states: California, Illinois, Michigan, New York, and Texas.* Washington, DC: United States Department of Health and Human Services. (Draft, November 5, 1993).

Yancey, A. (1998). Building positive self-image in adolescents in foster care: The use of role models in an interactive group approach. *Adolescence, 33*(130), 253–259.

Yoshikami, R. (1984). *Assessing the implementation of federal policy to reduce the use of foster care: Placement prevention and reunification in child welfare, vol. 1.* Washington, DC: Children's Bureau.

Yost, D. M., Hochstadt, N. J., & Charles, P. (1988). Medical foster care: Achieving permanency for seriously ill children. *Children Today, 17*(5), 22–26.

Youths in foster care speaking out to make a difference. (1994, March). *Virginia-Youth Advisory Council Newsletter* (3rd ed.).

Zamosky, J., Sparks, J., Hatt, R., & Sharman, J. (1993). Believing in families. In B. Pine, R. Warsh, & A. Maluccio (Eds.), *Together again: Family reunification in foster care* (pp. 155–178). Washington, DC: Child Welfare League of America.

Zill, N., & Coiro, M. J. (1992). Assessing the conditions of children. *Children and Youth Services Review, 14*(1/2), 119–136.

Zimmerman, R. (1982). *Foster care in retrospect.* New Orleans, LA: Tulane Studies in Social Welfare.

Zimmerman, R. (1988). Childhood depression: New theoretical formulations and implications for foster care services. *Child Welfare, 67*(1), 37–47.

Zlotnik, J. L. (1998). The adoption and safe families act of 1997: Implications for social work education. *The Prevention Report,*(2), 17–18.

Zuravin, S., Benedict, M., & Stallings, R. (1999). The adult functioning of former kinship and nonrelative foster care children. In R. Hegar & M. Scannapieco (Eds.), *Kinship foster care: Policy, practice and research* (pp. 208–224). New York: Oxford University Press.

Index

DATE